Ōsaka Archaeology

Richard Pearson

ARCHAEOPRESS ARCHAEOLOGY

Archaeopress Publishing Ltd
Summertown Pavilion
18-24 Middle Way
Oxford OX2 7LG

www.archaeopress.com

ISBN 978 1 78491 375 5
ISBN 978 1 78491 376 2 (e-Pdf)

© Archaeopress and R Pearson 2016

Cover image: The Daisen Ryō Kofun (upper) and Kami Ishitsu Misanzai keyhole shape tombs (*zenpokoenfun*), of the Mozu Tomb Group. Fifth century AD. The total length of the Daisen Ryō Kofun is 850 m. From Ōsaka Furitsu Chikatsu Asuka Hakubutsukan 2006: 86).
Courtesy of Ōsaka Furitsu Chikatsu Asuka Hakubutsukan and Sakai Shi Hakubutsukan.
Photo property of Sakai Shi Hakubutsukan.

All rights reserved. No part of this book may be reproduced,
Or transmitted, in any form or by any means, electronic, mechanical, photocopying or otherwise,
without the prior written permission of the copyright owners.

This book is available direct from Archaeopress or from our website www.archaeopress.com

Table of Contents

Acknowledgements vii

Chapter 1
Ōsaka Archaeology 1

Chapter 2
The Environment Of The Ōsaka Area And Its Changes 8

Chapter 3
Early Hunter Gatherers: the Palaeolithic and Jōmon Periods (ca. 20,000 BC to 950 BC) 13

Chapter 4
The Expansion of Agrarian Society; the Yayoi Period (950 BC to 240 AD) 15

Chapter 5
Consolidation of Political Power and Trade; the Kofun Period (240 to 600 AD) 23

Chapter 6
The Naniwa Port as a Regional Center; The Kodai (600 to 1185 AD) Period 53

Chapter 7
Ōsaka as a Commercial Center; The Chūsei Period (ca 1185 to 1603 AD) 61

Chapter 8
The Beginnings of Modern Ōsaka; The Kinsei Period (ca 1603 to 1868 AD) 75

Chapter 9
Ōsaka's Special Features 77

Appendix A
Site Descriptions 81

Appendix B
Sakai Historical Background 101

Appendix C
Ōsaka's Cultural Heritage and Selected Museums 104

Glossary 111

References Cited 116

Index 132

Table of Figures

Figure 1.1. Ōsaka, the Kinai Region, and Japan. Adapted from Barnes 2007: 11. Courtesy Dr. G.L. Barnes.................1
Figure 1.2. Archaeological chronology of Japan, Korea, and China. 2
Figure 1.3. Archaeological chronology of Japan. 3
Figure 1.4. Major sites mentioned in the text, and some significant historical bench marks. 4
Figure 1.5. Ancient projects described in the text..6
Figure 2.1. Rivers of Ōsaka. 8
Figure 2.2. Kawachi Bay, Lagoon, and Lake. Adapted from Kihara and Kajiyama 1986: 32, 48, 80, 96. Radiocarbon dates supplied by the authors were recalibrated using www.calpal-online.de, quickcal ver 1.5 accessed Nov 13 2013, and the dating of the three periods was adjusted slightly. 9
Figure 2.3. Changes in climate, vegetation and sea level from 13,000 BP to the fourth century AD. From Yasuda 1978a...10
Figure 2.4. Trees featured in pollen analysis, Ōsaka region..10
Figure 2.5. Environmental changes at the Uriūdō Site. From Yasuda 1980: 435. (upper) Late Jomon Period, salt water shoreline environment. (middle) Early to Middle Yayoi Period, freshwater shoreline paddies with villages on slightly higher ground. (lower) End of Middle Yayoi Period, shoreline was flooded and small villages were built on higher ground. Courtesy of Yasuda Yoshinori and the Ōsaka Fu Bunkazai Sentā. 11
Figure 2.6. Stratigraphic section of the Nagahara Site, Ōsaka, showing the entire span of occupation of the Ōsaka Plain from the Late Paleolithic Period to the present. Part of a display at the Ōsaka Museum of Natural History, November 2013. Courtesy of the Ōsaka Shi Hakubutsukan Kenkyūkai, Ōsaka Bunkazai Kenkyūsho. 12
Figure 3.1. Steps in the manufacture of the Kō Type Knife by the side blow technique. Adapted from Kinugawa 2008: 24. In Stage 1, a core is made from a pebble, by removing a piece from a pebble by percussion. In Stage 2, flakes are removed by the side blow technique. In Stage 3, the flakes are retouched for use as knives. Courtesy of the Ōsaka Shi Hakubutsukan Kyōkai, Ōsaka Shi Bunkazai Kenkyūsho. 13
Figure 3.2. The earliest Jōmon pottery found in the Ōsaka region, the Awatsu SZ Type. From Sugimoto 2008: 34. Courtesy of the Ōsaka Shi Hakubutsukan Kyōkai, Ōsaka Shi Bunkazai Kenkyūsho. 14
Figure 3.3. Slit earrings of jade found in burials at the Kō Site. Redrawn from Yoneda 2006. Total diameter approx. 5cm. 14
Figure 4.1. Earthenware storage and serving vessels found in a ditch at the Middle Yayoi Period Kuwazu Site, Ōsaka. From Ōsaka Shi 2008,: 61. Courtesy of the Ōsaka Shi Hakubutsukan Kyōkai, Ōsaka Shi Bunkazai Kenkyūsho. 15
Figure 4.2. Nagahara Type pottery, the oldest Yayoi pottery found in the Ōsaka area. Nagahara Site, Ōsaka. From Ōsaka Shi 2008: 43. Courtesy of the Ōsaka Shi Hakubutsukan Kyōkai, Ōsaka Shi Bunkazai Kenkyūsho......16
Figure 4.3. Map of rice paddies, Late Yayoi Period, Ikejima Fukumanji Site, Ōsaka. Adapted From Eura, 2012. Powerpoint presentation Slide 14. Courtesy of Eura Hiroshi. 17
Figure 4.4. Moated Precinct Burial No. 2, Uriūdō Site, Ōsaka. Middle Yayoi Period. From Sahara and Kanaseki 1975: Color Plate 16. Courtesy of Kōdansha...21
Figure 5.1. Tomb groups, individual tombs, and sites in the Kinai Region discussed in the text. Tomb Groups (in circled numbers): (1) Ōyamato. (2) Umami. (3) Saki. (4) Tamateyama. (5) Nagahara. (6) Furuichi. (7) Mozu. Individual Tombs: (8) Niwatoritsuka. (9) Kurohimeyama. (10) Koganetsuka. (11) Kumeda Kaifukuyama. Sites: (12) Hōenzaka. (13) Furu. (14) Karako Kagi. (15) Makimuku. (16) Nangō. (Redrawn from Ichinose 2005: 169). 24
Figure 5.2. Keyhole shape tombs in the Nara and Ōsaka regions, showing their chronological position and relative size. From Tanaka 1991: 278. Courtesy of Tanaka Migaku and Shūeisha Publishers. 24
Figure 5.3. Example of a triangular rim mirror with beast and deity decoration. 1. Sacred beasts, usually dragons and tigers. 2. Bands of sawtooth pattern separated by wave pattern. 3. Deities, usually Queen Mother of the West and King of the East. 4. Inner zone. 5. Outer zone. 6. Nipple. 7. Square hole for tassel. 8. Triangular outer rim. 9. Four or six nipples in the outer zone. Redrawn From Kondō, Yoshirō. 1981. Gongenyama 51 Kofun. Publisher and place of publication unknown. From Ōsaka Furitsu Asuka Hakubutsukan: 2013:11. Courtesy of Ōsaka Furitsu Chikatsu Asuka Hakubutsukan. 29
Figure 5.4. Storage Chest Type stone coffin (*nagamochigata sekkan*) recovered from the Tsudoshiroyama Kofun in AD 1912. From Ichinose 2009: 18. From Ōsaka Furitsu Chikatsu Asuka Hakubutsukan 2010: 150. Courtesy of Ōsaka Furitsu Chikatsu Asuka Hakubutsukan. 30
Figure 5.5. Major tombs in the Furuichi and Mozu Tomb Groups, the time period of the Five Kings of Wa, and

the succession of emperors outlined in the Nihon Shoki. Adapted from Nakakubo and Takahashi (eds) 2014: 63. Courtesy of the Ōsaka Daigaku Shuppankai. 34

Figure 5.6. Major *kofun* in the Furuichi Tomb Group. (1) Tsudō Shiroyama. (2) Ichinoyama. (3) Komuroyama. (4) Nakatsuyama. (5) Oka Misanzai. (6) Ariyama. (7) Konda Maruyama. (8) Niitsuka. (9) Hasamiyama. (10) Miyayama. (11) Konda Gobyōyama. (12) Nonaka. (13) Bokeyama. (14) Hakayama. (15) Minegatsuka. (16) Maenoyama. (17) Tsuka'ana. (18) Shirakayama. (19) Takashiroyama. From Ōsaka Furitsu Chikatsu Asuka Hakubutsukan: 2006: 11. Courtesy of Shiraishi Ta'ichirō. 35

Figure 5.7. Major kofun in the Mozu Tomb Group. (1) Tadeiyama. (2) Nagayama. (3) Daisen Ryō. (4) Nagazukayama. (5) Chino'oka. (6) Shichikanyama. (7) Nagazuka (8) Mozu Tori Gobyōyama. (9) Katonboyama. (10) Kami Ishitsu Misanzai. (11) Ōtsukayama. (12) Itasuke. (13) Shironoyama. (14) Haji Nisanzai. From Ōsaka Furitsu Chikatsu Asuka Hakubutsukan 2006: 11. Courtesy of Shiraishi Ta'ichirō. 36

Figure 5.8. Conformity of proportions of kofun. From Tsude (ed) 1989, 30. (1) Hashihaka Kofun, Nara Prefecture, end of third century AD. (2) Shibuya Mukōyama Kofun, Nara Prefecture, latter half of fourth century AD. (3) Konda Gobyōyama Kofun, Ōsaka Prefecture, early half of fifth century AD. (4) Nisanzai Kofun, Ōsaka Prefecture, mid fifth century AD. (5) Toriya Misanzai Kofun, Nara Prefecture, early half of sixth century AD. Courtesy of Kōdansha Publishers. 37

Figure 5.9 Decoration of a Middle Kofun Period Tomb with wood and clay *haniwa*. (1) Front portion of mound. (2) Rear portion of mound. (3) Moat. (4) House shape clay *haniwa*. (5) Wooden parasol. (6) Finned clay morning glory haniwa. (7) Finned clay tubular haniwa. (8) Torii gate. (9) Wooden birds. (10) Row of wooden shields (11) Wooden ritual fence. From Tanaka 1991: 270. Courtesy of Tanaka Migaku and Shūeisha Publishers. 40

Figure 5.10. Sueki vessels from the Sue Kiln Group, Senboku, Osaka, fifth century AD. From Tanaka 1991, 325. Courtesy of Tanaka Migaku and Shūeisha Publishers. 42

Figure 5.11 Methods of firing sueki vessels in a climbing kiln (*noborigama*), and level kiln (*hiragama*), 2006: 34. Courtesy of Shinsensha Publishers. 1. Firebox. 42

Figure 5.12. Replicas of Early Kofun Period iron tools used in cultivation. Originals from the Shikinzan Kofun. From left to right, axe, adzes, hoe blade, fork, reaping tools. From Ōsaka Furitsu Chikatsu Asuka Hakubutsukan 2013: 41. Courtesy of Ōsaka Furitsu Chikatsu Asuka Hakubutsukan. 45

Figure 5.13. Replicas of Early Kofun Period iron tools for woodworking and carving. Originals from the Shikinzan Kofun. . From Ōsaka Furitsu Chikatsu Asuka Hakubutsukan 2013: 41. Courtesy of Ōsaka Furitsu Chikatsu Asuka Hakubutsukan. 45

Figure 5.14. Iron cuirasses of the fourth and fifth centuries AD. (1, 2, 3,4, 7) Examples in which the iron plates are fastened with leather thongs. (1) Vertical oblong plates. (2) Rectangular plates. (3) Oblong plates. (4) Triangular plates. (7) Horizontal oblong plates. (5) Triangular riveted plates (6) Horizontal oblong riveted plates. From Kobayashi 1990: 143. Courtesy of Kōdansha Publishers. 47

Figure 5.15. Reconstruction of suit of armor from the fifth century AD. (1) Peaked helmet with visor. (2) Neck guard. (3) Shoulder guard. (4) Fore arm protectors. (5) Knuckle protectors. (6) Metal plates of upper and lower parts are fastened with leather thongs. From Kobayashi 1990: 145. Courtesy of Kōdansha Publishers. ..47

Figure 5.16. The Nangō Site Group. 1. Residences of immigrants. 2. Elevated 'palace' of paramount chief. 3. Area for water rituals. 4. Ritual structure for paramount chief. 5. Specialized workshop. 6. Commoners' cemetery. 7. Large storehouses. 8. Elite houses. 9. Chief's house. 10. Ancestors' burials. 11. Paramount chief's residence. Adapted from Ban 2009: 11. Courtesy of Shinsensha Publishers. 48

Figure 5.17. Fifth century AD storehouses at Hōenzaka, Naniwa, on the Uemachi Terrace. From Ōsaka Furitsu Chikatsu Asuka Hakubutsukan 2006: 63. Courtesy of the Ōsaka Fu Bunkazai Sentā and the Ōsaka Furitsu Chikatsu Asuka Hakubutsukan. 49

Figure 5.18. The northern part of the Ōsaka region in the sixth and seventh centuries AD. (Based on Kusaka 2012 frontispiece). Sites: (1) Eguchi. (2) Naniwa Horie. (3) Naniwa Port. (4) Naniwa Palace. (5) Tamatsukuri. (6) Sumiyoshi Shrine. (7) Sumiyoshi Port. (8) Nagayoshi Kawanabe. (9) Furuichi Tomb Group. (10) Mozu Tomb Group. (11) Ikegami Sone. (12) Sayama Reservoir. Rivers: (13) Yamato River. (14) Ishi River. (15) Present Yodo River course. (16) Present lower Yamato River course. Roads: (17) Naniwa Great Road. (18) Shihatsu Road. (19) Ōtsu Road. (20) Tajihi Road. Ditches: (21) Hariuo. (22) Furuichi. (23) Nagasone Ditch. The present shoreline of Ōsaka is indicated by dotted lines. Courtesy of Kōdansha Publishers. 50

Figure 6.1. Plan of the Shitennōji, built in AD 588. 54

Figure 6.2. Sites in the Uemachi terrace region, in the Kodai Period. Based on Ichikawa et al 2011, 13. (1) Tenjinbashi. (2) Shōen (Chūsei Period Tenma Honganji Site). (3) Ōsaka Castle (4) Hōenzaka and Naniwa. (5) Saishōyama. (6) Kudara Amadera. (7) Saikudani Site. (8) Kudaradera (9) Tennōji Old Site. (10) Tennōji. (11) Abenosuji. (12) Kuwazu. (13) Naniwa Great Road. (14) Old Sumiyoshi Precinct. (15) South Sumiyoshi

Site. (16) Ori Ono. (17) Kire Higashi (18) Uriwari Kita (19) Uriwari. Courtesy of the Ōsaka Shi Hakubutsukan Kyōkai, Ōsaka Shi Bunkazai Kenkyūsho. 56

Figure 6.3. Reconstruction of the Naniwanomiya, Early Period (AD 652 to 686). From Ueki 2009: 2. Courtesy of Dōseisha Publishers. 57

Figure 6.4. Reconstruction of the Naniwanomiya, Late Period (AD 726 to 732). From Ueki 2009: 2. Courtesy of Dōseisha Publishers. 57

Figure 6.5. The sluice of the Sayama Dam. On both sides of the wooden sluice are two rows of recycled Kofun Period stone coffins, as well as a block of Izumi sandstone, with an inscription commemorating Priest Chōgen. From Ichikawa 2009: 106. Courtesy of Ichikawa Hideyuki...59

Figure 7.1. Reconstruction of a metal casters' village, twelfth to thirteenth centuries AD, Trench 1, Hiki Shō, Sakai City (from Sukigara 1999: 368). (A) Excavation area showing diagonal trench and rectangular boundaries of the old jōri field system, village sites in shaded areas, with building remains indicated by triangles and metal casting remains by circles. Old watercourses are shown as irregular lines. (B) Excavation plan. C. Reconstruction of site in Trench I. (1) Dwelling. (2) Storehouse. (3) Trench. (4) Hearth. (5) Trench. (6) Melting hearth. (7) Work area. (8) Well. Courtesy of Sukigara Toshio. 63

Figure 7.2. Stratigraphy and chronology of disasters affecting Sakai (from Morimura 1989: 50). Courtesy of Morimura Ken'ichi. 65

Figure 7.3. The moated city of Sakai and localities described in the text and grid areas A, B, and C. From Ōsaka Fu 2007: 2. Courtesy of Tsuzuki Shin'ichirō. 66

Figure 7.4. Reconstruction of Sakai from the mid fifteenth century to early sixteenth centuries. Adapted with permission from Tsuzuki 1994: 100. Courtesy of Tsuzuki Shin'ichirō...67

Figure 7.5. Reconstruction of Sakai from sixteenth century to the beginning of the seventeenth century. Adapted with permission from Tsuzuki 1994: 100. Courtesy of Tsuzuki Shin'ichirō. 67

Figure 7.6. Reconstruction of residences, shops, and three storey storehouses. From Morimura 2002: 279). Courtesy of Morimura Ken'ichi and the Kokuritsu Rekishi Minzoku Hakubutsukan..68

Figure 7.7. Plan of basement construction of storehouses, using a line of vertical tiles (senretsu). From Ōsaka Fu Bunkazai Sentā 2007: 2. Courtesy of Ōsaka Fu Bunkazai Sentā. 69

Figure 7.8. Detail of incised drawing on a grey rectangular tile of Chinese style boats of the type that visited Sakai in the latter half of the sixteenth century AD. Total width of drawing approx. 26 cm, Recovered from SKT3, Sakai. From Ōsaka Furitsu Yayoi Bunka Hakubutsukan 2008: 50. Courtesy of Ōsaka Furitsu Yayoi Bunka Hakubutsukan and Sakai Shi Kyōiku Iinkai. 69

Figure 7.9. Reconstruction of Ōsaka castle as it developed from 1583 up to the burning of AD 1615. Remains of the huge stones of the walls constructed under Hideyoshi are circled. Courtesy of Chikurinsha Kenkchiku Kenkyūsho. 74

Figure 7.10. Reconstruction of Ōsaka Castle after the rebuilding of AD 1620 up to 1868. Courtesy Osakajō Tenshukaku Hakubutsukan. 74

Figure A.1. The Ikegami Sone Site and surrounding sites of the Middle Yayoi Period. Redrawn from Ishigami 1985, 15. (1) Marsh, shoreline. (2) Sand bar. (3) Alluvial fan with natural terracing. (4) Flood plain. (5) Fan area. (6) Slope, natural terrace. (7) Old river course. (8) Recent reservoir. (9) Natural levee. Courtesy of Kubosō Kinen Bijutsukan. 81

Figure A.2. Yayoi Period sites mentioned in the text. The present shoreline of Ōsaka Bay, consisting of huge areas of landfill, is indicated, while the thick grey line shows the shoreline of the Early Yayoi Period. (1) Ama. (2) Higashi Nara. (3) Kitoragawa. (4) Uriūdō. (5) Ikeshima Fukumanji. (6) Kyūhōji. (7) Kamei. (8) Uriwari. (9) Nagahara. (10) Onchi. (11) Hajinosato. (12) Yotsuike. 82

Figure A.3. Plan of Ikegami Sone site, showing features dating to the latter half of the Middle Yayoi. adapted from Akiyama 2006: 30. Courtesy of Shinsensha Publishers. 82

Figure A.4. The large central building of the Ikegami Sone Site, November 2013. R. Pearson photograph. 83

Figure A.5. The Konda Gobyōyama keyhole shape tomb (zenpokoenfun) of the Furuichi Tomb Group. From Ōsaka Furitsu Chikatsu Asuka Hakubutsukan 2006: 15. Courtesy of Ōsaka Furitsu Chikatsu Asuka Hakubutsukan...84

Figure A.6. Waterbird haniwa from the moat of the Konda Gobyōyama Kofun, Furuichi Tomb Group, fifth century AD. Tokyo National Museum. Courtesy of TNM Image Archives. 85

Figure A.7. The Daisen Ryō Kofun (upper) and Kami Ishitsu Misanzai keyhole shape tombs (zenpokoenfun), of the Mozu Tomb Group. Fifth century AD. The total length of the Daisen Ryō Kofun is 850 m. From Ōsaka Furitsu Chikatsu Asuka Hakubutsukan 2006: 86). Courtesy of Ōsaka Furitsu Chikatsu Asuka Hakubutsukan and Sakai Shi Hakubutsukan. 86

Figure A.8. Daisen Ryō Kofun. Total length of the mound is 512 m, and total length of the site with moats and ridges is 512 m. Surrounding (satellite) tombs. (1) Chayama. (2) Dai'anjiyama. (3) Gen'eimon. (4)

Figure A.9. The Konda Gobyōyama Kofun, Furuichi Tomb Group, showing surrounding satellite tombs. From Tanaka 2001, 149. (1) Higashiyama. (2) Ariyama. (3) Ōtorizuka. (4) Konda Maruyama. (5) Kyukinzuka. (6) Nitzuzuka. (7) Bazuka. (8) Kurizuka. (9) Inner moat. (10) Inner ridge. (11) Outer moat. (12). Outer ridge (13) Ditch facing outer ridge. From Tanaka 2001: 149. Courtesy of Gakuseisha Publishers. 89

Figure A.10. Gilt bronze saddle bow from the Konda Maruyama Kofun, Furuichi Tomb Group. Fifth century AD. From Ōsaka Furitsu Chikatsu Asuka Hakubutsukan 2006: 50. Courtesy of Konda Hachiman Shrine and Ōsaka Furitsu Chikatsu Asuka Hakubutsukan. 90

Figure A.11. Iron cuirasses, shoulder protectors and helmets found in the Nonaka Kofun. From Takahashi and Nakakubo 2014: 2. Courtesy of Osaka Daigaku Kōkogaku Kenkyūshitsu. 91

Figure A.12. Artifacts from metal working workshops associated with Naniwanomiya; clay tuyeres (bellows valves), slag, whetstones, stone bases, and small containers. From Ōsaka 2008: 161. Courtesy of the Ōsaka Shi Hakubutsukan Kyōkai, Ōsaka Shi Bunkazai Kenkyūsho. 93

Figure A.13. Map of sites in the area of the Kodai Period Naniwanomiya and Chūsei Period Ōsaka Castle, showing ravines and locations of finds of seventh century AD, Silla and Paekche ceramics. Original prepared by Terai Makoto, Ōsaka Rekishi Hakubutsukan. From Ōsaka Furitsu Yayoi Bunka Hakubutsukan 2008, 78. Courtesy of Terai Makoto and the Ōsaka Furitsu Yayoi Bunka Hakubutsukan. 94

Figure A.14. Ceramics from Layer 3, SB 302, SKT 39, Sakai. From Morimura 2002: 280. Rubbings of the grooved surfaces of the tea mortar (upper right) are shown. The locations of some object are not indicated. The Chinese white, and blue and white, ceramics were produced in Jingdezhen Jiangxi Province (JDZ), and Zhang Zhou (ZZ), Fujian Province, China. Courtesy of Kokuritsu Rekishi Minzoku Hakubutsukan. ..96

Figure A.15. Floor plan of Layer 3 of SKT 39, Sakai, showing location of buildings SB 301 and SB 302. From Morimura 2002, 279. In the front of the property, near the road, were residential buildings with raised floors set on wooden pillars on stone bases. (Indicated as Stone Base). In the rear were multi storey storehouses, with tile lined basements (indicated as Tile). From Morimura 2002: 280. Courtesy of Kokuritsu Rekishi Minzoku Hakubutsukan. 97

Figure A.16. Tea related ceramics from Sakai sites. From Sakai Shi Hakubutsukan 2006. (1) Chinese Longquan celadon bowl, mid fourteenth century AD (found in Locality SB 3). (2) Black Oribe ware tea bowl, Mino Kilns (SKT 39). (3) Bizen ware water jar (SKT 39). (4) Shigaraki ware water jar (SKT 61). (5) Seto Mino flower vase (SKT 39). (6) Korean grey glazed jar (SB 301). (7) Blue and white box, Zhang Zhou Kilns, Fujian Province, China (SKT 794). (8) Karatsu ware tea bowl (SKT 230). (9) Vietnamese jar (SKT 230). (10) Group of blue and white bowls, Zhang Zhou Kilns, Fujian Province, China (SKT 230). Courtesy of Sakai Shi Kyōiku Iinkai and Sakai Shi Hakubutsukan..98

Figure A.17. Stoneware plate of South China Three Color Ware, found in SS201 Furitsu Yayoi Bunka Hakubutsukan and Sakai Shi Kyōiku Iinkai., Sakai. Early seventeenth century AD. From Ōsaka Furitsu Yayoi Bunka Hakubutsukan 2008: 28. Courtesy of Sakai Shi Kyōiku iinkai. 100

Figure C.1. Reconstructed storehouse at Hōenzaka, in front of the Ōsaka Museum of History. Photo by R.Pearson...105

Figure C.2. The exterior, stepped surface of the Ōsaka Furitsu Chikatsu Asuka Museum, designed by Andō Tadao. The museum is set in a large garden of flowering plums, designed by the architect. Photo by R. Pearson. 106

Table of Boxes

BOX 4.1.
    Yayoi Chronology, with reference to the Ōsaka Region 16

BOX 5.1
    Keyhole shape tombs 23

BOX 5.2
    The "Imperial Tombs" of Japan 25

BOX 5.3
    Triangular rim mirrors 27

BOX 5.4
    Historical texts and the Five Kings of Wa 33

BOX 5.5
    Haniwa 39

Box 5.6
    Sueki 41

BOX 5.7
    Cuirass 46

BOX 7.1
    Tea Ritual 71

BOX 7.2
    Shūinsen: the Red Seal Trade 72

Acknowledgements

The research for this project began about a decade ago, when I became interested in Japanese mediaeval archaeology, a field rarely published in the west. Further research was supported in 2007 and 2008 by the Sainsbury Institute for the Study of Japanese Arts and Cultures. I offer sincere thanks to the Institute and to Dr. Nicole Roumaniere, Director. Dr. Simon Kaner suggested many improvements to a preliminary draft. Thanks are also offered to Mr. Morimura Ken'ichi of the Sakai Senboku Suemura Shiryōkan, Mr Kotani Hiroshi of the Kotanijō Museum, Mr Tsuzuki Shin'ichirō of the Sakai City Museum, and Ms. Nakanishi Yumiko of the Cultural Properties Protection Division, Ōsaka Prefectural Board of Education, Mr Hirose Yukishige of the Ōsaka Furitsu Chikatsu Asuka Museum, and Mr. Okamura Katsuyuki of the Ōsaka City Cultural Properties Association. Professor Shiraishi Ta'ichirō, Director of the Ōsaka Furitsu Chikatsu Asuka Museum generously sent me precious research materials. I greatly appreciate the cooperation of the institutions that gave permission to use their illustrations in this book. They are acknowledged in the figure captions. Special thanks are offered to the Interlibrary Loan Office, University of British Columbia Library, who efficiently facilitated my use of books from North American libraries. Professor Gina Barnes reviewed the work in progress, providing detailed editorial and scholarly comments on two drafts, and motivated me to complete this project.

Chapter 1
Ōsaka Archaeology

This book is an archaeological study of the Ōsaka region from the about 20,000 years ago to 1868 AD. Its purpose is to introduce the recently excavated rich archaeological heritage of the Ōsaka area and to show how archaeology contributes to our general knowledge of Ōsaka in unique ways. While I provide minimal historical background in some sections, the book focuses on excavations, environmental data, sites, and artifacts and their interpretation.

From reports of recent excavations and environmental studies, I describe the unusual features of the region and its people. Located at the terminus of the Silk Route that extended from Europe through central Asia to maritime Asia and Japan, Ōsaka was the gateway to the Kinai hinterland of western Japan (Figure 1.1) and became a kind of economic powerhouse. I contextualize discoveries in terms of some established topics of anthropological archaeology, such as trade and social complexity. I also introduce the topic of Ōsaka cultural heritage management and provide introductions to some of the interesting archaeological museums in the region.

In the first chapter I introduce Ōsaka archaeology and its place in Japanese archaeology and point out its specific strengths and contributions to the study of Ōsaka. A comparative chronology of Japan, Korea, and China is given in Figure 1.2, a chronology of Japan in Figure 1.3, and a list of major sites in Figure 1.4.

The general significance of Ōsaka archaeology

A narrow coastal plain roughly 20 km x 20 km, now the center of Ōsaka City, has been a cultural and economic center of power of Japan for a very long time. It is the geographic center of the Kinai region, which extended from the shore of Ōsaka Bay through a network of rivers to the basins of Nara, Kyōto, and Omi. It played a critical role in industrial production and economic exchange from the end of the Jōmon Period around 1000 BC to the present.

While the entire Kinai region can be seen as the center of Japanese culture until the rise of Tōkyō and the Kantō region after 1615 AD, I argue that one sub region, the Ōsaka Plain, played a primary role. It was an area of vigorous Palaeolithic and Jōmon culture, the center of a network of large villages during the Yayoi Period, and the political center of Japan for parts of the Kofun, Asuka and Nara Periods. Later it was an area of rich and powerful manors in the Heian and Kamakura Periods.

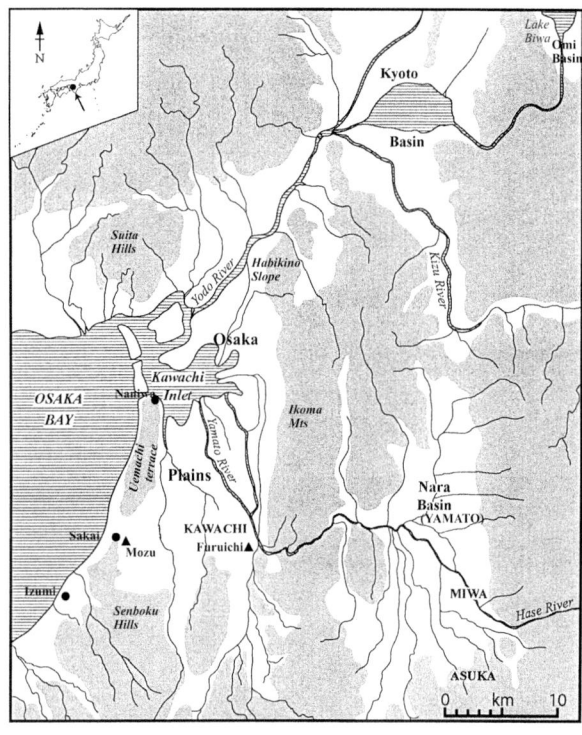

FIGURE 1.1. ŌSAKA, THE KINAI REGION, AND JAPAN. ADAPTED FROM BARNES 2007: 11. COURTESY DR. G.L. BARNES.

Unquestionably it worked in tandem with the adjacent Nara and Kyōto Basins, conveying people, ideas, and goods from continental Asia via the Inland Sea. Its ports were essential for the development of inland political centers. In the Chūsei (Mediaeval) Period, the city of Sakai emerged as the financial and cultural center of Japan. In the Azuchi-Momoyama Period, Ōsaka Castle dominated the region. In the Tokugawa Period Ōsaka continued to be a commercial center although the political center moved to Edo (Tōkyō).

As in every area of Japan, the past four decades witnessed the production of an incredible amount of new archaeological information, as archaeologists struggled to explore sites before they were destroyed in the path of economic development. Of course, key sites have been protected. Enormous rescue archaeology projects have been carried out since the 1970's, when Ōsaka was modernized with urban railway lines, sprawling highways, shoreline land reclamation, suburban housing and commercial centers, and an island airport. These developments, following the destruction caused by World War II bombing, left a concrete landscape with few vestiges of the past except the enormous "Imperial

	JAPAN (OSAKA)	KOREAN PENINSULA	CHINA
Late Palaeolithic	30,000 to 14,000 BC	Late Palaeolithic c. 30,000 to 8000	Late Palaeolithic 30,000 to 8500 BC
Jōmon	(6 periods) 14,000 to 1000 BC	Chulmun 8000 to 1500 BC	Neolithic c. 8500 to 2100 BC Xia c. 2100 to 1600 BC
Yayoi	Initial 950 to 780 BC Early 780 to 380 BC Middle 380 BC to 1 AD	Mumun 1500 to 300 BC Proto Three Kingdoms 300 BC to 300 AD Ko Choson ?108 BC to 300 AD	Shang c. 1600 to 1046 BC Zhou 1045 to 256 BC Qin 221 to 206 BC
Kofun	Late 1 to 240 AD Early 240 to 400 AD Middle 400 to 500 AD Late 500 to 600 AD	Chinese Commanderies c. 108 BC to 313 AD Koguryo 37 BC ? to 668 AD Paekche 18 BC ? to 660 AD Silla 57 BC ? to 935 AD	Han 206 BC to 220 AD Three Kingdoms 220 to 280 AD Jin 265 to 420 AD Southern and Northern 420 to 589 AD
Kodai	Asuka 600 to 710 AD Nara 710 to 794 AD Heian 794 to 1185 AD	Kaya Confederacy 42 to 562 AD	Sui 581 to 618 AD Tang 618 to 907 AD
Chūsei	Kamakura 1185 to 1333 AD Muromachi 1333 to 1568 AD Azuchi Momoyama 1568 to 1603 AD	Koryo 918 to 1392 AD Choson 1392 to 1897 AD	Song 960 to 1279 AD Yuan 1271 to 1368 AD Ming 1368 to 1644 AD
Kinsei	Tokugawa 1603 to 1868 AD		Qing 1644 to 1911 AD

FIGURE 1.2. ARCHAEOLOGICAL CHRONOLOGY OF JAPAN, KOREA, AND CHINA.

Tombs" which have no public access. To their credit, local governments have created many museums to commemorate the vanished archaeological sites. Some of these museums, and the general problems of heritage management and public archaeology, are introduced in Appendix C. A regional approach to archaeology will hopefully link sites to their landscapes and to each other, balancing the treatment of artifacts and stratigraphy with human communities and environment. My work is partially based on invaluable Japanese compilations such as those provided in Ōsaka Shi Bunkazai Kyōkai (2008) and Higashi (2009) that provide site summaries and descriptions of the most important finds.

Drastic changes to the shoreline of Ōsaka Bay, and the demolition of the Senboku upland to provide fill for the Kansai Airport have obliterated the original landscape. Smaller burial sites have been destroyed and the region has become completely built over. To show how the buried history of the region is maintained and interpreted, I have selected case studies for each period, describing the most dramatic discoveries and pointing out their significance. Figure 1.3 lists the major sites discussed in each chapter.

A brief summary of Japanese archaeology

In assessing the contribution of archaeology to understanding Ōsaka, it is important to set the region in the context of Japanese archaeology.

The archaeological framework consists of seven broad cultural periods, Palaeolithic, Jōmon, Yayoi, Kofun, Kodai, Chūsei, and Kinsei. Since many readers will prefer to link archaeological discoveries to familiar historical periods these are also included. I employ a mix of two chronological frameworks (Figure 1.4).

Japan was first occupied around 30,000 to 40,000 years ago. By around 5000 BC the Jōmon people reached a level of social complexity known as complex hunting and gathering, distinguished by social ranking (but not stratification into classes) and production of elaborate crafts, including fine pottery and lacquer covered objects. They began to experiment with horticulture of native plants. Around 1000 BC immigrants from the Korean peninsula moved into Kyūshū Island, bringing new ideas and artifacts that initiated the Yayoi Culture. This new culture spread to the Kinai and Kantō

Cultural Period	Sub Period or Historical Period	Dates
Palaeolithic	Late	30,000+ to 14,000 BC
Jōmon	6 periods	14,000 to 950 BC
Yayoi	Initial Early Middle Late	950 to 780 BC 780 to 380 BC 380 BC to 1 AD 1 to 240 AD
Kofun	Early Middle Late	240 to 400 AD 400 to 500 AD 500 to 600 AD
Kodai	Asuka Nara Heian	600 to 710 AD 710 to 794 AD 794 to 1185 AD
Chūsei	Kamakura Muromachi Azuchi Momoyama	1185 to 1333 AD 1333 to 1568 AD 1568 to 1603 AD
Kinsei	Tokugawa	1603 to 1868 AD

FIGURE 1.3. ARCHAEOLOGICAL CHRONOLOGY OF JAPAN.

regions. Yayoi people began intensive irrigated rice cultivation in lowland valleys and were organized into confederacies in some areas. Continental methods of cultivation, pottery making, weaving, and metallurgy were adopted through contacts with the adjacent Asian continent. In the subsequent Kofun Period, complex chiefdoms, characterized by paramounts that controlled subject chiefdoms, ruled with the help of immigrant clans who brought all kinds of new knowledge with them. These paramounts controlled the flow of iron and other valuable materials. Central authority shifted among several power groups in the Kinai region. In the sixth century AD Buddhism was introduced, and new forms of Chinese governance were adopted. In the Asuka and Nara Periods, the early part of the Kodai Period (see Figure 1.2), a Chinese bureaucratic model of a centralized state was introduced along with Tang Chinese civil and penal codes. Although it was based on Chinese forms, the actual operation of the model in Japan was less centralized and less coercive. It has been termed a galactic polity (Piggott 1997); the surrounding chiefdoms were loosely federated with a central cultural and ritual court. By the Heian Period the Chinese model, which had been imposed over an earlier form of familial authority (Hall 1966, Hurst 2009), lost its power. This familial authority can be seen in the growth of the estate (*shōen*) system, indirect rule by regents of the powerful Fujiwara Clan and retired sovereigns, and the rise of feudal warrior bands of *samurai* who were bound by patron client relations to royal and noble houses (Hurst 2009: 33). The Chūsei or "Mediaeval" period extends from the late Heian Period to the late Muromachi Period. During this period military rulers (*shōgun*) assumed political leadership. They first ruled in Kamakura, in the Kamakura Period (1185 to 1333 AD), and later in Kyōto in the Muromachi Period. Muromachi Period society has been described as capitalist-agrarian (Grossberg 1981: 14), in which the predominant activity was agriculture but cash crops, beyond the requirements for local consumption, were produced for markets. Beginning in the Yamato area in the fourteenth century and spreading throughout central Japan thereafter, concentrated, compact settlements developed; these have continued until the present day. Many villages established between the tenth and thirteenth centuries AD were extinct by 1300 AD, while those established in the fourteenth century and later coincide with present villages. In the late fourteenth century double cropping and conversion of dry fields was active, as small independent farmers appeared and the role of *shōen* manors declined (Troost 1997: 94-98). In the sixteenth century AD de facto power was held by the *shōgun*'s deputy (*kanrei*), until the warrior Nobunaga usurped the power of the *shōgun*'s office in 1573 AD.

From 1568 to 1598 AD, warring factions were pacified and political consolidation occurred. In the Kinsei or Pre Modern Period (1603 to 1867 AD) Japan became a network of feudal polities tightly controlled by the Tokugawa Clan, who fostered a vigorous domestic commercial sector.

The Contributions of Archaeology

What are the distinctive contributions of archaeology to the understanding of the past of Ōsaka and Japan in

Sites	Links to historical documents/events
Chapter 2 Morinomiwa, Final Jōmon to Early Yayoi Furuike, Final Jōmon Kitoragawa, Yayoi to Chusei Uriūdō, Yayoi to Kodai Kamei, Yayoi to Muromachi Uriwari, Palaeolithic to Muromachi Onchi, Yayoi	
Chapter 3 Kō Nagayoshi Kawanabe, Final Jomon Ikegami Sone, Early to Late Yayoi Higashi Nara, Yayoi to Kofun Ikeshima Fukumanji, Karako Kagi, Yayoi to Kofun Makimuku, Yayoi Ama, Yayoi	Chinese *Wei Zhi*, written c. 265 AD (Himiko account)
Chapter 4 Tamateyama Kofun Group, 4th cent AD Furuichi, Mozu Groups, mostly 5th cent AD Takaida Corridor Tombs, late 6th cent AD Suemura Kiln Group, 5th, 9th,10th cent AD Furu, 5th cent AD Nangō, 5th cent AD Haji no Sato, Palaeolithic to Nara AD Ōgata, 5th to 8th cent AD Tanabe, 7th to 8th cent AD Hōenzaka, 5th cent AD Narutaki, 5th cent AD Ōtsu, Nankai, Nagasone Ditches, 5th cent AD and later	Chinese *Song Shu*, written c. 492 AD (Five Kings of Wa) Adoption of Buddhism, c. 538 AD Construction of Shitennōji, c. 588 AD
Chapter 5 Early Naniwa Palace, 652 to 686 AD Late Naniwa Palace, 726 to 784 AD Sayama Reservoir, 7th century AD Senpukuji Sutra Mounds, 10th to 11th cent AD Dotō, 8th century AD	Taika Reforms, 646 AD *Kojiki*, written c. 712 AD *Nihon Shoki*, written c. 720 AD
Chapter 6 Shinpukuji Metal Casting Site, 13th cent AD Hiki Shōen sites Hine Shōen sites 13th to 15th cent. AD Sakai Moated City, 13th cent. AD to present Ishiyama Honganji, 1532 to 1580 AD Ōsaka Castle, 1583 to 1615 AD, later rebuilt	*Engishiki*, written c. 927 AD Defeat of Heike (Taira) Clan, 1185 AD Refurbishing of Tōdaiji, Chōgen, c 1200 Onin Wars, 1476-1477 AD Portugese arrive Tanegashima, 1543 AD Death of Oda Nobunaga, 1582 AD Death of Toyotomi Hideyoshi, 1598 AD
	Burning of Osaka, Sakai, 1615 AD Beginning of Sakoku Exclusion 1639 AD

Table 1.2. Major sites mentioned in the text, in relation to important historical documents and events.

general? The strongest contributions of archaeology concern environment, land use, economy, and spatial organization.

1. Archaeological excavation has uncovered stratigraphic and sedimentary data used by palynologists and geomorphologists to discover changes in landscape, vegetation, sea level, drainage patterns earthquakes and subsidence.

2. The interaction of Jōmon and Yayoi populations can be documented through the study of spatial patterning of distinctive artifacts such as pottery and stone tools. Social organization and patterns of authority can be inferred from village layout. The ditches discovered at Yayoi sites form the basis of speculation on defense and inter village relations, and the discovery of unusual large buildings has generated new theories on collective rituals and power. Buried field systems of Yayoi sites illuminate agricultural practices and technology.

3. The nature of prestige systems and economic exchange can be studied through changes in the types of artifacts and from spatial patterns of the distribution of artifacts in village sites and burials; for example, bronze mirrors and stone ritual ornaments gave way to armor and weapons on the Kofun Period.

4. Burial mounds of the Kofun Period provide rich data for inferring social organization and belief systems. Relative mound size and location show both social hierarchy and heterarchy, and the discovery of formulae concerning proportions reveals codes of construction shared by confederates and subordinates. The nature and placement of grave goods and tomb furnishings such as *haniwa* show religious beliefs (Wada 2014), while the uncovering and mapping of ancient roads and ditches illuminates the nature of the regional infrastructure, commerce, and communication. Studies of the chronology, manufacturing technology, and distribution in sites and regions of new forms of ceramics and metal objects show the key role played by immigrants, whose settlements can be documented by distinctive architecture and imported ceramics.

5. Exploration of ancient port areas of the Kodai Period shows the roles of foreigners and domestic power groups who sponsored temple construction. Evidence of coinage production in foreign enclaves suggests that foreigners played key roles in the economy, and excavations of ditches and reservoirs give an indication of improvements in engineering.

6. In the Chūsei Period abundant sherds of exotic ceramics graphically document the expansion of commerce, both domestic and foreign, plus the growth of social activities such as tea consumption. Changes in the composition of ceramic assemblages reflect changes in the source areas of ceramics and imported goods such as China or Vietnam, and the rise of local Japanese ceramic production.

7. Archaeology of the Kinsei Period contributes to knowledge of the layout and construction of industrial, administrative and residential sites.

Theoretical Orientation

What conditions led to the preeminent position of Ōsaka? A central location within the Japanese Islands, a rich river delta and ancient lagoon, and a busy port were important prerequisites. However, the Ōsaka region became pre eminent through the mobilization of social capital. Informed by the contributions of North (1981), Earle (1997), Robb (2010), (Campbell 2009), Schram (2010), and Schortman (2014), I propose that increases in productivity, power, and social complexity were achieved by entrepreneurs who participated in and mobilized social networks to initiate and execute projects which expanded the economy and contributed to the rise of the region.

An entrepreneur may be defined as a business leader, an innovator of new ideas and business processes, characterized by risk taking. Entrepreneurs act as catalysts for economic change. They introduce new technologies, increase efficiency or productivity and generate new products or services. For the purposes of this book, "business" may be considered broadly to be the realm of social and economic exchange. Schramm (2010: viii) distinguished productive entrepreneurship that enhances the growth of the economy from unproductive entrepreneurship that exploits opportunities for personal gain. In my opinion, improvements to transportation, such as roads and canals, and expansion of agricultural land and irrigations systems, are productive, while the construction of monumental tombs is unproductive, taking resources out of circulation. Entrepreneurs act in social arrangements or institutions, finding opportunities for change. Broadly speaking, institutions are any structure or mechanism of social order or co-operation governing the behavior of a set of individuals within a given community. According to the economic historian Douglass North, "institutions are a set of rules, compliance procedures, and moral and ethical behavioral norms designed to constrain the behavior of individuals in the interest of maximizing the wealth or utility of individuals" (North 1981: 201). North (1981: 205) proposed that

> "A political economy consists of a complex of interrelated institutions, specifying a pattern of wealth and income distribution and a system of protection among competing states, and a framework

of operating rules to reduce transaction costs in the economic sector."

The activity of entrepreneurs is specific to a set of relations; it takes place within institutions. Entrepreneurs are effective because they mobilize those around them in ways specific to each culture and landscape. There is a dialectic relation between structure and action, and agency is defined within particular historical settings (Robb 2010: 498-500). People's activities may be organized into projects. The concept of project is useful for the archaeological study of co-ordinated collective activities that leave sites such as remains of irrigation systems, large central dwellings, mausolea, capital complexes, etc, and is used in this book to explore the significance of archaeological sites. Industrial innovations such as metal working and coinage production leave distinctive physical sites; whereas trade missions and markets may be inferred from the distribution of goods changing hands under their auspices. In the following chapters I describe the major discoveries for each period, grouping them around the idea of projects, that expand the economy, extend trade and social networks, create new power systems, incorporate new social groups, and lead to new kinds of cultural expression. (I acknowledge that concept of 'projects' may difficult be difficult to apply to Palaeolithic and Jōmon activities but still propose that certain individuals were responsible for the invention and dissemination of new tool making tools and ritual objects.) The projects described in this book are listed in Figure 1.5.

A focus on networks is useful because it stresses actual human action in social and political settings instead of debating the degree of evolutionary complexity or the suitability of labels such as state or early state. Campbell recommends recontextualizing ancient polities as bundles of relationships within fields of culture, economy, and power (2009: 823). While Ōsaka shared a cultural repertoire with the rest of Japan, it was the economic and political center in the Kofun, Kodai, and Chūsei Periods. The region's economic systems extended to the Korean peninsula in a distinctive manner. Two perspectives have been identified by Schortman (2014: 167-168), one placing the emphasis on the pre-existing network, within which people take action, and the other on the actions of people, which create and change the network. People and groups used networks to build, maintain, and transform regional hierarchies. The study of how this was achieved is based on the identification of information, goods, and materials that were exchanged and their sources, changes in their volume and intensity, and the mechanisms of exchange.

Summary of contents

After this brief introduction in Chapter 1, I describe the environment of the Ōsaka Plain in Chapter 2. In

Palaeolithic Setouchi technique and Kō knife
Jomon Production of ritual objects Large Villages
Yayoi Adoption of wet rice cultivation Construction and expansion of irrigated field systems Construction of large villages, wells, ritual pits, ditches Centralization and co-ordination of rice storage Exchange of prestige goods Limited production of weapons and ritual items Construction of moated burial precincts
Kofun Monumental tomb construction Trade in iron ingots, weapons and armor Sponsorship of new technologies and craft production: ceramics, metal working, bead production Expansion of storage facilities Construction of roads and canals Construction of elite residential compounds
Kodai, Asuka Port construction in Naniwa area Construction of Naniwa capital Integration of foreign specialists into economic system Construction of first Buddhist temple, Shitennoji Reservoir construction, improvement of irrigation Construction of sutra mounds
Chūsei Craft production on estates Shift to commerce and diversification of economy Establishment of moated independent trading city Sakai Construction of religious center Ishiyama Honganji Construction of fortified political center Ōsaka Castle
Kinsei Promotion of new industrial techniques Warehousing

FIGURE 1.5. ANCIENT PROJECTS DESCRIBED IN THE TEXT.

Chapter 3 early hunter gatherers of the Palaeolithic and Jōmon Periods are introduced and their innovative lithic technologies and exchange systems are summarized. In Chapter 4, the adoption and expansion of irrigation technology and the rise of large central villages are described. In Chapter 5 the imposing tombs of Mozu and Furuichi are the main theme, but there are other sites that give an idea of the nature of power on the Ōsaka Plain in the Kofun Period. In Chapter 6 the main focus is the Naniwa Palace of the Kodai Period, with brief mention of early Buddhist sites. In Chapter 7, the scene shifts to the archaeology of production sites and the rise of mediaeval trading ports, particularly Sakai, a unique site which embodies the mentality of Ōsaka entrepreneurs and provides an introduction to the huge enterprise of mediaeval archaeology in Japan. Historical background of Sakai is presented in Appendix B. In the late sixteenth and early seventeenth centuries, as Sakai reached the height of its prosperity, two enormous cultural centers were built in rapid succession, at a central location where the delta of the Yodo River meets the Uemachi Terrace. These two huge sites, the Ishiyama Honganji Buddhist center and Ōsaka Castle, were started and destroyed in less than a century: they typify Ōsaka as a powerful center in the decades leading up to the formation of pre modern Japan, in the Tokugawa Period (1603 to 1867 AD). In Chapter 8, remains of warehouses and industrial processes show that Ōsaka continued to play an important role after the political center shifted to Tōkyō. In Chapter 9 the interaction of entrepreneurs, institutions and environment in the rise of Ōsaka is discussed. Summaries of sixteen excavations discussed in the text are grouped together in Appendix A. In Appendix B, the historical background of the mediaeval moated city of Sakai is presented, and Appendix C contains a discussion of Ōsaka's cultural heritage and selected museums.

Chapter 2
The Environment Of The Ōsaka Area And Its Changes

This chapter provides a brief discussion of the ancient environment of the region, derived primarily from the study of sediments found in archaeological sites. This environment afforded various opportunities as well as obstacles. A substantial portion of the Kinai region, the ancient cultural heartland of Japan, lies in the drainage system of the Yodo River, the eighth largest in Japan. This drainage system includes the Ōsaka region, Lake Biwa, the Kyōto Basin, the Ueno valley of Mie Prefecture, the northern portion of Nara Prefecture, and the Yamato River area (Ōsaka Shi Bunkazai Kyōkai 2008: 46). The Ōsaka region consists of the Yodo and Yamato Rivers, the Uemachi Terrace, the Kawachi Plain, and Suita and Senboku Hills to the north and south respectively. Rivers draining the Ōsaka region are shown in Figure 2.1.

The Kawachi Plain consists of a coastal and deltaic region, bounded by mountains and slopes. It is bounded on the north by the mouth of the Yodo River and the Senri Terrace, on the east by the Ikoma Mountain Range that separates it from the Nara Basin, and on the south by the Izumi mountains separating Ōsaka from the Kii River valley. The lower western slopes of the Ikoma Mountain Range, near modern Higashi (East) Ōsaka, are about 30m above sea level. The plain itself is 10km in length from the Ikoma Mountain Range to the coastal Uemachi Terrace. In ancaient times the central area, now a low lying section of Ōsaka City, was the delta of the Yamato River that drains the northern portion of the Nara Basin and flows through a narrow valley cutting through the Ikoma Range. It was an embayment during the earlier part of the Holocene as described below. In 1704 AD the Yamato River was artificially realigned to flow directly west from the Ikoma Range to Ōsaka Bay. The main portion of the Uemachi Terrace is approximately 10km long and 2 to 3km wide. For most of its length, from the vicinity of Ōsaka Castle to the Tennōji area, it is about 15 to 25m above current sea level. It has a central portion and lower slopes, which have been eroded into ravines (Ichikawa et al 2011).

To the northeast and east, respectively, of the Uemachi Terrace is the delta of the Yodo and ancient Yamato Rivers. Shifting sand bars divided the delta into many channels and narrowed access from Ōsaka Bay. To the east of the Uemachi Terrace the embayment mentioned above was a body of water until the end of the first millennium AD. As it filled in through alluviation and sea level change, it created rich areas for paddy cultivation and even pasture for horse rearing in the Kofun Period. This area has four components; alluvial fans, natural levees, flood plains

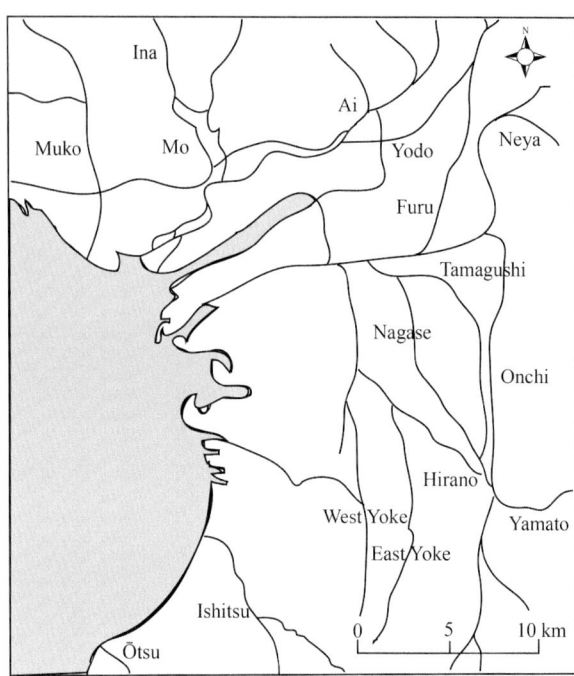

FIGURE 2.1. RIVERS OF ŌSAKA.

and lagoonal lowlands. While the Yamato River lacks a typical alluvial fan because the sediment it transports is composed of very fine detritus, there are still many small alluvial fans exiting along the foot of Mount Ikoma. Flood plains are lowlands more than 5m above sea level between the natural levees. They are generally covered with brown silt or silty clay more than 1m thick. Lagoonal lowlands are lowlands below 5m. They are covered with dark grey humic clay of the lagoon bottom (Yasuda 1978a: 225). The lagoonal lowlands and subsequent lake bottom were prime locations for paddy fields and could support both wet and dry cultivation depending on their preparation. They are surrounded by adjoining hills such as the Senboku Hills in the area of Sakai City.

Geomorphological Changes, Bay, Lagoon, Lake

A number of important geomorphological changes affected the delta area of the Yamato/Yodo Rivers and its back marshes as it changed from a marine bay to a fresh water lagoon and finally dry land (Yasuda 1977, 1978b, 1980a,b, hct.zaq.ne.jp 2014). Around 9000 to 8500 BP, a large marine bay covered the lowlying central portion of Kawachi. With climatic amelioration of the mid Holocene Period, the sea level rose rapidly and area

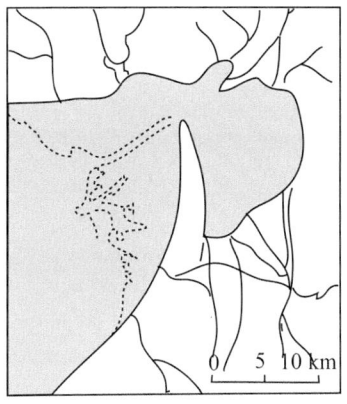 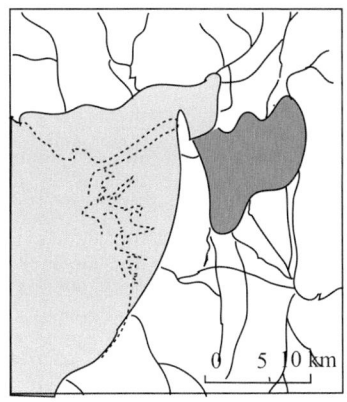 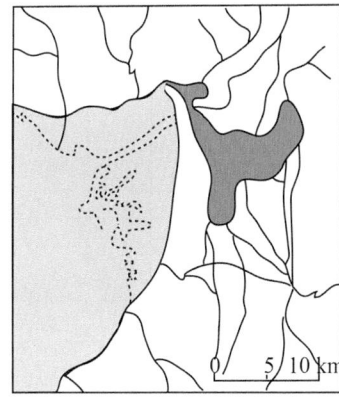

Kawachi Bay I (about 7500 to 6500 BP)   Kawachi Bay II (about 5500 to 4500 BP)   Kawachi Lagoon about 3000 to 2000 BP

FIGURE 2.2. KAWACHI BAY, LAGOON, AND LAKE. ADAPTED FROM KIHARA AND KAJIYAMA 1986: 32, 48, 80, 96. RADIOCARBON DATES SUPPLIED BY THE AUTHORS WERE RECALIBRATED USING WWW.CALPAL-ONLINE.DE, QUICKCAL VER 1.5 ACCESSED NOV 13 2013, AND THE DATING OF THE THREE PERIODS WAS ADJUSTED SLIGHTLY.

of the bay expanded. By 3000 BP the bay had contracted to expose lobes of the delta of the Yamato River. Sites dating from the Middle Jōmon (around 5500 BP) to the latter half of Late Jōmon contain salt water shells, indicating that the waters of Kawachi Bay were saline. In the early centuries of the first millennium BC at the time of the Final Jōmon and Early Yayoi, a shift from a salt water bay to a freshwater lagoon occurred. These shells include strawberry conch (*Conomurex luhuanus* Jap. *magakigai*), salt water clam (*Meretrix lusoria*, Jap. *hamaguri*), and marine snail (*Cerithideopsilla cingulata* Jap. *henatari*). Sites dating to the Final Jōmon and Early Yayoi (roughly 3000 to 2500 BP), such as the Morinomiwa Shellmound, contain freshwater shells such as basket clam (*Corbicula sandai* Jap. *setashijimigai*) (Odagi 2008 b, Yasuda 1978a, 212). By 2700 BP Yayoi villagers cultivated rice in the lowlying areas while living in villages in slightly higher regions. Alluvial deposits in the lowlying Kawachi area below 5m above current sea level are composed of clay and organic material that formed at this time on the bottom of the Kawachi freshwater lake, while those above 5m above sea level are composed of brown silt from the Yamato River. Kajiyama and Ichihara (1986) summarized the sea level changes as follows: Kawachi Bay (salt water), 7000 to 4000 years ago; Kawachi Lagoon (3000 to 2000 years ago; and Kawachi Lake (fresh water) 1800/1600 years ago to the fifth century AD (Figure 2.2). These dates have been adjusted to match recent radiocarbon recalibration.

Vegetation Changes

Yasuda (1978a,b, 1980a,b) describes vegetation changes of the Kawachi Plain (Figure 2.3). In the Late Jōmon Period much of the Kawachi Plain was swampy lowland composed of deposits of brown humic clay. The surrounding hills and mountains were covered by evergreen broadleaf forest composed of trees such as evergreen oaks and umbrella pine. At the beginning of the Latest Jōmon Period there was substantial flooding and blue grey sand and gravel were deposited to a depth of more than 50cm. The lobed delta of the Yamato River extended over the southern part of the Kawachi Plain. The surrounding dry land was composed of sand and gravel, while the marshy lowland was rich in humic soil. This geomorphological change was caused by sea level regression. Yayoi people lived in the higher areas and farmed the lowlying humic soil. The margins of the Kawachi Plain were wooded. Trees such as hackberry and muku tree were adapted to the emerging flood plains.

According to Yasuda (1980b: 235) all of the wooden artifacts found in sites in the lobed delta area are finished products, whereas many unfinished products are found in sites at the edge of the plain. People who living in villages in woodland at the edge of the Kawachi Plain produced artifacts and supplied them to villages in the delta, where soils were too wet to support thick forest. In the pollen diagram of the Furuike site, Izumi City, Ōsaka, the horizon dated 2940±85 BP shows high values of hackberry and muku trees that make up more than 40% of the arboreal pollen. The subsequent Yayoi farmers cleared the bottomlands and removed the hackberry forests (Yasuda 1980b: 242). In the Early and Middle Kofun Periods potters used the wood of trees such as oak for the firing of grey stoneware but after the sixth century AD they changed to red pine, secondary vegetation from forest clearance. Upland trees such as oak were valued for tools and construction projects (Yasuda 1980b: 243). The major tree species found in pollen analyses are listed in Figure 2.4.

Period	Vegetation	Sea level
13,000 to 10,200 BP	Dominant vegetation was coniferous subalpine forest	
11,800 to 11,000 BP short warm period	Increase in temperate species, of oak, elm, hornbeam	Sea level 22 m lower than present
10,200 to 9,000 or 8500 BP	Grass pollen is prominent, indicating low density of forest	
9000/8500 BP	Temperate trees such as oak, hackberry, Muku tree, elm, hornbeam increased rapidly, indicating climatic amelioration	Sea level rose rapidly, shoreline transgressed into the Kawachi Plain (Kawachi Bay)
ca 3000 BP		Kawachi Lagoon (brackish water), 3000 to 2,000 BP. Shoreline regressed, climate was slightly cooler and wetter than at present
Late Yayoi Period (date)	Lowland trees including *Celtis* and *Aphananthe* were cleared for paddy cultivation. Decrease in pollen of umbrella pine used for coffins and large buildings (Osaka Shi 2008, 46).	Flooding, covering sites with lake deposit
Early Kofun Period	Expansion of pine forests, arboreal pollen including broadleaf evergreen oak decreases	Contraction of Kawachi lake

FIGURE 2.3. CHANGES IN CLIMATE, VEGETATION AND SEA LEVEL FROM 13,000 BP TO THE FOURTH CENTURY AD. FROM YASUDA 1978A.

English name	Japanese name	Scientific name
Alder	*hasonoki*	Alnus japonica
Elm family	*keyaki*	Zelkova
Hackberry	*enoki*	Celtis japonica
Hornbeam	*shide*	Carpinus
Muku	*mukunoki*	Aphananthe aspera
Oak	*shii* etc	Quercus glauca, gilva, etc (Cyclobalanopsis)
Red pine	*akamatsu*	Pinus densiflora
Umbrella pine	*koyamaki*	Sciadopytis

FIGURE 2.4. TREES FEATURED IN POLLEN ANALYSIS, ŌSAKA REGION.

Paddy cultivation on the lake margins began in Yayoi Periods I and II (Murakawa and Kobayashi 1995: 31) as seen in the early evidence of paddies at Kitoragawa. In Yayoi Period II, sand transported by river flooding appears on top of the alluvium on the natural levees (*teibō*). The vegetation on these levees consisted of various willows, trees of the elm family, and Japanese alder. In the Yayoi Period III water levels were relatively stable. At the end of Period III or at the beginning of Period IV a period of flooding began, producing a yellowish white clay layer on top of a dark grey clay layer. Yayoi sites in the area are found buried below the present surface because of subsequent flooding. The area was covered with water to a depth of more than 1.5m, judging from pollen of species found in a deposit of black peat some 80 cm deep deposited during this flooding. At the end of the Yayoi Period the area was re-occupied (Yasuda 1980b: 235). Was the flooding exacerbated by extensive forest removal caused by the expansion of Yayoi cultivation? A similar situation was reported by Kusaka (2012: 29-33), who noted that in the Ikegami Sone area, small valleys were buried with sediment containing sherds dating to the Middle Yayoi Period. Early Kofun Period villages were built on these bars of gravel and sand. Kusaka attributed this alluviation to deforestation caused by clearing for cultivation in the Late Yayoi Period. However, some subsidence also occurred, allowing for changes in drainage patterns and marine incursions.

Flooding of the Kawachi Plain

Yasuda noted that there is absence of Yayoi sites dating from the end of the Middle Yayoi to Late Yayoi in the lowlying areas of the Kawachi Plain. Also, he noted that at sites such as Uriūdō, occupation layers from the end of Middle Yayoi were covered by clay and organic material created by the lake. In the Uriūdō site report he offered a reconstruction of landscape change from the Late Jōmon Period (roughly 1500 BC) to the end of the Middle Yayoi Period (Yasuda 1980a: 435) (Figure 2.5).

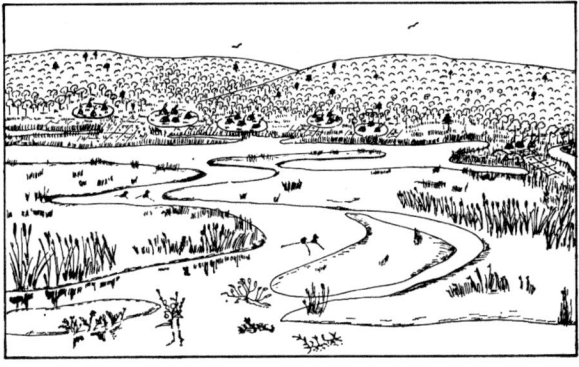

FIGURE 2.5. ENVIRONMENTAL CHANGES AT THE URIŪDŌ SITE. FROM YASUDA 1980: 435. (UPPER) LATE JOMON PERIOD, SALT WATER SHORELINE ENVIRONMENT. (MIDDLE) EARLY TO MIDDLE YAYOI PERIOD, FRESHWATER SHORELINE PADDIES WITH VILLAGES ON SLIGHTLY HIGHER GROUND. (LOWER) END OF MIDDLE YAYOI PERIOD, SHORELINE WAS FLOODED AND SMALL VILLAGES WERE BUILT ON HIGHER GROUND. COURTESY OF YASUDA YOSHINORI AND THE ŌSAKA FU BUNKAZAI SENTĀ.

Archaeologists found evidence of an earthquake of Magnitude 7 that occurred at the end of Middle Yayoi, followed by subsidence in the area (Higashi Ōsaka Shi Kyōiku Iinkai 2009: 27). Subsequent habitation layers date to the end of Late Yayoi, and are deposited on brown silt and greyish white sand from riverine deposits. Nearby sites at similar elevations, such as Kamei and Uriwari, were not occupied from the Middle Yayoi to the late sixth century AD and during this hiatus, were covered by alluvial deposits. Yasuda (1978a: 224) proposes that the discharge of the Kawachi lagoon was blocked by newly forming sand bars at the mouth of the Yodo River and slowed by the rising of sea level in relation to the lake level. This disparity in water level could have occurred either through a rise in sea level or subsidence of the Kawachi Plain, or both processes. At another site, Nagahara, the entire span of occupation of the Ōsaka Plain can be seen in the cross section (Figure 2.6).

The dramatic demise of important low lying sites at the end of Middle Yayoi may have been a major factor in the shift to settlement in smaller sites at higher elevations. An increase in warfare has generally been considered the main cause of this change (Yasuda 1978a: 211) but multiple factors must have been involved. Kawachi Lake remained until the Heian Period, when it was reduced to river courses. Ichihara (1975) recognized two periods of Kawachi Lake, from roughly 1800 years ago to the fifth century, and from the fifth century to the eighth and ninth centuries AD. In the fifth century AD flood control and improved access to Ōsaka Bay were achieved by digging a channel, the Horie, through the northern part of the Uemachi Terrace.

In the southern part of the Ōsaka Region in the modern city of Izumi Ōtsu similar results were derived from analyses by Kusaka (1980: 175-216) of pollen and diatoms in sediments, obtained by boring. In the approximate time range of 7000 to 6000 BP there was evidence of the Jōmon Transgression in the form of black clay with organic materials. In the pollen analysis deciduous broadleaf trees predominated, indicating a cooler climate than at present, and there was evidence of a shift from fresh to brackish water and back to fresh water. From 6000 to 3000 BP broadleaf evergreen forest predominated. Rice pollen dated to the Yayoi Period is found, and in the latter part of the Yayoi Period temporary climatic cooling is interpreted from a decrease in the pollen of broadleaf evergreen trees and an increase in conifer pollen, although these changes could be the result of human forest clearance. There is also evidence of a marine incursion similar to the one that occurred in the Kawachi area. Small lower valleys were buried from erosion caused by clearance on the slopes, and Yayoi Period sites are covered by up to 120cm of soil.

In samples from the Onchi Site, pollen analysis showed that at the time of the first development of the paddy system, pollen from broadleaf evergreen trees such as oak and chestnut from the surrounding forest was abundant; but later, the pollen of hackberry and deciduous secondary forest species increased as clearing of the plain continued. Analysis of charcoal in the samples shows that these species increased after burning. They were later replaced by the spread of red pine secondary forest in the Kofun Period (Yasuda 1980b). The Onchi and Uriūdō sites were flooded in the Middle Yayoi

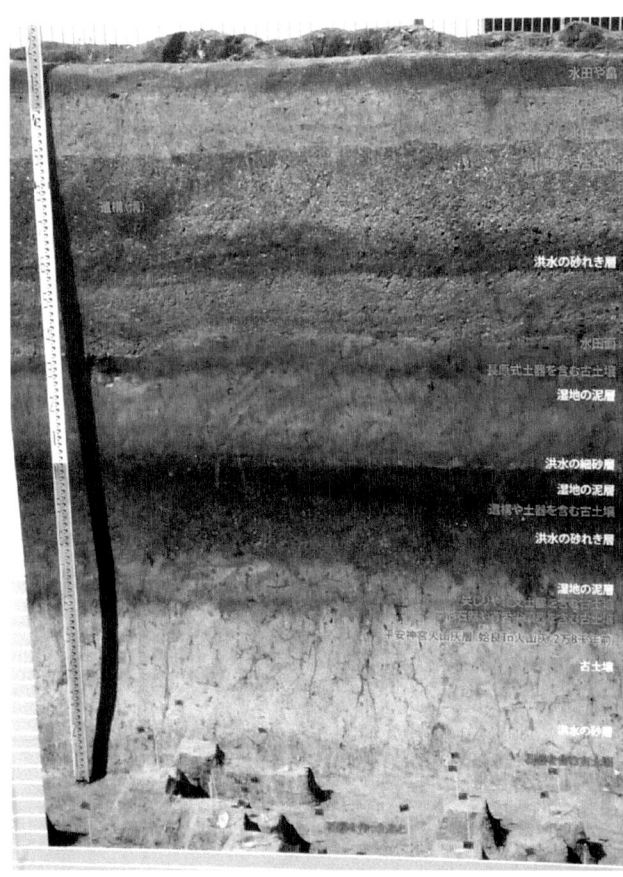

FIGURE 2.6. STRATIGRAPHIC SECTION OF THE NAGAHARA SITE, ŌSAKA, SHOWING THE ENTIRE SPAN OF OCCUPATION OF THE ŌSAKA PLAIN FROM THE LATE PALEOLITHIC PERIOD TO THE PRESENT. PART OF A DISPLAY AT THE ŌSAKA MUSEUM OF NATURAL HISTORY, NOVEMBER 2013. COURTESY OF THE ŌSAKA SHI HAKUBUTSUKAN KENKYŪKAI, ŌSAKA BUNKAZAI KENKYŪSHO.

Period. Paddies were relocated to higher areas and the submerged areas could not be occupied until the end of Late Yayoi.

Chinese data show a warm peak around AD 200 but temperatures declined rapidly in the third century and around 270 AD the temperatures of the Kofun Cold Period reached their minimum (Tanioka 2008: 87). In the Kofun Period pollen of pine trees increased, indicating the spread of secondary forest through forest clearing and ceramic production (Chapter 5). There is evidence of brackish water diatoms, indicating flooding during very strong typhoons or a temporary rise in sea level (Kusaka 1980: 212). By 800 AD the Kinai periphery was stripped of suitable timber. The construction boom of 600 to 850 AD was not sustainable (Totman 1989: 27).

Chapter 3
Early Hunter Gatherers:
the Palaeolithic and Jōmon Periods (ca. 20,000 BC to 950 BC)

Palaeolithic Period

Settlement in the Ōsaka area began as early as 23,000 to 18,000 years ago, judging from finds of small camps found on marine terraces (Kinugawa 2008a). Footprints of some of the prey animals of these hunters, deer and Nauman's elephant, have been recovered from ancient mud deposits as early as 20,000 years ago (Chō 2008).

The Kō Site, located near the junction of the Yamato and Ishi Rivers, within the Kofun Period Furuichi Tomb Group mentioned in Chapter 5, is famous as a production site of the Kō Knife, a specialized stone knife fashioned from local sanukite, a tough volcanic stone found in the nearby Mount Ikoma area. This type of artifact dates to roughly 19,000 to 13,000 years ago, in the Late Palaeolithic Period (Kinugawa 2008b). It first appears in the Kinai area and later was adopted in other parts of Japan. In order to make tools from such dense stone, which is much more difficult to work than glassy obsidian or silicious chert, the inhabitants devised a means of using an oblong stone core, from which thick flakes were removed by percussion by the side blow technique, known as the Setouchi (Inland Sea) Technique (Figure 3.1). As early at 1917, the Kyōto University archaeologist Kita Sadakichi noted that at the Kō Site, these artifacts occurred in a layer below the Jōmon Layer, and questioned whether they might pre date it. Kita's observations (academics3, 2014) are intriguing since the Japanese Palaeolithic was not formally recognized until after 1945, at the Iwajuku Site in Gunma Prefecture. Other forms of stone tools include finely flaked stemmed points of sanukite, dating from 16,000 to 11,000 years ago. They were hafted to spears for hunting (Odagi 2008a).

Jōmon Period

With the advent of the Jōmon Period (ca. 14,000 to 1950 BC) innovations include pottery making and new forms of stone tools as well as new methods of food gathering, preparation, and storage. Jōmon people produced various kinds of ornaments and ritual objects that show a rich social and ceremonial life. The oldest types of Jōmon pottery found in the Ōsaka region include the Awatsu SZ Type, decorated with the edge of a bivalve shell or bamboo spatula but often called finger nail impressed dating to the Initial Jōmon (Sugimoto 2008a) (Figure 3.2), and the Kijima Type, a deep jar decorated with roller stamp impression (*oshigata mon*). In the first half of the Earliest Jōmon Period, small villages occurred along the foot of the Ikoma Range, inland from Kawachi Bay. They consisted of four to six pit houses and about ten outdoor cooking hearths. The pottery is of the *oshigata*

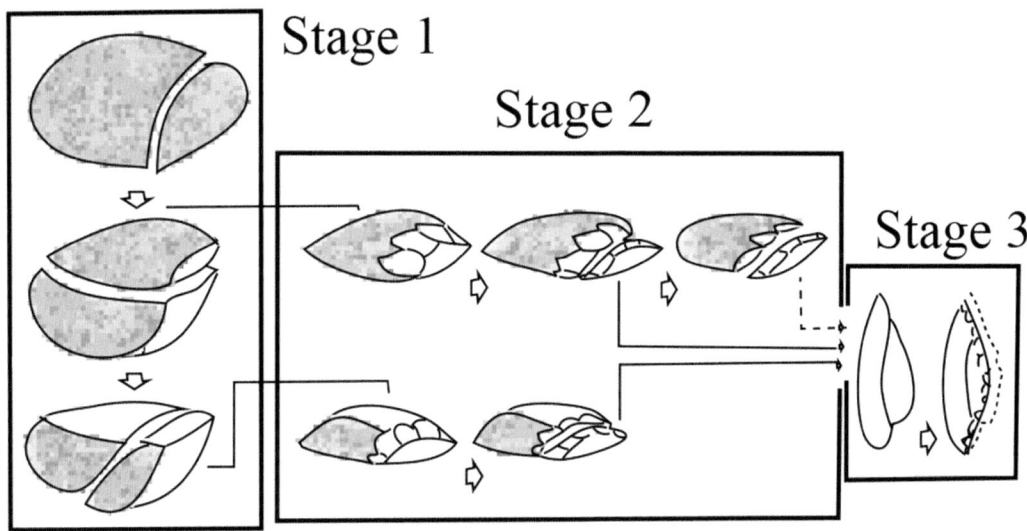

FIGURE 3.1. STEPS IN THE MANUFACTURE OF THE KŌ TYPE KNIFE BY THE SIDE BLOW TECHNIQUE. ADAPTED FROM KINUGAWA 2008: 24. IN STAGE 1, A CORE IS MADE FROM A PEBBLE, BY REMOVING A PIECE FROM A PEBBLE BY PERCUSSION. IN STAGE 2, FLAKES ARE REMOVED BY THE SIDE BLOW TECHNIQUE. IN STAGE 3, THE FLAKES ARE RETOUCHED FOR USE AS KNIVES. COURTESY OF THE ŌSAKA SHI HAKUBUTSUKAN KYŌKAI, ŌSAKA SHI BUNKAZAI KENKYŪSHO.

FIGURE 3.2. THE EARLIEST JŌMON POTTERY FOUND IN THE ŌSAKA REGION, THE AWATSU SZ TYPE. FROM SUGIMOTO 2008: 34. COURTESY OF THE ŌSAKA SHI HAKUBUTSUKAN KYŌKAI, ŌSAKA SHI BUNKAZAI KENKYŪSHO.

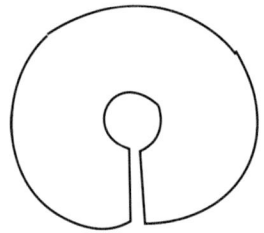 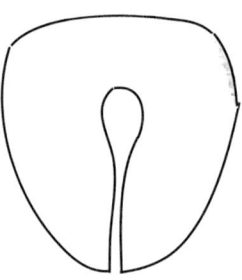

FIGURE 3.3. SLIT EARRINGS OF JADE FOUND IN BURIALS AT THE KŌ SITE. REDRAWN FROM YONEDA 2006. TOTAL DIAMETER APPROX. 5CM.

mon (roulette impressed) type in which a small carved stick is rolled or impressed on the surface of the pottery, and stone tools include stemmed points and abraders, as well as triangular concave based points (Kashiwara Shiritsu Rekishi Shiryōkan 1994). Stone querns have also been found. The sites appear to be base camps from which people travelled on a seasonal round to collect and process local foods.

A particularly large and important site, Morinomiya, is located on the old shore of Kawachi Bay near the modern subway station of the same name. It was occupied from 4000 to 2000 years ago (Odagi 2008b, Matsuo 2008a). In layers dating to the Final Jōmon Period shellfish species indicate the transition from salt water to fresh water as indicated in Chapter 2. Fishing gear, ornaments and a local type of Jōmon figurine were also found. In the Late Jōmon Period pottery types from the Kantō, Hokuriku, and Kyūshū regions show that the Ōsaka area became an important center for exchange. This central position was maintained in the Yayoi and later periods.

The Kō Site mentioned above is stratified, with cultural layers from the Jōmon, Yayoi and later periods in addition to those of the Palaeolithic. From excavations in 1917 slit ring jade earrings were found in Early Jōmon Period burials dating to roughly 6500 to 5500 years ago. These have been registered as Important Cultural Properties and are held in the Archaeological Museum of Kansai University. There has been a long debate on the origins of this type of earring, since similar types have been found in Jiangsu Province in China. The relative antiquity of the earrings in the two areas changes as new finds and dating techniques are reported. However, it would seem likely that interaction between the Yangtze River and Kinai regions already occurred at this time period. In Japan, clay and antler forms have also been found (Yoneda 2006). Jade occurs in the Itoigawa area of Niigata Prefecture. Slit earrings first appear in the Initial Jōmon Period and by Early Jōmon are found in various parts of Japan, but are always rare. Perhaps 100 specimens have been found in total. They were probably used in communal ritual rather than being personal property or prestige goods (Fujiidera Shi 2015).

It is striking that a small area at the junction of the Yamato and Ishi Rivers should reveal so many forms of evidence of interaction between Ōsaka and the continent, from the time of Jōmon hunter gatherers. This area was truly significant in Ōsaka prehistory and history.

Accomplishments of the Palaeolithic and Jōmon Periods include the development of distinctive tool making techniques and participation in wide spheres of interaction. The diverse environment of the Kawachi Bay/Lagoon, marine shore terraces, and surrounding mountains also presented challenges to hunter gatherer populations. In particular, unpredictable flooding of the Yodo River system caused much hardship.

Chapter 4
The Expansion of Agrarian Society; the Yayoi Period (950 BC to 240 AD)

The Yayoi Period is marked by the development of warfare and social ranking and the introduction of continental style pottery and bronze objects. New techniques of weaving and metal working were adopted as well as many continental concepts in religion, architecture and engineering. These include systems of measurement, new styles of buildings, and cosmological concepts. Yayoi people made distinctive pottery often finished with smoothed surfaces and based on a different shape such as vessels with constricted waists, flared pedestals, and narrow mouthed jars. Well known examples the come from the Kuwazu Site (Figure 4.1).

In the Ōsaka region the Yayoi Period began around 950 BC (Box 4.1). The arrival of farming groups expanding from North Kyūshū through the Inland Sea Region to the Kinai Region brought about the transition to farming on the alluvial lowlands of the Ōsaka Region and the establishment of an agrarian society fundamentally different from that of the Jōmon Period. Political alliances that relied on religious power and charisma rather than on military control linked villages into networks around nodes of power (Mizoguchi 2012, 2013). Yayoi settlement was exceptionally dense in the Ōsaka Plain, despite its relatively small size. In the latter half of Middle Yayoi, large central sites were relatively numerous compared to other regions (Wakabayashi 2009: 37). Key debates about the Yayoi Period in the Ōsaka Region concern the process of adoption of cultivation and its timing, the nature of very large Yayoi settlements and exchange networks, and the relationship of Ōsaka Yayoi communities to those in the adjacent Nara Basin. Synergy between these two areas was important in early state formation. Why did some sites increase in size and what was the nature of their central buildings? What factors led to the decline of large central sites in the Late Yayoi Period? How did leadership change at the end of the Yayoi Period? Did new ideologies play an important role?

The transition from Jōmon to Yayoi in the Ōsaka area

The process by which Yayoi farming began in the Kinai region of Japan involved new crops, people, technology, and worldview. The transition to intensive rice cultivation took several steps.

1. Jōmon people were already familiar with cultivation of various plants in dry field horticulture. The shift

Figure 4.1. Earthenware storage and serving vessels found in a ditch at the Middle Yayoi Period Kuwazu Site, Ōsaka. From Ōsaka Shi 2008,: 61. Courtesy of the Ōsaka Shi Hakubutsukan Kyōkai, Ōsaka Shi Bunkazai Kenkyūsho.

from Jōmon to Yayoi was not a shift from hunting and gathering to cultivation, but rather a shift from horticulture to paddy cultivation, Of course hunting and gathering continued to be an important source of food in the Yayoi Period.

In the Late Jōmon Period rice and beans were grown in areas of Kyūshū, where storage pits have yielded the remains of the rice weevil, *Sitophilus linearis,* which eats crops such as wheat, sorghum, and barley in addition to rice (Fujio 2011: 133). Around 3000 years ago, at the time of the Jōmon Kurokawa Type of pottery of northern Kyūshū, cultivators began to modify water courses into

ŌSAKA ARCHAEOLOGY

> **BOX 4.1.**
> **Yayoi Chronology, with reference to the Ōsaka Region**
>
> Akiyama (2006: 65) proposed the following chronology for the Yayoi Period of the Ōsaka region: Initial, 950 to 780 BC; Early, 780 to 380 BC; Middle, 380 BC to 1 AD; Late, 1 to 240 AD. The revised dating is based on the compilation of new AMS dates and recalibration using recent curves (Fujio 2009: 2011; Akiyama 2006: 65, Takesue et al 2011: 8). Cross dating of artifacts and sites has revealed inconsistencies that have been taken into account. For instance, some artifacts clearly derived from proto types found in the Korean peninsula have been found in contexts dated earlier than the Korean proto types, suggesting that the Korean proto types need to be re-dated, and some Chinese mirrors kept as heirlooms in Japan for several centuries are found in contexts much later than their date of manufacture (Takesue et al 2011). Based on the new dates, Fujio (2011: 20-22) described major changes in the current conception of the Yayoi Period. Rice paddy cultivation in Japan began as early as the ninth to tenth centuries BC in northern Kyūshū and was carried out without iron tools until around 400 BC. The total length of the Yayoi Period has been extended from 500 to about 1200 years, meaning that each pottery type lasted much longer than previously believed (Fujio 2009). Before the revision of the dating, some archaeologists believed that each pottery type lasted about one generation, and that houses with the same pottery type found directly on their floors must have been occupied at the same time. Based on these assumptions, archaeologists estimated village population size based on a proposed rate of five persons per house, times the number of houses occupied simultaneously. However if each pottery type lasted for a longer duration, houses with such pottery directly on the floor (not deposited later) may not have been occupied at the same time. Thus villages were occupied for longer periods of time by fewer people. This finding affects estimates of population growth and the rate of spread of migrants and practices such as paddy cultivation.

FIGURE 4.2. NAGAHARA TYPE POTTERY, THE OLDEST YAYOI POTTERY FOUND IN THE ŌSAKA AREA. NAGAHARA SITE, ŌSAKA. FROM ŌSAKA SHI 2008: 43. COURTESY OF THE ŌSAKA SHI HAKUBUTSUKAN KYŌKAI, ŌSAKA SHI BUNKAZAI KENKYŪSHO.

small natural marshes using river oxbows and alluvial regions. In the Initial Yayoi of the Sora Plain of northern Kyūshū, paddy fields were developed in the lower and middle river valleys while dry fields were opened up in the upper areas (Fujio 2011: 133).

2. It took about 300 years for rice cultivation to spread from northern Kyūshū to the Kinai Region (Fujio 2011: 20-22). Jōmon horticulturalists of the Kawachi area used the Nagahara Type of pottery (Figure 4.2), which retains Jōmon features such as the horizontal ridge (*tottaimon*).

Sherds of this type of pottery from the Nagayōshi Kawanabe Site, dated to the Final Jōmon Period, contain rice impressions (Ōsaka Shi Bunkazai Kyōkai 2008: 42). Presumably villagers received rice from Yayoi people in the area, or were beginning to make their own paddies independently. Migrant farmers who practiced irrigation brought with them the Ongagawa Type of pottery, distinguished by Yayoi features such as a flat foot, bulging lower section, constricted upper body or neck, and a short collared rim. Sites yielding this pottery type have produced charred rice grains, wooden agricultural tools for opening up and maintaining rice paddies such as shovels and hoes, stone reaping knives, actual remains of paddy fields, and rice pollen (Akiyama 2007: 35). In some cases groups using Ongagawa pottery lived within Jōmon villages. In others, Jōmon villages identified by Nagahara Jōmon-type pottery were found within 500m of villagers of Ongagawa pottery users. There were also Jōmon villages where Ongagawa pottery was rare or completely absent and also villages with only Ongagawa pottery. In some 23 sites reported up to 2007 (Akiyama 2007:191), Jōmon figurines and stone rods indicative of Jōmon religious practice were found. They continued to be used in the Early Yayoi Period, indicating that Jōmon ritual practices were retained in the Yayoi Period, after the adoption of Yayoi type pottery, and that there was a period of several centuries of cultural mixing (Akiyama 2007: 112-148).

The Expansion of Agrarian Society

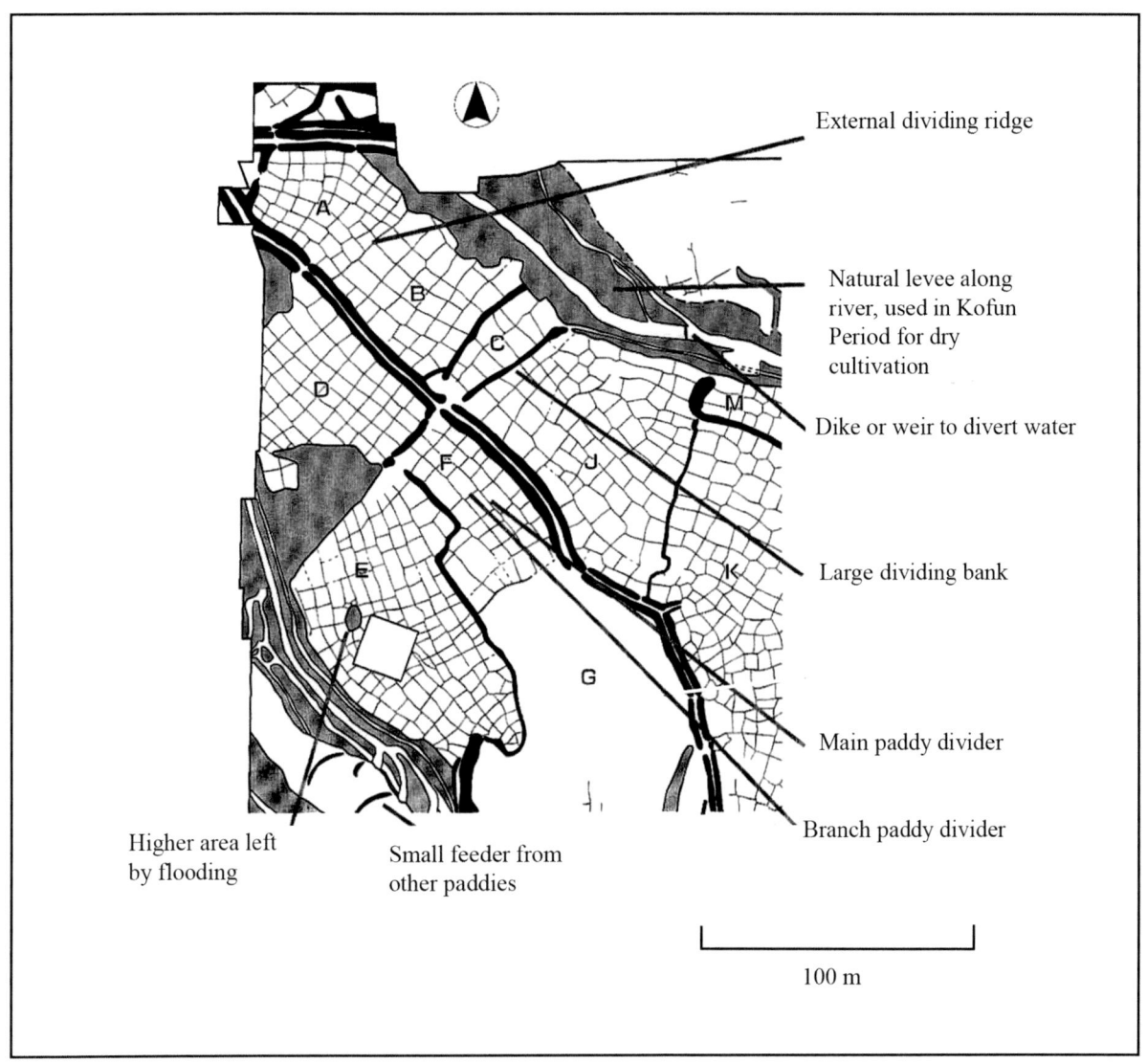

Figure 4.3. Map of rice paddies, Late Yayoi Period, Ikejima Fukumanji Site, Ōsaka. Adapted from Eura, 2012. Powerpoint presentation slide 14. Courtesy of Eura Hiroshi.

Yayoi cultivation

The geomorphology of the Ōsaka Plain, discussed in Chapter 2, is key to understanding the progression of Yayoi cultivation. Two river systems, the Yodo and the Yamato, drained into a single basin. At times areas were submerged and covered with a black organic layer containing shells, while past flooding brought layers of sand. The cycle of flooding in later periods actually protected ancient field systems until the advent of archaeologists in the 1970s, who cleared and mapped wide areas of ancient paddy fields in huge excavations. These paddies are difficult to discern in narrow trench style excavations.

Natural levees composed of brown silt or silty fine sand are found along the old courses of the Yamato River. Alluvium began to form along the rivers and between the natural levees in the Later Jōmon Period with lower sea levels in Kawachi Bay. Small elongated rice paddies were constructed and were watered by erecting dams and diverting water into channels (Inoue 2007: 24). In the latter half of Final Jōmon, early farmers could not control the abundant water lying in the lowest areas, which were prone to flooding.

One of the most extensive paddy systems to be investigated was found at the Late Yayoi Period Ikeshima Fukumanji Site, in the vicinity of Yao City in the southeastern part of the Kawachi Plain (Figure 4.3).

Excavation of an area of 120,000m² took place between 1981 and 1986, in preparation for flood control construction projects along the Onchi River (Eura 1996:

2012). Layers of flood deposits some 4m deep separate the Yayoi layers from the present ground surface. Three or four separate Yayoi layers could be discerned. In the Late Yayoi Period hexagonal paddies were efficiently arranged to increase the paddy area fed by each irrigation channel.

From the end of Middle Yayoi, large central villages declined in size and number. At first this was interpreted as a kind of collapse or depopulation, attributable to an increase in warfare or displacement by floods. While both of these probably affected the livelihood of people in the Late Yayoi Period, Wakabayashi (2006, 2009) proposed that what actually occurred was a steady increase in population with a reorganization of demography. He stated that throughout the Yayoi Period there were three basic site location types; marine terraces, riverine alluvial terraces, and hilltops. The number of sites on the marine terraces, such as Ikegami Sone remained stable, although the size of the settlements declined while sites on riverine alluvial terraces and hilltops increased. Lowland flooding in the latter half of the Yayoi Period may have reduced the carrying capacity of the large sites, forcing some segments to relocate on higher land (Mizoguchi 2013: 180). Cultivation seems to have become dispersed, the farmers living in small settlements occupied by single consanguineous groups. Murakawa and Kobayashi (1995: 113) concluded that the increase of upland sites may indicate agricultural expansion created by a steady population increase but in fact the increase in upland sites is balanced by a decline in large villages on the river terraces.

Hirose stated that in the Yayoi Period, irrigation technology included the diversion of water from natural streams to artificial ditches, the construction of artificial ditches, and the combination of these in the same system (1984). While he proposed that these occurred in an evolutionary progression, it seems more likely that different techniques depended on the environmental situation. In some cases lines of stakes set in a river bed supported a weir that diverted water into paddies, as at the Nishiurahashi Site, where water was diverted from the Wada River, some 10 to 20m wide and 2m deep. In other sites such as Makimuku, mentioned below, manmade ditches were dug. In the Asuka and Kodai Periods, discussed in Chapter 6, large man made watercourses and reservoirs were constructed.

The Archaeology of Large Villages

One of the first excavations of a very large Yayoi site took place at Higashi Nara, Ibaraki City (Ōsaka). The site was rectangular, being 1km on each side. The most dramatic finds were fragments of at least six sandstone molds for casting ritual bells (*dōtaku*), fired clay molds for making glass curved pendants (*magatama*), and fired clay bellows valves showing that high temperatures could be achieved by using forced air (Tanaka 1991: 140). Another famous site, Kamei, occupied from the early part of Middle Yayoi to early Late Yayoi, yielded bronze arrowheads and fragments of bronze bells (*dōtaku*) (Sugimoto 2007: 53). Specialized craft production sites of this type are quite rare in the Ōsaka area. As well as metal objects, fine pottery for ceremonial use was definitely produced in large centers.

The discovery of very large Yayoi villages in the Kinai region, northern Kyūshū, and possibly the Nagoya region has led to vigorous debates about the nature of Yayoi village life, political organization and production. These sites have been termed central or stronghold villages (*kyōten shūraku*). In the Middle Yayoi Period of the Kinai region about 50 of these sites have been recorded (Ikegami Sone Shiseki 1996: 68). Evidence of moats is often present. In Sakai's model (Sakai 2001) the central site sits in a series of catchments, being surrounded by small agricultural villages, about 5km distant.

Hirose (1998) proposed that the sites were actually urban centers, showing dense habitation, centralized power, social stratification, craft specialization, and economic co-operation among hunters, fishers, traders, and religious specialists. He defined the Yayoi Period urban center as " space where people who carry out the reproduction and maintenance of a group of a certain region live, and where the functions of religious, economic and political centers were situated under the leadership of a chief" (1998: 56). He identified four distinguishing features of Yayoi urban centers: a concentration of population, a functional division of labor, the presence of chiefs, and the existence of a shrine to symbolically unify the population. The presence of a moat was also found to be important. He noted that the contents of the ditches show dense human settlement since they were filled with large amounts of garbage containing insects associated with human refuse (Hirose 1998: 38). It should be noted that bronze casting is usually restricted to one locality within each site. Wakabayashi (2009: 50) concluded that Ikegami Sone was a large central settlement, with population concentration, but there was no evidence of social hierarchy within the site, or a non-farming population, or an administrative class found in an urban center (2009: 50). He noted that spatially separate burial precincts were established by kin groups, not social classes, and that the agricultural systems showed little intensification. Mizoguchi (2012: 2013) refers to Yayoi society as resisting trends to stratification. Mametani (2012: 14) considers the idea of the chief's residence inside a square, discussed by Hirose and Iba (2006) to be 'wishful thinking' (Jap. *kitai*). These are not substantiated archaeologically in the Ōsaka area. (The postulated chief's house is distinct from the large central building, '*shinden*' referred to above). Wakabayashi (2008) found that the large central sites (*kyōten shūraku*) are actually amalgamated, compound agricultural villages, not urban centers. They consist of a number of zones of habitation, but did not consist of a single group that had been reconfigured by a chief (Wakabayashi 2009: 33-37). Villagers belonged to clans or sodalities, the members of which inhabited hamlets in several villages. The clans or sodalities were endogamous but marriage partners from other clans could be found in large villages (Mizoguchi 2013: 124).

The best known Yayoi site in the Ōsaka area is Ikegami Sone, described in Appendix A.1. The site covered a huge area and was occupied by several communities, separated by ditches. A central building is thought to be a storehouse. Nearby small pits containing ritual offerings were discovered. The site shows the consolidation of communal storage and the celebration of agricultural rituals, as well as the construction of large family tombs. At Ikegami Sone, the production of stone hoes, spade/plow (*suki*), and reaping knives took place but it is debated whether artifacts were exchanged with other villages (see below). Fujiwara (2002) concluded that the surrounding available agricultural land could not provide enough rice to support the settlement, based on a proposed population between 500 and 1000. He used historical documents to reconstruct land use and to estimate the rate of consumption of rice at the time. He concluded that surrounding hamlets contributed food for the central settlement. The long campaign to save the Ikegami Sone site from destruction and the building of its associated Yayoi Museum (Ōsaka Furitsu Yayoi Hakubutsukan) provided an important focus for these debates engaging the public and many academic specialists.

Large buildings, moats and ditches

As mentioned above, one of the most important aspects of large central villages is the presence of a single very large elevated building. These are known not only from the remains of their huge supporting posts but also from depictions incised on pottery vessels, the most famous being the multi storied building with decorated roof found on a pottery sherd from the Makimuku Site. A detailed description of the largest excavated example is included in the discussion of the Ikegami Sone Site in Appendix A.1.

Hosoya's study of these buildings included the analysis of plant macrofossils through the flotation of soil samples (Hosoya 2009: 162). The analysis showed an overwhelming predominance of rice, both chaff and grains, indicating rice processing and storage. She proposed that the large building was a center for agricultural ritual, organized by the chief, and functioned as a granary. It was a center for collective daily activities, such as preparing rice for storage, located in a central position in the living area of the settlement, with unrestricted access. It was more than a political or religious center, functioning in various aspects of the agricultural cycle and daily activities. Mizoguchi (2013) noted that these buildings were not spatially connected with any one group of houses (sub village) within the village. These special buildings had an independent pillar to support the ridge pole, a feature that appears in only 5% of the raised floor buildings so far found in Yayoi contexts. There is never more than one of these special buildings in a village at a given time. This style of building, termed *shinmei*, can be seen in the oldest extant Japanese shrine at Ise (Hosoya 2009: 115-118). Both Hosoya (2009: 161-165) and Shitara (2009: 55) note that these large buildings were communal in character in the Middle Yayoi Period but became the exclusive space for the chief, isolated by ditches and fences, in the Kofun Period. Shitara (2009: 55-58) noted that in the Kinai area they were associated with ancestors and were located in the habitation area rather than in the burial area, but in Northern Kyūshū they were sometimes erected over a burial chamber. In the Late Yayoi Period Hōkenoyama Site, Nara Prefecture, the large building is on top of a roughly rectangular burial mound.

It is not only the large buildings that have generated debate. The defensive purpose of ditches been questioned. Were they intended to protect important centers?

Morii (2001) summarized the evidence for moated villages in the Kinai region. He grouped the total of 116 sites into five size ranks, the smallest and most numerous being 0.2ha to 1.5ha in area. The largest, in Rank V, contained 800 to 1600 persons and were inhabited in the Middle and Late Yayoi. Many villages had multiple moats but it is not clear that the moats actually functioned to surround the entire village or to separate sections. In many cases the remains of several consecutive ditches have been found but it is not clear that they encircle the entire settlement. In some cases the excavators could not investigate enough of the site to uncover the entire ditch. Although the Yotsuike Site is entirely moated, house remains have been found both inside and outside the moat. While ditches may have encircled the sub villages within the large central village the concept of an entire large village protected by a single moat, dominated by a chief's residence, is not considered to be tenable by Wakabayashi (2001:48). Were ditches in the Kinai area used for defense in times of warfare? As noted above, ditches in the Kinai region were often shallow and discontinuous. It appears that there is more evidence of warfare in large centers in North Kyūshū where some Yayoi sites have deep ditches and palisades, than in the Kinai region (Matsugi 1995, Hashiguchi 1995).

Important Yayoi Sites in the Nara Basin, Karako Kagi and Makimuku

The Ōsaka Plain and the Nara Basin present an interesting historical combination. The Nara Basin, 20km north-south and 15km east-west, is larger than the

Kawachi Plain (estimated to be 10km x 20km). They are part of the same drainage system of the Yamato River that provides an entryway through the Ikoma Mountains from Kawachi to Nara. Yayoi paddy farmers arrived first in Kawachi from the Inland Sea region, but moved quickly into the Nara Basin. It appears that the density of both Early Yayoi agricultural villages and central village sites (*kyōten iseki*) is greater in Kawachi than in Nara up to the time of extensive flooding in Kawachi at the end of Middle Yayoi. This could be an artifact of greater urban development and excavation around Ōsaka, but Nara has also undergone intensive scrutiny. In the Early Kofun Period, the Nara Basin was the center of Yamato power but as described in Chapter 5, the Kawachi Plain became the political center in the Middle Kofun Period (fifth century AD). By the seventh century Nara was again the center. The Karako Kagi and Makimuku sites of the Nara Basin provide reference points for understanding the debates surrounding the Ikegami Sone Site and Yayoi 'urbanism' discussed below. Karako Kagi is noted for its extensive ditches, the remains of two large buildings, and production areas for wooden agicultural tools and bronze molded objects (Fujita 2012). The Makimuku Site, occupied from the late second century to the first half of the fourth century, yielded abundant exotic pottery from surrounding areas in the Japanese Islands indicating intensive interaction at the end of the Yayoi Period. The remains of large elevated building probably used for the administration of a confederation of chiefs, and a chief's residence, were found (Barnes 2007: 124-125, Ryan 2011, Ishino 2005a,b, Hashimoto 2010, archaeology.jp.2014a).

Production and Exchange

The degree of economic interdependence of Yayoi villages on the Ōsaka Plain is a topic of debate. In the 1970's, when the new huge excavations of sites began, an ideal picture of heavily interdependent, regularly spaced centers and satellites was proposed. The control of the exchange networks was seen as a source of power (Takesue et al 2011: 74-76). Tsude (1989a) proposed that the large central sites were distribution points for lithic materials. In the north of the Kinai region, slate (Jap. *nenbangan*) was used, while in the south crystalline schist (*kesshōhengan*) was used. In the 1990's archaeologists concluded that the large central sites were linked in exchange systems, but they debated the degree of their interdependence and self sufficiency. Judging from the presence of debitage and partially completed stone reaping knives, they concluded that knives were made in a few large centers, such as the Ama Site, Takatsuki City, and Ikegami Sone. Sakai (2001) proposed that the reaping knives were stored in Ikegami Sone for distribution. Similarly, since semi-processed specimens of large polished stone adzes were found only in the Ikegami Sone Site the site was thought to be a center from which they were distributed. However Akiyama (2007: 626, 636-637) showed that all of the large central sites contained all of the production stages of the reaping knives. Akiyama found that about 20% of the total stone assemblage in each site in the central Ōsaka area consisted of exotic lithic material that was not locally available, indicating that while there was exchange of raw material, the sites were not centers for redistribution of finished or semi processed stone artifacts.

Special types of wood were transported from mountain slopes to the center of the alluvial plain. Coffins for the moated burial precincts were made of the umbrella pine (*Sciadopytis*) found at present at elevations of 500 to 100m above sea level. It has been proposed that wooden agricultural tools such as spades and hoes were made at sites such as Kitoragawa and sent to sites such as Uriūdō where no incomplete tools have been found. Akiyama (2007: 660-668) introduced the results of wood identification studies that show that Uriūdō was supplied from many surrounding sites.

Bronze casting appears to be limited to a few large central sites such as the Kitoragawa Site, Yao City, Higashi Nara, and Karako Kagi (Murakawa and Kobayashi 1995: 105, Kōeki Zaidan Hojin 2012), from which the products were distributed as far as the Japan Sea coast and Shikoku (Takesue et al 2011: 27). Evidence of bronze casting has also been found at Ikegami Sone (Appendix A.1). The sandstone used for making molds for *dōtaku* is found in the Izumi area (Sakai City) and Kobe. In the Late Yayoi Period, clay molds were adopted (Tsude 1989a: 365-368). Tsude proposed that in the Yayoi Period bronze casting was performed by itinerant craftsmen who possessed specialized knowledge, whereas in the Kofun Period there were specialized craft communities. On the other hand, Kurosawa (2012) considered bronze artifact production to have been under the control of the chief, who had resources to secure bronze material for casting and the expertise required to make and use molds. It is interesting that Late Yayoi workshops for iron were in small outlying villages rather than in centers (Imai and Morioka 2012), suggesting that they were independent from chiefly control.

Iizuka has argued in favor of distribution from production centers to surrounding villages. Data from parts of Japan outside of the Kinai region show that in the Yayoi Period wooden tools may have been exchanged among villages, as various authors cited above have proposed for the Ōsaka region. Partially prepared wooden tools were soaked in wet areas or artificial small ponds and were made by specialists for distribution to surrounding villages, Small scale production of metal objects may have followed a similar pattern according to Iizuka (2004: 51).

FIGURE 4.4. MOATED PRECINCT BURIAL NO. 2, URIŪDŌ SITE, ŌSAKA. MIDDLE YAYOI PERIOD. FROM SAHARA AND KANASEKI 1975: COLOR PLATE 16. COURTESY OF KŌDANSHA.

Continental Contacts

Yayoi communities and their contemporaries on the Korean peninsula were in constant contact (Takesue et al 2011: 89). In the Early Yayoi Period a suite of new artifact types arrived in Kyūshū and ultimately in the Kinai region, from the continent. These included wooden spades and forked tools, new types of querns and stone knives, new forms of burials such as stone cists and wooden coffins, and spindle whorls. Polished stone weights excavated in 1981 from the Kamei Site, Ōsaka, were recently found to represent a system based on multiples of 2,4,8,16, and 32 times 8.7 grams (Morimoto 2012, Ōsaka Fu Bunkazai Sentā 2013a). This discovery shows that not only discrete kinds of tools, but entire systems of new knowledge arrived.

At the end of the Early Yayoi Period and the first half of the Middle Yayoi, bronze weapons and Chinese mirrors were imported. From the Middle Yayoi Period, villagers began to construct a new kind of burial facility, based on continental mound burial, but with distinctive Japanese features. These square mounds with discontinuous surrounding ditches (*hōkei shūkōbo*) have been termed moated precincts by Gina Barnes (1988: 95-106). They appear to be family tombs, containing up to three generations of burials of male/female pairs, usually in wooden coffins (Wakabayashi 2005). Other burial areas in the same villages contain simple earth burials. At Uriūdō, one of the moated precincts, No. 2, is 9.7m E/W, and 14.8m N/S, with a height of 1.2m. It contained 6 grave pits, each with a coffin made of assembled pieces of wood. Grave goods were a few pieces of utilitarian pottery (Figure 4.4). One area of moated precincts at Uriūdō, 500m N/S and 300m E/W, contained 60 of these family mounds (Murakawa and Kobayashi 1995: 112, Higashi Ōsaka Kyōiku Iinkai 2009: 27).

A system of social ranking of elite and commoners existed, but among the elite, a formal hierarchy did not emerge until the end of the Yayoi Period when some segments of lineages became very powerful and were linked in a network. Their burials took the form of keyhole tombs, marking the beginning of the Kofun Period discussed in the next chapter. They competed for access to continental elites, who were the source of new social forms and legitimation.

Conclusion

Discoveries from the Yayoi Period show the undertaking of projects concerned with agricultural expansion and storage, useful for consolidating and expanding chiefly power. There is also evidence for localized production of bronze ritual objects and probably specialized agricultural tools made of desirable kinds of wood. Stone raw material, found in restricted locations was also exchanged.

Large central villages, sometimes moated, are an outstanding feature of the Middle Yayoi Period in the Ōsaka area. There are active debates about the extent of social hierarchy among and within villages, the exchange of goods among them, and the presence of defensive systems. It appears that they are actually agglomerations of smaller units, lacking urban features, and their central buildings are communal and ceremonial edifices rather than chiefs' compounds. They appear to have been used for harvest rituals and storage. Was there a change in agricultural productivity in the Late Yayoi Period that led to the disappearance of these sites? Environmental data indicate flooding, a substantial earthquake, and possible climatic cooling, and historical data suggest an increase in village warfare. The Middle Yayoi was a high point for the Ōsaka region. In subsequent centuries the Nara Basin was the scene of social change with a concentration of political power in its southeastern corner. However the Ōsaka region rose to prominence in the fifth century and a very different cultural landscape was created at that time.

Chapter 5
Consolidation of Political Power and Trade; the Kofun Period (240 to 600 AD)

Introduction

The Kofun Period is named for a system of burial in an earth mound (*kofun*) practiced in the region from Kyūshū to Tōhoku from about 240 AD to the seventh century AD. Part of a much larger tradition of mounded tombs found throughout East Asia (Okauchi 1986, Barnes 1993: 222-245), this burial system signifies a new political ideology with well-defined rules of ritual and hierarchy. In this period the Ōsaka region surpassed other regions in the Japanese Islands in the scale of monumental tomb construction, trade in iron ingots, weapons and armor, and the sponsorship of new technologies and craft production. In the Middle Kofun Period Japan experienced a large scale technological revolution precipitated by close contact with the continent and the arrival of large numbers of immigrants who brought with them advanced techniques for producing iron goods and stoneware ceramics, new forms of architecture, and engineering expertise for improving irrigation systems (Tanaka 2001: 13, Ban 2009: 110-130, Hishida 2010a, Suzuki 2002).

The creation of a new ideology is one of the most striking activities of entrepreneurs of this period. Archaeologists describe the new burial ritual and prestige goods exchange, but surely these are only a small part of a new social and religious order involving many aspects of daily life. For instance, architectural programs stipulating conformity of tomb dimensions may reflect cosmic beliefs. This ideology held together various regions from Kyūshū to Tōhoku under the control of the central authority in the Ōsaka region. Just as in the Yayoi Period, expanded storage facilities reflect economic growth. While Kofun Period chiefs' residences are not well known in the Ōsaka region, an example from Gose in the Nara Basin provides a general impression of the kind of multifunctional residential compound which will be found in future in the Ōsaka region. Instead of the single storehouses of the Yayoi Period, groups of storehouses dating to the Kofun Period show a huge increase in storage capacity. These structures may have been used for weapons in addition to foodstuffs. Roads and canals linked settlements, palaces, tombs, craft production areas, and ports from at least the fifth century AD. Obviously these were indispensable for the development of the local economy and improvement of the standard of living.

Typical elite tombs consisted of a circular rear mound and an attached rectangular or trapezoidal front area (Box 5.1). The most typical, and very largest mounds, all have the characteristic "keyhole" (*zenpōkōenfun*) shape. The term, keyhole, refers to the old fashioned western style keyhole with a round top and flaring trapezoidal bottom. Mizoguchi (2013: 244) provides a detailed exegesis of tomb types. In the Kinai region, an unusual form of front and rear square mound (*zenpōkōhōfun*)

BOX 5.1
Keyhole shape tombs

Of a total of 5200 keyhole tombs in the Japanese islands about 35 are over 200m in total length. Thirty-two of these occur in the Nara Basin or the adjacent areas of Kawachi, Settsu, and Izumi in Ōsaka (Hirose 2004a: 10). In the five main groups of large keyhole tombs in the Kinai region (Yamato-Yanagimoto, Saki, Umami, Furuichi and Mozu) there are 303 tombs over 100m long (Figures 5.1, 5.2).

Another 140 tombs of this size are found in the adjacent areas of Hyogo and Kyōto. Of the very largest tombs, 23 are over 200m long and most of these are concentrated in the Kinai region (Hirose 2004b). Within the ten chronological sub periods of the Kofun Period, spanning some 350 years, the so-called royal tombs of Mozu and Furuichi, discussed below, dominate time periods 4 to 7 (Hirose 2004b: 20). In the Middle Kofun Period (roughly fifth century) the Kinai region was the center of military power, judging the concentration of iron weapons found in the satellite mounds (*baichō*) of the very largest tombs in Kawachi.

The Ōsaka rulers controlled the flow of iron ingots and finished weapons and appear to have derived great wealth from trade. With the construction of the largest tombs in Japan in the Kawachi area in the Middle Kofun Period, royal power was concentrated there. However in the sixth century AD the power base shifted back to the Nara Basin, while Kawachi remained a vital economic center. Barnes (2007: 7-18, 2015: 342-352) provides a succinct review of the Kofun Period and its chronology and internal development.

ŌSAKA ARCHAEOLOGY

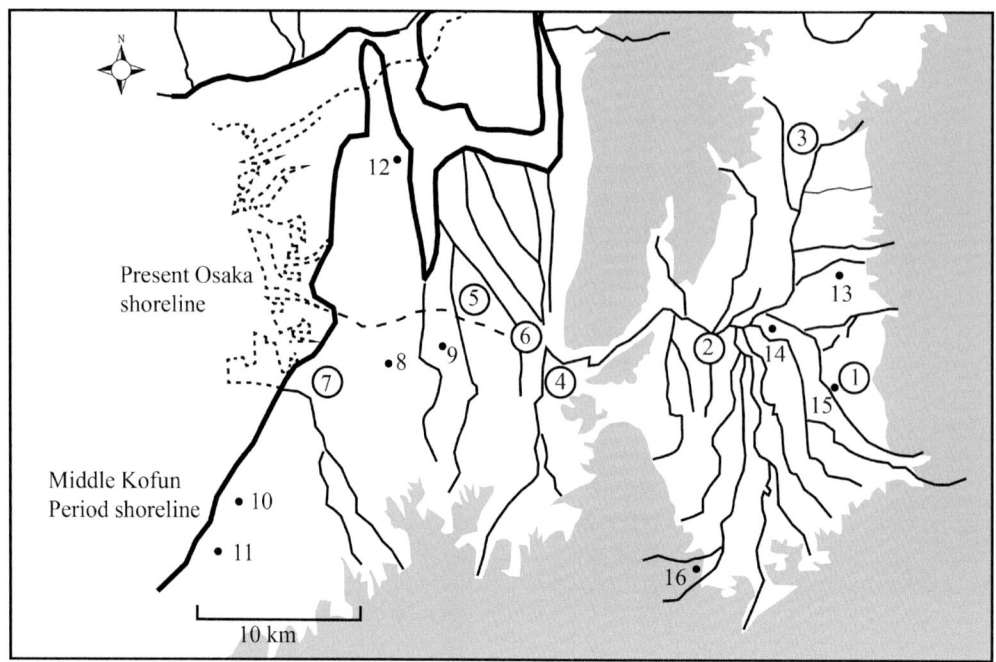

FIGURE 5.1. TOMB GROUPS, INDIVIDUAL TOMBS, AND SITES IN THE KINAI REGION DISCUSSED IN THE TEXT. TOMB GROUPS (IN CIRCLED NUMBERS): (1) ŌYAMATO. (2) UMAMI. (3) SAKI. (4) TAMATEYAMA. (5) NAGAHARA. (6) FURUICHI. (7) MOZU. INDIVIDUAL TOMBS: (8) NIWATORITSUKA. (9) KUROHIMEYAMA. (10) KOGANETSUKA. (11) KUMEDA KAIFUKUYAMA. SITES: (12) HŌENZAKA. (13) FURU. (14) KARAKO KAGI. (15) MAKIMUKU. (16) NANGŌ. (REDRAWN FROM ICHINOSE 2005: 169).

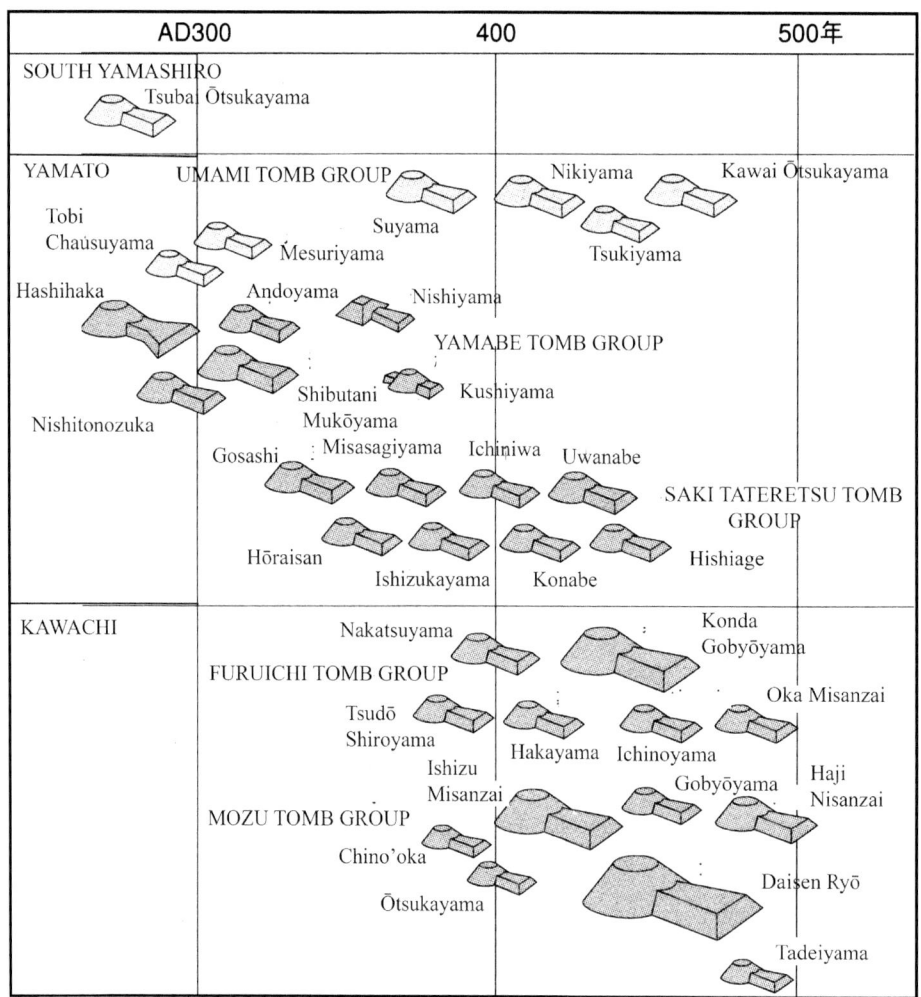

FIGURE 5.2. KEYHOLE SHAPE TOMBS IN THE NARA AND ŌSAKA REGIONS, SHOWING THEIR CHRONOLOGICAL POSITION AND RELATIVE SIZE. FROM TANAKA 1991: 278. COURTESY OF TANAKA MIGAKU AND SHŪEISHA PUBLISHERS.

> **BOX 5.2**
> **The "Imperial Tombs" of Japan**
>
> The fact that a substantial number of Kofun Period tumuli are under the protection and control of the Imperial Household Ministry of Japan, whose main concern is their preservation as religious sites, has a substantial effect on their study. Some 900 tombs thought to belong to previous Japanese emperors and their relatives in various parts of Japan, including the Nara Basin and Ōsaka Region, are included (Edwards 2000). There are a total of 188 burial mounds thought by some scholars to belong to senior members of the imperial family, dating back to the legendary founder, Jimmu Tennō (Harunari 1975). The list is based on traditions and ancient documents, such as the eighth century *Nihon Shoki* and *Kojiki* and the *Engishiki*. Considerable scholarship on the textual identification of the tombs was carried out during the Edo Period when a list of the rulers and the postulated burials was created. In 1871 AD the Imperial Household Tomb Office was established and legislation prohibiting excavation of the so-called Imperial Tombs was put in place from 1874 AD. It is significant that in the 1890s the Meiji historian Miyake Yonekichi disagreed with this ban on excavation on the grounds that it could yield valuable evidence for their appreciation and interpretation, and resigned from the Tōkyō Imperial University in 1893 (Pai 2013: 60). Criteria for assigning imperial status include the large size of the mounds and local legend. The presence of a particular style of chest-shaped stone coffin, the *nagamochigata sekkan*, and *haniwa* (clay tomb ornaments) in the form of water birds, have been taken to indicate ruler's tombs. (*Haniwa* are described in Box 5.5). There has been no conclusive archaeological confirmation of the identity of the occupants of any imperial tomb through epitaphs, buried texts, or DNA studies. No excavation or detailed survey is permitted, although recently groups of specialists have been invited to accompany officials for brief site visits. Most archaeologists refer to these sites by their archaeological site name rather than the name of the proposed occupant. I follow this practice in this publication, but provide the most widely accepted list of occupants in Table 5.1, which shows the relative temporal positions of major tombs, the Five Kings of Wa, and some of the emperors mentioned in the *Nihon Shoki* (Takahashi and Nakakubo 2014: 63).
>
> Although the present system of protection was implemented as part of the new regime in the early Meiji Period (1867 to 1912 AD), a number of illegal excavations took place in the late nineteenth century. In addition, not all very large *kofun* have been given imperial designations. A few undesignated *kofun*, both large and small, have been excavated scientifically, and discoveries have also been made during the maintenance of the moats of protected mounds.

occurs: from a total of 36 examples of this type four are over 100 m in total length, indicating that their occupants possessed considerable power. Some kind of social group must have chosen this special form, but its exact nature is not known (Urabe 2006). A small group of chiefs living in the Yongsan River Valley, Cholla Province, Korea actually constructed *zenpkoenfun* burial mounds and embellished them with cylindrical *haniwa* made in the Kinai style, showing their participation in the Kinai prestige system (Ban 2009: 289-290, Lee 2014).

The monumental mounds of the Kofun Period are unusual in world archaeology, since many of them are thought to belong to the ancestors of the present Japanese imperial family (Box 5.2) They are termed the Imperial Tombs. In this chapter it will be shown that although such tombs cannot be excavated at present, a huge amount of information on Kofun Period burials is already available.

There are many debates concerning Kofun Period social and political organization. Does the building of monumental tombs and large structures necessarily imply state organization? What is state organization? Archaeologists propose that it is a complex social and political system in which social classes are controlled by an elite that monopolizes production and uses military force. Some scholars state that literacy is required to control large populations and organize labor and production. Many archaeologists and historians propose that in third century Japan, Himiko was the ritual head of a pre-state confederacy of powerful chiefs while in the fifth century AD, an "early state" economy is indicated by discoveries of monumental tombs and groups of large storehouses (Tsude 2006, Edwards 2006, Fukunaga 2014). By the seventh century codification of state law and the construction of large administrative capitals with substantial administrative components indicate that state organization was consolidated. How centralized was control in the Kofun Period? Shifts in power within the Nara Basin and on the Ōsaka Plain suggest that political organization may have taken the form of a complex paramount chiefdom, in which power circulated among high ranking hereditary chiefs, rather than among residing within one dynasty. Tsujita (2014) proposed three steps in state formation. In the third to fifth centuries AD, a confederacy of chiefdoms spread over a wide area. Membership was confirmed by participation in prestige goods systems based on bronze mirrors, weapons, armor, and other regalia. In the early to mid sixth century, control of the central Kinai area was centralized. Government-sponsored clans (*be*) operated sections of the economy under state overseers (*miyake*). In the seventh and eighth centuries, the social and political *ritsuryo* system indicated centralized political control.

Translation from Japanese to English of writing on this period can be confusing because of the use of terms such as ō (king) or *dai ō* (great king) or *ōbo* (royal tomb) (Ichinose 2005) or *jōbigun* (standing army) (Tanaka 2010: 81) for the Middle Kofun Period, when the rulers were actually paramount chiefs.

Chronology

The Kofun Period spans roughly 350 years, from 240 to 600 AD. Usually it is divided into three sub periods, Early (240 to 400 AD), Middle (400 to 500 AD), and Late, 500 to 600 AD). Archaeological dating is based on changes in burial assemblages and burial treatment, and changes in the styles of ceramics. In general the center of power in the Early Kofun Period was in the Nara Basin, as well as in local centers such as northern Kyūshū and Okayama. In the Middle Kofun Period a supra regional center, marked by the construction of tombs much larger than those in other areas, arose in the Kawachi region. In the Late Kofun Period, the Nara Basin seems to have regained its supremacy. In a finer grained chronology of ten periods each of about 35 years in length, the royal tombs of Furuichi and Mozu dominate Periods 4 to 7 (Hirose 2004b: 20). In the early and Middle Periods, burials were placed in a chamber dug into the top of the mound and lined with stones, while in the Late Kofun Period, a horizontal chamber was built at ground level, with side access, and the earth mound was added later.

The excavation of smaller tombs in various parts of Japan has provided material for building chronologies based on changes in the kinds of grave goods and tomb structure. The Early Kofun Period burial assemblage contains bronze mirrors, stone ornaments and assembled scepters fashioned from green tuff, bronze whorl-like ornaments (*tomoegata*), and bronze tubular socket like artifacts. About 2cm in diameter and 10 to 15cm long, these appear to be sockets for some kind of emblematic wooden staff. About 73 specimens have been found in elite graves in Japan. They are not found in association with triangular rim mirrors, although they are contemporary. They occur in southern Korea as well as Honshū, Shikoku and Kyūshū. They appear to have been distributed among a limited group of confederates (Tanaka 2009: 143-20).

With the beginning of the Middle Kofun Period in the fifth century AD the grave goods described above are replaced by armor and weapons. In the Late Kofun Period, smaller, more numerous burial mounds yield a diverse assemblage of weapons and ornaments, many of continental origin, reflecting in some cases immigrant groups from the continent. The gold ornaments and glass objects found in the Niizawa Senzuka mounds are an example (Kashihara Kōkogaku Kenkyūsho 1977).

Changes in burial treatment are also helpful in dating. Coffins were fashioned from wood, clay, and stone. The most enduring form of coffin, lasting from the Yayoi Period to the Asuka Period consisted of assembled planks. Other forms were made by hollowing a log, resembling a dug out canoe, or a section of split bamboo. The wooden coffin was often encased in clay, termed a *nendokaku*, in the latter half of the Early Kofun Period and the Middle Kofun Period. Wada (2014) proposed two basic types of coffins; those that were portable (*mochihakobu kan*) and those which were immovable, or set in place (*suetsukeru kan*). The latter involved multiple treatments, such as sealing with clay. Wada also noted that the burial chamber, as well as the coffin, could be a sealed one, or one that was open, as in the case of the horizontal burial chambers of the Late Kofun Period. The belief systems that motivated these different forms remain unknown. It seems that the indigenous Japanese pattern was one of enclosing and sealing, while continental forms favored open space around the coffin.

Dating the tombs by the presence of grave goods such as mirrors and armor is difficult because the life of these valuables, before their deposition, may be long and variable. Three imponderables were mentioned by Shimogaki (2012); length of time between manufacture and procurement of the object, time from procurement to deposition (that could be several generations), and length of the lifetime of the individual buried with the goods. These variables affect attempts to reconstruct networks sharing the same type of artifact, or attempts to show that a group of mounds represents rulers who were descendants of the same family. Ceramic objects such as *haniwa*, or *sueki* (described below), produced and deposited on a tomb in a short period of time, may provide a better picture of chronological succession. DNA studies to determine genetic relationships of tomb occupants have not been possible for tombs in the Ōsaka area because of a lack of suitable skeletal specimens. The presence of hard fired grey stoneware, *sueki*, introduced at the beginning of the fifth century AD, indicates that the site postdates the Early Kofun Period, which is dominated by Furu type earthenware, a ware marking the transition between the Yayoi and Kofun Periods. *Haniwa* and *sueki*, two types of ceramics developed in the Kofun Period, are useful for chronologies. Details of their production are discussed later in this chapter, under craft production. *Haniwa* were placed on the surface of the tomb mound, following its construction. Thus surface finds can be used for dating, even if excavation is not possible. Variations in shape and surface treatment can be used for relative dating, and can also be linked to radiocarbon dates. *Sueki* type designations such as TK 73, refer to the site where the particular type was first recognized.

The Beginning of the Kofun Period: Dramatic Changes in the Mid Third Century AD

Recent excavations in the Nara Basin elucidate the transition from a ritual confederacy under Queen Himiko in the third century AD to a more centralized system of political power. Japanese scholars refer to this as the transition from the Country of Yamatai (Yamataikoku) to the Power of Yamato (Yamato Seiken). The adoption of new burial rituals was a factor in this centralization. Chiefs opted into the new system, members of which constructed keyhole mounds and distributed new continental prestige goods to gain power in their communities and participate in a wide confederacy. Whereas previous religious artifacts were sacred non-circulating local products such as bronze bells (*dōtaku*) and rare weapons, the new goods were bronze mirrors and stone ritual objects (Fukunaga 1999). Fukunaga proposes that participation in the mirror exchange and burial ritual likely based on Chinese Daoist concepts, was an active agent in the centralization of political power.

By the end of the Early Kofun Period, ritual practice became diverse in outlying areas, indicating the relaxing of central control (Fukunaga 1999: 60-67). Archaeologists propose that Himiko, who ruled the country of Yamataikoku, lived at the Makimuku Site, and was buried in the nearby Hashihaka Kofun (Terasawa 2005). The historical account of the *Wei Zhi* (referred to above) states that Himiko sent tributary missions to Wei in 238 and 243 AD and received tributary gifts, including a large number of a specific type of cast bronze mirror decorated with beasts and and deities, and marked by a distinctive triangular sectioned rim (Kidder 2007, Barnes 2007, Piggott 2009) (Box 5.3). Himiko is thought to have ruled over a voluntary confederacy of chiefdoms, unified in ritual, without sufficient military power to rule by force (Mizoguchi 2009). Her recognition by the rulers of Wei was given with the intention of 'containing' Korean polities. Wei subsequently realized that Himiko had no power to play such a military role (Wang 2005: 4). However her recognition by Wei must have enhanced her prestige in the Japanese Islands.

BOX 5.3
Triangular rim mirrors

A distinctive type of cast bronze mirror has been the subject of some of the most intensive research in Japanese archaeology. It is termed the triangular rim mirror with deities and beasts (*sankakuen shinjūkyō*). This type has a distinctive triangular outer rim cross-section not found in other types of the same period from Japan or the continent and an average diameter of over 20 cm, substantially larger than other mirrors that average about 14 cm (Mizuno 2006, Mizuno and Ishino 2006 a,b, Ishino 2006). It has been proposed that the distinctive triangular rim was adopted to strengthen the rim of the oversize mirrors.

From a total of about 4000 mirrors found in sites of the Kofun Period, about 520 triangular rim mirrors have been found, of which 390 are thought to have been made in China (*hakusaikyō*), while the remaining 130 were made in Japan (*boseikyō*) from molds made from Chinese specimens (Fukunaga 2005). Decoration on the back of the mirrors consists of outer concentric rings of raised geometric or meander decoration and intermediate ring which often has an inscription in raised characters, in the form of a felicitous phrase, a reign date from AD 239 to around 270, and/or the maker's surname. In the inner circular zone, the raised decoration consists of mythical beasts, deities, chariots, standards, and other motifs. Two figures interpreted as the Chinese Daoist deity Queen Mother of the West and her consort, King of the East, are common (Barnes 2007, 179: 2014) (Figure 5.3). Barnes (2014) proposed that specific Chinese concepts of the Queen Mother of the West, whose image appears on bronze mirrors, entered the Japanese Islands in the late second and third centuries AD, and played a role in the religion and legitimization of power in the Early Kofun Period. Reading the actual meaning of motifs on the mirrors, in addition to organizing them typologically, sheds light on their use as prestige goods. However, Fukunaga (2005) has stressed that the representations are related to third century Wei Dynasty Buddhism, in which Daoist and Buddhist iconographies were mixed. Fukunaga concluded that Daoist ideology was not used strategically (2005: 203). It has been proposed that these mirrors were part of a diplomatic gift recorded in the third century Chinese historical account History of the Wei Dynasty *Wei Zhi*, to Himiko in 239 AD (Kidder 2007). Wa sent tribure missions to Wei in China in 239, 243, 247, and 266 AD; (Fukunaga (2005: 91) has proposed that different sub types were produced for these missions.

Although most Japanese scholars conclude that this type of mirror was made somewhere near the Wei Dynasty capital of Luoyang (Fukunaga 2005, Shimogaki 2010), it has never been found on the Chinese mainland, leading the Chinese archaeologist Wang Zhongshu to conclude that they were made in Japan by immigrant Chinese artisans from the state of Wu in the Yangtze River region (Wang 1992). The state of Wu which did produce triangular rim mirrors, was destroyed in 280 AD. Prior to its demise it was in contact with the Gongsun Dynasty of North Korea and Lelang (Tsujita 2007: 226-227).

The production of Chinese triangular rim mirrors (*hakusai sankakuen shinjūkyō*) ended around 270 AD, with the fall of Wei. Subsequently Japanese made copies of triangular rim mirrors (*bosei kyō*) were produced until the early fourth century. It is likely that some craftspersons migrated from the continent and provided technical assistance. Sets of identical mirrors, produced either from the same clay mold or a second generation mold made from an existing mirror, were produced and distributed to leaders in widely dispersed part of central and western Japan, leading Kobayashi (1976, 2006) to conclude that a central authority rewarded subordinates by bestowing these mirrors.

Kobayashi's model of distribution from a Yamato center to outlying confederates is exceptionally influential. However alternative interpretations should be noted. Barnes (2007: 22, 23) has questioned whether the distribution was necessarily centrifugal from the Yamato center, since the distribution of exotic pottery in Makimuku shows contributions from outlying areas to the center. No centralized workshop of mirror production has been found. The existence of pairs of identical mirrors shared by locations distant from the Yamato center suggests alliances based on kinship and marriage (Barnes 2007: 23).

A huge number of subtypes have been identified and the number of studies is bewildering (Nishikawa 2006). They are very rare on the Ōsaka Plain, but are common in surrounding areas, being reported only from the Koganetsuka Kofun in the Izumi area. Other types of beast and deity mirrors were produced in small quantities in workshops in several localities in China and were traded to Japan through separate trading networks (Morishita 2007).

How were the mirrors cast and how were identical sets created? Stone molds were used for some mirrors with geometric decoration, including Korean fine line mirrors with multiple knobs, but usually a clay mold was employed. It could be made by pressing a bronze mirror directly into wet clay, or by making a clay mold from a wax model. While several castings from a stone mold are possible, the mold deteriorates quickly. Multiple molds could be produced in clay and pre fabricated sections such as molds of beasts and deities could be inserted into the molds or wax models. The clay mold could be made in two pieces for re use. In making the mold, a hole was cut in the central boss for the wax to pour out. The precise location and the hole was shared by all objects from the same mold. After use for perhaps five to ten times, more copies could be made from a new mold made from a wax model fashioned from the old mold (Kishimoto 1989, Fukunaga 2005: 138-141).

At the end of the Yayoi Period, around 200 AD, a mirror with a concentric zone of decoration (*gamontai*) has been identified by Fukunaga as the precursor of the triangular rim mirror and the first type to be found in the Kinai region. It is thought to have been produced by the Gongsun Clan of North Korea, while the triangular rim mirrors were produced after their decline (Fukunaga 2005: 154). (It should be noted that earlier types of continental and Japanese mirrors were produced in the Yayoi Period, particularly in Kyushu, but these do not figure in the discussion of Osaka).

Mirrors gained significance as they were transformed from objects of collective ritual to symbols of rank at the end of the Yayoi Period. However, they continued to have great collecetive ritual importance in the creation of a new ideology of the early state or complex chiefdom (depending on the level of complexity one infers for the Kofun Period). Fukunaga stressed the importance of a unified ideology in the formation of what he termed a secondary state (2005: 327). In the third to fourth centuries, Wei/Jin Chinese mirrors were of foremost importance. They were superceded by the rise of armour and weapons and trade with Kaya on the Korean Peninsula in the late fourth to fifth centuries. From the mid to late fifth century new forms of mirrors were given to dignitaries in Japan and Korea by the Southern Dynasties. In the fifth and sixth centuries, new forms of horse gear and tomb architecture were received from Paekche. The precise political and social meaning of the motifs on the mirrors and their relation to local political strategies is difficult to determine from archaeological evidence but the fact that the beast and deity mirror dominates at the time of the rise of the rise of a power center in the Kinai region suggests that Chinese Daoist and Buddhist spirit world concepts played a key role in social and political integration in the Kofun Period.

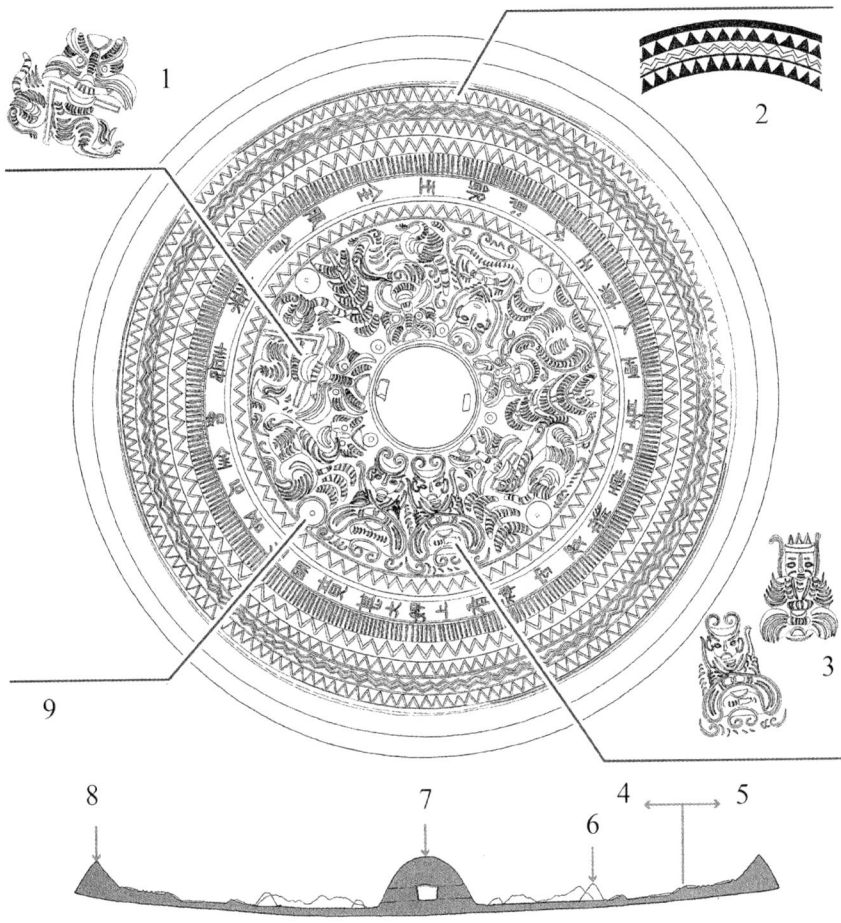

FIGURE 5.3. EXAMPLE OF A TRIANGULAR RIM MIRROR WITH BEAST AND DEITY DECORATION. 1. SACRED BEASTS, USUALLY DRAGONS AND TIGERS. 2. BANDS OF SAWTOOTH PATTERN SEPARATED BY WAVE PATTERN. 3. DEITIES, USUALLY QUEEN MOTHER OF THE WEST AND KING OF THE EAST. 4. INNER ZONE. 5. OUTER ZONE. 6. NIPPLE. 7. SQUARE HOLE FOR TASSEL. 8. TRIANGULAR OUTER RIM. 9. FOUR OR SIX NIPPLES IN THE OUTER ZONE. REDRAWN FROM KONDŌ, YOSHIRŌ. 1981. GONGENYAMA 51 KOFUN. PUBLISHER AND PLACE OF PUBLICATION UNKNOWN. FROM ŌSAKA FURITSU ASUKA HAKUBUTSUKAN: 2013:11. COURTESY OF ŌSAKA FURITSU CHIKATSU ASUKA HAKUBUTSUKAN.

Himiko died around 247 AD and following temporary burial *(mogari)* was possibly interred in the keyhole shaped Hashihaka Kofun around 250 AD. Hashihaka is a designated Imperial Tomb and has not been excavated. However, radiocarbon dating of residues from pottery recovered from the moat of the tomb has provided recalibrated dates with mid points ranging from 240 to 260 AD (Harunari et al 2011). This burial mound, some 277m in length, has a stepped form consisting of four tiers. In comparison with other rulers' tombs in East Asia, Hashihaka's size is substantial. Generally the tombs of the Chinese Warring States Period (475 to 221 BC) were square mounds about 100m on each side while the famous Qin Shi Huang Tomb of the third century BC was 485m east –west and 515m north-south. Tombs of the Han Dynasty (206 BC to AD 220) varied from 170 to 240m on each side (Fukunaga 2014: 37-43). The upper portion of the rear circular mound was paved with flat stones and embellished with special pottery vessels with stands produced in the Okayama region. Tubular *haniwa* were also included in the arrangement.

The burial of top elites in keyhole tumuli represents a huge change from elite family burials in moated precincts in the Yayoi Period as outlined in Chapter 4. The construction of a single huge burial facility for a single ruling generation, rather than many smaller family facilities for a large group of elites, reflects increasing social complexity and a level of hierarchy above local chiefs.

If Hashihaka Kofun is Himiko's burial place, then it seems likely that the Nishitonozuka Kofun belongs to Himiko's successor, Toyo, according to Shiraishi (2006: 9). The third in the sequence, Tobi Chausuyama Kofun and the fourth, Mesuriyama Kofun, have both been robbed. In

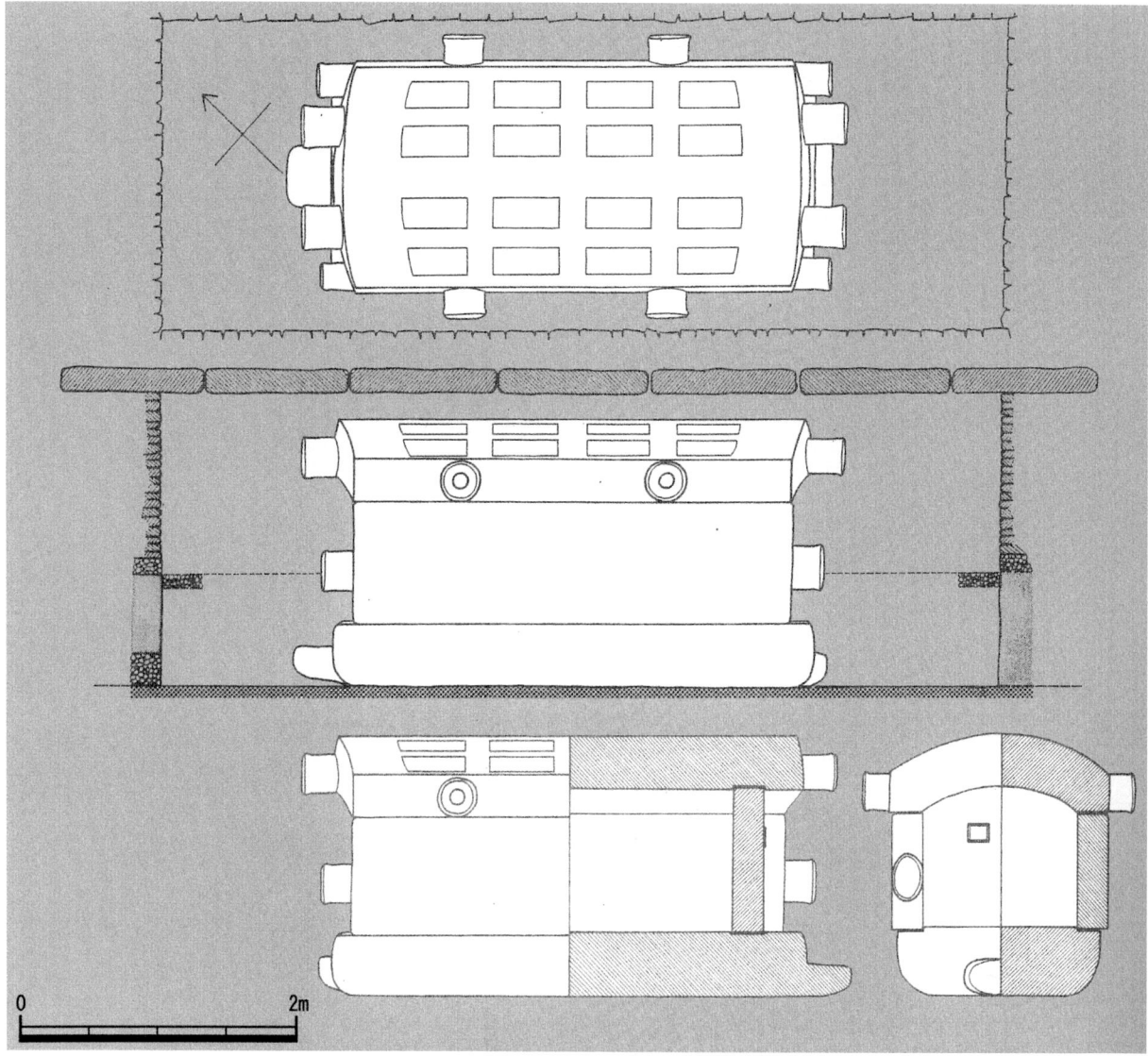

FIGURE 5.4. STORAGE CHEST TYPE STONE COFFIN (*NAGAMOCHIGATA SEKKAN*) RECOVERED FROM THE TSUDOSHIROYAMA KOFUN IN AD 1912. FROM ICHINOSE 2009: 18. FROM ŌSAKA FURITSU CHIKATSU ASUKA HAKUBUTSUKAN 2010: 150. COURTESY OF ŌSAKA FURITSU CHIKATSU ASUKA HAKUBUTSUKAN.

the rear circular part of these *kofun* there was a vertical stone chamber, and iron weapons have been recovered. Judging from the occurrence of these weapons, it is likely that these were burials of male political/military leaders. Little is known about the Andoyama and Shibuya Mukōyama burial mounds thought to belong to the fifth and sixth generation leaders. Kishimoto (2008: 2013) and Ishimura (2010) have proposed that throughout the Kofun Period there was a dual system of religious and political/military authority. The dual system, postulated some time ago derives support from the Chinese account that Himiko was a religious leader. The fact that the largest tombs appear in chronological pairs of roughly the same date, based on *haniwa* typology, and that there are differences in grave goods, where excavation has taken place, between assemblages rich in ritual objects and ornaments and those rich in weapons and armor, as well as differences in the size range, makes it seem this hypothesis seem worth considering. In the Early Kofun Period, the postulated military leader's tombs are in the range of 280 to 310m long, while the range for the ritual leaders' tombs have the same size range. The ritual leader could be male or female. For the Early Kofun Period in the Ōyamato Kofun Group, the succession of ritual leaders' tombs is proposed to be Hashihaka, Nishitonozuka, and Andoyama, while that of the military leaders' tombs is Sakurai Chausuyama, Mesuriyama, and Shibuya Mukōyama. On the other hand, Mizoguchi (2013, 273) notes the size differences in contemporary pairs of largest tombs but proposes that this is an indication of fluid, competitive, heterarchical power relations among paramount chiefs of similar rank and power.

Shiraishi (2006, 9) proposes a line of successive rulers of Yamato, the polity succeeding Yamatai, buried in the following huge kofun in the Nara Basin, Hashihaka, Nishitonozuka, Sakurai (Tobi) Chausuyama, Mesuriyama, Andonyama, and Shibuya Mukōyama. He does not propose two separate lines of ritual and military/political rulers. Instead, he proposes that in some keyhole mounds, military rulers were buried in the rear round mound and religious specialists were buried in the front square portion. Together they constituted religious and political authority (Shiraishi 2009: 38). There are many debates concerning the nature of power and membership of elite groups in the Kofun Period.

In the Saki Tomb Group, four leaders' tombs are proposed by Shiraishi (2006: 10) in the following order of construction. Goshaji, Horaisan, Saki Ryōsan (imperial), and Saki Ishitzuyama (imperial). Kishimoto (2008: 460) proposes that these tombs fall into a ritual leaders' group, consisting of the Horaisan and Goshaji Kofun, and a political/military leaders' group, consisting of the Saki Ryōsan and Saki Ishizukayama Kofun. Shiraishi proposes that in some cases both functions may have been expressed within one burial mound, rather in two separate lines; there may be a local military chief in the rear mound and a ritual chieftainess in the front mound (2009: 38).

For individuals of highest status, stone coffins were preferred. A hallmark of the fifth century AD in Kawachi was a stone coffin resembling a wooden storage chest, (*nagamochigata sekkan*) (Figure 5.4). Most were made of exotic stone quarried on Mt. Ikoma or mountains on Shikoku Island. This type was replaced in the Late Kofun Period by the house shaped coffin (*iegata sekkan*) (Makabe 1994), often fashioned from volcanic tuff from the Harima region of Hyogo Prefecture (Wada 1986). Stone coffins indicate a social rank higher than those buried in wooden coffins sealed in clay. They were often used for main burials in smaller mounds, and have also been found in side burials in the largest mounds. We do not know the precise nature of coffins and burial chambers of the main burials in the largest 'imperial' tombs because they are unexcavated.

Hirose (2013) found that usually all of the main burials in the rear summit area of large *zenpōkōenfun* of the Early to Middle Kofun Period are of the same rank indicating that all of the burials belonged to members of the chiefly class.

A formalized burial ritual with rigid regulations regarding mound shape and size, and grave design and offerings, demonstrated participation in Yamato power relations and adherence to Yamato ideology.

The Power Shift from the Nara Basin to the Kawachi Plain

The Ōsaka region often complemented the Nara Basin as a commercial center, occasionally eclipsing Nara as a power center, as in the Kodai and Mediaeval Periods. In this section I discuss the shift in power from Nara in the Early Kofun Period to Ōsaka in the Middle Kofun Period. In the fourth century AD the political center in the Kinai region was in the Nara Basin. Shiraishi has termed this the Yamato political power (2009: 34). This power can be seen in the concentration of very large tombs at the foot of Mt. Miwa in southeastern Nara. From north to south within a total span of 4km, there are the Ōyamato, Ryūōzan, and Hashinaka (sic) Kofun Groups, Other *kofun* groups in the Nara Basin also contain large mounds at this time, indicating that power was rather dispersed.

Some archaeologists propose that at the end of the fourth century AD, the royal tombs of Wa moved to the Furuichi and Mozu Tomb Groups of Kawachi (Kishimoto 2010b: 47). Paramount chiefs shifted their power base from the Nara Basin to the Ōsaka region, and established imposing cemeteries at two locations, Furuichi and Mozu (Shiraishi 2011). What was involved in this apparent shift in power? What was the relationship of the newcomers to the existing fourth century Kawachi elites? Is it possible that a central authority in Nara remained in control of several groups in the Kinai area, including the Kawachi rulers? This was the conclusion of Kondō Yoshirō (1983) who stated that although the locus of royal burial in the Middle Kofun Period shifted to Kawachi, the center of power remained in the Southeastern part of the Nara Basin. On the other hand, Shiraishi (1989, 2008) regarded the construction of the huge *kofun* of the Middle Kofun Period in the Kawachi Plain as evidence that the supreme political center shifted to that area.

In the Early Kofun Period, Kawachi communities appear to have been subordinate to groups in the southern Nara Basin. Burial mounds have been found in Central Kawachi near the confluence of the Yamato and Ishi Rivers, as well as in coastal areas such as Sakai, Kishiwada and Izumi. The tombs occur individually or in small groups, indicating small chiefdoms. The predominant forms of burial are the clay encased wooden coffin (*nendokaku*) and the vertical stone chamber, and grave goods consist of the usual ritual objects found in the Kinai in the fourth century AD, such as stone bracelets, beads, and mirrors. In a few cases early types of the storage chest type of stone coffin (*nagamochigata sekkan*) were also found. The adoption of this type of stone coffin is thought to indicate induction into the Yamato hierarchy and allegiance to the Yamato rulers.

The Chino'oka Kofun (length 155m), located 1km west of the fifth century Furuichi Kofun Group (discussed later in this chapter), indicates that a chief with substantial power lived in the area before the advent of the great Furuichi tomb builders. The front portion of the *kofun* is damaged but the rear portion yielded an early type of stone chest shaped coffin, encased in clay. The flat lid of the coffin, resembling the lid of an assembled coffin, shows that it is of an early type (Kohama 2006; 21). In Izumi City, the Koganetsuka Kofun (length 94m), excavated in 1950-51, yielded three clay encased wooden coffins (*nendokaku*) in the rear portion. Associated with the central burial was a bronze triangular rim mirror decorated with deities and beasts, with an inscription dated to 239 AD (see Box 5.3). In the eastern burial, which contained an assembled wooden coffin covered with red ocher, there were five iron knives and an eroded coin, thought to be a *Goshu* coin, most likely minted in the Western Han Period (206 BC to 9 AD) and retained as an heirloom. A cuirass of early type composed of triangular pieces, cap, a piece of armor for the neck (*okabe yoroi*), and bronze whorl-like ornaments (*tomoegata*) were also recovered from a separate burial (Kohama 2006: 22-24). This tomb represents an important locus of power on the Ōsaka Plain in the Early Kofun Period, in which both ritual and military objects occurred together in the burial, whereas Middle Kofun Period grave goods were primarily weapons and armor. Nine iron adze heads and an iron sickle, as well as five long narrow iron ingots were also found, as well as an assortment of beads of semi-precious stones and glass, including curved pendants (*magatama*) (Shimada 1985: 45-47).

In the region of the confluence of the Yamato and Ishi Rivers, an unexcavated Early Kofun Period keyhole tomb, the Matsuokayama Kofun (length 130m to 150m) (Fukunaga 2008: 440) is surrounded by six small round Early Kofun Period mounds which yielded burials associated with mirrors and stone ornaments. Nearby on a ridge there is linear group of eighteen keyhole shape and round burial mounds, the Tamateyama Kofun Group (Yasumura 2008a,b). Some have been excavated and destroyed in the wake of recent development of the area. Tamateyama No. 9 is a keyhole tomb 65m long, with a vertical stone chamber ritual stone grave goods. It has yielded the oldest type of cylindrical (*entō*) *haniwa* in the south Kawachi area, placing it in the Early Kofun Period.

Tanaka (2001: 31) states that the group represents a short time span in the Early Kofun Period and that since there are too many mounds for there to be one for each successive generation, the group who made them must have consisted of several lineages. Several tombs may have been constructed within one generation (Shimogaki 2012: 68-70). Two of the keyhole mounds are 130m and 101m long respectively, indicating that the builders had considerable power in the area.

What is the relation between the Tamateyama builders of the Early Kofun Period and the succeeding Furuichi builders of the Middle Kofun Period? Yasumura (2008b: 471) states that it is likely that people buried in the Tamateyama group were replaced by later arrivals, but that much more research is required.

Other Early Kofun Period tombs show the existence of local elite centers in the Kawachi area. Two examples are the Kumeda Kaifukuyama Kofun in Kishiwada City and the Niwatori Kofun of Habikino City. The Kumeda Kaifukuyama Kofun is a *zenpōkōen* mound, 130m long. In the front square area a wooden clay-encased coffin was found, and in the back portion there was a vertical stone chamber. It was robbed, but the following finds were recorded; bracelets, wheel shape stone bracelets (*sharinseki*), hoe shape bracelets, tubular beads, bronze arrowheads, iron arrowheads, and single and double edged swords. The material for the stone coffin comes from the Yoshinogawa River area of Tokushima Prefecture Shikoku Island, showing close relations with the Inland Sea area, and the ceramics show close relations to southern the Korean peninsula (Ōsaka Furitsu Chikatsu Asuka Hakubutsukan 2006: 18).

The Niwatori Kofun, investigated in 2005, a *zenpōkōen* 50m long, stands by itself on the left bank of the Ishi River. It yielded an assembled log coffin encased in clay. Inside the coffin, above the head, a triangular rim mirror and an iron knife, and near the head, a double edged short sword and jade *magatama* were placed. Outside the coffin on the east side, there were iron and bronze arrowheads, two bronze tubular artifacts, an iron spearhead, bronze gauntlet, and another imported triangular rim mirror. Two bronze tubular pieces were either fittings for the base of a long spear or for a hand held scepter. As mentioned above, the individual buried in the mound, in similar fashion to the Izumi City Koganetsuka burial, seems to be linked to the center of power in southeast Yamato and is said to represent newly emerging military power in the area (Ōsaka Furitsu Chikatsu Asuka Hakubutsukan 2006: 28).

Archaeologists have concluded that construction of the royal tombs of Wa in Kawachi at the Mozu and Furuichi Tomb Groups began at the end of the fourth century AD (Shiraishi 2008). In the first half of the fifth century AD the royal tombs became much larger. (Not only were there large tombs in Kawachi but also in other locations such as Okayama.) Chronologically the first tomb is Tsudō Shiroyama, Fujiidera City (Ōsaka Furitsu Chikatsu Asuka Hakubutsukan 2006: 48). Since this tomb overlaps with the latest tombs from Saki, there must have been an abrupt political shift from one area to the other. All of the subordinate chiefs loyal to Saki must have shifted over to Kawachi in the coup d'etat of Homutawake (also transcribed as Hondawake), whose posthumous name was Ōjin. The first year of his reign was probably AD 390. The elite Kawachi group had tombs in Kawachi before Ōjin but it was Ōjin who completed the shift of power (Kishimoto 2010b).

Important Tomb Groupings

The Furuichi and Mozu Tomb Groups

The most imposing archaeological sites of the region are the Furuichi and Mozu Tomb Groups, built in the fifth century, thought to contain the mausolea of the Five Kings of Wa, recorded in Chinese records from 413 to 502 AD, and other members of their dynasty (Figures 5.5, 5.6, 5.7). They contain the largest tombs ever built in Japan; and the Daisen Ryō Kofun, is said to be the largest in the world. Three very large mounded tombs, Tadeiyama Kofun, Daisen Ryō Kofun, and Kami Ishitzu Misanzai, are lined up on a terrace above the old shoreline of Ōsaka Bay. Foreigners travelling from the Asian continent via the Island Sea would have seen these tombs when they landed at the old port of Sakai Ura, and would have passed by them on the Ōtsudō and Tajihidō roads to Naniwa. Their great height (the rear mound of the Daisen Ryō Kofun Kofun is 35m high) and fresh stone facing along with the massive wooden palaces of Naniwa would have added to the impressive nature of the center (Izumori 2006: 93-94). The area of the Daisen Ryō Kofun is 47,000m². Including its three surrounding ditches and ridges its total length is 850m. Its construction is thought to have taken 2000 workers 15 years 8 months (Ueda 2007: 4-12). Mounded tombs such as Daisen Ryō contain burials of individuals at the very apex of Kofun Period society. Since the tombs are virtually unexcavated, information on the number and nature of the burials in these mounds is not available. Some important officials may be buried in auxiliary tombs termed *baichō* (discussed later in this chapter).

BOX 5.4
Historical texts and the Five Kings of Wa

Two bodies of historical records shed faint light on this period. The first are Japanese historical accounts, the *Kojiki* and *Nihon Shoki* of the early eighth century AD, and the *Engishiki* of the tenth century AD. The historian Joan Piggott (1997) has discussed these sources in detail. The second are Chinese dynastic chronicles, such as the *Wei Zhi (Annals of the Wei Dynasty)*, published in the late third century AD (Tsunoda and Goodrich 1951, 8-21) describe "Queen" Himiko and her kingdom in some detail, but Himiko is not mentioned by her name in the Japanese texts, nor can the location of her kingdom or grave be precisely determined from excavations at present (Kidder 2007). The *Song Shu* (History of the Liu Song Dynasty) (Tsunoda and Goodrich 1951: 22-27) contains brief notes on the "Five Kings of Wa" with dates of their tributary missions to China, but the single character names that they were given cannot be correlated with Japanese sources. The great tombs in which they are thought to be buried might some day be dated on a calendrical time scale by tree ring dating, if excavations are ever permitted. Since this study concerns archaeological, rather than historical data, I can only introduce these problems and refer the reader to experts such as Piggott (1997) and Kidder (2007). In the fifth century AD very large keyhole tombs appear for the first time beyond the mountainous border of the Nara Basin, on the Kawachi alluvial plain. Although the historical identity of the tombs' owners has not been identified by excavation or the presence of epitaphs, it is certain that among the largest of these keyhole mounds are the tombs of the so called Five Kings of Wa, which are mentioned in the Chinese history of the Liu Song Dynasty, *Song Shu, (History of the Liu Song* (Tsunoda and Goodrich 1951: 22-17). The *Kojiki* (Asao et al 1999: 7) states that three of the five king's tombs were built in the Mozu group – those of Nintoku, Richū, and Hanzei, while the tombs of the other two kings, Ōjin and Yūryaku, were built in the Furuichi Group, described below. In the Chinese records these kings are referred to as San, Chin, Sai, Ko, and Bu. Around 425, San petitioned the Liu Song court for diplomatic recognition, which was granted. Later his brother and successor, Chin, also received recognition, along with a number of his generals. In 443 AD, a third ruler, Sai, also received military titles from the Liu Song court. His son, Ko, and the final ruler of the Five Wa kings, Bu, brother of Ko, also received military titles in 462 and 478 AD respectively (Tsunoda and Goodrich 1951: 22-27). Earlier in the fifth century, 416 and 420 AD respectively, the kings of Koguryo and Paekche were given Chinese military titles; this custom was not limited to the Kings of Wa but extended to rulers in the Korean peninsula (Murakawa 1991: 68). These titles were bestowed to make it appear as if the newly founded Liu Song Dynasty had many allies; in fact, these were nominal titles of little consequence (Wang 2005: 23).

According to Piggott (1997, 47), "historians....posited that early in the fifth century a "Kawachi Dynasty" of paramounts presided over a maritime confederacy incorporating the Kii peninsula and Kibi" assuming supremacy over the previous rulers of the whose center was the Miwa region of the Nara Basin. The confederacies of the Nara Basin and Ōsaka alluvial plains merged to form an integrated political entity. The record in the *Song Shu* is primarily a record of the

Tomb in Mozu, Furuichi	Chronology	5 Wa Kings	Emperor Reign from Nihon Shoki
Tsudō Shiroyama *F			Ōjin
Nakatsuyama *F	391 Wa advances in Korean Peninsula		
Kami Ishitsu Misanzai *M	400 Koguryo advances south		Nintoku
			Richū
Hakayama			Hanzei
	413 Wa send tribute to Eastern Jin?		
Konda Gobyōyama *M	420 Eastern Jin falls, Song founded		
	421 Wa San sends tribute to Song?	San	
	425 Wa San sends tribute to Song?		
	430 King of Wa sends tribute to Song		
Mozu Gobyōyama	438 Wa Chin sends tribute to Song	Chin	Ingyō
	443 Wa Sai sends tribute to Song		
Daisen Ryō *M	451 Wa Sai sends tribute to Song		
		Sai	Ankō
Haji Nisanzai *M			
Ichinoyama *F	462 Wa Ko sends tribute to Song	Ko	
Karusato Ōtsuka	475 fall of Paekche capital Hansong	Bu	Yūryaku
	477 Wa sends tribute to Song		
	478 Wa Bu sends tribute to Song		
Oka Misanzai *F			Seinei
			Kenzō
Shirosagiyama	493 Northern Wei capital to Loyang		Ninken
			Buretsu
Bokeyama			Keitai

FIGURE 5.5. MAJOR TOMBS IN THE FURUICHI AND MOZU TOMB GROUPS, THE TIME PERIOD OF THE FIVE KINGS OF WA, AND THE SUCCESSION OF EMPERORS OUTLINED IN THE NIHON SHOKI. ADAPTED FROM NAKAKUBO AND TAKAHASHI (EDS) 2014: 63. COURTESY OF THE ŌSAKA DAIGAKU SHUPPANKAI.

titles given to these rulers by Song authorities. There is no proof that they were lineal descendants. Most likely they were competing paramount chiefs.

At the end of the fourth and early fifth centuries AD Wa was involved in long periods of warfare on the Korean peninsula and there was internal warfare among Korean states. Wa diplomacy extended to all of the small countries of East Asia at that time (Suzuki 2002: 34). The fact that Himiko also sent tributary missions to China and received titles around 240 AD, indicates that the Nara/Kawachi area was closely connected to the continent in both the Yayoi and Kofun Periods.

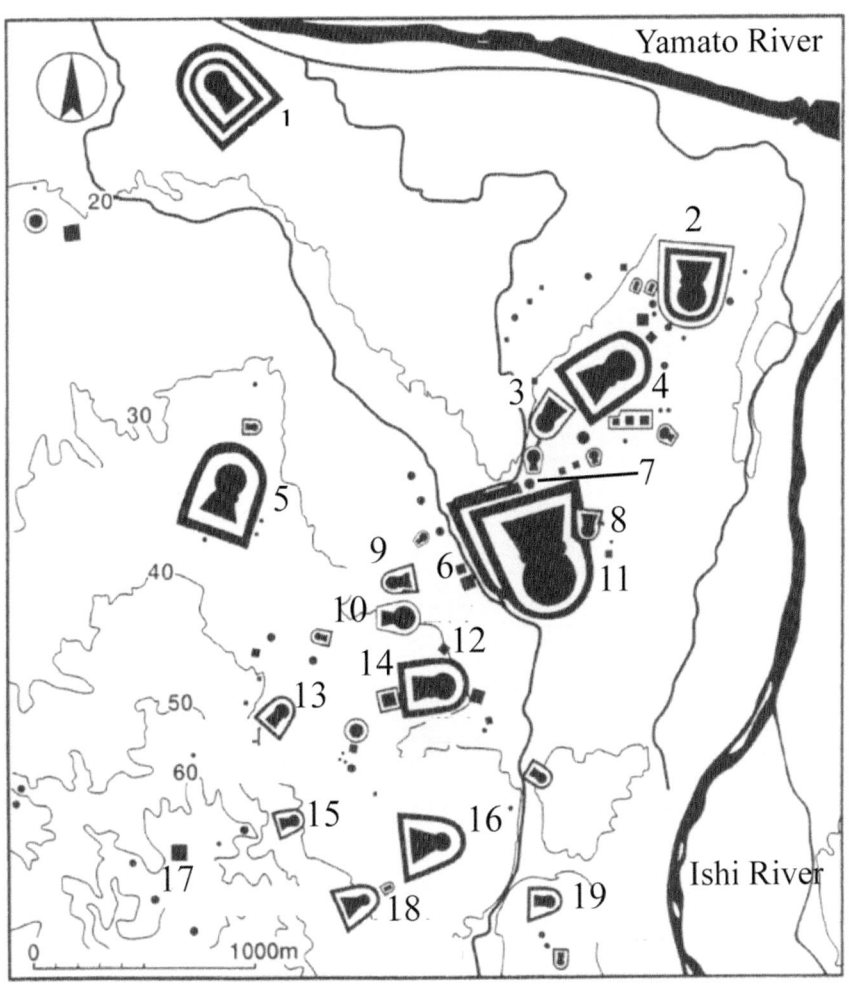

FIGURE 5.6. MAJOR KOFUN IN THE FURUICHI TOMB GROUP. (1) TSUDŌ SHIROYAMA. (2) ICHINOYAMA. (3) KOMUROYAMA. (4) NAKATSUYAMA. (5) OKA MISANZAI. (6) ARIYAMA. (7) KONDA MARUYAMA. (8) NIITSUKA. (9) HASAMIYAMA. (10) MIYAYAMA. (11) KONDA GOBYŌYAMA. (12) NONAKA. (13) BOKEYAMA. (14) HAKAYAMA. (15) MINEGATSUKA. (16) MAENOYAMA. (17) TSUKA'ANA. (18) SHIRAKAYAMA. (19) TAKASHIROYAMA. FROM ŌSAKA FURITSU CHIKATSU ASUKA HAKUBUTSUKAN: 2006: 11. COURTESY OF SHIRAISHI TA'ICHIRŌ.

Both of these tomb groups fit into a rectangular area about 14 km east west and about 20 km north south, excluding the Tsudō Shiroyama Kofun of the Furuichi Group (Ueda 2007: 4-12, Ichinose 2009: 81). Although many of the great tombs are protected from excavation as Imperial Tombs, a surprising amount of digging has occurred and nearly half of the tombs in each group have been destroyed.

The Furuichi Tomb Group extending from the northwest of Habikino City to Fujiidera City, about 4km east west and about 3km north south, is dominated by a nucleus of very large royal tombs. One of these, the Konda Gobyōyama Kofun is the second largest in the country, 416m in total length. Others are the Oka Misanzai, 242m long, and the Ichinoyama Kofun, 230m long. There are a total of 19 keyhole (*zenpōkōenfun*) tombs, 1 *zenpōkōhōfun* tomb, and 25 round mounds. Of the 19 keyhole tombs in the group there are 6 over 200m long. Most of the tomb construction occurred in the fifth century AD (Ōtsuka and Kobayashi 1984: 272). Data from three large tombs, Tsudō Shiroyama, Konda Gobyōyama, and Minegatsuka are summarized in Appendices A.2 to A.4.

The Furuichi Group commands the Yamato River drainage and access to the Nara Basin, while the Mozu

FIGURE 5.7. MAJOR *KOFUN* IN THE MOZU TOMB GROUP. (1) TADEIYAMA. (2) NAGAYAMA. (3) DAISEN RYŌ. (4) NAGAZUKAYAMA. (5) CHINO'OKA. (6) SHICHIKANYAMA. (7) NAGAZUKA (8) MOZU TORI GOBYŌYAMA. (9) KATONBOYAMA. (10) KAMI ISHITSU MISANZAI. (11) ŌTSUKAYAMA. (12) ITASUKE. (13) SHIRONOYAMA. (14) HAJI NISANZAI. FROM ŌSAKA FURITSU CHIKATSU ASUKA HAKUBUTSUKAN 2006: 11. COURTESY OF SHIRAISHI TA'ICHIRŌ.

Group is close to the shore of Ōsaka Bay and commanded maritime trade routes (Kishimoto 2010b: 47-75). While figures vary slightly in different descriptions, the Mozu Group originally was comprised of 23 *zenpōkōenfun* mounds, 9 scallop shape mounds, 8 square mounds, and 54 round mounds (Sakai Shi Kyōiku Iinkai 2008, 2009). By 2013 only 48, roughly half of the mounds were still extant (bell.jp 2014). Four large tombs yielding substantial information, Chino'oka, Daisen Ryō, Ōtsukayama, and Kurohimeyama, are described in Appendices A.5 to A.8.

Construction of the Mozu and Furuichi large tombs took several decades. As with all *kofun* it involved complex administrative organization and the recruitment of technical experts (Ichinose 2005). In the sixth century AD the rulers stopped building the very large tombs in Mozu but in Furuichi three more very large *zenpōkōenfun* about 130m long were built, Bokeyama, Shirahayama, and Koyashiroyama, even though there was a trend to build smaller *kofun* at that time (Shiraishi 1989: 103).

So called imperial tombs in Furuichi and Mozu are often substantially larger than the largest tombs of the Nara Basin, with vertical chambers containing massive stone coffins, double or triple surrounding moats, and the use of special bird form *haniwa*. Strict adherence to the prescribed proportions of the 'keyhole' shape (*zenpōkōenfun*) tombs is a feature of most of the tombs of the highest rulers. Building these huge monuments to strict proportions required substantial expertise. Ichinose (2005) states that the proportions of the Tsudō Shiroyama Kofun in Furuichi are as follows: diameter of rear mound at middle step, length of front square portion, and length of whole mound are 1,1,1.8. This is termed the Tsudō Shiroyama Type. The Haji Nisanzai Kofun is 1.959 times the length of the Tadeiyama Kofun, and the ratio of the width of the rear mound to the total length is 0.513 for the Tadeiyama Kofun and 0.517 for the Haji Nisanzai Kofun. In both tombs the ratio of the width of the front mound to the width of the rear mound is 0.69 (Izumori 2006: 93) suggesting that a master plan or standard unit of measurement was used. Within the Mozu Group, some of the tombs are exactly half the size of others, indicating strict rules of protocol for construction (Izumori 2006: 92). Tsude (1989b: 30) showed that there was striking consistency in the proportions of the width of the steps of the rectangular front and circular rear portions of the great mounds of the Kinai Region in examples from the end of the third century AD to the beginning of the sixth century AD (Figure 5.8). Precise mapping of the fourth largest *kofun* in Japan, Tsukuriyama Kofun in Okayama, using a total station, has allowed archaeologists to deduce the original unit of measurement, the *shaku* (0.2331m). The consistency in proportions of different tombs is the result of careful calculations of dimensions using standard units of measurement that differed slightly by time period and region rather than simple copying

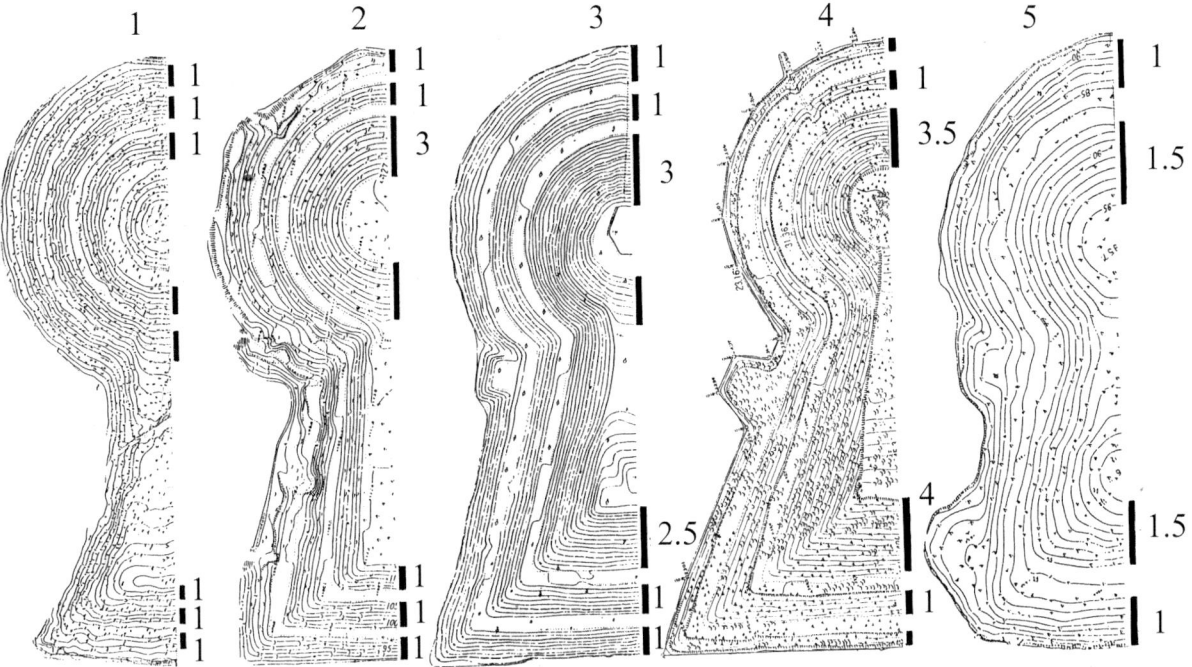

FIGURE 5.8. CONFORMITY OF PROPORTIONS OF KOFUN. FROM TSUDE (ED) 1989, 30. (1) HASHIHAKA KOFUN, NARA PREFECTURE, END OF THIRD CENTURY AD. (2) SHIBUYA MUKŌYAMA KOFUN, NARA PREFECTURE, LATTER HALF OF FOURTH CENTURY AD. (3) KONDA GOBYŌYAMA KOFUN, ŌSAKA PREFECTURE, EARLY HALF OF FIFTH CENTURY AD. (4) NISANZAI KOFUN, ŌSAKA PREFECTURE, MID FIFTH CENTURY AD. (5) TORIYA MISANZAI KOFUN, NARA PREFECTURE, EARLY HALF OF SIXTH CENTURY AD. COURTESY OF KŌDANSHA PUBLISHERS.

of existing designs (Niiro 2011). The relative power of local rulers can be measured by the degree of perfection of compliance to this ratio in their tomb construction.

Many of the large tombs included in this discussion are unexcavated or partially excavated, often a long time ago. One example, the Minegatsuka Tomb, excavated in the 1980s, is of interest because it is of intermediate size, perhaps indicating a lesser royal figure; it yielded a wide variety of grave goods that are not well known from other sites in the two royal cemeteries. It is described in Appendix A.4.

The first tomb in the Mozu group is Chino'oka, built while the center of power was still in the Saki area of Nara. In the Ōsaka Plain the very large tombs thought to be imperial tombs are Nakatsuyama, Ishitsuoka Misanzai, Konda Gobyōyama, Daisen Ryō, Haji Nisanzai, and Oka Misanzai. Kingship is thought to have alternated between the Mozu and Furuichi groups. The first royal tomb to be built in the Mozu Group was the Kami Ishitsu Misanzai Kofun, followed by Daisen Ryō Kofun, and subsequently Haji Misanzai. If we compare the chronologies of Furuichi and Mozu, in the gap between Furuichi Nakatsuyama and Konda Gobyōyama, the Mozu Kami Ishitsu Misanzai fits, and in the gap between the Furuichi Konda Gobyōyama and Oka Misanzai, the Mozu Daisen Ryō and Haji Nisanzai fit (Shiraishi 1989: 96).

It is proposed that the Okinaga and Wani Clans of Furuichi provided queens for the Katsuragi in Mozu (Shiraishi 1989: 99). It may ultimately be possible to outline the sequence of political succession through archaeological relative dating, but determining the actual kin relations of rulers is much more difficult (Shimogaki 2012: 57).

Descriptions of individual tombs in the Furuichi and Mozu Tomb Groups are given in Appendix A.2 to A.15.

Satellite Tombs (baichō)

Tombs for retainers or officials, thought to be associated with largest tombs rather than occurring in separate cemeteries, are a feature of the Middle Kofun Period in the Kawachi Plain. In general there is a wide range of mound sizes and shapes in Furuichi and Mozu. The presence of large numbers of smaller, apparently subordinate mounds near very large burial mounds is a key feature of these groups. The satellite mounds are considered by their general proximity to larger mounds to be dependent on the former, rather than independent burial facilities. Two types are recognized, those with grave offerings as well as human burials, and those with grave offerings alone. The latter may contain offerings given to the occupants of adjacent large mounds, or they may be retainers' graves in which the human remains have for some reason not been found. They are often square in horizontal plan and the burials occur in wooden coffins rather than stone chambers with stone coffins. The satellite tombs are considered to be a class separate from the small, medium, and large free standing tombs. There are also cases of satellite tombs related to medium mounds as well as large ones (Tanaka 2001: 55). The assigning of tombs with burials to satellite status seems to depend on a subjective assessment of their spatial relationship to large tombs. In addition, the absence of human burials is a deciding factor. However from limited excavation or accidental exposure it is not always possible to be sure that a tomb does not contain a burial which has not been found. These burials, rather than being offerings to personages in the main tombs, may be 'cenotaphs' to individuals whose remains could not be buried in their home territory.

In the Early Kofun Period, at the time of the early fourth century Hashihaka Kofun, Nara, the large keyhole shape tombs stand alone, without associated smaller tombs or satellites. In the subsequent Yamato Yanagimoto Tomb Group of the Nara Basin, middle size tombs appear in addition to large ones and there appear to be some satellite tombs. In the Saki Tomb group of the Nara Basin (end of Early Kofun), there are three or four distinctive tomb groups but the ratio of satellite and medium tombs is low. In the Mozu and Furuichi tombs of the fifth century, the diversity of mound sizes greatly increases, with a ratio of many small, medium, large, and satellite tombs per huge tomb. Tanaka (2001: 49) concludes that this indicates a sudden increase in social complexity and the number of social ranks. Some archaeologists have proposed that the satellite tombs were the burials of administrative officials (Tanaka 2001: 50-55, Ban 2009: 96). Suzuki (2002: 68-72) interprets the satellite tombs as the burials of a "primitive administrative class" (*genshiteki kanryo*). It is interesting that the grave wealth of this class seems to consist of utilitarian objects, perhaps produced under sponsorship of paramount chiefs.

Tanaka (2001: 50) notes that the contents of satellite tombs are variable. In Mozu and Furuichi they contain weapons or agricultural tools, tombs such as Shichikanyama, Ariyama, and Nonaka. Others such as Katonboyama contain many stone replicas and jade objects (Tanaka 2012). Descriptions of five of the best documented examples of satellite tombs, Konda Maruyama, Nonaka, Tsukamawari, Shichikanyama, and Katonboyama, are given in Appendix A.9 to A.13.

This discussion of the Kofun Period focuses on particularly large mounds. Many smaller tombs dot the Ōsaka landscape. For instance, over two hundred smaller tombs, dating to the fifth and sixth centuries AD, thought to belong to lesser officials, are situated to the northwest of Furuichi in the Nagahara Tomb Group. Some spectacular *haniwa*, including two types of boat, come from Nagahara Takamawari (Kyōshima 2007a).

Takaida Corridor Tomb Group

The decline and disappearance of *zenpōkōenfun* in the late sixth century AD reflect profound social changes in the Ōsaka region, in which local groups appear to have become independent from central authority. Ideological changes also accompanied the introduction of Buddhism around 538 AD. New burial practices can be seen in the key region near the confluence of the Yamato and Ishi Rivers, at the Takaida Corridor Tomb Group, where some 160 to 200 chambers were cut out of volcanic tuff, to bury members of a corporate group who presumably controlled the area (Kashiwara Shiritsu Rekishi Shiryōkan 2012). Each tomb consists of an entry corridor that expands into three or four chambers, 170 to 180cm high, containing individual burials in wooden plank coffins. Nails from these coffins have been found on the chamber floors. In some cases an open rectangular stone coffin was carved from the wall of the artificial cave. Groups of burial chambers on the same slope, in vertical arrangement, seem to indicate successive generations of the same family. Grave goods include gold or silver plated bronze earrings, steatite beads, and sets of *sueki* vessels. Smaller elevated cups were placed in the chamber while heavily decorated elevated vessels were set on top of the tomb (Morimoto 2011). The Takaida burial chambers are famous for their wall decorations incised on the soft tuff. These depict people, houses, birds, and an individual in a boat.

While Late Kofun Period dug out corridor tombs are widespread in Japan from southern Tōhoku to Miyazaki, the Takaida Site is the only example in the Ōsaka region. Perhaps the elite practitioners of the *zenpōkōenfun* system resisted the adoption of practices from outlying areas, and the people of the Takaida group chose to be distinctive, or innovative. After the close of the Kofun Period, in the seventh century AD, square mounds with a wide entrance leading to a cut stone chamber were constructed for persons of high status. Some are imperial tombs.

Ishisuka Tomb Group

The third largest tomb group in the Ōsaka region is the Ishisuka Tomb Group, located in the uplands of the Chikatsu region. It was the burial place of elite immigrants from China and Korea. Dating from the first half of the sixth century to the mid seventh century 262 graves occur in 23 clusters on a gradual mountain slope. They are mostly circular mounds 10 to 20m in diameter with a small number of square examples. Most of them have an interior stone chamber with a side entrance and contain wooden coffins, but a few contained simply a small chamber that served as a coffin. A single large mound, 30m in diameter contained a house shaped stone coffin in a stone chamber and grave goods of *sueki*, miniature jars, glass beads, iron swords and horse gear.

Gilt bronze earrings and fragments of a gilt bronze crown indicate the presence of a local chief (Ichimoto 2014).

Craft Production

Hishida (2010a,b) noted that virtually all innovations in craft production were introduced by migrants from the continent (*toraijin*). These include iron working, *sueki* production, horse gear manufacture and horse raising (Sugiyama 2010), and salt production. Improvements in weaving, difficult to document archaeologically, must also have been introduced.

The Kawachi region was a center for craft production, particularly of ceramics such as *haniwa* and *sueki* ceramics, iron products, stone beads, and salt. Around the tombs were found workshops for beads, iron working, and *haniwa* production, as well as warehouses for tools and food. Haji no Sato, located in Fujiidera City near the Nakatsuyama Kofun, is thought to have been a center of the Haji Clan of artisans and engineers, and a *kofun* construction site. The products of *haniwa* kilns in the area went to the Ichinoyama and Konda Gobyōyama mounds. Although this site was occupied at various times from the Jōmon Period to the Chūsei Period, the two major periods of occupation were during the Kofun Period and the subsequent Asuka Period, when the Buddhist Temple, Hajidera, was constructed. While commoners' pit houses are abundant, there are no remains of the houses of the elite members of the Haji Clan who managed the huge projects.

Surely textile production must also have been of major importance, although archaeological traces of its progress are difficult to detect. The expansion of craft production was stimulated by elite demand and the arrival of immigrants from the Korean peninsula in the fifth century AD. They settled in the Habikino slope and south Kawachi area. With their base in this area they spread to the Yamato River area and Naniwa Port, and to the west, overland, to the Sumiyoshi area, to the port of Suminoue no tsu and to the mouth of the Ishitsu River, in the area of Sakai (Kishimoto 2010b: 47-75). Workers were organized into occupational groups (*be*) under the control of supervisors (Asao et al 1999: 20). Specialized craft production was maintained and supervised by *gozoku* (aristocratic lineages) (Hishida 2007: 57). Who actually managed these activities and extracted tribute from them? Did foreign elites control production and turn over proceeds to Wa chiefs?

An unusual find of two V-shaped wooden sledges for hauling very large stones or coffins was made in the moat between two large square mounds, the Yashimatsuka Kofun and the Nakayamatsuka Kofun, on the south side of the Nakatsuyama Kofun. They are roughly 9m and 3m long respectively (Ōsaka Furitsu Chikatsu Asuka Hakubutsukan 2006: 54, 88-91).

Haniwa and Sueki

Haniwa and *sueki* were two kinds of luxury goods produced under central supervision. *Haniwa* kilns have been found near a number of *kofun*. The *haniwa* were made close to their intended final locations, from locally available clay. The Shin'ike kilns provided *haniwa* for the Ima Shirozuka Kofun in Takatsuki City, Ōsaka. On the north side of the Furuichi Tomb Group the Haji no Sato site yielded *haniwa* kilns (Hishida 2010a: 233). *Haniwa* kilns near the Konda Gobyōyama developed in the fifth century, and production shifted to the Nonoue kiln in the sixth century. In the Mozu Tomb Group, kilns produced *haniwa* for the Daisen Ryō Kofun, including the Ume chō kiln and kilns in the Hiki Shōen area (Box 5.5).

BOX 5.5
Haniwa

The custom of placing earthenware grave furniture (*haniwa*) on the exterior of the mound began in the Late Yayoi Period with the use of decorative ceramic stands and vessels in the Okayama region. In the Early Kofun Period, cylindrical (*entō*) *haniwa* were set in arrangements and from the Middle Kofun Period a diverse array of forms including replicas of houses, umbrellas, quivers, and *haniwa* in human form were produced. The idea of representing humans must have been introduced from the continent to the Kawachi area.

Large earthenware ornaments in the form of jars, stands, shields, umbrellas and other forms, were placed on the tops and edges of the mounds Figure 5.9). Large wooden ornaments, serving the same function as *haniwa* have been preserved in moats and ditches. They have been termed wooden *haniwa* (Tanaka 1991: 269). Note that they were placed on the exterior surfaces and boundaries of tombs, rather than on the inside. Both tubular and representational *haniwa* had a cylindrical base set in the ground. Although the top portion of each *haniwa* collapsed long ago, sherds remain on the mound surface and remains of the base can be seen with minimal clearing. The chronology of *haniwa* is based on four sets of attributes; scraping of the surface, external ridges, nature of firing, and shape and location of perforations (Sekimoto 2011). These cut-out sections on *entō haniwa* change in shape from triangular to rectangular to circular. Five periods extend from the fourth century to the latter half of the sixth century. In addition Early Kofun Period types of tubular *entō haniwa* have exterior vertical flanges or 'fins', which disappear during the Middle Kofun Period. A broad division can be made between *haniwa* fired in the open, which have dark specks of carbon in their paste, and those fired in enclosed kilns adapted from kilns for *sueki* after its introduction at the beginning of the fifth century AD, which lack the carbon specks. The *haniwa* chronology allows archaeologists to assign rough dates to unexcavated tombs from sherds found on their surface.

From the fifth century these included representations of humans and animals. Most large mounds had an arrangement of *haniwa* in the form of a circle within a square on the summit of the rear circular mound. The square was often demarcated by *haniwa* figures while the circle could be marked by stones or circular *haniwa* (Figure 5.9). Such an arrangement is said to have Chinese cosmological origins. The placement of the *haniwa* on the round mound was one of the final steps in the burial ritual, which began with the keeping of the deceased in a special structure *(mogari)* prior to burial. Vessels for food and drink, model houses for the temporary repose of the spirit, and symbols of rank such as *haniwa* umbrella, swords, quivers, and shields, were used.

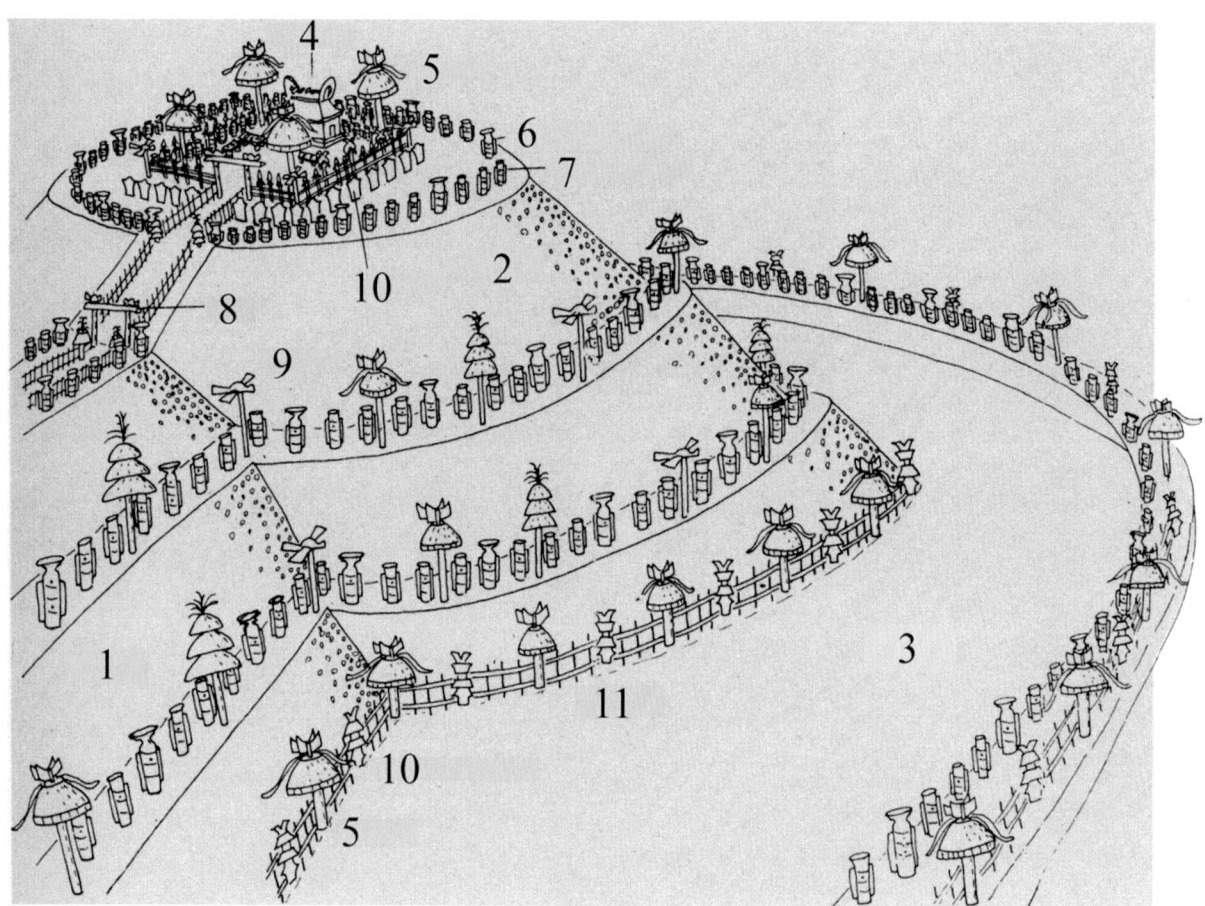

FIGURE 5.9 DECORATION OF A MIDDLE KOFUN PERIOD TOMB WITH WOOD AND CLAY *HANIWA*. (1) FRONT PORTION OF MOUND. (2) REAR PORTION OF MOUND. (3) MOAT. (4) HOUSE SHAPE CLAY *HANIWA*. (5) WOODEN PARASOL. (6) FINNED CLAY MORNING GLORY HANIWA. (7) FINNED CLAY TUBULAR HANIWA. (8) TORII GATE. (9) WOODEN BIRDS. (10) ROW OF WOODEN SHIELDS (11) WOODEN RITUAL FENCE. FROM TANAKA 1991: 270. COURTESY OF TANAKA MIGAKU AND SHŪEISHA PUBLISHERS.

In the fifth and sixth centuries local villages underwent important changes showing the development of *sueki* production. In the Ōbadera Site, at the earliest stage Korean style domestic pottery was abundant, indicating that the village was a center for Korean immigrants. In the slightly later Kosaka Site Koreans and Japanese lived together, judging from the presence of Japanese *haji* and Korean *sueki*. In the fifth century, at the time of the building of the largest tombs it appears that village settlements in the immediate area decreased. By the sixth century, Korean types of domestic pottery disappeared (Nakamura 2001: 103). In the sixth and seventh centuries at Ōbadera there are pit houses and elevated storehouses, and remains of a boundary ditch. The quantity of ceramics found in the village increases and is mostly comprised of *sueki*, used by the inhabitants. Some villages appear to have been inhabited by ceramic specialists while others were inhabited by farmers. The Yagai Site appears to have specialized in *sueki* production, Within 100 years, from the latter half of the fifth century AD the village expanded and did not have its own fields. It appears that in the sixth century, when tomb building declined, *sueki* production was reorganized and potter's villages became less specialized and more self sufficient (Shiraishi 2004:104) (Box 5.6).

Burials of *sueki* and *haniwa* producers

Distinctive burial practices for skilled craft artisans are a feature of the Late Kofun Period. Craftsmen had their own distinctive modes of burial, and must have been relatively privileged, to receive mound burial (Miyaoka

---

Box 5.6
Sueki

Sueki is a bluish grey stoneware fired in a reducing atmosphere at more than 1000 degrees Centigrade. Some vessels were fashioned using the coil method and were beaten to thin their walls, and often shaped on a slow turn table, while others were thrown, with bowls exhibiting string cut bases. Many different shapes were produced, including bowls, plates, platters, barrels, pitchers, steamers, handled vessels, twin jars, and high pedestalled jars. Many forms were containers of food and drink for burial offerings, but the ware was also used as elite tableware, its quality being rigidly controlled. The chronology of *sueki* production is undergoing constant revision. In the Kinai area, the oldest type, TG232, found in the Uji area, is dated to the late fourth century, while the types found in the Konda Gobyōyama Tomb, TK216 and TK73, are dated to the first half of the fifth century AD (Shiraishi 2011: 15). Morimura (2014) concluded that permission to produce *sueki* was granted by the Southern Song court to Nintoku, and was actually embedded in the East Asian tributary system but production definitely started much earlier than Suemura where large scale production seems to have begun around 450 AD, which confirms accounts that craftsmen came from the continent and established those kilns under the control of Nintoku.

The peak of occurrence of *sueki* in the Kinai tombs was the latter half of the fifth and early sixth centuries AD. After the decline of *sueki* production for tombs the main production shifted to everyday life and ritual objects and spread throughout Japan (Asao et al 1999: 17). *Sueki* vessels for elite and ritual use were rejected if they were imperfect in form or color as seen in refuse heaps associated with kilns (Morimura Ken'ichi personal communication). In the area to the west of the Ishitzu River greater control by the central authority is indicated by a higher level of standardization of production than in other areas (Sugahara 2006). Sites associated with *sueki* include kilns, clay digging sites, villages and burials sites.

The Suemura Kiln Site Group, located on the Senboku Slopes, was excavated in the 1970's and 1980's, at the time of the transformation of the region and the movement of huge quantities of fill for construction of the Kansai Airport on a artificial island in Ōsaka Bay (Nakamura 2006). Some 800 kilns covered an area of 9km x 11km. in the region of Sakai City at an elevation of 50 to 130m above sea level (Shiraishi Koji 2004, 96-108). The kilns are mostly of the tunnel type, dug into slopes or ravine edges of seven long hills running east to west, although some are level kilns (Figures 5.10, 5.11). Often the sites border on river courses and sherds are found in the river bed. Using local marine clay, Suemura began production in the fifth century and continued until the ninth and tenth centuries AD. Sites such as Ōbadera, Ume 231, and Ume 232, dating to the early fifth century, have yielded early *sueki*. At present, the oldest *sueki* production site is Ume 232, (early 5th century AD) which yields *sueki* with decoration similar to that found on Kaya ceramics from the Korean peninsula. While westerners often think of *sueki* as ritual ware for burial, excavation of the Suemura Kilns showed that the majority of vessels produced were large jars (*kame*), valued for their dense hard body suitable for water containers. Footed stands and covered bowls were found in both residential areas and tombs (Nakamura 2001, 159, 166-167) (Figure 5.10). Shallow clay pits, about 50 cm deep and 1 or 3 m square, have been found near kiln sites. Although the Ōsaka Marine Clay Layer is extensive in the Kawachi area, it is often deeply buried (Nakamura 2006: 44).

Figure 5.10. Sueki vessels from the Sue Kiln Group, Senboku, Osaka, fifth century AD. From Tanaka 1991, 325. Courtesy of Tanaka Migaku and Shūeisha Publishers.

Figure 5.11 Methods of firing sueki vessels in a climbing kiln (*noborigama*), and level kiln (*hiragama*), 2006: 34. Courtesy of Shinsensha Publishers. 1. Firebox, 2. Combustion chamber, 3. Firing area, 4. Flue, 5. Back wall, 6. Firewall, 7. Smoke chamber.

2012). In the Sakai area a group of sixth century AD small circular burial mounds is thought to contain burials of *sueki* producers (Sakai Shi Kyōiku Iinkai 1984a: 14). The group of some 30 mounds is adjacent to a small keyhole shape tomb, Goboyama Kofun, 30m in total length and 4m high as if they were politically subordinate to the ruler. Details on the burials in the large mound are unknown but some of the smaller mounds have been excavated. In 1950 there were about 30 small circular mounds in the group, but by 1970 only 10 remained. No. 29, a small circular burial mound was excavated. In the main burial there was a tubular coffin of *sueki* ware. Such coffins are extremely rare. At the time of reporting in the 1980's there were some 30 cases known, from various parts of Japan. In particular they are numerous in Shizuoka and Ōsaka. There were twelve cases in Ōsaka mostly in the Wada and Ibaraki areas. In many examples there is evidence that the entire coffin was burned after placement in the burial chamber. There were different styles of surface treatment on different parts of the coffin, as if it was made by a group of artisans.

A particular kind of burial using a specially made tubular cylindrical coffin of *haniwa* ware was the mark of the Haji Clan, engineers and artisans (Seike 1999). It is found in mounds of intermediate size and was not used by commoners. Discoveries have been made in the Furuichi, Mozu, Saki, and Umami Tomb Groups. In the area near Haji no Sato, (see above), more than 100 of these coffins have been found. Stylistically they are dated to the latter half of the fifth century AD but in a few cases the grave goods inside the coffins date to the early seventh century. Why did the use of these coffins persist after the construction of the large tombs ended in the sixth century? Many of these graves do not contain offerings and are difficult to date. In some parts of Japan distant from the Kinai, burials in *haniwa* ware coffins are found in the peripheries of large mounds and may indicate the presence of craft specialists attached to the main occupant of the burial mound.

Salt Production

The Izumi area of Kawachi was a center of ceramic and salt production (Sekiyama 2004). Salt making originated in the latter half of the Middle Yayoi in the Inland Sea region, and was introduced from there to the Kawachi region, judging from similarities in elevated stands and round bottom vessels in the two regions. From the Late Yayoi Period, pottery with a distinctive clay body strong enough to be used for boiling salt water has been found. This distinctive pottery marks the appearance of salt making as a specialized activity, at sites such as the Minato Site on the lower reaches of the Sano River in Izumi Sano City (Kaigawa 2013). This site, with access to coastal resources, contains layers from the Palaeolithic Period to the Kinsei Period (Nakaoka 2012: 14). Early salt making communities were also involved in fishing, which included deep sea species. Since some salt making sites have yielded very early types of grey stoneware, salt making must have flourished at the same time as the largest tombs in the Furuichi Group, expanding in the Early and Middle Kofun Periods. In the Middle Kofun Period (fifth century AD) specialized sites appear to have been devoted to salt production. Many smaller production sites have been found all along the coast, within 10 km of the old shoreline (Tanaka 2001: 434-439). Tanaka found that the decline in specialized pottery for salt production coincides with the decline in the Mozu and Furuichi tomb groups. In the Kojima Higashi Site, in the Izumi area, large scale salt production died out after the Middle Kofun Period (Tanaka 2001: 434).

Production of iron goods

Iron production can be recognized archaeologically by the presence of large hearths, slag, bellows valves, iron fragments, whetstones and incomplete iron objects. While iron working or smithing, as distinct from smelting or refining, goes back to the Yayoi Period, the production of iron goods in large quantities began in the Early Kofun Period. Although it is common for fifth century *kofun* to contain large quantities of weapons it should not be forgotten that third century Tsubai Ōtsukayama contained many weapons in addition to the 36 famous mirrors, 1 set of cap and cuirass, 20 swords, 200 iron arrowheads, and more than 16 bronze arrowheads (Tanaka 1991: 321).

Iron was imported and exchanged in the form of ingots, as well as finished goods. At least two sizes of ingots were produced. The small size is 14cm long, with a maximum width of 3cm, and a thickness 1.5cm. while the large form is roughly 36cm long, with a maximum width of 12cm and a thickness of 2cm. Both forms were found in the Yamato No. 6 Kofun, satellite tomb (*baichō*) of the Unabe Kofun of the Saki Group, dating to the first half of fifth century. A total of 872 ingots were found in a wooden box. The origin of these iron ingots is iron ore, not iron sand, indicating that they were imported from the Korean peninsula. This type has been found in 25 *kofun* in Japan yielding roughly a total of 1000 ingots; and seven localities in the Kinai region have yielded over 90% of this total (Tanaka 1991: 323-324, Ichinose 2005: 13).

Extracting iron metal from iron sand and iron ore began in the late fifth century or early sixth century (Hishida 2010a: 212-238). Most likely the technical aspects of iron extraction were introduced and managed by people from the Korean peninsula (Kashiwara Shi Kyōiku Iinkai 1997: 17-18) and Yamato may well have encouraged Kaya iron specialists to immigrate, as suggested by some of the fifth century guild workers' names (Barnes 2000: 89). By the mid sixth century and Kaya's defeat by Silla, iron was no longer flowing to the Japanese islands from the southern Korean peninsula, and Japan established the beginnings of a regional iron smelting process historically referred to as *tatara*, which used iron sand as its raw material (Barnes 2000: 89).

Evidence of iron working and bead production is often found in villages with remains of Korean style houses. A new type of building, derived from the Kongju area of Korea, the center of the Paekche Kingdom, had walls attached to stout posts set side by side in a trench (*ōkabe tatemono*). While this type of construction was most common in the area near Lake Biwa it also occurred in the Ōsaka Region. These were distinctive from local buildings supported by dispersed posts. These 'large wall buildings' occurred in sets with local style buildings, indicating an immigrant elite house compound. The central house was protected by a surrounding wall. The Nagahara Site (Figure 2.4), yielded fifth century evidence of iron working along with Korean pottery types and early forms of *sueki*, indicating that it was inhabited by Korean immigrants. Evidence of bead making and horse rearing was also found. Nearby is a group of some 200 small *kofun*, thought to be burials of immigrant functionaries.

The change from smithing imported iron to smithing locally smelted iron from iron sand for the production of iron agricultural tools occurred in the latter half of the fifth century. The small, dispersed production sites of the Yayoi and Early Kofun Periods were replaced by larger centers, spatially concentrated in special areas inside villages and elite residential centers (*jūkan*). By the sixth century, production of iron goods was concentrated in a few very large sites in both the Kawachi Basin and the Nara Basin. Through co-operation between Korean and Wa groups, cuirasses and helmets were produced (Hanada 2002: 357). Iron and *sueki* production of the fifth century both indicate mastery of high firing techniques. The use of iron for military weapons strengthened the power of elites and hastened state formation but iron was also critical for iron tools such as the edge or bit of wooden hoes and sickles.

Iron Working Sites

Some 68 sites were recorded by Hanada in the Ōsaka Bay Region out of a total of 79 in the entire Kinai area (Hanada 2002: 7). The smaller sites were associated with elite residences, very large tomb sites and in some villages, where small scale, short term metal working facilities have been found. Iron working sites associated with the construction of large tombs include the Haji Minami Ryō and Higashi Ueno sites in the Mozu Tomb Group and the Haji no Sato and Konda Shiratori sites in the Furuichi Group. Iron working tools have been found in the Nonaka Kofun of the fifth century and in small mound burials of the Kinai region dating to the sixth and seventh centuries AD; these include pliers, hammers, and cold chisels (Hanada 2002: 133) (Figures 5.12, 5.13).

The Haji no Sato Site was occupied in the fifth and sixth centuries AD. It was associated with the construction of the Mozu Tomb Group, and was abandoned when the tombs were completed. The sites yielded remains of elevated buildings, ditches, wells, *haniwa* tubular coffins, *komochi magatama* and salt making pottery. Iron slag and tuyeres were found on the east side of the excavation (Hanada 2002: 121). There were some 40 iron working localities in two groups around the Daisen Ryō Kofun as well (Hanada 2002: 8-9).

The Ōgata Site Group is probably the largest iron working site found on the Kawachi Plain to date. It is strategically located at the confluence of the Yamato and Ishi Rivers, within 2km of the Furuichi Tomb Group. A large excavation was undertaken prior to the laying of an underground water pipe. Some 200kg of slag were found in an area of 140m^2. and a total of 386 tuyeres were found, along with abundant whetstones for finishing cast objects (Kashiwara Shi Kyōiku Iinkai 1997: 1-12, Kashihara Kōkogaku Kenkyūsho 2013). Many excavations in the 1980s uncovered the largest site of its type in the Kinai region, comprising an area 800m x 200m. Covered by 3m of overburden, it was used from the Middle Kofun Period to the Nara Period, the greatest density occurring in the Late Kofun Period. The association of Wa type sword fittings and Korean style pottery indicated that there was a Korean artisan group in a Wa community. According to Hanada, the Ōgata area was under the control of the Mononobe Clan, a powerful clan that controlled the Ōgata area in the seventh century. They must have sponsored groups of immigrant specialists

The Tanabe Site appears to succeed the Ōgata Site, suggesting that the iron workers of Ōgata may have moved to Tanabe. The main occupation at Tanabe is a village of the seventh to eighth centuries, associated with the Tanabe abandoned temple. Situated on the south bank of the Yamato River near the Matsuokayama Kofun group, the region was the center for the Tanabe Clan. A smaller site, the Ryōnan Kita Site, on the Ishitsu River, dating to the middle and late fifth century AD, contained evidence of the production of wooden artifacts such as sword sheaths as well as evidence of iron working (Hanada 2002: 121).

In the Nara Basin, sites include the huge fifth century AD Furu Site Group and the Nangō Site Group. It has been proposed that the Furu Site was a production center of the Mononobe Clan (Hanada 2002: 12-17) and the Nangō Site belonged to the Katsuragi Clan (Hishida 2010a: 224). Extending 1.5km east-west and 1km north-south, the Furu Site contained a dwelling area, ritual area, production area, and chief's residence. The association of the chief's house with production seems to indicate

Consolidation of Political Power and Trade

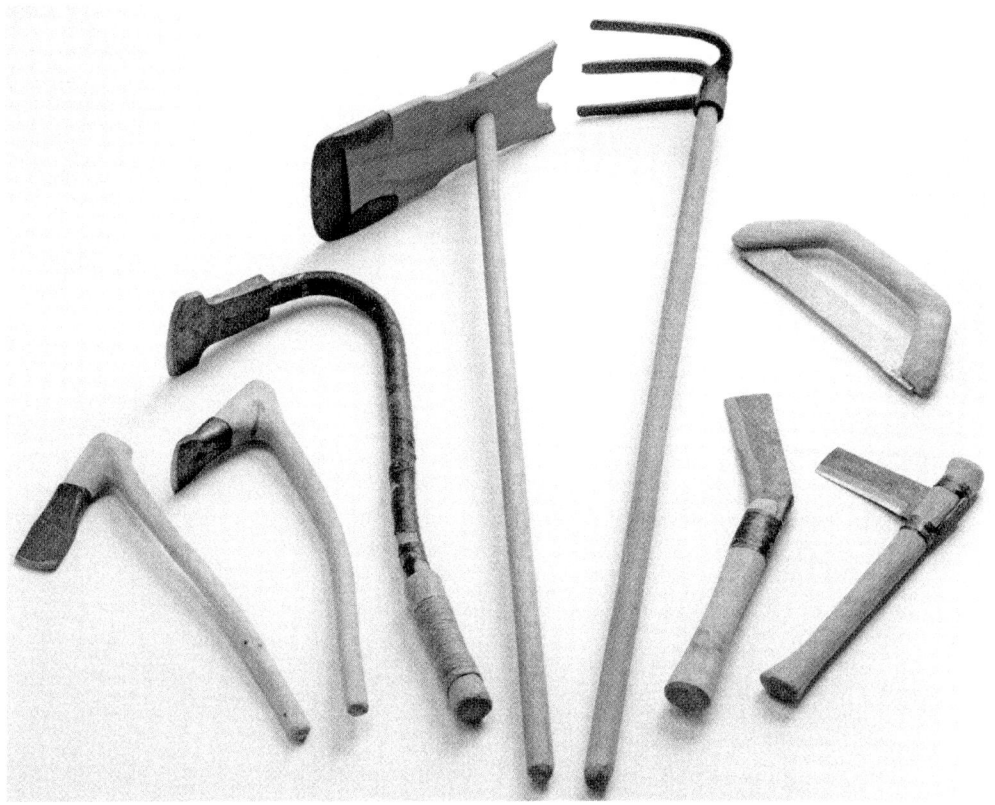

Figure 5.12. Replicas of Early Kofun Period iron tools used in cultivation. Originals from the Shikinzan Kofun. From left to right, axe, adzes, hoe blade, fork, reaping tools. From Ōsaka Furitsu Chikatsu Asuka Hakubutsukan 2013: 41. Courtesy of Ōsaka Furitsu Chikatsu Asuka Hakubutsukan.

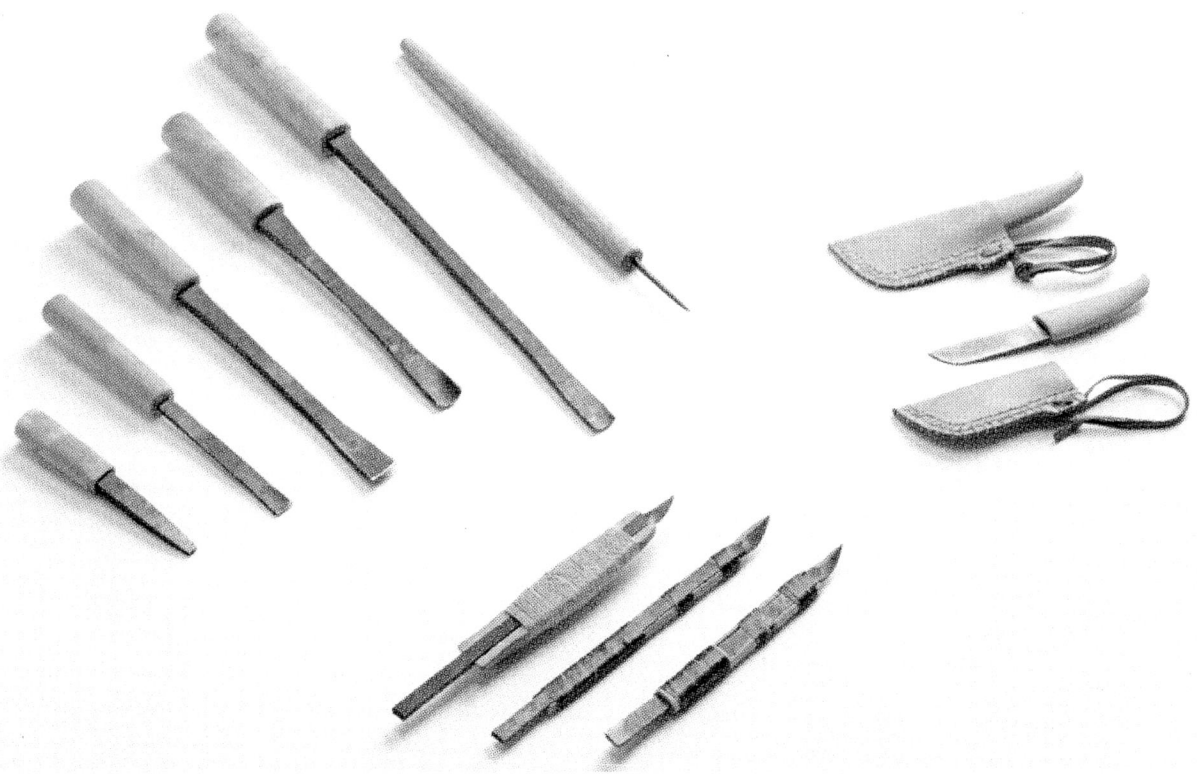

Figure 5.13. Replicas of Early Kofun Period iron tools for woodworking and carving. Originals from the Shikinzan Kofun. . From Ōsaka Furitsu Chikatsu Asuka Hakubutsukan 2013: 41. Courtesy of Ōsaka Furitsu Chikatsu Asuka Hakubutsukan.

that production was regulated by local elites. The site yielded abundant evidence of new artifacts, including Korean pottery. New methods of production were imported from Korea. Workshops on the site processed glass, jade, and wood. Abundant bellows valves confirm the production of metal objects. Remains of wooden scabbards and lacquered sword handles painted with a design reserved for persons of high status, the composite curvilinear *chokkomon*, were also found (Ōsaka Furitsu Sayama Hakubutsukan 2007: 12, Yamauchi 2008). The ritual area contained a group of pits filled with *haji* and *sueki* as well as beads in all stages of manufacture. These pits, about 2m² in area, were covered with paving stones. Nearby, a cemetery of 20 small mounds dating from the fifth to seventh centuries AD was found. In at least two mounds, grave goods of iron working tools and slag indicated the occupation of the deceased (Tenri Gareri 2013).

Armor Production

The Kawachi area was an important armor making center. Although there was no intensive iron smelting in Japan until the sixth century (Fujio 2000: 97) manufacture of Japanese armor by working imported iron began in the late fourth to fifth centuries and a particular style of Japanese armor was produced in the Kinai region in the fifth century using raw material which was imported from southeastern Korea as ingots (Barnes 2000: 62). The central Yamato powers probably controlled armor manufacture as well as the importing of iron from the Kaya region; they may also have imported specialists from Kaya (Barnes 2000: 69-89) (Box 5.7).

Ban (2009: 131) describes three general levels of iron production. Very large central workshops such as Ōgata, described above, were under the direct control of the paramount chiefs. There were smaller centers for weapons production managed by aristocratic immigrant lineages, as well as small scale village workshops for the production of agricultural tools.

Wada (2003) proposed that in the Middle Kofun Period the manufacture of prestige goods such as armor, iron tools, beads, *sueki*, and stone coffins, was dominated by the central authority of the Kinai region. In the Late Kofun Period the production of specialized artifacts was no longer monopolized by the center and local chiefs started manufacturing these artifacts, specializing in the production of one kind of product, to offer to the center as tribute. Such specialization made it difficult to reorganize production into a centralized "industrial complex" of the state until the late Asuka Period of the seventh century AD; the Asuka Ike Site, Nara, of the latter half of the seventh century AD yielded evidence of a broad range of techniques for the working of iron, copper, gold, mercury, agate, amber, and tortoise shell in one center (Wada 2003: 53). In addition to new metal technology, new agricultural knowledge and techniques came to Kawachi. As mentioned above iron agricultural tools were found in the Ariyama and Nonaka satellite mounds of the Konda Gobyōyama Kofun (Ōtsuka and Kobayashi 1984: 13, 245).

Settlements and Infrastructure

Residential Compounds

With the exception of the Hōenzaka Storehouses of the Naniwa area mentioned below, no remains of large

---

BOX 5.7
Cuirass

The fifth century has been termed 'the century of the cuirass', a vest made of assembled iron plates, attached to a rigid frame resembling a series of barrel hoops (Edwards 2013: 15). Differences in the style of cuirass have been used for dating. The shape of the individual plates of the cuirass changed from triangular to rectangular.

A set of armor (*kachū*) consisted of a helmet (*kabuto*) and cuirass (*tankō*) In early examples from the fourth and early fifth centuries the plates were attached with leather thongs but in the middle of the fifth century the iron plates were held together with rivets (Fujita 2006, 22). From the predominance of horizontal band cuirasses in Yamato compared to Kaya this style may have originated in Japan (Barnes 2000: 65) (Figures 5.14, 5.15).

The custom of burying cuirasses as grave offerings is of great interest. Composed of iron plate about 1.5cm² in area and 2 mm thick, a cuirass weighed about 30kg, ruling out the possibility that their wearer could actually engage in combat. Were they, along with horse gear, ritual objects for burial, indicating that the ruler was protected but did not actually fight (Nishikawa 2010: 43-44)? While there are about 20 cuirasses recorded for all of Japan in the Early Kofun Period, about 500 specimens have been recorded in the Furuichi and Mozu Tomb Groups in the Middle Kofun Period (Tanaka 2010: 83). Production sites for armor have not been found. Metal working in general leaves few traces compared to ceramic production because all waste metal can be recycled. The styles of the first half of the Kofun Period were produced in Korea. From the middle of the Early Kofun Period, it is thought that armor production in Japan was supervised by immigrants from the continent (*toraijin*) (Tanaka 2010).

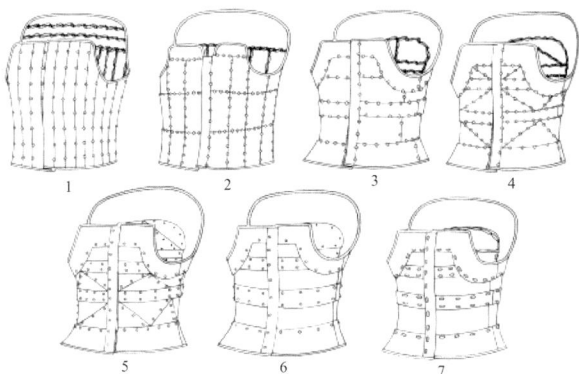

Figure 5.14. Iron cuirasses of the fourth and fifth centuries AD. (1, 2, 3,4, 7) Examples in which the iron plates are fastened with leather thongs. (1) Vertical oblong plates. (2) Rectangular plates. (3) Oblong plates. (4) Triangular plates. (7) Horizontal oblong plates. (5) Triangular riveted plates (6) Horizontal oblong riveted plates. From Kobayashi 1990: 143. Courtesy of Kōdansha Publishers.

buildings dating to the Kofun Period have been reported in the Ōsaka region. However, recent excavations of the Nangō Site Group in the southwestern corner of the Nara Basin near Gose City provide clues about what we might expect to find in the Ōsaka area in the future (Mizoguchi 2013: 293). The site group, dating primarily from the fifth century AD, is linked to the Katsuragi Clan, who migrated from the Korean Peninsula. Historical sources record them as providers of consorts for the rulers buried in the Furu and Mozu Tomb Group. The Katsuragi are thought to have been buried in the Umami Tomb Group in the Nara Basin. The Nangō Site Group is located on the slope of Mt. Katsuragi that adjoins the Kongō Mountain Range, separating southern Nara from southern Ōsaka. Dozens of sites are spread out on the slope (Ban and Aoyagi 2011, bunarinn.fc2 web.com 2014). From south to north, some of the most significant sites include two residential compounds of paramount chiefs, separate hamlets of commoners and headmen, a commoners' cemetery, remains of metal working, and an adjacent group of large elevated storehouses. Continuing to the south, there are remains of a berm for a small dam and wooden sluices. Over the main sluice was a structure which may have protected the conduit, but also served as a place for rituals related to water, judging from finds of wooden ritual artifacts. At the extreme north of the slope was the site of a large elevated building at the Gokurakuji Hibiki Site, fashioned from *hinoki* cypress. This is the largest wooden structure known for the Kofun Period, in all of Japan. The floor area is 284m² and the building was protected on two sides by a wooden fence. It is situated on a terrace overlooking the surrounding area. The area below the terrace was approached by an earth ramp. To the east is an open plaza, at the edge of which was a small elevated building. In the same compound there were five pit house buildings which had been renovated

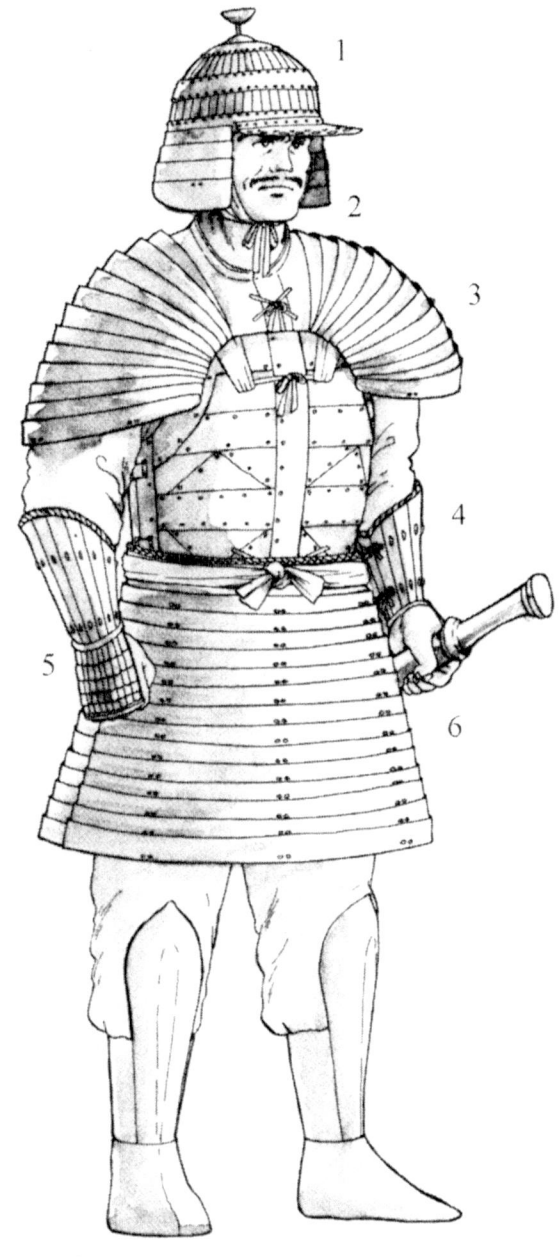

Figure 5.15. Reconstruction of suit of armor from the fifth century AD. (1) Peaked helmet with visor. (2) Neck guard. (3) Shoulder guard. (4) Fore arm protectors. (5) Knuckle protectors. (6) Metal plates of upper and lower parts are fastened with leather thongs. From Kobayashi 1990: 145. Courtesy of Kōdansha Publishers.

several times. They were used by groups in charge of the area and its rituals. The large building is thought to have been used for administration and ritual, rather than residence. Next to the large raised floor building on the southern edge of the site was a group of large pit houses which appear to have flues for heating part of the floor, similar to the *ondol* system of heating found in the Korean Peninsula. A small nearby cemetery contained secondary burials in jars placed mouth to mouth. These

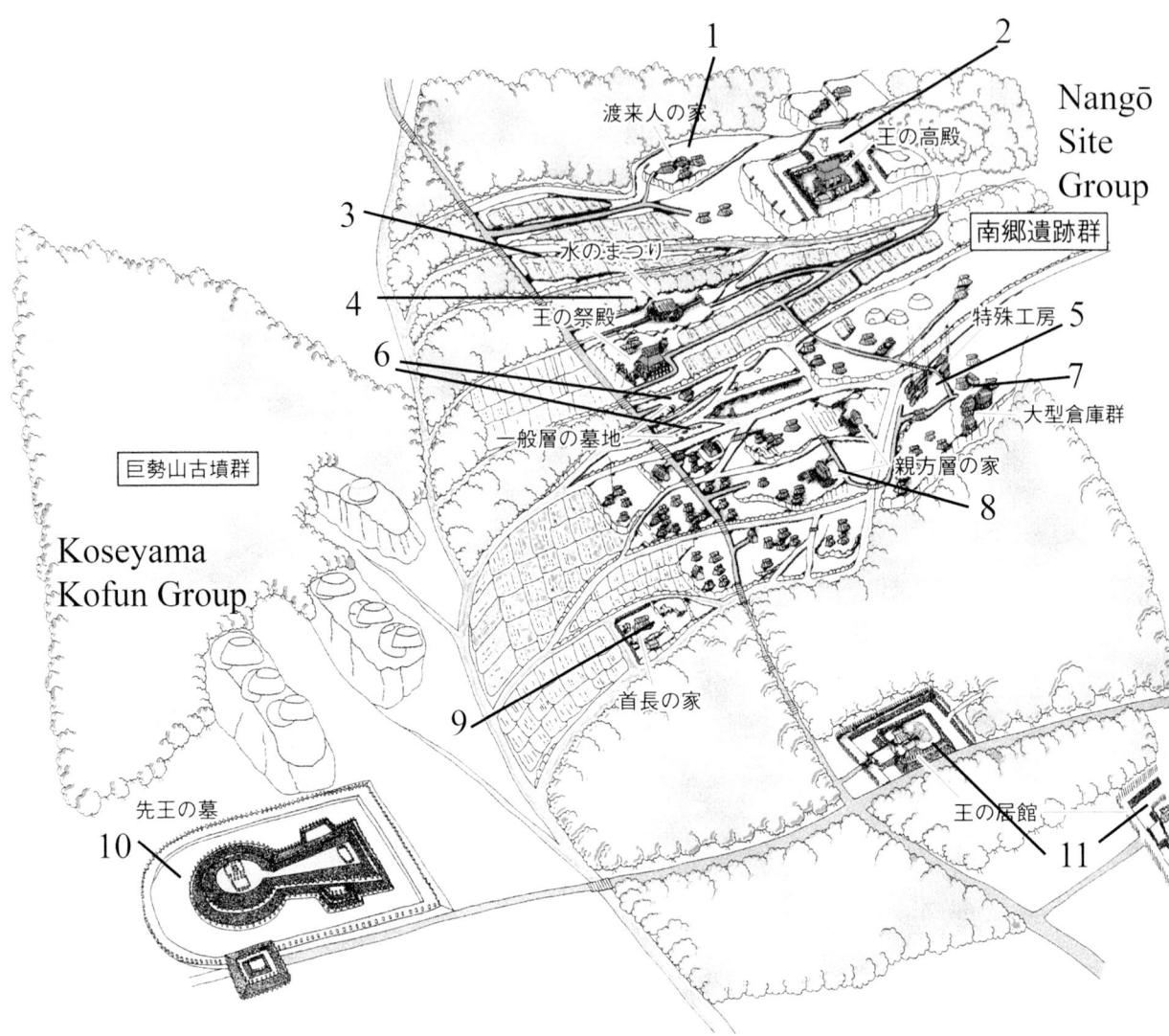

Figure 5.16. The Nangō Site Group. 1. Residences of immigrants. 2. Elevated 'palace' of paramount chief. 3. Area for water rituals. 4. Ritual structure for paramount chief. 5. Specialized workshop. 6. Commoners' cemetery. 7. Large storehouses. 8. Elite houses. 9. Chief's house. 10. Ancestors' burials. 11. Paramount chief's residence. Adapted from Ban 2009: 11. Courtesy of Shinsensha Publishers.

are similar to examples from Korea, and are different from the primary burials in large jars found in Kyūshū in the Yayoi Period. Across from these sites, on an adjacent flat, is a large keyhole tumulus (Figure 5.16).

One would expect that the residential sites of the Kawachi rulers will be found to have roughly the same combination of features: raised floor buildings, ritual, craft production and storage sites, and residences of immigrant specialists. Such residential compounds constituted displays of power in their large visible buildings, as well as evidence of increasing centralization of administration and the inclusion of foreign elites.

Storehouses

In Chapter 4, Yayoi Period storehouses for agricultural produce, located in large central villages were discussed. In the Kofun Period, much larger storehouses were constructed adjacent to shipping routes. They may have been used for weapons or other kinds of tributary goods.

Two fifth century storehouse groups, Hōenzaka and Narutaki, provide evidence for the redistribution of strategic goods and the economic strength of the Kinai rulers. Narutaki is near the Zenmyōji Temple in Wakayama City, on the southern shore of the lower reaches of the Ki River, on the route from the southern Nara Basin to the Inland Sea. It consists of remains of seven raised storehouses, their function confirmed by the presence of extra support pillars under the central parts of the building to bear weights heavier than those created by residences. The seven buildings were not identical; the five in the western group ranged in floor area from 56 to 62m^2, while those on the east were larger, the largest being 81.9m^2. In the area of these remains,

Figure 5.17. Fifth century AD storehouses at Hōenzaka, Naniwa, on the Uemachi Terrace. From Ōsaka Furitsu Chikatsu Asuka Hakubutsukan 2006: 63. Courtesy of the Ōsaka Fu Bunkazai Sentā and the Ōsaka Furitsu Chikatsu Asuka Hakubutsukan.

sherds of large buried *sueki* jars (*kame*) were dated to the first half of the fifth century. At Hōenzaka, on the northern tip of the Uemachi terrace adjacent to the site of Ōsaka Castle constructed in the sixteenth centeury, 16 raised storehouses in two east-west rows were excavated (Figure 5.17). Their floor area ranged from 82 to 98m², with a total area 1400m². Since the usual floor area of storehouses of the Kofun Period was about 30 m², these are very large. Their total area was three times the area of the Narutaki storehouse total (Sugiyama 2010: 161-181). They face the Akashi Strait, where the Sumiyoshi Shrine is located. Sumiyoshi deities are strongly related to the state; they were devoted to the protection of sea travellers, but they also became state military deities (Asao et al 1999: 10-17). The warehouses show the strength of the Kinai rulers. The fact that Korean ceramics have been found in this area indicates interaction with the Korean peninsula. Hanada (2002, 355) concluded that Korean ceramics found in the Hōenzaka Site indicated that Korean immigrants played a role in the administration of the port, bringing new kinds of technical knowledge from the continent. Occupying the same general area in succession, Hōenzaka, Naniwanomiya, Ishiyama Honganji, and Ōsaka Castle are all on a spit at the terminus of the Inland Sea and the complex delta of the Yodo and Yamato Rivers. They are key to understanding the pre eminence of Ōsaka. The latter three sites are described in Chapters 6 and 7.

Roads and Canals

Roads linked settlements, palaces, tombs, craft production areas, and ports from at least the fifth century AD. While reliable documents date only from the seventh century or later, specialists such as Kusaka and Morimura are confident that the infrastructure was established in the Kofun Period. It seems likely that there were a palace and administrative center in the Naniwa area during the Kofun Period, somewhere in the vicinity of the Hōenzaka storehouses described above.

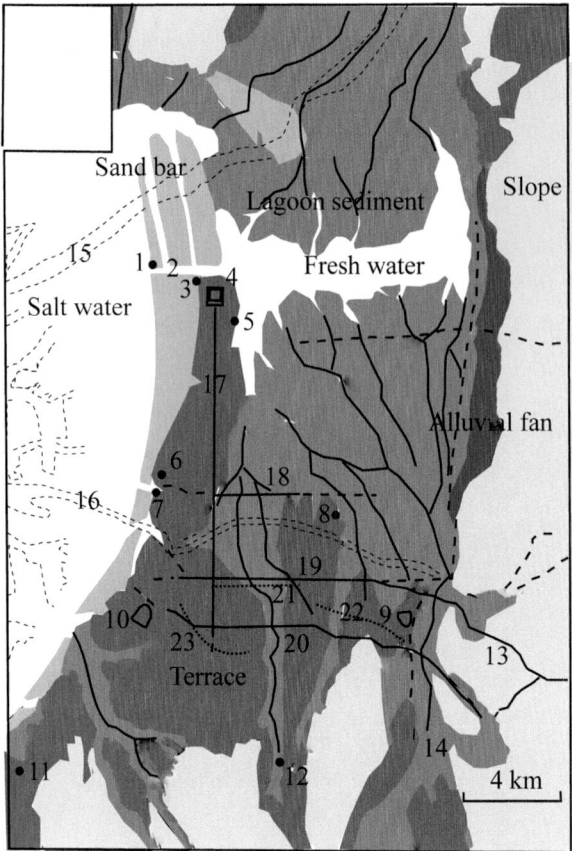

FIGURE 5.18. THE NORTHERN PART OF THE ŌSAKA REGION IN THE SIXTH AND SEVENTH CENTURIES AD. (BASED ON KUSAKA 2012 FRONTISPIECE). SITES: (1) EGUCHI. (2) NANIWA HORIE. (3) NANIWA PORT. (4) NANIWA PALACE. (5) TAMATSUKURI. (6) SUMIYOSHI SHRINE. (7) SUMIYOSHI PORT. (8) NAGAYOSHI KAWANABE. (9) FURUICHI TOMB GROUP. (10) MOZU TOMB GROUP. (11) IKEGAMI SONE. (12) SAYAMA RESERVOIR. RIVERS: (13) YAMATO RIVER. (14) ISHI RIVER. (15) PRESENT YODO RIVER COURSE. (16) PRESENT LOWER YAMATO RIVER COURSE. ROADS: (17) NANIWA GREAT ROAD. (18) SHIHATSU ROAD. (19) ŌTSU ROAD. (20) TAJIHI ROAD. DITCHES: (21) HARIUO. (22) FURUICHI. (23) NAGASONE DITCH. THE PRESENT SHORELINE OF ŌSAKA IS INDICATED BY DOTTED LINES. COURTESY OF KŌDANSHA PUBLISHERS.

Kusaka's seminal map, published as the frontispiece of his popular book in 2012 (Kusaka 2012), displays sites of the sixth and seventh centuries, but I would propose that the infrastructure of roads and ports was established in the Kofun Period (Figure 5.18). This map will serve as a transition to the Kodai Period, 600 to 1185 AD, discussed in Chapter 6.

Important roads connected the five tomb groups of the Nara Basin to Mozu and Furuichi and the ports on the shore of Ōsaka Bay (Morimura 2008a). Kusaka (2012: 242) noted that three ports, Ōtsu, Sumiyoshi, and Naniwa, are mentioned in historical sources dating to the late fifth century AD. While Ōtsu and Sumiyoshi ports were largely natural ports, Naniwa was planned and man-made. It is discussed briefly in Chapter 6.

The Ōtsu Road, also known as the Nagaō Road, links sites built in the fourth quarter of the fifth century such as the Tadeiyama Kofun, and the Ōtsukayama Kofun. Excavations in 1983 showed that the road bed was 1.7m wide and 0.3m deep.

Morimura (2006a) traced another route, the Ōtsu North Road, by examining Meiji Period maps, modern roads, and known sections of the jōri field system of the Kodai Period (Chapter 6). This may have been the route for hauling the *nagamochigata* stone coffins to the Tsudō Shiroyama Kofun in Fujiidera City from a port in the Kawachi Lagoon. Sections of an east west road, the Tajihi Road or Takenouchi Road, connected the Konda Gobyōyama Kofun and Daisen Ryō Kofun with the Nara Basin. This road, later known as the Takenouchi Road, connected the Naniwa Port to Asuka and was the route for delegations from continental Asia travelling to the capital. In fact, it was the last lap of the continental Silk Road. On the way to Nara it travelled through the Kawachi Region on the west side of the Ikoma Range, the "Chikatsu Asuka" (Near Asuka) region.

The most imposing of all was the Naniwa Great Road that extended along the crest of the Uemachi Daichi, connecting Shitennōji with the Naniwa Palace. The road had a width of 17m with 1m ditches on the side. Morimura (2006a) concluded that this road, and another extending from Naniwa to the Koganetsuka Kofun in Izumi City, were in use by the end of the fourth century AD. These various roads connected the great burial tumuli of the Kinai Region to the East Asian continent through ports in Sakai and Naniwa, fostering the movement of goods, information, and international exchange. The Nankai Road, from Naniwa to Wakayama and Mt Koya may also have been in existence by this time.

A channel cutting across the Uemachi Terrace, linking Ōsaka Bay to the Kawachi Lake, is said to have been dug in the reign of Nintoku in the fifth century AD. While the date of its initial construction is uncertain, there seems to be no doubt of its importance by the sixth and seventh centuries AD. It cut through three parallel sand bars, separated by narrow lagoons, immediately to the north of the northern tip of the Uemachi Terrace (Figure 5.18). The total length of the artificial canal is 3km. Canals were also used for transportation in the lowlying areas of the Ōsaka region. One can imagine how important water transport would have been for various huge projects. The Nagasone Ditch appears to have been a major waterway. Some 500m of the length of the ditch were excavated (Sakai Shi Kyōiku Iinkai 1999). From the occurrence of fifth century *sueki* sherds in the bottom of the ditch, which was 4m wide and 1m deep, Morimura (2006a) dated it to the late fifth century AD.

Discussion

Key projects of the Kofun Period were the building of burial monuments, sponsorship of new technologies and engineering techniques, importing of iron, manufacture and distribution of weapons, armor, and tools, construction of elite residential compounds, expansion of storage and distribution facilities, and construction of roads and canals.

Mizoguchi (2013, 328) proposed that the Kinai region (he terms it the Kinki core region) was dominant because of its central position in a set of nodes. I propose that topological position, plus cultural, historical, and physical environment contributed to its pre eminence.

Buried weapons and armor are important in archaeological interpretations of the period. Kawachi rulers controlled the distribution of iron and weapons whereas earlier rulers of the Nara Basin controlled the distribution of ritual artifacts such as mirrors, soapstone miniatures, and bronze tubular artifacts. Finds of iron artifacts in small and medium size burial mounds indicate that they were bestowed on local chiefs to create a military power system. But what can we actually know of military organization and warfare from grave goods? Was there a military class or a standing army? Did military officials evolve from outstanding local chiefs or from immigrant groups? Or were the military weapons and armor part of a system of ritual display? A typological comparison of iron weapons buried with and without accompanying inhumations showed that the latter included miniature swords and complex shaped arrowheads thought to be for ritual use, which were different from the types accompanying inhumations. This difference lends support to the interpretation that the *baichō* were votive mounds, and were not evidence of the existence of a standing army as interpreted by Tanaka Shinsaku (2010, Tanaka and Nishikawa 2010, Toyoshima 2000). Did large immigrant clans such as the Mononobe, play substantial military roles (Nishikawa 2010, 18)? Were farmers conscripted and armed? Up to the Middle Yayoi Period raiding was carried out with the aid of bows and arrows and rare short double edged short swords. Although bronze weapons increased and diversified in the Late Yayoi Period it was only in the Kofun Period that iron weapons increased substantially.

While many districts in the Kinai region and other parts of the Japanese islands were settled by migrants at this time, the Ōsaka region was particularly transformed. The formation of service groups (*be*) by foreigners was not simply a matter of craft specialization; continental knowledge and religious observances were also imported (Barnes 1987). For instance the Mononobe were not only skilled artisans but were also introducers of religious observances from the Chinese festival calendar, such as the use of *hitogata* human effigy figures for exorcising impurities. Such rituals were carried out for the ruler, the metal effigies being thrown into the sea at Naniwa (Como 2009: 117).

Why did military power become so critical in the Middle Kofun Period? Political instability on the Chinese mainland in the fourth to seventh centuries must be an important factor. New World archaeologists have observed the transition from "Classic" to "Post Classic" civilizations in Mexico and Peru, in which groups expressing strong religious connections through iconography were transformed by rapidly spreading military groups (Willey and Phillips 1958). The rise of military rulers seems to be an important step in the evolution of social complexity. Such a change seems to have occurred in the change in burial assemblages and ideology from the Early Kofun to Middle Kofun Periods. In the transition from Saki in the Nara Basin to Kawachi on the Ōsaka Plain, political fission among rival groups in Saki, as well as the pull of international contacts through Ōsaka ports and the development of agricultural land around Lake Kawachi and on nearby terraces must have been factors.

From the center of power in the Kinai Region, irrigation technology and all kinds of engineering skills were diffused to areas such as Gunma Prefecture in eastern Japan in the Early and Middle Kofun Periods. Large and medium size keyhole tombs conforming to the Kinai norms of construction indicate that this area was tied to the system of power of the Wa paramounts, and exotic pottery types show the presence of continental immigrants (Wakasa 2007: 285).

Why was so much energy devoted to tomb construction? Expanding social networks funneled labor and resources into the Ōsaka area. To confirm and maintain their superior position, Kofun Period rulers were involved in intense social competition with other regional paramount chiefs. Despite the huge size of the burial mounds most archaeologists propose that they were built by voluntary labor. There appear to be no traces of construction camps or village around them, except for traces of workshops for producing ritual paraphernalia, such as *haniwa*. Mizoguchi proposes that the construction of the tombs celebrated "communal well being" (Mizoguchi 2013: 280-305). With the shift from kin to class organization in the Late Kofun Period, domination and subordination became the chief organizing principles.

Archaeology of the Kofun Period in the Ōsaka region is unusual, since the capital and royal residences are undiscovered and the largest burial sites are unexcavated. While these sites will some day provide a more complete picture, it is important that they are preserved for future generations, after recent enormous excavations have been adequately compiled and interpreted.

What events or social processes brought about the end of the burial system of the Middle Kofun Period? What kind of system replaced it? For about five decades, from AD 550 to 600, a small group near the present city of Takaida, buried their dead in artificial caves, as mentioned above. Why was this type of burial, common in other parts of Japan, used by one particular group in Ōsaka? These are questions for which I have been unable to find answers in current Japanese literature. I hope that future investigation of social processes in the Kofun Period will lead to interesting interpretations.

Enormous political and cultural changes in the seventh century, including the fall of the Paekche Kingdom of southwestern Korea and the unification of the peninsula under Silla Kingdom of southeastern Korea as well as the unification of China under the Sui and Tang Dynasties brought new forms of social and artistic expression to the Ōsaka area.

The greatness of the Kofun Period in the Ōsaka region can be seen in monumental burial and production sites. In the subsequent period major discoveries are the finds of the capital of Naniwa and its surroundings, discussed in Chapter 6. Old elites adapted to a very different world.

Chapter 6
The Naniwa Port as a Regional Center; The Kodai (600 to 1185 AD) Period

During this long period huge changes took place in Japan, particularly in the Nara Basin. These include the consolidation of state organization, introduction of Buddhism as well as the establishment of capitals in the Ōsaka region, Nara and Kyōto. The Naniwa area of Ōsaka, at the outflow from Kawachi Lake, was already developed in the Kofun Period with the construction of early palaces (not yet discovered) and storehouses. It continued to thrive as a port and commercial area in the Kodai Period. The capital of the Yamato State was moved to a new location in the Kansai region every few decades. It was located in Ōsaka at Naniwanomiya on two occasions in the seventh and eighth centuries. The construction of the buildings, as well as the reorganization of administrative and logistical networks created opportunity for local development. Buddhism was adopted as a state religion in the sixth century. Following cultural and economic networks linked to the continent, specialists brought new technology as well as iconography. Elites from Korea, such as the Paekche royal clan, settled in Ōsaka and contributed to economic and cultural development, even being involved in official activities such as the minting of coins.

Although the Ōsaka area ultimately lost its preeminent position in favor of inland areas, it was the site of an important capital at Naniwanomiya for several decades and its ports continued to provide key access for the flow of goods and ideas to the capitals. While it was not until the end of the Chūsei (Mediaeval) Period, discussed in Chapter 7, that Ōsaka regained its primary position, its role in the Kodai Period was far from negligible. Specific site groups dealt with in this chapter are the Naniwa Palace, Shitennōji Temple, the Sayama Reservoir, and the Buddhist sites of Dotō and Sefukuji Sutra Mounds.

The exploration of the earliest archaeologically confirmed capital site in Japan, the Naniwanoiya or Naniwa Palace, situated on the northern tip of the Uemachi Terrace was a huge contribution to Japanese archaeology. How did the palace relate to the growing town that surrounded it? What was the role of immigrant groups, including powerful aristocrats from the Korean Peninsula? Although its immediate antecedents are unknown, the fact that it was built on the Uemachi Terrace confirms the central significance of this area, which later became the site of Ōsaka Castle and the center of modern Ōsaka. This area, the northern portion of the Uemachi Terrace, in the vicinity of Ōsaka Castle, was referred to as Naniwa in ancient times. In addition to the Naniwanomiya, the nearby Sumiyoshi Shrine and Shitennōji (Temple) are briefly discussed. The expansion of roads and the improvement of agriculture on alluvial terraces were also important projects of this period. Opening of upland areas and improvement of irrigation systems benefitted the growing centers of Ōsaka and Sakai. The Sayama Reservoir is not only an early example of Japanese hydraulic engineering but also the site of an innovative excavation and museum. The finding of a group of significant sutra mounds contributes to our knowledge of this practice and underlines the growing importance of trade with China at the end of the Kodai Period.

There are many opinions on the dating of the Kodai Period. The beginning could be pushed back to as early as 538 AD, the traditional date of the introduction of Buddhism; however archaeologically much of the sixth century is better considered as the Late Kofun Period. I extend the period to the beginning of the seventh century AD, when the Japanese islands were dominated by an imperial system with regulated control of religion and economy.

Naniwa in the Sixth and Early Seventh Centuries AD.

The northern tip of the Uemachi Terrace was a center of administration and commerce in the Asuka Period and the early part of the Kodai Period. Its strategic location adjacent to the delta of the Ō and Yamato River systems with access to overland routes into the Kinai region was important. In ancient times, the Yodo River was referred to as the Ō River (Ōkawa).

It should be noted that the Naniwa area of Ōsaka was an important administrative center from the fifth century, long before the establishment of the Naniwa Palace (Naniwanomiya), as indicated by the Hōenzaka storehouses and associated administrative buildings (Kihara 2000, 2007). In the layers under the Naniwa Palace there are remains of small villages and a local administrative center, possibly associated with immigrants. Korean ceramics have been found (Naoki and Nakao 2003: 134, Eura 2007, Nakao 2007). In the sixth and early seventh centuries it was still important as a storage area and port. Archaeological evidence spans the transition between the Kofun and Asuka Periods, and sets the stage for the important role of the area as the primary political center of Yamato in the late seventh century (Miyamoto 2010, Ueki 2009: 22).

Dating from the first half of the sixth century to the first half of the seventh century, remains of 69 elevated buildings have been found. There were dwellings and storehouses, the latter having more support posts under the raised floor than the former. The building remains can be divided into three time periods, (1) first half of the sixth century, (2) end of the sixth century and early seventh century, and (3) first half of the seventh century AD. In Period 1 there was a transition from pit house to elevated buildings; the size of the village was small and there were relatively few houses. In Period 2 the number of buildings increased and some large buildings were erected. In Period 3 some buildings were as large as 45m² and the number of buildings increased. A particular kind of earthenware, distinguished by wiping and finishing with fingers called Naniwa Type, is found in Periods 1 and 2. In Period 3 this ware was replaced by a kind of fine earthenware *hajiki* from south Kawachi. This ware, also found in Minami Kawachi and Asuka, was produced for official use by administrative offices (*kangai shisetsu*) in the region (Ueki 2009: 21-23). Also a particular kind of clay net weight for small fishnets was found, indicating the importance of the adjacent fresh water Lake Kawachi. Sumiyoshi port had important state related functions. From Sumiyoshi port the direct overland route to Asuka was shorter than from other ports. In close proximity was the Sumiyoshi Shrine, a very important site for Japanese history and culture. Since it is not possible to excavate in close proximity to such an important Shinto Shrine, little is known about its archaeology. It enshrines the legendary empress Jingū and her son, Emperor Ōjin, said to have been buried in the Konda Gobyōyama Kofun in the Mozu Tomb Group. Sumiyoshi port is as old as Naniwa, being important from the late fifth century. The Hōenzaka storehouses described in Chapter 5 served the port.

The nearby Shitennōji (Temple) is also of enormous importance. It was first excavated in the 1950's after its most recent destruction in World War 2. It was built in 588 AD under the direction of architects from Paekche, Korea. It follows a strict axial plan, used on the Asian continent, in which there is a single pagoda in front of the Buddha Hall (Figure 6.1). This strict symmetry was abandoned in favor of an indigenous temple plan followed in subsequent temples in Nara such as the Hōryuji (Paine and Soper 1981: 291-293). On the north side of Shitennōji was an important market area. In the area surrounding Shitennōji many finds of roof tiles from the Asuka and Heian Periods have been made. They have also been found in the lowest layers of the Naniwa Palace and Ōsaka Castle Sites. In many cases the roof tiles are of the same type, made from the same mold, indicating close interrelationships among the temples along the main road from the Naniwa Palace Site to the Shitennōji and further to the south, to the general area of the Sumiyoshi Shrine, a distance of some 10 km. These include tiles from the Hōryuji in Nara. Abundant ceramics and lacquer objects from the Nara

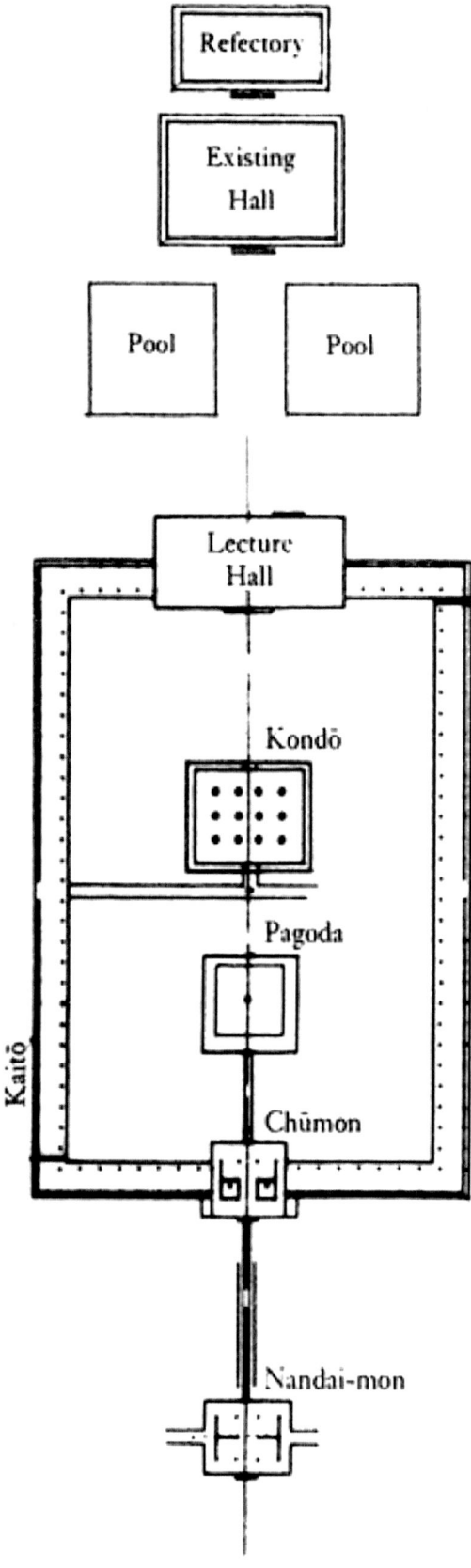

FIGURE 6.1. PLAN OF THE SHITENNŌJI, BUILT IN AD 588.

to Edo Periods have also been discovered (Zaidan Hojin Ōsaka 1996).

In addition to the Naniwa Palace, official temples, houses of officials, and aristocrats were concentrated near the man made outlet of the Naniwa Horie in the seventh and eighth centuries AD. There were residences and storehouses of the Mononobe and Soga clans, estates belonging to the Tōdaiji and Hōryuji, and facilities for trading with the Korean Peninsula. Seagoing ships carrying cargoes weighing up to 20 to 30 *koku* (roughly 3600 to 5400kg) docked in the area of the Naniwa Horie, where their cargo was transferred to flat bottom river boats, about 9m long. Both private and state trade went through the Naniwa Horie (Nakao 2010: 9-15). Diplomatic missions to China from the fifth century to the eighth century (*Kentōshi*) departed from the Naniwa Horie. These tribute ships carried 150 people and travelled in convoys of two to four or more ships.

The exact location of the port is debated. While historical texts hint that it was immediately north of the Naniwanomiya, analysis of sediments by boring indicates that this section of the Ō (Yodo) River was unsuitable for a port and that a location to the east, inside Kawachi Lake, near the present location of the modern bridge, Kōraibashi, is more likely (Naoki and Nakao 2003: 48-53). Sediment samples from boring in the area of historic Kawachi Lake in modern West Ōsaka showed that in the seventh and eighth centuries AD the lake, which extended from the Uemachi Terrace to the foot of the Ikoma Mountain Range was 4 to 5m deep in the west and 6 to 7m deep in the east (Kihara 2007).

In 660 AD, with the defeat of Paekche by Silla, the Paekche royal clan migrated to the Naniwa area. They resided in the western part of the Uemachi Terrace, to the south of the Naniwa Palace (Sekiyama 2010a). Migrants from Silla also resided in the Ōsaka area. In addition to many types of Korean ceramics, a particular type of building with a continental type of wall construction is found in the Kinai Region (referred to in Chapter 5).

Excavation of the Saikudani site, near the Kudara Amadera (Convent), produced important information on this period (Kyōshima 2007b, Ōsaka Fu Bunkazai Kenkyūsho 2014a) (Figure 6.2). It contained a workshop site operated by members of the Paekche Clan. Most significant were remains of metal casting, including the production of official (Japanese) coins. A branch mold for casting *Wadō Kaichin* (AD 708), and 18 intact coins of this type were found, as well as thin copper plate, granules and chunks. Slag was also recorded. There is no textual evidence of the production of coinage in the Naniwa area (Sekiyama 2010a: 138). Also found was a *mokkan* (ink inscribed wooden slip) that appears to be an official pass to the Amadera Convent. In a separate pit a rare example of a *Fuhonsen* coin, thought to have been used on ritual occasions (trussell.com 2015), was found. Strong evidence of the participation in metal casting of immigrants from Silla is also abundant. At the Oi Site, Mihara Chō, Sakai, a metal casting site dating to the eighth century AD yielded fine Silla ceramics (Ōsaka Furitsu Yayoi Bunka Hakubutsukan 2008: 13). This casting activity set the stage for later specialization in the Mihara Chō area in the Chūsei Period, discussed in Chapter 7. Another clan temple site, of the Tanabe Clan, was found near the Tanabe Kita subway station. Roof tiles with lotus decoration dated to the eighth century were recovered (Odagi 2007a).

The Naniwa Palace (Naniwanomiya)

The Early Naniwanomiya (Early Naniwa Palace), completed in 652 AD, (Figure 6.3) was used by the emperors Kōtoku and Tenmu, burned in 686 AD, the year of Tenmu's death, and rebuilt from 726 to 732 AD at the time of Emperor Shōmu. The latter is known as the Late Naniwa Palace (Figure 6.4). In 784 AD the capital was moved to Nagaoka. The stratigraphy is complex and there is some debate concerning the interpretation of the layers (Naoki and Nakao 2003: 157-159). This palace was particularly large for its time (Naoki and Nakao 2003: 142). Details of the excavations are provided in Appendix A.16. The site contained space for the ruler's residence, ceremonies, audience halls, administrative offices storehouses, gardens, and workshops.

Why did the Naniwa Palace lose its central position, following the shift of the political center to Nagaoka and subsequently Kyōto? Silting of the adjacent port may have been a factor. From the 760s, Silla and Bohai delegations came to ports on the Japan Sea, not to Naniwa (Ōsaka Shi Bunkazai Kyōkai 2008: 132). The decision to establish the capital in the Kyōto region in 794 AD may have been influenced by the Hata Clan, Chinese foreign immigrants whose power base was in the area of Kyōto and Lake Biwa (Como 2009). Nevertheless Naniwa's importance continued in the eighth and ninth centuries, despite the move of the palace. Since the custom of designating multiple capitals was adopted in Japan in the eighth century, the Fujiwara Capital overlapped with the Early Naniwa Capital for a brief period and the Late Naniwa Capital overlapped with the Nagaoka Capital.

Immediately to the north of the Naniwa Palace a channel, the Naniwa Horie, excavated in the late eighth century, ran to the mouths of the Yodo and Yamato Rivers. Remains of the posts of elevated buildings from the eighth and ninth centuries were found in the area near the Horie, where there was a zone of temples and manors of temples strategically placed to control maritime trade at the transfer point between Inland Sea ships and river boats. The port contained facilities devoted to importing goods for state institutions in Nara, which relied heavily on trade for their support. Large temples in the Nara

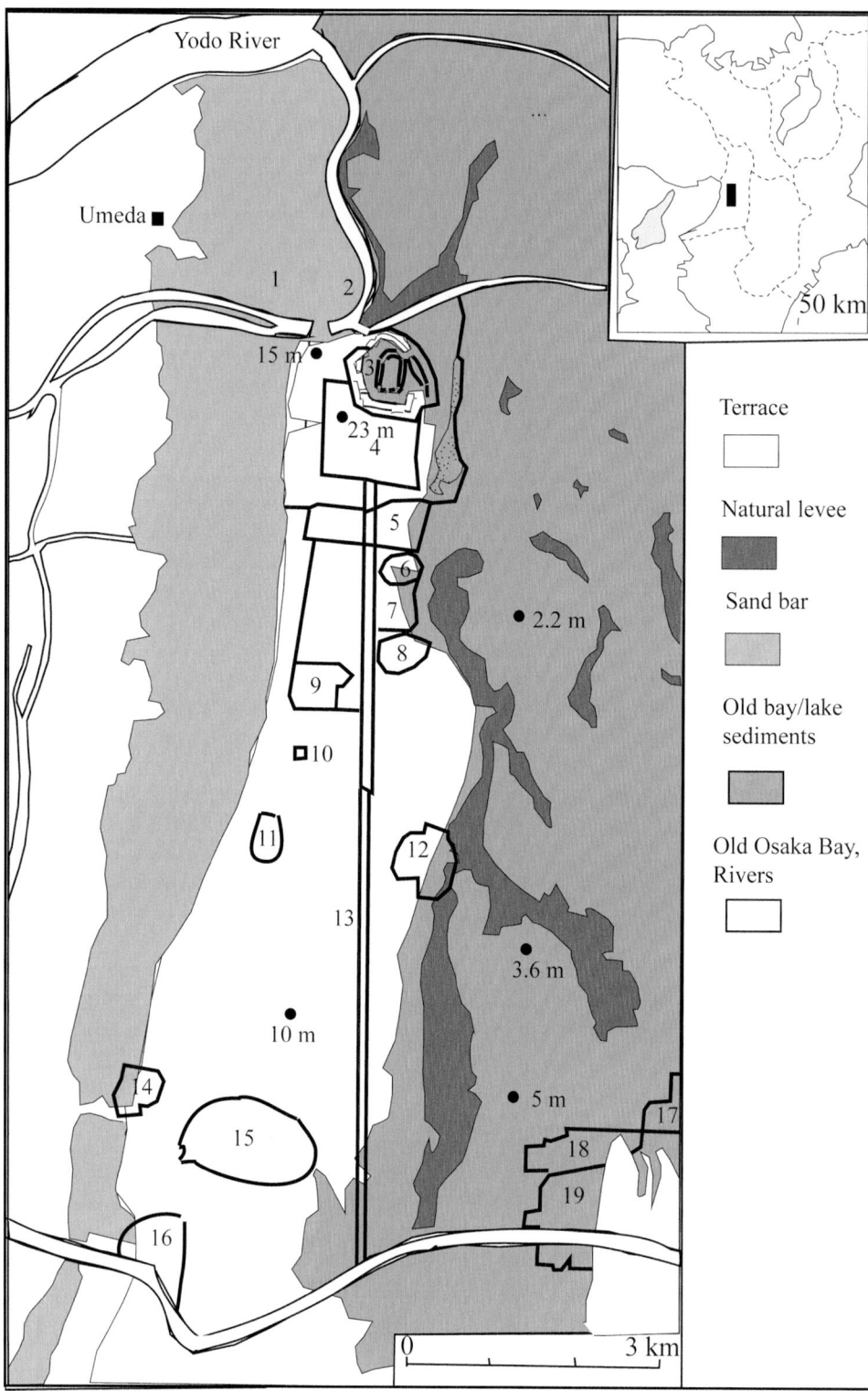

FIGURE 6.2. SITES IN THE UEMACHI TERRACE REGION, IN THE KODAI PERIOD. BASED ON ICHIKAWA ET AL 2011, 13. (1) TENJINBASHI. (2) SHŌEN (CHŪSEI PERIOD TENMA HONGANJI SITE). (3) ŌSAKA CASTLE (4) HŌENZAKA AND NANIWA. (5) SAISHŌYAMA. (6) KUDARA AMADERA. (7) SAIKUDANI SITE. (8) KUDARADERA (9) TENNŌJI OLD SITE. (10) TENNŌJI. (11) ABENOSUJI. (12) KUWAZU. (13) NANIWA GREAT ROAD. (14) OLD SUMIYOSHI PRECINCT. (15) SOUTH SUMIYOSHI SITE. (16) ORI ONO. (17) KIRE HIGASHI (18) URIWARI KITA (19) URIWARI. COURTESY OF THE ŌSAKA SHI HAKUBUTSUKAN KYŌKAI, ŌSAKA SHI BUNKAZAI KENKYŪSHO.

Basin such as the Tōdaiji, Dai'anji. Hōryuji, and Shin Yakushiji are mentioned in documents concerning the area (Ōsaka Shi Bunkazai Kyōkai 2008: 144). To the north of the Horie was an estate (*shōen*), Shiragi e Shō, controlled by Hōryuji. In the seventh and eighth centuries in the vicinity of the Naniwa Horie there were official and aristocrats' manors and temples. Ocean going ships with crews of about 50 people could be pulled up on the beaches of bay-like areas, protected by rock-faced berms (Ōsaka Shi Bunkazai Kyōkai 2008: 142, 143). At the same time, contributions of rice and fish from local farmers and fishermen were important for the large estates of Nara and Kyōto (Kawane 2002: 138).

At the entrance to the Kanzaki River goods arriving by sea were transferred to river boats. In the twelfth century

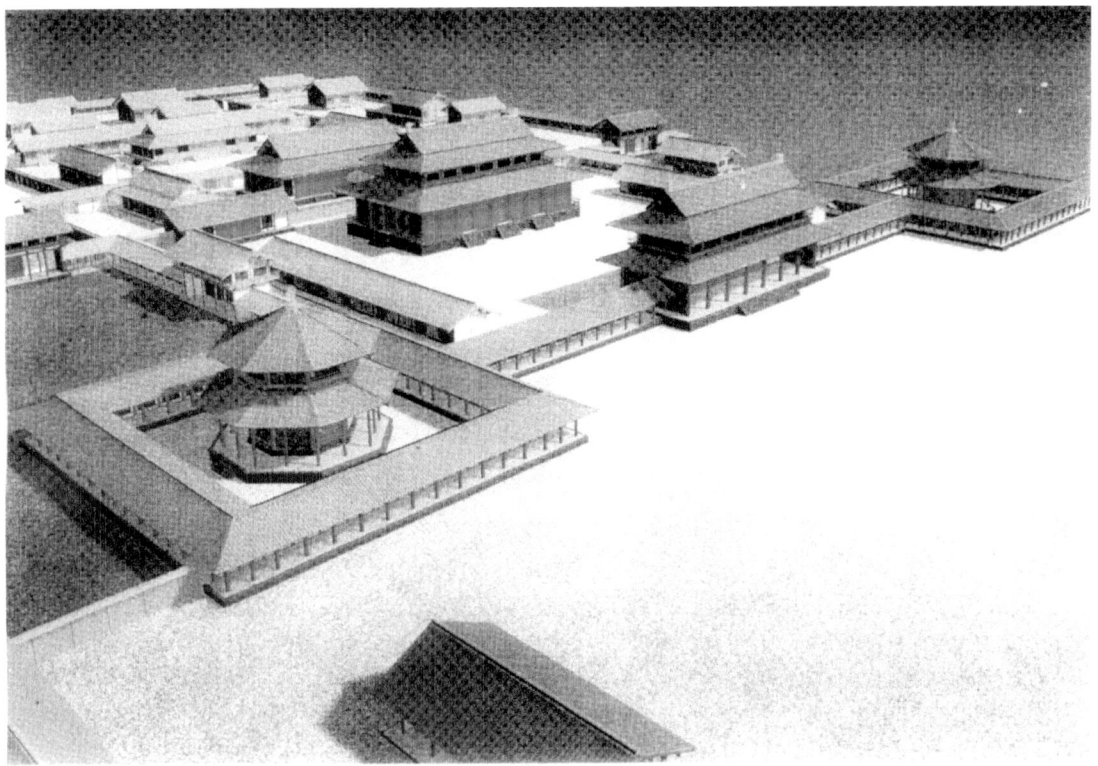

FIGURE 6.3. RECONSTRUCTION OF THE NANIWANOMIYA, EARLY PERIOD (AD 652 TO 686). FROM UEKI 2009: 2. COURTESY OF DŌSEISHA PUBLISHERS.

FIGURE 6.4. RECONSTRUCTION OF THE NANIWANOMIYA, LATE PERIOD (AD 726 TO 732). FROM UEKI 2009: 2. COURTESY OF DŌSEISHA PUBLISHERS.

AD Watanabe Tsu became the main port, not only for commercial activity but also for religious pilgrimages from Kyōto to the sacred mountains of Koya and Kumano in modern Wakayama Prefecture (Kawane 2002: 11, 138).

Naniwa was also linked to the Nara Basin by a series of roads traversing the Ōsaka Plain. The main route Naniwa Great Road (Naniwa Daidō) proceeded directly south from Naniwa to a point east of Shitennōji, and across the plain to the confluence of the Yamato and Ishi Rivers, where a bridge estimated to be 300 to 350m long was built between 730 and 740 AD (Kashiwara Shiritsu Rekishi Shiryōkan 2013). Artifacts left by immigrants from the continent are abundant in this area. Six substantial Buddhist temples were built in the eighth century. Roof tiles for their eaves, typical of the period, bear exquisite molded eight petal lotus flower motifs (Ōsaka Fu Chikatsu Asuka Hakubutsukan 2013b: 148-153). On the south bank of the Yamato River, a section of the Naniwa Daido was recently excavated. Dated by associated ceramics to the mid seventh century, the road was 18m wide and had flanking ditches (Shibata 2011).

Agricultural development, ditches and ponds

As mentioned in Chapter 4, Yayoi farmers diverted natural streams and constructed water courses. In the Asuka and Kodai Periods, expansion of upland agriculture was accomplished with the construction of irrigation ditches such as the Furuichi and Nagasone Ditches. The Furuichi Ditch was previously thought to have been constructed in the fifth century but the fact that it cut the edges of fifth century tumuli, and the absence of any *sueki* types earlier than TK 217, led Hirose to conclude that it was constructed some time between the very early seventh and eighth centuries AD. Since the ditch extends for more than 10km, with an average width of 3.5 to 5m and a depth of 2m, it would have required considerable engineering skill to ensure the flow of water. It branched off from the Old East Yoke River to join the Ishi River, a branch of the Yamato River, and it was probably connected to small holding ponds (Hirose 1983: 55). Seasonal corvee laborers used iron edged tools to excavate the ditch.

In the Izumi area, an excavation of 17,000m^2 at the Ikedadera Site, dating from the beginning of the seventh century to the first half of the tenth century yielded 76 house remains, as well as evidence of ditches and reservoirs (Hirose 1984: 57). These are simply examples of countless excavations of sites of this period.

The Sayama Reservoir

The western slopes of Kawachi, removed from Ishi and Yamato Rivers flowing on the eastern side, suffered from lack of water for cultivation. In the early Asuka Period (first half of seventh century), the Amano River and Imakuma Rivers were dammed to create Sayama Pond, from which the water flowed by gravity to a huge area of lower slopes. In the stratigraphy of the berm there were 12 layers. Tree ring dating of timber from Layer 12, the bottom layer of construction, gave a date of 616 AD (Ichikawa 2009: 38). The berm was strengthened through the inclusion of a dense layer of branches, as well as sand bags, using continental construction techniques. At present the surface area of the pond is 17.9km^2. The construction post dates the Kawachi rulers of the Middle Kofun Period. However in the Ikejiri area adjacent to the pond there are the remains of Kofun Period dry fields, leading archaeologists to ponder whether there was an earlier pond in the area.

In 762 AD, a major renovation and expansion created Layer 10 of the berm. Historical sources state that 83,000 persons were employed at that time (Ichikawa 2009: 62), suggesting that rotating groups of corvee labor completed the project. In the renovation of 1202 AD, undertaken by the famous priest Chōgen, who supervised the repairs to the Tōdaiji of the same period (Rosenfield 2010), the main massive wooden sluice was equipped with side channels composed of two tiers of recycled stone coffins of the Kofun Period, perforated to permit the flow of water. A large block of Izumi sandstone, inscribed with 300 characters, commemorates Chōgen's project. It probably postdates his work by several centuries (Figure 6.5).

Substantial waterways or canals completed in the Kofun Period were also used in later periods (Morimura 2008a). The Furuichi Canal is 8.5 to 9.5m wide, 4 to 5m deep, and 10km long. Since it runs among the great tumuli of Furuichi, rather than under them, it is thought to postdate their construction and to have been built in the late fifth century AD. It remained in use until the eighth century AD. The Tajihi Canal, in the vicinity of the Tajihi Road, was also used for the same time period. A third canal, in Sakai City, the Nagasone Canal dating to the seventh century AD, was traced by excavation for about 500m (Sakai Shi Kyōiku Iinkai 1999). These waterways must have been used to transport heavy building materials and also had ceremonial use.

Local Buddhist Sites

Earlier in this chapter the Shitennōji was described. The study of Buddhist sites is an enormous field, which can only be touched upon here, In addition to many temples, other types of monuments have been discovered. An unusual type of site is the sutra mound.

Sutra mounds are important Buddhist sites of the Kodai and Chūsei Periods. An earth mound, sometimes covered with protective stones, protected a burial in a stone lined pit, in which a copy of a sutra, usually the Lotus Sutra,

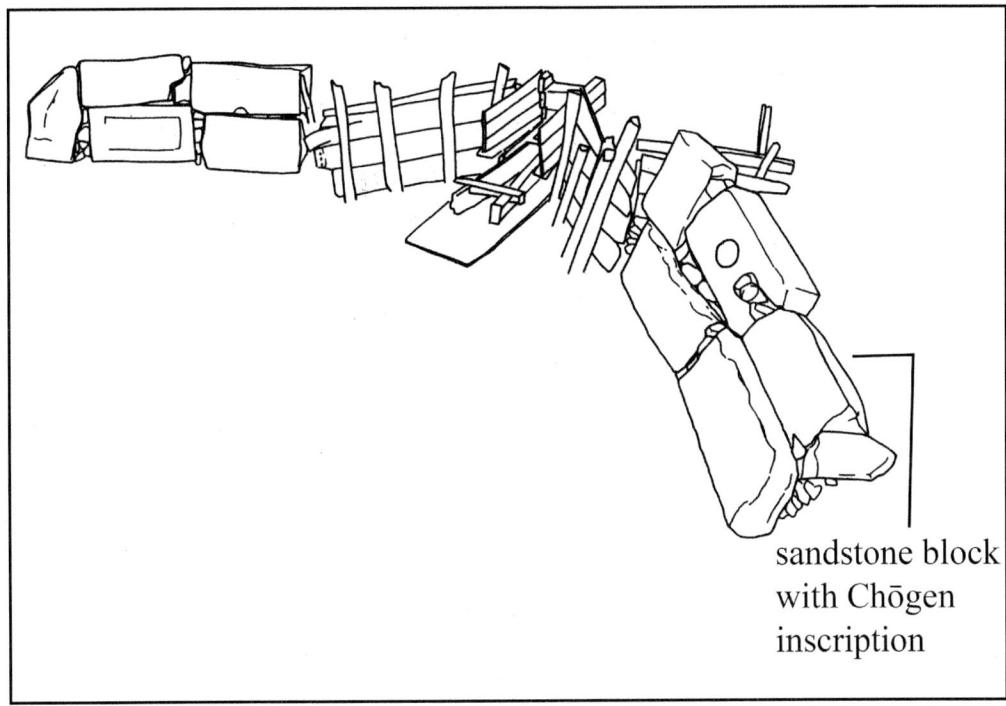

FIGURE 6.5. THE SLUICE OF THE SAYAMA DAM. ON BOTH SIDES OF THE WOODEN SLUICE ARE TWO ROWS OF RECYCLED KOFUN PERIOD STONE COFFINS, AS WELL AS A BLOCK OF IZUMI SANDSTONE, WITH AN INSCRIPTION COMMEMORATING PRIEST CHŌGEN. FROM ICHIKAWA 2009: 106. COURTESY OF ICHIKAWA HIDEYUKI.

was buried within a protective container, and associated with offerings. In the latter part of the Heian Period, Japanese believed that Mappō, the degenerate third stage of Buddhism, said to begin 2000 years after the Buddha's death and last for 10,000 years, was imminent, and buried copies of sutras to preserve them for future generations. This custom continued into the Chūsei Period.

A group of seven Sutra Mounds was excavated in a salvage operation in 1962 at the Sefukuji in the Izumi area, at the foot of the Katsuragi and Kongō Mountains. In a pit covered with stone slabs, a bronze container containing a copy of a sutra was found. The bronze container was placed inside a grey glazed ceramic container and an outer cylinder of fine sandstone. The pit was lined with stone slabs. One bronze mirror was placed inside the ceramic container and another was placed in the pit along with a long sword. On top of the stone slabs offerings of mirrors, swords, Chinese white ware ceramic boxes and vessels produced in Jingdezhen or Fujian were placed. Other offerings included mold made bronze ritual bowls and an incense burner, a water dropper and an inkstone. The other sutra burials contained similar assemblages, as well as a square Chinese Huzhou type bronze mirror, Chinese bluish white (*seihakuji*) ceramic wares and fragments of glass bottles (Akiyama 1985). An unusual "earth pagoda" (*dotō*) constructed by the famous priest Gyoki in 727 AD at the Onodera Temple site, Sakai, was investigated from 1998 to 2002. Clay slabs 30 cm square, inscribed with a donor's name, were piled up in twelve stories and an eight-sided wooden structure was constructed on their top. The entire pagoda was constructed on a base of tiles 53m square (Kondō 2011).

Discussion

Naniwa and its surrounding area were important in the development of the early Japanese state. Large excavations have uncovered two the remains of two periods of the royal residence and administrative offices of the Naniwanomiya. Surrounding this center were temples, shrines, storehouses, estates of important temples in Nara, and port facilities along the artificial channel, the Horie. The fall of Paekche in 660 AD brought new immigrants, including the Paekche royal clan, who played an important role in technological advancement. Following the abandonment of the Naniwa Palace in the eighth century the area still remained because of its ports and temples. The sutra mounds of the Sefukuji, Izumisano, show not only the importance of Buddhism along the pilgrimage routes to Mt Koya and Kumano, but also the growing importance of trade in Chinese ceramics from major kiln sites in Jiangxi (Jingdezhen) and Fujian. Excavations of the Sayama Reservoir and the Furuichi and Nagasone Canals show how local entrepreneurs increased the productivity of the terraces of the Ōsaka region through irrigation. I have not been able to cover many small Buddhist sites of this period, which should be treated in a separate study. The region became prominent in the Chūsei Period as the nexus of domestic and foreign trade, discussed in Chapter 7.

Chapter 7
Ōsaka as a Commercial Center; The Chūsei Period (ca 1185 to 1603 AD)

This chapter is concerned with mediaeval craft production, trade, and the rise of religious and political centers, ending with the rise and fall of the merchant city of Sakai and Ōsaka Castle. Ōsaka merchants played a key role in the rise of mediaeval commerce. In this period, the ports of Ōsaka in the delta region flourished and provided important services for inland areas of the Kinai region. They were ideal locations for storage, commercial transactions, and craft production.

A feature of Japan in the Kodai and Chūsei Periods was the institution of estates (*shōen*). These were substantial properties that afforded aristocrats and religious institutions with revenues and resources that were directed to their coffers, instead of being paid to the central government. In the Kodai Period these estates gradually became independent and turned to craft production to supplement their income. Metal casting was a specialty of some estates in the Ōsaka region. While trade and exchange within the Japanese Islands and with the Korean Peninsula were carried out from at least the Yayoi Period, overseas trade with more distant regions expanded dramatically in the Chūsei Period. Merchants from Sakai were able to invest their capital in tribute missions to China organized by the government in Kyōto and powerful clans to reap very substantial profits as brokers and financiers. These merchants also expanded private trade networks to include the Ryūkyū Islands, Taiwan, and Vietnam. Archaeological evidence of this trade includes abundant luxury ceramics and the remains of warehouses. At the end of this period a huge religious center of the Honganji Buddhist Sect was built near the old site of the Naniwa Palace and finally, the enormous fortified Ōsaka Castle was built on the ruins of this center, commanding the delta and riverine access to Kyōto. The Ōsaka area was the pre eminent mediaeval economic hub of the Japanese Islands.

As mentioned in Chapter 1, Japanese history can be divided into broad historical eras or specific historical periods (Figure 1.3). In the former scheme, the Chūsei (Mediaeval) Period of Japanese history constitutes the transition from the Kodai (Ancient) Period (ca 600 to the twelfth century AD) to the Kinsei (Early Modern) Period (1603 to 1867 AD). It is marked by the growth of military and merchant classes, decline in central authority and rise of local powers. From 1467 to 1568 AD Japan was wracked by internal strife and shifting power among local rulers loyal to the central power and those seeking local autonomy. This is the period of the building of fortified castles in Japan, termed the Warring States or Sengoku Period. The Chūsei Period came to an end with unification under military rulers, whose power was consolidated in the Kinsei Period (1603 to 1867 AD). Despite the occurrence of political upheavals throughout the period there were three centuries of economic growth between 1250 and 1550 AD (Totman 2000: 160-175).

In the fourteenth and fifteenth centuries, during the Little Ice Age, cooler climate affected agricultural production. Although adverse climatic fluctuations occurred, there was a general increase in agricultural productivity brought about by double cropping and the introduction of sub tropical Champa rice that has a short growing season (Yamamura 1990: 394). In some areas including the Ki River valley of Wakayama Prefecture, immediately south of Ōsaka, farmers developed a method to mitigate the effects of drought by partitioning rice paddies to reduce the irrigated portion, while using the rest for simultaneous (not sequent), dryland cultivation (*nimōsaku*) (Isogai 2001). The trend to increasing nucleation of villages began in the thirteenth century and progressed rapidly in the fourteenth century, as farmsteads were grouped into clusters. Moated nuclear villages developed around irrigation systems and holding ponds *(tameike)* with the regional expansion of arable land, primarily rice fields.

The discovery of these trends is based on the archaeological investigation of old village sites and ditches dated by associated artifacts and the intensive study of old maps (Yamakawa 1998).

A separate period, the Azuchi Momoyama Period (1568 to 1603 AD), has been designated by historians to distinguish the prosperity and high culture of the late sixteenth century AD. At this time the Ōsaka region was the scene of tumultuous political events. During this time three generals sought to pacify warring factions. In the early part of this period the city of Sakai in southern Ōsaka continued to prosper, building on the momentum it had achieved in previous centuries. Its prosperity led to the flowering of merchant culture. A short distance away in the Naniwa area, the enormous temple fortress of Ishiyama Honganji, a center of the Honganji Buddhist sect that flourished among the merchants and entrepreneurs, was built, then destroyed, and Ōsaka Castle was erected over it, only to be destroyed in 1615 AD. At the same time Sakai was burned. Subsequently the political center shifted to Edo (Tōkyō) and the Ōsaka area lost its supremacy.

What were the factors and processes in the rise of mediaeval commercialism? How have recent excavations illuminated early industrial development? What were the roles of the central government in Kyōto and institutions such as temples, and what was the effect of dynamic commercialism in China? How did merchants rise from *shōen* officials? How did Ōsaka people find opportunity in the rise of warring factions?

In this chapter I discuss the archaeological evidence for the urban development of the Naniwa area, metal casting in the Hiki Shōen and Mihara Chō, Hine Shōen, the moated city of Sakai, and two huge centers constructed at the end of the period, the Ishiyama Honganji and Ōsaka Castle.

Prosperous ports in the Naniwa area

At the head of Ōsaka Bay several ports became prosperous in the Chūsei Period. The mouth of the Ō (a section of the Yodo) River downstream from the junction with the Yamato River, was an active area of riverine commerce; however the archaeological picture is not clear because of changes in the river channels and heavy alluviation. In the latter half of the eleventh century AD the mouth of the Ō River became clogged with sediment and navigation was dangerous. The site of Watanabe Tsu, an important port in the extreme northwest of the Uemachi Terrace on the shore of the Ō River, has not yet been located conclusively. It was an important transfer point for pilgrims travelling to Kumano in Wakayama in the early mediaeval period. In the area of Watanabe Tsu the Watanabe Clan controlled local commerce passing into the river from the Inland Sea. This change in the estuary must have been a factor in the rise of the port of Sakai. Although shallow offshore depths at Sakai made it necessary for large ships to anchor and be offloaded, Sakai's rise to prominence was based on its access to the Pacific route to China and Southeast Asia that followed the Pacific coast of Shikoku to Kagoshima in southern Kyūshū, the Ryūkyū Islands, and Taiwan. These regions gave it a distinctive hinterland and range of products. In the second half of the fifteenth century the population of Sakai is estimated to be at least 20,000 (Yamamura 1990: 381).

The Mediaeval Religious Center of the Uemachi Terrace

In the Mediaeval Period Shitennōji (Temple) was the center of the cult of Prince Shōtoku Taishi, an important statesman of the seventh century AD, and the Eastern Gateway to the Pure Land across the sea in Pure Land Buddhism. For the head of the Ishiyama Honganji, Rennyo, proximity to the Shōtoku cult center was an important factor in relocating from Kyōto to Ōsaka (Osawa 2006). Up to 1995, 37 excavations uncovered ditches, wells, post holes and hearths around Shitennōji (Matsuo 2006:150-152). South of Shitennōji several metal casting sites were found, showing the close relationship between crafts and services and large temples. In the fifteenth and sixteenth centuries AD, population density and economic activity increased in the northern part of the Uemachi Terrace, just prior to the construction of Ishiyama Honganji. Matsuo (2006:150) describes the area as '*toshi-teki*' (urban-like). From a broad area, soapstone cauldrons, imported Chinese ceramics and Japanese Koseto and Tokoname wares have been found.

Shōen and craft production

At the end of the Heian Period around the end of twelfth century, the organization of craft production shifted to estates (*shōen*) rather than specialized craft groups (*be*) under direct control of central authority. *Shōen* were autonomous estates or manors belonging to officially sanctioned temples or shrines and the great aristocratic families who supported them (Amino 2012). They were free from paying taxes to the central government and their revenues were devoted to the support of the institutions that controlled them. They existed from the eighth to fifteenth centuries, and perhaps much earlier. *Shōen* produced all kinds of crafts and local specialties as tribute to their sponsors but also for outside buyers, and often possessed stands of protected valuable timber used in construction projects. They provided all kinds of supplies for ritual ceremonies in the political and religious center of Kyōto, as well as people who served in rotation in functionary positions such as guards and attendants. They also supplied the court in Kyōto with items such as sea bream and vegetable oil from the Sakai area (Colcutt 1990: 99). Local officials responsible for remitting specialties to the *shōen* supervisor (*jitō*) gradually became independent merchants and brokers in the Chūsei Period. The control of *shōen* by their owners and agents was reduced as the government despatched its own constables to take over fiscal administration (Ryavec 1978). The *shōen* system is considered by Yamamura to provide the initial conditions for Japanese mediaeval commerce (Colcutt 1990: 347). In port areas such as the Yodo River, *shōen* were involved in trans-shipping.

Craft Production in The Hiki Shōen

New techiques for casting large metal objects came from the continent during the long span of the Kodai Period. Intensive excavation and survey of the Hiki Shōen area, located to the east (inland) from Sakai, showed some aspects of the life of metal casters (Sukigara 1999: 305-347). Artifact assemblages from the Nara, Heian, and Chūsei periods were recovered. These were identified by numerous distinctive types of ceramics. Sites occupied from the ninth to eleventh centuries AD yielded *hajiki*,

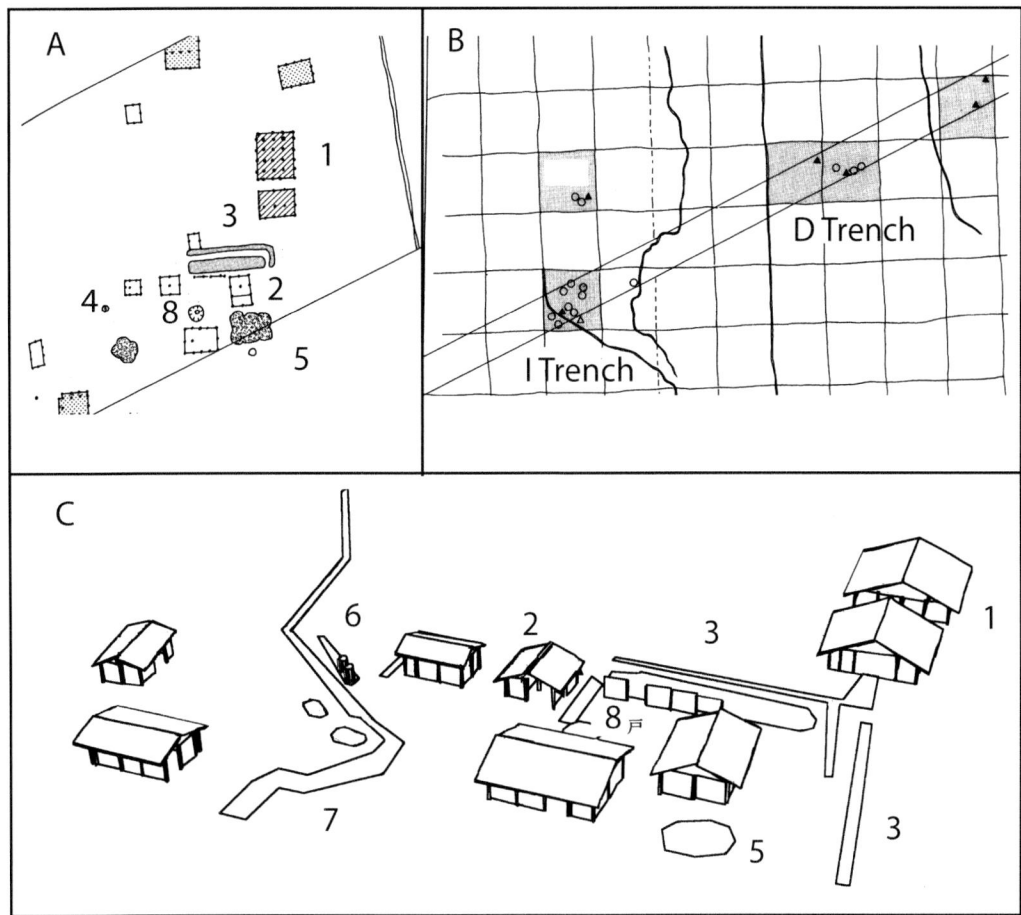

FIGURE 7.1. RECONSTRUCTION OF A METAL CASTERS' VILLAGE, TWELFTH TO THIRTEENTH CENTURIES AD, TRENCH 1, HIKI SHŌ, SAKAI CITY (FROM SUKIGARA 1999: 368). (A) EXCAVATION AREA SHOWING DIAGONAL TRENCH AND RECTANGULAR BOUNDARIES OF THE OLD JŌRI FIELD SYSTEM, VILLAGE SITES IN SHADED AREAS, WITH BUILDING REMAINS INDICATED BY TRIANGLES AND METAL CASTING REMAINS BY CIRCLES. OLD WATERCOURSES ARE SHOWN AS IRREGULAR LINES. (B) EXCAVATION PLAN. C. RECONSTRUCTION OF SITE IN TRENCH I. (1) DWELLING. (2) STOREHOUSE. (3) TRENCH. (4) HEARTH. (5) TRENCH. (6) MELTING HEARTH. (7) WORK AREA. (8) WELL. COURTESY OF SUKIGARA TOSHIO.

sueki, and soft greyware (*gashitsu doki*), while sites from the twelfth and thirteenth centuries were distinguished by Chinese trade wares, consisting of white ware and celadon.

Archaeologists plotted the distribution of ceramics in the excavation area, century by century, searching for patterns that might indicate the period of occupation, the nature of activities, and the relative density of population. They estimated the latter by plotting the density of cooking cauldrons in the five sub periods. In general the results showed a network of small agricultural villages with a few villages inhabited by specialized craftspersons.

Casting Village No.1 of the Hiki Shōen is an archaeological example of a settlement of specialized craftspersons (Figure 7.1). The modest nature of the archaeological record in I Trench belies the impact of such a community on the larger region. There were two groups of buildings, a casting area and a residential area, separated by a small ditch about 90 m long. In the work area, two sequential technical steps, melting (*yōkai*) and forming (*zōkei*) took place. Casting probably required five workers to carry out various functions such as maintaining the fire, pouring of the molten metal, and removing ashes (Sukigara 1999: 353-355). It is thought that three extended families comprised a village. The site yielded remains of sixteen buildings from two time periods. Two of the buildings were 75 sq m in area; five were 35 to 40 sq m, and nine were less than 10m². Only the largest would have been residential, while most were probably sheds and roofed areas. From the relatively large residential area and the occurrence of a relatively high percentage of Chinese ceramics, such as a four-eared white ware jar (*tsubo*) (a symbol of high status), it seems likely that the eldest male in the group would have been a headman (*nanushi*) as distinct from a farmer (*kobyakusho*).

Metal Casting at Mihara

An important product of Japanese casters was the iron cauldron, for boiling food. These cauldrons were particularly in demand by elites; commoners used soapstone or ceramic stoneware. While it is known from historical sources that cauldrons were cast in the Kodai Period, little archaeological evidence is available, since the metal could be repeatedly recycled, leaving few archaeological traces. An archaeological study by Isogawa (1992) examined heirloom specimens and consumption and production sites but found few examples that could be dated earlier than the fourteenth century. Heirloom pieces often lack datable context.

Local groups of craft specialists such as the *Kawachi imoji* of the Mihara Chō region of Sakai developed throughout the Kinai Region. They produced cauldrons and iron pots for daily use and bells for temples, travelling throughout the regions to sell their wares. Although probably few of these craftsmen had the capital to set up operations away from their villages, some artisans travelled by ship to undertake larger projects. In the Middle Heian Period, their specialty was the *Kawachi nabe*, an iron cauldron, and also articles for the nobility in Kyōto (Isogawa 1992: 79). Casting sites consisted of pits, burned earth areas, slag and bellows valves.

At the time of the reconstruction of the Tōdaiji in Nara, under the famous priest Chōgen, local artisans lacked knowledge to cast such a large object as the Great Buddha that was destroyed in a fire in AD 1180. Therefore the casting group consisted of Song Chinese specialists and fourteen local casters (Jap. *Kawachi imoji)*. The *Kawachi imoji* also cast the huge iron bath water container for the Todaiji (Ōsaka Furitsu Sayamaike Hakubutsukan 2007: 24-27). The highly specialized and successful Kawachi casters were much in demand and established centers in other parts of Japan.

From the site of Shinpukuji, Mihara, archaeologists found a complex set of pits; one of these, No. 2, was 3.25 m e/w, 2.7 m n/s, with a depth of 0.15 m. On the bottom of the pit there are five ridges on which the heavy clay mold for the bell was set. Since two ridges are needed to prop up one mold, the pit was used for more than one firing. The pit area yielded slag and crucible fragments, fragments of the exteriors of cauldron and bell molds, fragments of other molds, and bellows valves. The remains of two buildings with elevated floors date to the latter half of the thirteenth century. The bell at the Chōshōji in Kagawa Prefecture has an inscription indicating that it was cast in AD 1275 in the Mihara area in the Shimokuroyama area. It must have been cast in a mold similar to the Shinpukuji example (Sakai Shi Mihara Chō Rekishi Hakubutsukan 2012).

Chōgen worked with the Kawachi *imoji* for 20 years and was responsible for the redevelopment of Sayama Reservoir in 1202 AD. From the latter half of the thirteenth century Kawachi casters established centers in Kantō and Kyūshū. From 1252 to 1262 AD, they participated in the casting of the Great Kamakura Buddha. They also established a center in North Kyūshū and cast bells as far south as Satsuma in southern Kyūshū (Ōsaka Furitsu Sayamaike Hakubutsukan 2007: 29, Ueda 2011). Of a total of 81 extant bronze bells cast in the twelfth and thirteenth centuries, fifty are known to have been cast in Kawachi (Uchida 2004). Did the Kawachi *imoji* play a role in sword production or was it the work of other groups? It is clear from historical sources that huge numbers of swords were shipped from Ōsaka to China in the fifteenth and sixteenth centuries AD (Kobata 1939, 1941) (Appendix B). The contribution of sword making to the local economy was extremely significant. However archaeological evidence of this huge enterprise is lacking.

The Hine Shōen Sites

On the extreme southern edge of Ōsaka, in an interior mountain valley, the Hine Shōen flourished in the thirteenth to fifteenth centuries, being founded in AD 1234 (Nakaoka 2006, weblio.jp 2014, hineno.org 2014, geocities.jp 2014). Because the valley is beautifully preserved with many undisturbed historic sites it has been selected for preservation as a heritage landscape. The valley floor was covered with rice paddy, while upland areas were used for dry farming. Historical accounts confirm the presence of temples and shrines, and the ancient locations can still be identified. An old market area is also known. In the thirteenth century four villages were founded. Two were inland, while two were near the coastal road runninng from Ōsaka to the Kumano Shrine in the deep mountains of present day Wakayama Prefecture. In the fourteenth century, local society was divided into a lower stratum of farmers, fishers, and craftspersons, and a higher stratum of administrators and *samurai*. Wealthy farmers lived in house compounds with storehouses and animal pens, surrounded by stout fences. While the owners of the estate lived in Kyōto, local administrators, often *samurai*, lived in the estate, in a separate walled hamlet dominated by a large elevated residence. Graves of the latter group were earth pits, containing a sword and a few dishes of earthenware for food offerings. Remains of tiny flakes of lacquer suggest that the officials' tall lacquered hats (*eboshi*) were buried with them along with their swords. Inscribed stone epitaphs were erected, not at the grave site, but as part of a group, near the temple site (Rekishikan Izumi Sano nd). In the fifteenth century the valley was controlled by the Kujō Clan, a branch of the aristocratic Fujiwaras (Ryavec 1978: 38). At that time the local Chōfukuji Temple prospered. The temple site has yielded rich artifacts. In the surrounding mountains,

Period	Date	Disaster
I	Ōei 6 1399	Fire, Ōei Disturbance (war) 10,000 houses burned
Ic	Bunmei 7 1475	High tide several thousand houses destroyed
	Bunmei 18 1486	Fire Kita Shō area, 100 houses destroyed
Id	Mei'ei 4 1494	Fire Minami Shō area, extensive burning
	Eishō 5 1508	Fire, Minami Shō area, several thousand houses burned
II	Tenmon 1 1532	Fire, Kita Shō area completely burned, Minami Shō, 1/3 or 4,000 houses burned
III	Tenmon 22 1553	Fire, 2/3 of houses burned
	Tenmon 22 1553	Remaining portion burned
	Eiroku 5 1562	Fire, 500 houses destroyed
	Eiroku 7 1564	Fire, 1000 houses destroyed
IV	Tenshō 3 1575	Large fire
IVa	Keichō 1 1596	Earthquake, 600 people killed
V	Genwa 1 1615	Ōsaka summer war, 20,000 houses destroyed
VI	Empō 8 1680	Fire, 480 houses destroyed
	Kansei 10 1798	Fire, 18 houses burned
	Meiji 1 1868	Fire in north part of city
	Shōwa 20 1945	Second World War bombing, 18,000 houses destroyed

FIGURE 7.2. STRATIGRAPHY AND CHRONOLOGY OF DISASTERS AFFECTING SAKAI (FROM MORIMURA 1989: 50). COURTESY OF MORIMURA KEN'ICHI.

fortifications consisting of small ridge top enclosures separated by defensive ditches have been extensively mapped (Nakaoka 2013).

The moated city of Sakai

About 1000 excavations at the trading city of Sakai, Ōsaka, carried out over some 35 years, provide insights of changing land use, economy, politics, and culture. They show the role of financiers who became munitions dealers as well as cultural arbiters, seizing opportunities in the growth of markets and the loosening of government control. They were also involved in the production of counterfeit coinage. Sakai played a pivotal role in the economic and cultural life of Japan from the mid 1460's to AD 1615, becoming a financial and cultural center despite earthquakes and fires (Figure 7.2, Morimura 1989, 2009a).

Sakai sits at the boundary of three old provinces (*kuni*), Kawachi, Settsu, and Izumi. Settsu included the area of present northern Ōsaka and part of adjacent Hyōgo Prefecture. In the twelfth and thirteenth centuries large portions of this region were manors (*shōen*) providing produce and other raw materials to large temples in Kyōto and Nara. In the the thirteenth century Sakai served as a port for the transshipment of annual payments from *shōen* estates of the Inland Sea area to their proprietors, the temples and shrines of Nara and Mount Koya. There were markets and guilds in Sakai at this time but the principal activity was storage and exchange, in transactions involving large amounts of coins (Von Verschuer 2006: 110). Sakai merchants used their liquid wealth to invest in overseas missions to China, as they expanded their activities in the early fourteenth century. The boundary between Settsu and Izumi was marked by a major east-west road, running from Sakai on the shore of Ōsaka Bay, across the plain and through the Ikoma Mountains to the mountains to the Nara Basin and beyond. This road intersects with the coastal road from Ōsaka to the religious pilgrimage center of Kumano that ran through the center of Sakai. The present shoreline of Ōsaka Bay, transformed by landfill, is approximately 1200m seaward from the mediaeval shoreline and the boundary of the mediaeval city was about 50m from the sea at that time (1500 to 1600 AD). The maximum height above sea level of the mediaeval city of Sakai varies from 1 to 5m (Sakai Shi Hakubutsukan 2006: 5).

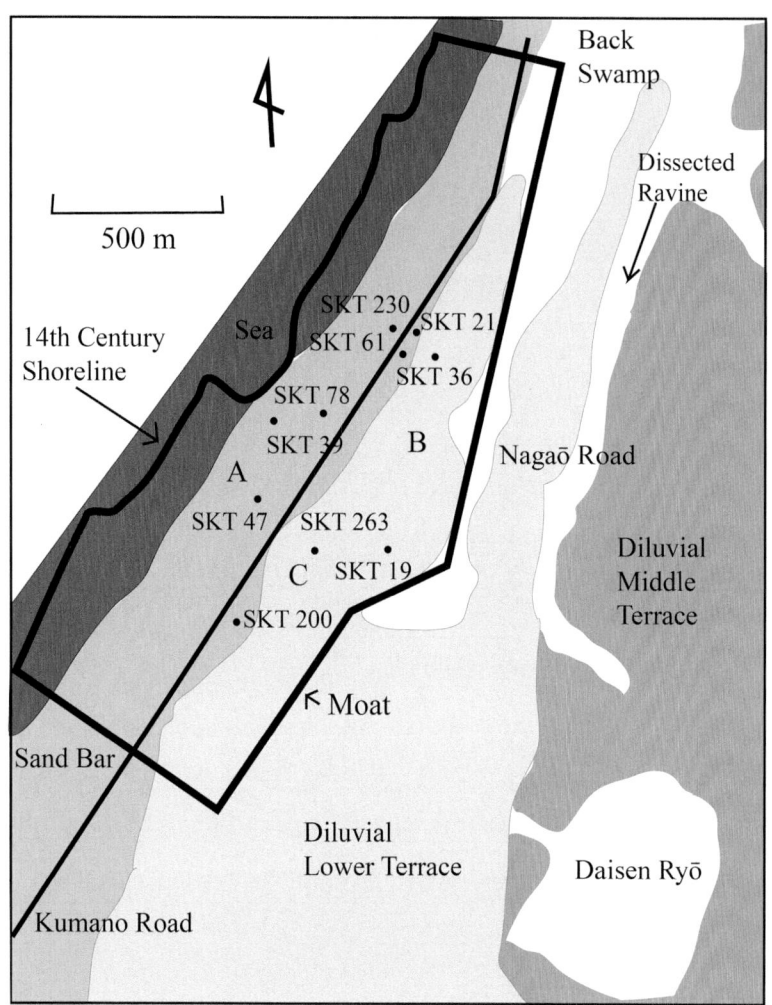

FIGURE 7.3. THE MOATED CITY OF SAKAI AND LOCALITIES DESCRIBED IN THE TEXT AND GRID AREAS A, B, AND C. FROM ŌSAKA FU 2007: 2. COURTESY OF TSUZUKI SHIN'ICHIRŌ.

Sakai is close to an important religious landmark, the Sumiyoshi Shrine. In mediaeval times, a network of Sumiyoshi shrines, devoted to mariners and traders, extended throughout Japan with the main Sumiyoshi Shrine of Ōsaka at its apex. In the fourteenth century, the shrine market at Sumiyoshi was referred to as the *takara no ichi* (Jewelled Market) (Wakita 1999: 38) because of its wide catchment, association with pilgrimage, and luxury goods. In 1332 AD, Emperor Godaigo Tennō sponsored an overseas trading mission to China to finance repair work on the Sumiyoshi Shrine (Von Verschuer 2006: 100). The Sumiyoshi Shrine not only generated local wealth but also stimulated overseas trade (Miyamoto 2008).

Sakai had access by road to the Kii Peninsula beyond Wakayama, the Nara Basin, Ōsaka, and Kyōto. From the twelfth century it was a terminus for land routes and a transfer point to sea routes of the Inland Sea (Asao et al 1999: 62). It faced the Inland Sea, but it also had sea access to the Ryukyus and Southeast Asia via the Pacific coast of Shikoku and Kyūshū (Asao 2004: 260).

Local river traffic must have moved on flat bottom boats, similar to one found in 1878 AD. Fashioned from a single log, it was some 11m long and more than 1meter wide.

A drawing of the boat is held by the Tōkyō University Museum. The undated original specimen was destroyed in the bombing of Ōsaka in 1945 (Tsujio 2000).

Site layout

The moated city is about 1 x 3km and contains 3 zones with differing orientations of the grid patterns of streets and buildings (*jōri*) (Tsuzuki 1993, 1994) (Figure 7.2). Area A, closest to the sea, is the area of the old port, which has not been archaeologically recovered. However a well for agricultural use, dating from the late twelfth or early thirteenth century suggests that there was a small shoreline community in this area at this time period (Tsuzuki 1994: 85). The main shoreline road from Ōsaka to Kumano runs through Area A. In the late sixteenth century this area became the center of Sakai with a concentration of storehouses, residences and tea pavilions of the richest merchants (Figures 7.4, 7.5). Some merchants had up to five storehouses on their property. In this area, the Sekiguchi Shrine, facing the Kumano Road, was an important feature, from the early fifteenth century to 1615. A new residential area grew on the inland side of the warehouse area, and secondary roads appeared. The double moat was at its deepest around 1569 AD, in preparation for Oda Nobunaga's

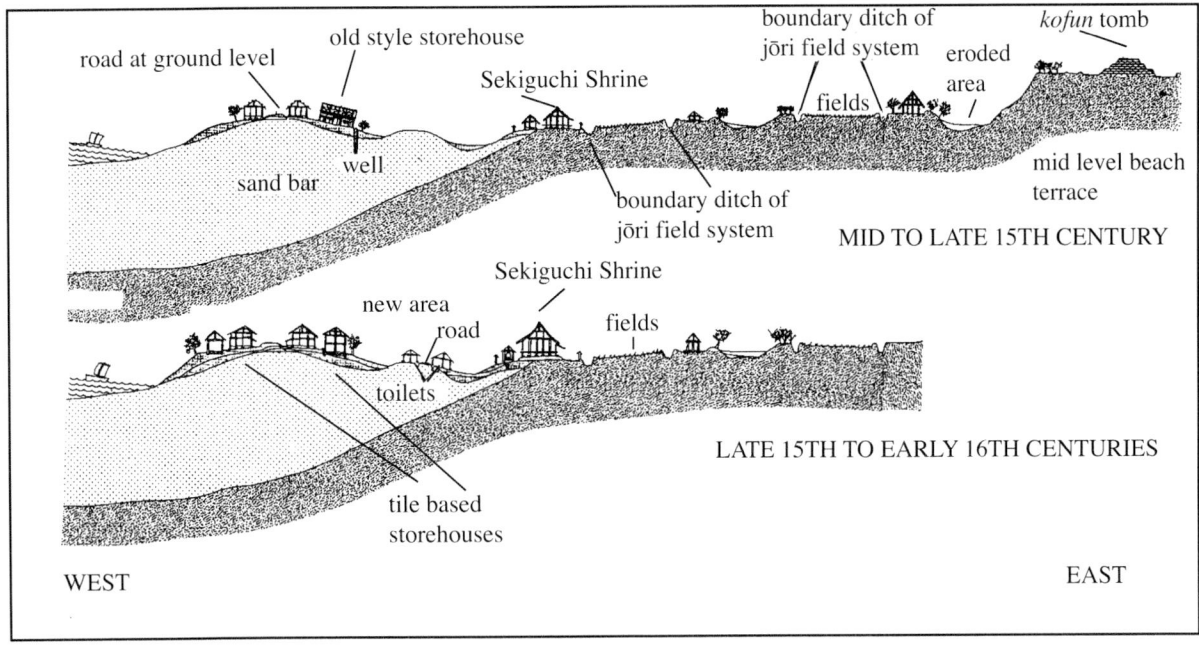

FIGURE 7.4. RECONSTRUCTION OF SAKAI FROM THE MID FIFTEENTH CENTURY TO EARLY SIXTEENTH CENTURIES. ADAPTED WITH PERMISSION FROM TSUZUKI 1994: 100. COURTESY OF TSUZUKI SHIN'ICHIRŌ.

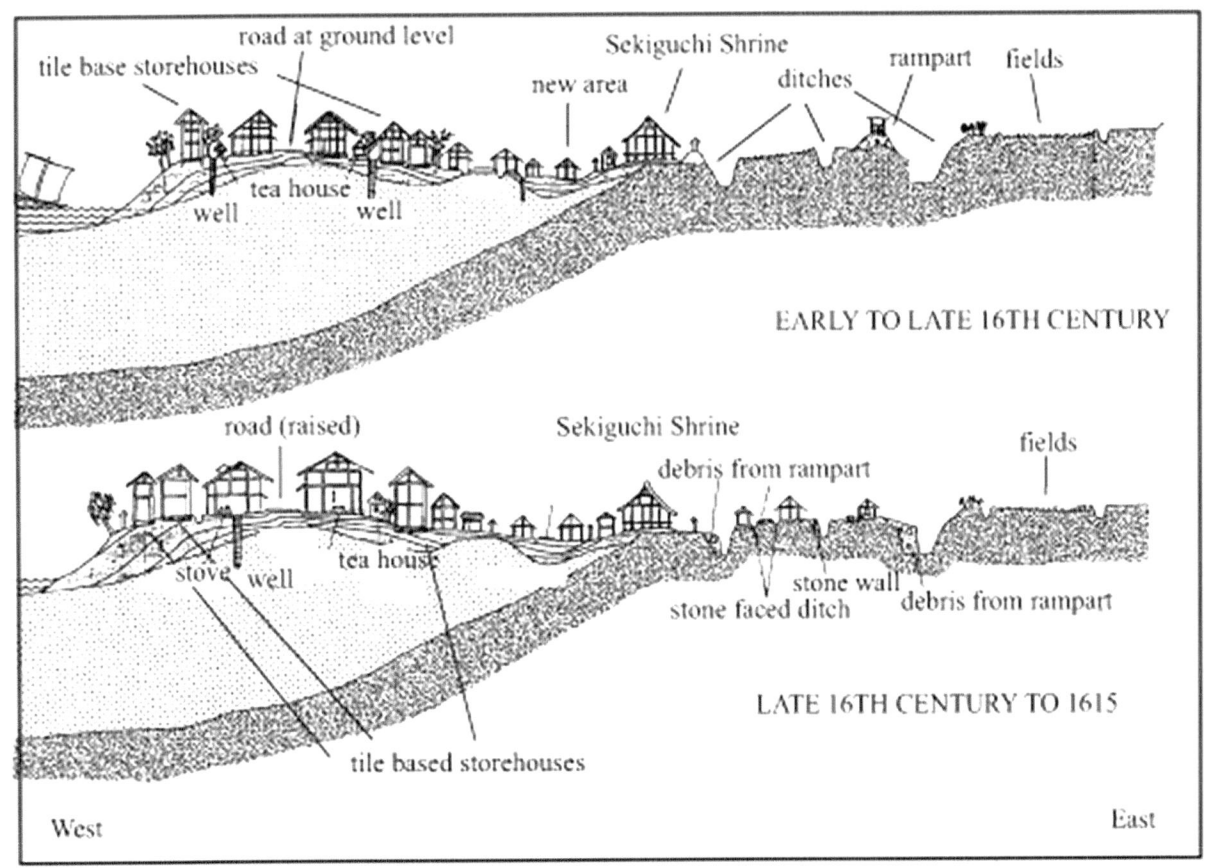

FIGURE 7.5. RECONSTRUCTION OF SAKAI FROM SIXTEENTH CENTURY TO THE BEGINNING OF THE SEVENTEENTH CENTURY. ADAPTED WITH PERMISSION FROM TSUZUKI 1994: 100. COURTESY OF TSUZUKI SHIN'ICHIRŌ.

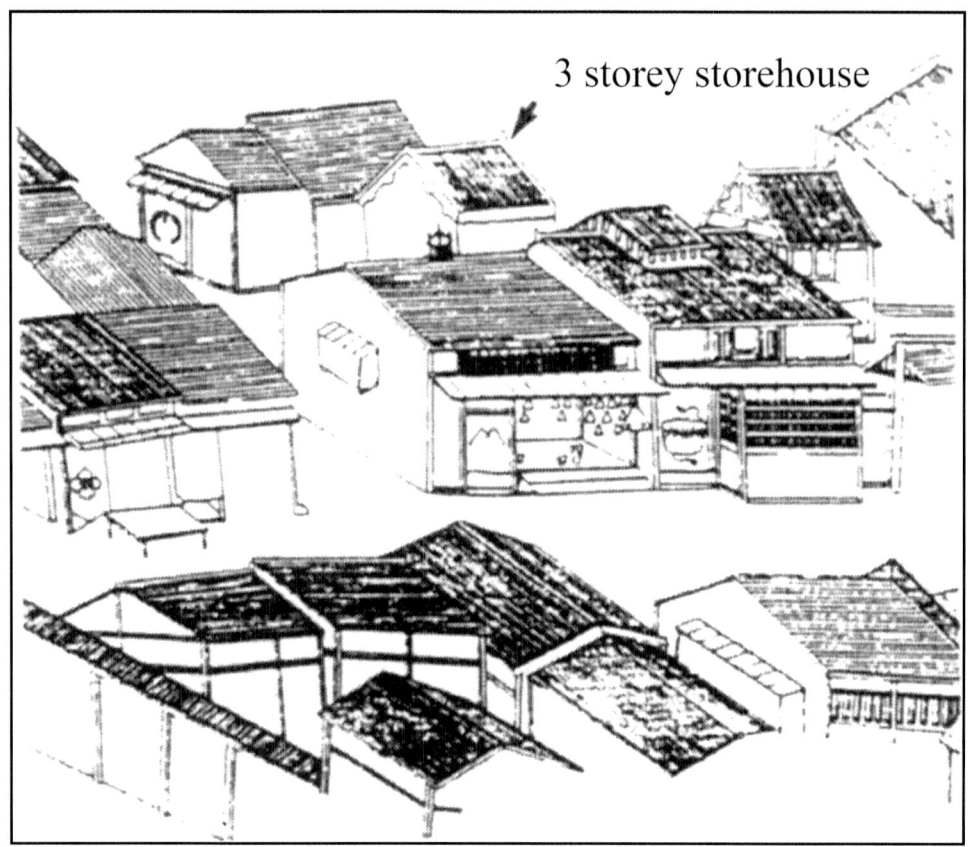

FIGURE 7.6. RECONSTRUCTION OF RESIDENCES, SHOPS, AND THREE STOREY STOREHOUSES. FROM MORIMURA 2002: 279). COURTESY OF MORIMURA KEN'ICHI AND THE KOKURITSU REKISHI MINZOKU HAKUBUTSUKAN.

reprisals, and was later partially filled in by Hideyoshi, when the rampart to the north of the moat was dismantled (Shimatani 2010). A site of metal casting, SKT 361, was found in the area inside the moat, dating from the late fifteenth century to AD 1615. Nearby is another metal casting site, SKT 39 (Tsuzuki 1993: 72-73).

In addition to historical descriptions there are pictorial representations of Sakai, the most famous being the folding screen entitled *Sumiyoshi Sairei Zu Byōbu* (Folding Screen Showing Rituals at Sumiyoshi) (Tsuzuki 1990: 149). It is dated to just before the destruction of 1615 AD, at the height of the prosperity. Buildings were grouped into sets consisting of a two storey main house with associated warehouses and a tea house. Within the house compound there were a small garden, and path. Trees were often planted within the compound. The storehouses were plastered and white washed and usually had tile roofs, while other buildings often had roofs of cypress bark. Some houses had a shop in the front or a front room for conducting business (Figure 7.6). Goods were often lined up on a bench-like shelf in front of the shop. From excavations of sites of the Keichō Period (1596 to 1615 AD), the city lots were long and narrow, with a frontage of 4 to 8m and a depth of 20 to 26m (Morimura 2004a). Construction in every period in Sakai was based on a raised floor supported on posts or pillars, set on granite stone bases. While Sakai merchants used local Izumi sandstone from quarries that they controlled, for ornamental carving, they used granite from the Inland Sea for pillar bases and artifacts such as tea mortars. After 1615 AD, the granite was under the control of the Tokugawa rulers, who used it to build the base of Ōsaka Castle (Morimura 2005a).

Stratigraphy of Sakai

Excavations within the moated city have yielded a series of thin, compacted living layers interspersed with thicker layers of ash and burned debris, left by widespread fires. These have been grouped into 6 periods (Figure 7.2) and correlated with historically recorded fires (Morimura 2006b). Other disasters that beset Sakai were flood tides and earthquakes (Morimura 2009a: 50). The land surface of the mediaeval city was 1.2 to 3.5m lower than the present surface.

Morimura (1989) provides a summary of the detailed archaeological chronology of Sakai. There are slight differences in the boundaries of Periods II and III in different parts of Sakai. The main chronological markers are the surfaces left from historically recorded fires. Summaries of major localities within Sakai are given in Appendix A-16.

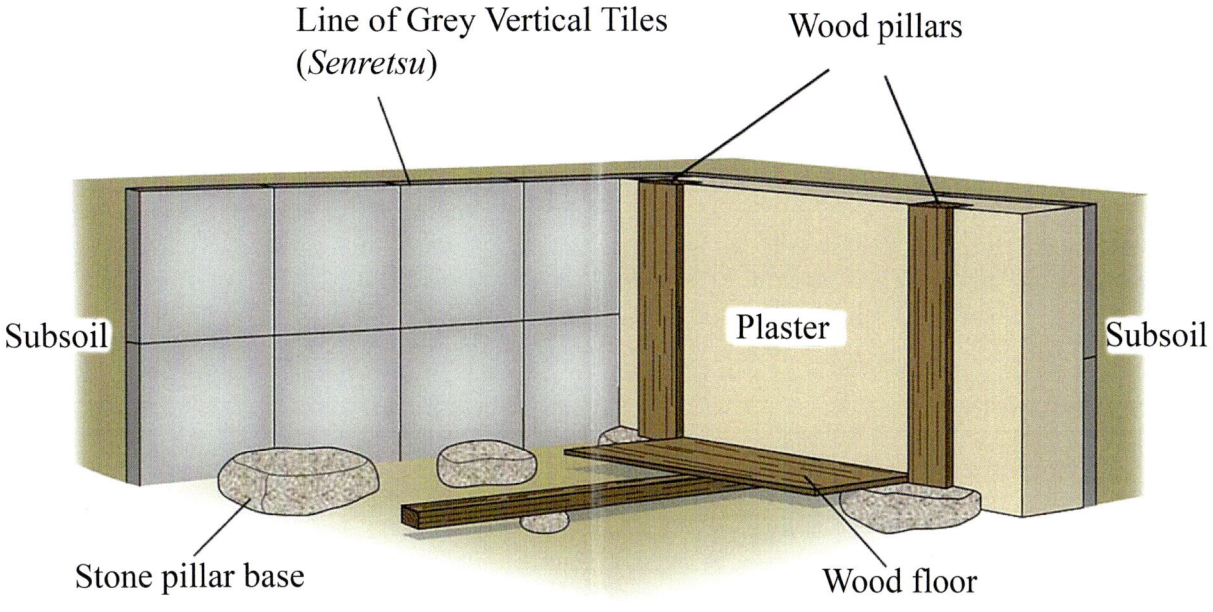

FIGURE 7.7. PLAN OF BASEMENT CONSTRUCTION OF STOREHOUSES, USING A LINE OF VERTICAL TILES (SENRETSU). FROM ŌSAKA FU BUNKAZAI SENTĀ 2007: 2. COURTESY OF ŌSAKA FU BUNKAZAI SENTĀ.

Period I. Early Fourteenth Century to 1475 AD

Although settlement occurred as early as the ninth century little is known about Sakai before the fourteenth century when it became the port of the shōgunate in Kyōto. In this period Sakai's defense system and its commercial role were established. In 1336 AD the former *shōen* (estate) of Sakai became the domain of the Sumiyoshi Shrine. The city was surrounded by a single outer moat. House construction was of wood, without plaster. The city contained about 10,000 households at the time of the fire in 1399 AD. Roads were at the same level as adjacent living surfaces. Large jars of Tokoname Ware were used for water storage and tubular well shafts of tile-like ware were also noted (Tsuzuki 1993: 70). Burials were concentrated in two locations near Buddhist temples. Refuse was thrown into the moat.

Period II. 1494 to 1532 AD

This is the period of the rise of warring factions of local rulers (*sengoku daimyo*). In this period white washed plaster walls were universal. Latrines consisted of 2 or 3 large buried jars in one location. In Periods II and III the city had both an inner and outer moat. From Periods II to IV the main roads were one step higher than the surrounding living areas and were separated by a ditch. In this period the first storehouses appear. These were small multi storied buildings of sturdy construction and plastered walls, used for the storage of valuable

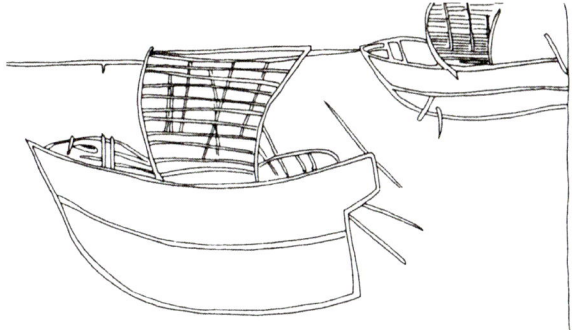

FIGURE 7.8. DETAIL OF INCISED DRAWING ON A GREY RECTANGULAR TILE OF CHINESE STYLE BOATS OF THE TYPE THAT VISITED SAKAI IN THE LATTER HALF OF THE SIXTEENTH CENTURY AD. TOTAL WIDTH OF DRAWING APPROX. 26 CM, RECOVERED FROM SKT3, SAKAI. FROM ŌSAKA FURITSU YAYOI BUNKA HAKUBUTSUKAN 2008: 50. COURTESY OF ŌSAKA FURITSU YAYOI BUNKA HAKUBUTSUKAN AND SAKAI SHI KYŌIKU IINKAI.

commodities. They were 3 to 5 m long on each side. A rectangular basement was first excavated and lined with vertical rows of square grey tiles covered with clay. On the excavated floor wooden posts for supporting the building were set on stone bases. The lining of the foundation with vertical tiles eliminated moisture and burrowing rodents (Ōsaka Fu Bunkazai Sentā 2007, Tsuzuki 2010a) (Figure 7.7). A tile from the basement of Site SKT3 was decorated with an incised drawing of a Chinese trading ship of the latter half of the sixteenth century (Figure 7.8)

Period III. 1532 To 1553 AD

In 1532 AD there were 15,000 households in Sakai. The Portugese missionary, Francis Xavier, visited in 1550 AD (Appendix B).

Period IV. 1553 to 1575 AD

This was the period of maximum prosperity and political independence. The number of three storey storehouses rapidly increased. Disturbances and a fire in Hakata, Kyūshū, a rival port of Sakai, gave Sakai a substantial commercial advantage. In Period IV there was a double outer moat and an inner moat.

Period V. 1596 to 1615 AD

Sakai remained very prosperous. At the time of the great fire of 1615, there were 20,000 households in Sakai. Despite the density of settlement, it appears that many prosperous house sites had a side garden. Changes to the city initiated by the general Toyotomi Hideyoshi included the filling in of portions of the moat, and the division of the city into ten wards. Land holdings were arranged in long lots with narrow frontage (*tansaku*). Sakai merchants sent ships to Siam and Luzon; incense and sugar were important imports from these areas. From 1573 to 1591 AD there was a Japanese community in Luzon, Philippines, with ties to Sakai. In Period V burial took place outside of the city but in Period VI it was inside the city in temple cemeteries. The city was unified and organized into blocks created by major streets whereas previously, it had been organized around temples and shrines (Morimura 2004a: 190). Morimura (1989: 55) identifies this period as the time of transition from Chūsei Period to the Kinsei Period.

Period VI. 1680 to 1707 AD

With the rebuilding after 1615, the city was re-surveyed and a new grid was established. Under the control of the Tokugawa government in Edo, Sakai was eclipsed by ports such as Nagasaki. It became a center for advanced manufacturing, although gun making declined under the peace created by the central control of the Tokugawa. It had an outer moat, 18m wide. Large differences in house size appear and many residences have no associated warehouses. Latrines were both public and private.

Metal Casting

There are several aspects of metal casting in the Sakai region, showing local proficiency of metal work and the importance of the area as a receiver and developer of new technologies.

As we have seen in other chapters, in the Kofun Period the inhabitants of the Kawachi Plain mastered the production of iron arms and weapons, as well as importing armor from the southern Korean peninsula. In the twelfth to fourteenth centuries the area that is modern Mihara Chō, inland from Sakai, was a center for the casting of bronze bells (Isogawa 2004, 226). In the sixteenth and seventeenth centuries Sakai itself was a center for casting coins and the metal parts of guns. In the Early Modern Period Sakai continued to be a center for metal casting and at present it is famous for its high quality knives and bicycles.

The manufacture of guns is not well known archaeologically, presumably because the production occurred outside the moated city and imperfect products were recycled rather than discarded. However the casting of coins took place within the moated city (Shimatani 2003). Although it is generally believed that Japan ceased production of coinage from 958 to 1636 AD and relied on imported Chinese coinage for raw material, Shimatani points out that the coins in circulation in the sixteenth century and early seventeenth centuries were actually a mix of Chinese coins and Japanese counterfeit. Local authorities identified the counterfeit coins as "bad coins" (*waruizeni*) and passed edicts against them (Shimatani 1999). However the use of coinage continued to increase in the latter half of the sixteenth century. For instance, Oda Nobunaga is said to have given 2,000,000 *mon* (1 mon equals 1000 coins) to repair damage to temples and shrines in Settsu Province, adjacent to Sakai, and 20,000,000 *mon* to religious institutions in Sakai (Brown 1951: 41). However on the same page Brown (1951: 41) states that Nobunaga demanded 20,000,000 coins from Ishiyama Honganji (Temple) and the city of Sakai.

Mold fragments have been found in Sakai, Kyōto, Kamakura, and Hakata. They are most numerous in Sakai. By 2003 six sites yielded tree form coin molds (coins were mold made, not struck from dies as in the west) and five more have produced evidence of metal working. The most abundant coins (25%) are copies of *Kaiyuan Tongbao* coins of the Tang Dynasty (618 to 960 AD). While copies of coins of the Hong Wu era (1368 to 1398 AD) were produced, no copies of coins of the subsequent Yong Le Era (1403 to 1424 AD) were produced, possibly in response to a prohibition (Shimatani 1999).

Shimatani (2003: 530) reported 202 mold specimens from Sakai. Coins cast in Sakai can easily be identified since they were cast in open molds and the reverse lacks any evidence of a mold, being completely plain. Normally the reverse should have at least a raised rim around the circular outer edge and the interior rectangular hole. Metallurgical analyses show that they are 98% copper, without tin or lead, both of which occur in Chinese coins. These plain coins were not produced in Kyōto or Kamakura. According to Shimatani, (2003: 537) the general rate of occurrence of counterfeit coins is very low, often below 1%; however a cache found at

Shinjō, Aomori City, yielded 6,433 counterfeit coins out of a total of 7019 (92% of the total cache) and Locality 448-3 of Sakai yielded 3,932 counterfeit coins out of a total of 4851 (81% of the total cache).

Changes In Ceramics

Ceramics constitute the most abundant artifact class, and illuminate patterns of trade and consumption. They reflect shifting contacts with surrounding areas, changes in customs relating to food and drink, and Sakai's transformation from a local to an international port. The ratio between local and imported wares fluctuated. Throughout the total period of occupation locally made disposable earthenware plates were often used for serving food. Cauldrons and large jars were of earthenware and stoneware. Jars for evaporating sea water to make salt were also found. In Periods V and VI iron cauldrons replaced ceramic examples. (The periods mentioned below were described earlier in this chapter.)

Imported ceramics show substantial changes (Morimura 1989, 1998). In every period, Chinese ceramics comprised more than 95% of the trade ceramics assemblage, while Korean and Southeast Asian ceramics were 3% and 2% respectively. Ninety percent of the Southeast Asian ceramics were storage vessels for luxury food items, while the Chinese ceramics were for serving food (Tsuzuki 2010d: 234). In Period I Chinese celadon bowls and plates predominated (Morimura 2005b). In Period II, Chinese blue and white wares become abundant, as well as Korean *punchong* ware rice bowls used as tea bowls by the Japanese (Morimura 2003b). In Periods I to III, Chinese ceramics (celadon, white wares, and blue and white) set the standard (Morimura 2005b). In particular celadon bowls from the Longquan kilns of Zhejiang province were highly valued. In the fifteenth century, blue and white wares from Jingdezhen, Jiangxi Province, increased (Tsuzuki 2010e, 2011a,b). Along with rare Thai and Vietnamese wares, they must have reached Sakai through private trade of Sakai merchants with the Ryūkyū Kingdom. These include famous black glazed jars with four ears on the shoulder, produced in Sri Satachanalai, and also products of the Menam Noi Kilns, about 70 km northwest of Ayuthaya. In Period V Southeast Asian ceramics were traded directly from Southeast Asia by Sakai merchants and demonstrate Sakai's expanding trade routes at the height of its power (Morimura 2004b, Tsuzuki 2007, 2012a). Large jars from Thailand were first used as containers for liquor or saltpeter. After their arrival in Sakai they were re-used as water containers. These jars often took on secondary roles as tea ceremony utensils along with small covered boxes used for incense (Morimura 2009c,d) (Box 7.1). Tall jars from Mi-Son, central coastal Vietnam, were originally sugar containers (Morimura 2004b). Japanese wares appear in Period II, with Seto and Mino types of oil spot glaze (*tenmoku*), as well as Bizen wares (Morimura 2005c, 2006d,e, 2011, Nagai 2010, Tsuzuki 2012b). Around 1570 AD Shino wares appear, and around 1590 AD, Shigaraki, Tanba, Karatsu, and other wares appear. After 1615 AD Japanese Imari blue and white can be found. Wilson (2003: 14) states that before the end of the sixteenth century, Seto and Mino wares were used only

---

BOX 7.1
Tea Ritual

Sakai was a center for the development of the "Tea Ceremony", and was the richest market for tea ceramics in Japan (Kanazawa 2004: 61). The Tea Ceremony provided a means for men of different social strata to meet, particularly warriors and merchants (Watsky 1995). During the mediaeval period, it underwent a series of transformations, recognizable by changes in the tea utensils found in archaeological excavations (Morimura 2006b). In the fourteenth and fifteenth centuries, the practice of tea was dominated by Zen priests and elite samurai warriors, who used Chinese *tenmoku* ("oil glaze") bowls placed on lacquer stands. In the late sixteenth century, low fired Japanese *raku* bowls expressed a different aesthetic, as Japanese influence became stronger. In the 'golden age' of Sakai (1596 to 1615 AD), many of the tea masters came to prefer tea decocted from leaves rather than tea leaf powder. This new form of drinking came from Fujian, China, along with blue and white ceramics (Morimura 2009b). According to Morimura (2006b; 2008b, 25) the Chinese style of tea consumption was brought to Sakai through the Ming tribute missions. Some Sakai merchants quickly adopted this innovation but others preferred older Chinese ceramics, such as celadon and *tenmoku* (Sen 1998: 159-160). From the Sakai excavations, Morimura (2000: 16-17) identified three periods of change in ceramics used for drinking tea. From 1580 to 1585 AD, Japanese Yellow Seto and Chinese Zhangzhou blue and white were introduced. From 1585 to 1596 AD, various vessels of Shino and Karatsu appear, and from 1596 to 1615 AD, green and black Oribe, Yellow Seto, and South China Three Color Wares were added. Large gatherings required sets of identical dishes in a variety of unusual shapes. Morimura (2002) notes that these new wares mark the beginning of Japanese Early Modern Period ceramics, emerging in a period of weak or absent central government control.

> **BOX 7.2**
> **Shūinsen: the Red Seal Trade**
>
> The general Toyotomi Hideyoshi and subsequently the Tokugawa Shogunate attempted to control Japanese piracy and trade in Southeast Asia by allowing only those with specific authorization from the ruler to go abroad for trade. The Red Seal system, in which each voyage had to be authorized with a special document, is thought to have begun as early as 1592 AD under Hideyoshi, but actually the earliest preserved Red Seal Permit is dated to 1604 AD. Tokugawa Ieyasu issued permits to his favorite feudal lords and principal merchants. With the permit came a commitment from the government to guarantee protection of the ships.
>
> Besides Japanese traders, 11 Chinese and 12 European residents including William Adams and Jan Joosten received permits. The ships, ranging in size between 500 and 750 tons, were equal or superior to European galleons but were one third the size of the Portugese carracks who sailed once a year from Macau to Nagasaki, carrying silk directly from China. Japanese residents exported silver, swords, and other artifacts. They were very active in Siam, with substantial royal influence. About 350 Red Seal voyages were recorded between 1604 and 1634. Sakai's role was significant only until 1615. The major export item was Japanese silver, a total of some 843,000 kg being carried by Red Seal ships, whereas Portugese carracks carried 650,000 kg. (Nagazumi 2001).

when continental wares were unavailable. However in the final decades of the sixteenth century, new Japanese ceramics challenged the authority of Chinese ceramics. These were produced at Mino, Gifu Prefecture, and were known as Shino and Oribe (Morimura 2004c). They displayed innovative shapes and color schemes. They exemplify social changes in which merchant culture flourished with a proliferation of art forms promoted by the merchants rather than by aristocrats or warriors (Morimura 2004c).

Relatively large Japanese bowls were used for tea produced from powdered tea. In a different way of enjoying tea, small Chinese blue and white bowls were used for tea prepared from leaves, and sets of brightly colored dishes of Japanese low fired wares were used for a particular type of meal in which delicacies were served (*kaiseki ryori*) (Morimura 2006f). With the increased interest in the Tea Ceremony and the building of small, urban gardens and tea pavilions, ceramics from Vietnam, Thailand, and coastal Fujian were prized (Morimura 2004a, 2009c).

Other mediaeval moated towns similar to Sakai existed in the Ōsaka region. One such example is Hirano (Odagi 2007b, 2008c). In the Chūsei Period it was surrounded by a double moat, inside which there were earth ramparts. Its residents were involved in the Red Seal Trade in the early seventeenth century AD (Box 7.2), and it was also a center for shipping cotton and rice from Kashiwara by boat along the Hirano River. The town was visited by the Portuguese missionary, Fiores, who also left accounts of Sakai. Although it was burned in 1615 AD, it was later rebuilt on the urban grid established at the time by Hideyoshi.

Temple and Castle

The final episode in this chapter is the almost surreal building and subsequent destruction two huge edifices, a Buddhist Temple fortress and Ōsaka Castle. For a period of about four decades in the late sixteenth and early seventeenth centuries, the old capital area of the Naniwa Palace once again became the political center of the Japanese Islands, while Sakai was the financial center. Matsuo (2003: 84-86) distinguishes three historical periods in the construction of Ishiyama Honganji and Osaka Castle; the Honganji Period (1496 to 1580); the Toyotomi Period (1580 to 1596), and the beginning of the Tokugawa Period, from 1603 to 1615 AD.

Ishiyama Honganji, a huge temple fortress

Higashi Honganji, formally known as Shinshū Honkyō, is the mother temple of the Shinshū Otani Branch of Jodo Shinshū, founded by the priest Shinran (1173 to 1262 AD) in Kyōto. The eighth successor of Shinran, Rennyo, revitalized the sect. In 1496 AD, he started a new temple near the old site of the Naniwa Palace in Ōsaka. After the destruction of his original center in Yamashina, Kyōto by the monks of Mt Hiei in 1532 AD, his new center, Ishiyama Honganji, became the main temple for Rennyo's sect, whose members included Sakai merchants. According to Amstutz (1991), Honganji was deeply connected to mediaeval commercialization and privatization, being heavily supported by merchants. From 1538 to the time of Nobunaga in the 1570s, the temple fortress was "possessed of complete tax and service exemption, was exempt from entry by governors agents, and was self governing and self policing" (Amstutz 1991:122). Around the temple were merchants' quarters, in Jinaimachi (Fujita 2000).

The plan of the site is debated but if it followed that of its predecessor at Yamashina, Kyōto, there would have been a religious hall for Amida worship in the east surrounded by two or three rings of moats, with adjacent administrative facilities. Surrounding the religious center were palisades and moats for protection against feudal lords such as Oda Nobunaga and also against rival Buddhist sects. The main entrance was gated and protected by towers (Amstutz 1991: 123). The center of the Ishiyama Honganji lies either under Enclosures I and II of Ōsaka Castle, (Tsujio 2000), or some distance to the south (Amano 1996). The actual plan of the Jinaimachi (temple compound) had a central temple and a surrounding commercial quarter. A very large ditch, some 8m wide and 5m deep, is thought to have served as an internal line of defense of the Honganji. For comparison, the outer moat of Ōsaka Castle, before 1615 AD, was 20m wide and 4 to 5m deep (Amano 1996: 39). It is important to distinguish between deposits belonging to the Ishiyama Honganji and subsequent, often intrusive deposits from Ōsaka Castle. Some areas have ceramic assemblages similar to those of Ichijōdani, Fukui Prefecture, destroyed by Nobunaga in 1573 AD and must date to the Ishiyama Honganji deposit, while others, containing the earliest forms of Kyūshū Imari ceramics dating to the early seventeenth century, Shoki Imari, must date to the time period of Ōsaka Castle.

From 1576 to 1580, the general Oda Nobunaga, who lived from 1534 to 1582, laid siege to Ishiyama Honganji, in an effort to establish his headquarters at the mouth of the Yodo River, which provided vital access to Kyōto and beyond to Lake Biwa. He completely destroyed the temple fortress in 1580 AD, with an enormous loss of life.

Ōsaka Castle

Excavation of Ōsaka Castle was complex because of existing modern buildings. The necessity to conduct very small excavations between these buildings, rather than large continuous wide areas has complicated stratigraphic correlation and site interpretation (Uchida 2000). The castle itself is situated on a plot of land roughly one square kilometer in area, to the north of the Uemachi Terrace on land which was originally lagoon (Figure 6.2). It is built on two raised platforms of landfill supported by sheer walls of cut stone, with small stones used to fill in the interstices. This method allows the individual stones to move slightly during earthquakes without causing damage. The building of Ōsaka Castle was completed in four stages from 1583 to 1598. These are Period I, 1583 to 1586, Enclosure I; Period II, 1586-1594, Enclosure II; Period III, 1594 to 1598, samurai and merchant quarters and Period IV, 1598, Enclosure IV (Nakamura 2000, 2001, 25-28). Transportation of the huge boulders for Enclosure I required 20,000 to 50,000 men, depending on the stage of construction. It was completed in two months. In about one Hideyoshi's year Enclosure I was ready for occupation. It included Hideyoshi's private residence, the Oku Goten, and northern (private) and southern (official) buildings. The Portugese missionary Fiores visited the site in 1586 AD, when he witnessed the construction of a massive ditch separating Enclosures I and II. The latter housed Hideyoshi's retainers and concubines. These two enclosures housed the basic functions of the castle. In Period III, the outermost area of the castle was constructed and in Period IV Enclosure III was constructed. It is separated from the other enclosures by a moat and palisade. Enclosure III contained very large *samurai* quarters. Enclosure III is located in the same area as the Hōenzaka Storehouses and the seventh century Early Naniwa Palace (Matsuo 2000). The later layers of the site are characterized by Japanese ceramics, Shoki Imari, Karatsu, Shino, and Oribe wares, as well as Fujian blue and white wares dating to the late sixteenth and early seventeenth centuries (Mori and Mametani 2000).

Matsuo (2003) divided The Toyotomi Period into Early (1580 to 1598 AD) and Late (1598 to 1615 AD). Oda was assassinated in 1582 AD. In 1583 AD Oda's successor, Toyotomi Hideyoshi (1537 to 1598 AD) began work on the construction of Ōsaka Castle, on the site of Ishiyama Honganji. In 1598 the townspeople of Jinaimachi were forcibly relocated to a new site on the west side of Ōsaka Castle to make room for the construction of a residential area for *samurai*. In the area of markets and merchants' quarters, two long rows of samurai quarters (*buke yashiki*) were constructed along the large main road (Daidō) from the Shitennōji Temple to Ōsaka Castle (Matsuo 2003, 89). This created a kind of artificial landscape of a capital city with retainers' dwellings at the foot of the castle. Extensive construction was carried out at the boat landing area immediately to the west of the castle. Ceramics and stone pillar bases have been recovered in that area. Surrounded by rivers and Ōsaka Bay on three sides, the site was difficult to subdue. Figure 7.9 shows a reconstruction of Ōsaka Castle as it existed from the time of its construction in the 1580's and 1590's until its destruction in 1615. Figure 7.10 shows the castle after it was rebuilt. It retained its general form until 1868 AD. It was transformed from a moated stronghold to an administrative structure surrounded by blocks of offices and residences.

Conclusion

In the Chūsei Period, commercialism and manufacturing, particularly metal casting, advanced rapidly. Production of metal goods, always important in the Ōsaka region, became a hallmark. Pilgrimage routes crossing the area were also significant. Sakai played an important role in cultural activities, mercantile wealth being poured into the Tea Ceremony. In the Naniwa area the long term importance of Shitennōji was a factor in attracting the

FIGURE 7.9. RECONSTRUCTION OF ŌSAKA CASTLE AS IT DEVELOPED FROM 1583 UP TO THE BURNING OF AD 1615. REMAINS OF THE HUGE STONES OF THE WALLS CONSTRUCTED UNDER HIDEYOSHI ARE CIRCLED. COURTESY OF CHIKURINSHA KENKCHIKU KENKYŪSHO.

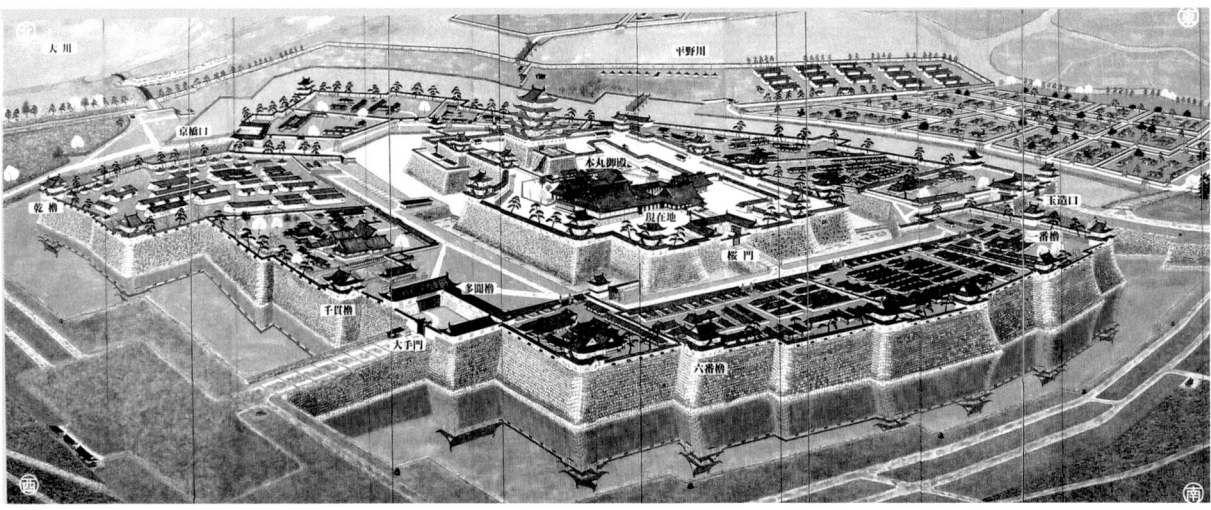

FIGURE 7.10. RECONSTRUCTION OF ŌSAKA CASTLE AFTER THE REBUILDING OF AD 1620 UP TO 1868. COURTESY OSAKAJŌ TENSHUKAKU HAKUBUTSUKAN.

Honganji and the construction of a huge temple fortress that was destroyed by the forces of Oda Nobunaga. Before long the same area was rebuilt as Ōsaka Castle, only to fall again. With the rise of the Tokugawa, the center of gravity moved to eastern Japan; but merchant culture survived and flourished.

Chapter 8
The Beginnings of Modern Ōsaka;
The Kinsei Period (ca 1603 to 1868 AD)

The Kinsei Period was a period of tightly centralized government described as feudal with modernizing tendencies (Hall 1991). Some 250 fiefdoms (*han*), ruled by regional lords, were controlled by the Tokugawa shōgunate. The dual system of shōgunate and emperor continued, with the establishment of the new capital in Edo (Tōkyō) and the political eclipse of Kyōto and Ōsaka. An extremely important transitional period from 1568 to 1603 AD forms a kind of prelude to the Kinsei Period. From 1543, the time of first European contact by the Portugese in Tanegashima, to 1639, when Japan was closed to outside powers excepting China, Korea, and Holland, was almost a century. During that time, there was substantial interaction with Asia and Europe. The brief archaeological discussion below highlights the flourishing commerce of Ōsaka.

Ōsaka after 1615 AD

In 1603 Tokugawa Ieyasu captured Ōsaka Castle. Superior fire power, in the form of cannons purchased from the British East India Company and Dutch Traders, played a decisive role in the Tokugawa victory. The Tokugawa attempted "peaceful routinization", allowing Hideyori, son of Hideyoshi, and his mother, along with a modest force of Toyotomi vassals, to stay on in the gigantic castle. However it became a center of resistance, and Ieyasu moved on the castle with a force of 100,000, whereas Hideyori had 90,000 soldiers (Totman 1993: 52). The castle was destroyed in the summer of 1615 and was reconstructed from 1620 to 1629 AD under the supervision of the Tokugawa government. The walls of the Toyotomi Period were covered with soil and new walls were built on top of them. Some sixty *daimyo* (local lords) of nearby areas such as Shikoku Island were forced to show their loyalty by contributing stone material for the walls. Some huge blocks bear the marks of the individual fiefdoms (Ōsaka Fu Bunkazai Sentā 2013b, 2014), whose contributions of labor and material are said to have drastically reduced their ability to rebel against the Tokugawa (Samurai archives 2015). The castle became the headquarters of the shōgunate's chief local administrator.

Ōsaka Warehouses

Ōsaka was a pre-eminent center for the distribution of all kinds of goods in the Edo Period. Large warehouses (dozō), about 34m long and 7.8m wide, set on stone blocks to raise the floors, lined the many small rivers of the delta. Four examples, three of which date to the eighteenth century, have been excavated. From historical records it is likely that they belonged to groups from Hiroshima, Saga, Takamatsu, and Kumamoto, although this could not be confirmed from the archaeological finds (Ōsaka Fu Bunkazai Kenkyūsho 2014). They were in use until the nineteenth century and were well maintained, leaving few deposits of debris that are so useful to archaeologists.

Sites of the Doshōmachi area

Excavations in the Doshōmachi area show narrow house lots spanning about 100 years from 1615 to the beginning of the eighteenth century. They became increasing dense, with decreasing garden and storage space. Remains of workshops and a fish market, identified by finds of wooden slips bearing fish names in black ink, were found (Minami 2008).

The Sumitomo Copper Refinery

The largest copper refinery in Japan in the Edo Period, the Sumitomo Copper Refinery, has been excavated since the 1990's (Ito 2008, Matsuo 2008b, 2010, Murakami 2008). The site consists of a factory, storage areas, and residences, which occupy a block of land on the Nagahara River. The location permitted water access for supplies and a supply of water for the refinery process. The Sumitomo Refinery used the Nanban Fuki Technique, by which an alloy of unrefined copper and lead is first formed; it contains silver. From this unrefined alloy, an alloy of silver and lead can be extracted at a lower melting temperature than the melting point of pure copper. The silver and lead can subsequently be separated. This technique allowed the Japanese to produce pure copper and silver themselves, whereas previously they had exported unprocessed copper overseas and lost the valuable silver (Sumitomo Group 2014). This foreign technique was mastered by Soga Riuemon, who worked in Sakai near the end of the sixteenth century. Soga passed the control of his business to his son, Tomomichi, who married a daughter of Sumitomo Masatomo and was adopted by the Sumitomo family. He built up a huge business centered on copper refining, importing of silk and financial services. The Shōgunate decreed that all copper intended for export must be silver free and processed at a single location in Ōsaka (Sumitomo Corporation News 1979: 13). By 1691 the company started to operate copper mines in several locations. Production at the Ōsaka site stopped in 1869.

The excavations produced substantial material dating to the seventeenth century and eighteenth centuries, up to the time of a major fire in 1724. Below the layer dating to this fire, a building with its own subterranean vault, 2.4 m north/south and 3.8 m east/west, was discovered. It was used for storing refined metal and important documents. The excavations yielded the largest assemblage of early Qing Period Chinese blue and white ceramics found in Japan, many occurring in identical sets of twenty or more vessels for serving food. Decorated Bizen ceramics were also found. These dishes were used for entertaining Tokugawa and Dutch officials. Some 70 specimens of ingots, as well as other metal debris were found. Analysis of samples from this site showed 99% pure copper with traces of silver and lead (Murakami 2008).

In the Kinsei Period Ōsaka flourished as a commercial center. Archaeology of this period, a relatively new field, has made some significant discoveries concerning modern industry and commerce. The continuous development of metal processing from the Kofun to Kinsei Periods was significant for maintaining its industrial pre-eminence.

Chapter 9
Ōsaka's Special Features

What makes the archaeological history of Ōsaka remarkable? A delta and coastal plain, 650km by boat from the Korean Peninsula, became a center of culture for the Japanese Islands for some two millennia. Few other areas show such sustained pre-eminence. How did ancient Ōsaka provide a base for modern Ōsaka? The historian, Miyazaki Ichisada, compared the Inland sea region to the Mediterranean, and Yamato to the Phoenicians. In particular he noted the combination of maritime and montane environments in both regions, providing good supplies of wood and other materials (Ogasawara 1995). Ecological conditions, immigration from the East Asian continent, and a particular entrepreneurial mentality to expand social and economic networks favored the development of Ōsaka.

Large composite villages and small hamlets existed in the Ōsaka region in the Yayoi Period. While it was closely linked to the Nara Basin, its access to the Inland Sea and the delta of the Yodo River system and the Kawachi Lagoon/Lake gave it a distinct advantage. The area became the pre eminent center of Japan in the fifth and sixth centuries AD, when it was the site of the imposing cemeteries of Furuichi and Mozu, the administrative center at Naniwanomiya, and many religious institutions such as Shitennōji and Sumiyoshi Shrine. Its rulers sponsored technological innovation in ceramics, metal working, engineering, and road building. In the Chūsei Period Sakai became a center of international trade and finance, its merchants supporting the growth of high culture and the tea ceremony. In the turbulent second half of the sixteenth century AD, the Ishiyama Honganji was built by a kind of protestant group persecuted by the old Buddhist establishment of Kyōto, and supported by the Ōsaka merchant community, only to be destroyed by the general, Oda Nobunaga. With the building of Ōsaka Castle, the dominance of Ōsaka was achieved, but could not be sustained when the political center was established in Edo (Tōkyō).

In Chapter 2, I outlined the unique topographical features of the Ōsaka region, including the extensive river system, delta, lagoon/lake with an extensive alluvial shoreline, and rich upland forests. The coastal area provided maritime connections to the Inland Sea, the Pacific Ocean, and coastal China while a critical trunk road extended to the Nara Basin.

In addition to its physical attributes, a second factor has been the flow of people and ideas from the East Asian continent. In subsequent chapters archaeological evidence for the role of the role of immigrants, particularly but not exclusively in the Yayoi to Kodai Periods, has been described. Local groups embraced immigrants and foreign ideas in bringing about innovation and change. This sustained, synergistic interaction between local elites and immigrants is a major factor in creating the vitality of Ōsaka. In the twentieth century Ōsaka experienced an inflow of Okinawans, Koreans and Taiwanese through Japan's colonial system. These people have made substantial contributions to the region. In the near future deeper co-operative ties, with continental East Asia under favorable political conditions could revitalize Japan in the twenty first century.

Ōsaka people are often characterized as energetic, proactive, and commercial. Could these traits have a long history predating the rise of Ōsaka merchants in the Kinsei Period (1603 to 1868 AD)? I propose that there is a mentality of entrepreneurship which can be seen in the long term history of Ōsaka.

In Chapter 1 I outlined the ideas of entrepreneurs, networks, and projects. How are these linked? Entrepreneurs create social capital and increase productivity. We see the results of their activity in projects interpreted from archaeological traces. Their activities are embedded in social relations, which are outlined below.

Ōsaka Yayoi Chiefdoms

In the Middle Yayoi Period focal settlements spaced 4 to 5 km apart were centers of relatively self sufficient communes (Fukunaga 2004: 141). Mizoguchi termed them nodal centers, which took on central roles in ritual and interaction, but were not centers of political control. Clans or sodalities (egalitarian clans) had members in several hamlets or parts of focal settlements (Mizoguchi 2013: 85). Local chiefs co-ordinated storage and distribution of crops, bringing together hamlets in co-operative projects such as the development of new rice paddies and the construction of large buildings and wells. They did not construct spatially separated residential compounds or burial facilities for their own use. The repeated building on the same spot of large granaries at sites such as Ikegami Sone was part of a ritual for regenerating the power of the ancestors as well as regenerating rice grains (Mizoguchi 2013: 132). The rituals pertaining to ancestors functioned to reduce conflict, maintain group cohesion and kin networks and stimulate agricultural production. There were few resources or services that could be monopolized to create social inequality except perhaps paddy soil and water; however agricultural villages could be encouraged to increase production as collectives. The splitting of water courses into sub-canals, at sites such as the Ikeshima Fukumanji Site (Chapter 4) promoted communal sharing, rather than monopolization of water (Mizoguchi 2013: 189, 212). There was no overall political control of the Ōsaka Plain or even portions of it.

However this system was not sustained, and in a period of less than a century, from the final stage of Middle Yayoi to the beginning of Late Yayoi, focal settlements were replaced by dispersed small to medium settlements. Most of the communal cemeteries that had been used for a long time were no longer continued, and bronze artifacts that had functioned to maintain social cohesion were no longer used and were buried. It has been proposed that there was a period of inter-village strife in the Late Yayoi Period, as well as a severe earthquake and flooding (Chapter 2).

In the Late Yayoi Period, trade in iron transported from the continent presented entrepreneurial opportunities for leaders who became members of a powerful elite stratum (Fukunaga 2004: 141-145). Yamato elites centered in the Nara Basin distributed mirrors as part of the creation of a federation just before the emergence of the keyhole tombs.

Entrepreneurial activities of Yayoi chiefs included expanding production through communal projects on a scale larger than in other parts of Japan through the construction of granaries and irrigation systems and promoting interaction with immigrant communities to benefit from their expertise. The finding of the sophisticated system of precise stone weights in the Nagahara Site (Chapter 4) sheds light on this process of using continental knowledge. Chiefs also sought out expanding networks for bronze ritual artifacts and lithic raw materials.

Kofun Period Early State

How did Ōsaka elites find opportunities in the political economy of the Kofun Period? There have been many debates about whether Kofun Period society was a paramount chiefdom or early state. Fukunaga (2004) and Hirose (2004c) conclude that the scale of organization required to construct huge tumuli and the wide degree of social conformity which persisted for 350 years required state organization, albeit with a relatively low degree of coercion and limited production, but Fukunaga considers the Kofun Period "state" to be a "theater state" or "galactic polity", loosely organized and without coercive capacity. Mizoguchi (2013) prefers to use the term paramount chiefdom.

At the beginning of the tomb period there was a sudden increase in mound size. In Nara, the Ishizuka Kofun immediately preceding Hashihaka had a length of 90m, while the Hashihaka Kofun had a length of 280m. After the construction of Hashihaka, mound lengths of over 200m became standard for tombs of paramounts. Tombs with similar dimensions, exactly one half, one third, or one sixth of the size of Hashihaka appeared. In addition tomb shape (circular keyhole, square keyhole, circular mound, and square mound), became formalized, and conformity in the use of grave goods became the norm, even though the contents of the assemblages changed frequently, However, Mizoguchi noticed similar "pairs" of tombs almost the same size in the same group and period, and questioned the conclusion that rigid regulation of size was of such great importance (Chapter 5). He thought that within each period and locality there was competition for the top spot, while other writers (Kishimoto 2010a,b) proposed that these 'tomb pairs' were occupied respectively by ritual and military rulers. From the time of the construction of the Hashihaka Kofun, tomb construction was based on kin based voluntary labor according to Mizoguchi (2013: 238-239). Participation fulfilled communal obligations and ensured communal prosperity. Even in the construction of the Middle Kofun Period burial mounds of Furuichi and Mozu, there are few traces of laborers' quarters or work camps, or permanent residences of construction crews, except for traces of workshops for producing paraphernalia such as *haniwa*.

Why did the Kinai region, and the Ōsaka region in particular, rise to prominence in the Kofun Period? Using topological theory Mizoguchi (2012, 2013), proposes that the emergence of his Kinai Core Area occurred because of its location in a system of communication nodes. As indicated above, I believe that it was the result of ecological conditions, historical migrations, and the formation of a particular competitive and entrepreneurial mentality that I have discussed in this book.

Fukunaga (2004) contends that the relations between the central and peripheral polities were not enforced by military means. Therefore the advantage of belonging to this system must have been in the realm of ritual and ideology. Similar conclusions about the significance of ritual and ideology were reached by Barnes (2007: 2014), but she differs from other writers in proposing that Queen Himiko used Daoist concepts to create a very particular ideology. If the principles of creating alliances were ritual rather than military, does this mean that the massive iron cuirasses buried in Middle Kofun burial mounds were for display and not for a standing army as contended by Tanaka (2010)? Variability in regional burial assemblages indicates weak powers of coercion by the center; there were regions where conformity to the burial ritual was not strict.

Characteristics of Kofun Period tomb construction were visibility, conformity, and hierarchy (Hirose 2004b: 253). He proposed that the deceased ruler became divine, the guardian of the communal group, as anthropologists have proposed for conical clans. In my opinion the construction of monumental mounds anywhere in the world is an example of unproductive entrepreneurship, a kind of negative aggrandizement common in history, in which millions of hours of labor and material are taken out of the economy and stored in mounds of earth. If the function of mound building was to create social solidarity, it seems that the circulation of prestige goods would be just as effective and less expensive. Not all of the entrepreneurial activities of the Middle Kofun Period led to greater efficiency, new services, or refinement of technology or learning. The prestige distribution system in Japan evolved from religious objects to ceremonial weapons, some of which were ceremonial but still celebrated warfare. For some reason violence and massive monument building emerges in various parts of the world as confederacies change into states and demagogues take over. Prestige goods are no longer enough to maintain centralized control. Perhaps it is necessary to bury the excess energy created in state formation, sometimes called surplus, because leaders are self centered and not creative enough to convert it into humanitarian projects directed to the common good, such as public religious structures, hospitals, schools, roads, and bridges. The fact that these mounds are part of the modern Japanese imperial cult means that they continue to drain energy from the political economy through the need for maintenance coupled with denial of public access.

In the second half of the Early Kofun Period there was a shift in the social identity of the chief from that of "the representative of the community's destiny to that of a powerful figure executing the will of the community by commanding its members" (Mizoguchi 2013: 261). According to Mizoguchi the custom of enclosing the top of the mound with a row of *haniwa* coincides with the disappearance of archaeological traces of mass feasting, and the exclusion of commoners from the mortuary rituals of the dead chief (Mizoguchi 2013: 265).

In the Late Kofun Period "the clan elite were no longer acting as representatives of the communal well being" (Mizoguchi 2013: 305) but ruled the community that by now was internally segmented into lineages or households, competing for favors from the ruling elite. As mentioned in Chapter 5, there is evidence that rulership was divided into ritual and military functions, a feature of later Japanese society.

Elites of the Kofun Period participated in iron exchange, promoting the local production of iron artifacts. They sponsored new technologies through links to immigrant communities.

The Yamato State and Naniwanomiya

The Naniwa area of Ōsaka functioned as the capital of the Yamato state for short periods in the seventh and eighth centuries AD. In the late eighth century the administrative center moved inland to Nagaoka, and subsequently to Kyōto. Roof tiles posts and beams were dismantled from the Late Naniwa Palace and were transported to Nagaoka for re-use (Van Goethem 2008, 114). Nevertheless, Naniwa retained its significance as a commercial and religious center, with substantial elite communities who fled political upheaval on the continent. Port facilities, temples, estates, and shrines were all situated in the river delta. The role of the Naniwa area as a maritime gateway was indispensable. Entrepreneurial activities include the construction of roads and port facilities, and improvement of agricultural infrastructure. The initiatives of sending tributary missions to China (*kentōshi*) promoted local prosperity through government spending. At the end of the Kodai Period Naniwa continued to be an important area for religious pilgrimages to the Kumano region.

Chūsei Period

In the Chūsei Period, manors or estates flourished in various parts of the Ōsaka region. Manors are an aspect of state organization in which powerful groups seek exemption from taxation in exchange for the support of the central authority. In the Kodai Period, it appears that local economic self sufficiency of manors may have led to a reduction in specialization and exchange. However, in the Chūsei Period, as commercial activity increased, their self sufficiency decreased and estate overseers assumed the role of traders of commodities such as ceramics and textiles. Coinage, some of which was produced in Sakai, was used in transactions. Trade with China brought ceramics, medicines, and books. The political economy of the Chūsei Period features a weak political center influenced by warriors, merchants, and very powerful temples. The Sakai elite made use of this fluid configuration, financing temples and managing official overseas trade.

The growth of markets was particularly important. In mediaeval times seasonal markets were often held in central places at regular intervals. The markets were places of retail and wholesale exchange and served as important locations for religious activities and all kinds of entertainment. They were usually sponsored by temples and shrines, and provided a means of economic innovation and economic expansion for retainers attached to the religious institutions. Vendors and peddlers may appear to have had limited economic power but as Braudel

(1982: 122) points out, they often were members of complex networks with considerable financial backing. According to Braudel, in mediaeval Europe shops grew out of markets, as permanent, specialized places for the purchase of staples and manufactured goods, often on credit (1982: 68).

The merchants of Sakai were the ultimate Ōsaka entrepreneurs. Despite the fact that Sakai lacked a deep water port, they took advantage of their location to develop a route to the Pacific coast of Shikoku, Satsuma, Ryūkyū, Fujian, and Southeast Asia, including Manila and Hoi An, where they established trading communities (Hirai 1988, Kikuchi 2003). They were able to convert their financial wealth into cultural capital by sponsoring the development of the tea ceremony and associated arts. A substantial proportion of its wealth was derived from military provisioning. While other ports in mediaeval Japan were highly developed, Sakai's international role was rivaled only by Hakata in Kyūshū. Religious institutions in the Sakai area sponsored all kinds of artistic and cultural production as well as overseas trade. They sponsored festivals and markets and functioned as effective nodes in commercial networks. The relationship between religious institutions and merchants is a topic to which archaeology can make important contributions in the future, through the detailed study of trade goods in temple and commercial sites.

The nature of the Ishiyama Honganji religious complex is not well known from archaeological evidence because of its rapid and total destruction and the building of Ōsaka Castle on the site. It is known that it attracted many followers and stimulated the growth of a substantial merchant quarter.

Ōsaka Castle Town

Another form of urban center surrounds a mediaeval castle. The commercial quarter was similar to those of other towns and cities; however the administrative area of officials was distinctive. Destructive personal competition and aggrandizement drained resources from economic expansion and the led to the rise of military leaders who centralized power and administration. Warehouse and production sites show the rise of a commercial center for redistribution different in scale from the warehouse site of the fifth century AD.

Japanese history is often seen as disjointed through rupture, with the appearance of new groups and cultural systems. By examining one region over a long span of time I hope I have shown important continuities. Through the notion of entrepreneurship I have attempted to give Ōsaka's archaeological history some relevance to the study of modern Ōsaka.

In 2010 Ōsaka became the center of the Kansai Innovative Comprehensive Global Strategic Special Zone, and in May 2014 it became a National Strategic Special Zone. These zones are given generous tax incentives, reductions in red tape, and stimulation in international competitiveness and cooperation. *Nature* magazine reported that Ōsaka represents the largest and densest science cluster in Japan (Nature 2014). The article featured a section on 'building innovation on tradition', mentioning that the merchants of the Doshōmachi and their warehouses, some of which specialized in domestic and imported herbs in the Tokugawa Period. The approach of long term history and mentality employed in this book provides important context for this recent development.

Appendix A
Site Descriptions

1. Ikegami Sone Site

Ikegami Sone is one of the most important sites in Japan. In its largest manifestation at the height of its prosperity it was the fifth largest moated Yayoi site discovered thus far (Yoshifusa 2001: 191), and it contained the largest Yayoi structure in the Ōsaka region. It underwent extensive excavation in wide areas, which permitted comprehensive interpretation, and was the subject of a vigorous campaign to preserve the site and construct a unique museum devoted to Yayoi Culture, The Ōsaka Prefectural Museum of Yayoi Culture. Although there are many imposing Yayoi sites in the Ōsaka Region, such as Uriūdō, Uriwari, Kamei, Higashi Nara, Kitoragawa, and Ikeshima Fukumanji, each the subject of many excavation reports. I deal intensively with only this one site, as an example. Although moated village sites are found from Kyūshū to the Kantō area their number is small compared to the total number of Yayoi villages.

The site is located on an old marine terrace, 8.5 to 13m above sea level. Two large and important Yayoi Period sites are located about 5km distant; the Yotsuike Site to the north, and the Kishiwada Einoike Site to the south. Upland sites such as the Late Yayoi Period Kannonjiyama, Izumi City, are found on the slope to the east (Ikegami Sone Shiseki 1996: 18). Occupied over a span of 500 years from Yayoi Periods I to V, the area of the Ikegami Sone Site varied in area from period to period, and occupations were partially overlapping. In Akiyama's descriptions (2006: 27) Early Yayoi is equivalent to Yayoi I, Middle Yayoi to Periods II to IV, and Late Yayoi, to Period V. Sites in the immediate vicinity are shown in Figure A.1 while other sites mentioned in the text are shown in Figure A.2.

In Yayoi Period I the area of the site was 30,000m², including limited adjacent paddy. Inui (2006) estimates the maximum population was 1000 persons at the time of its largest population in Yayoi IV. The actual area of the site is debated: however Takesue et al (2011: 314) consider that its maximum area in Yayoi IV was 81,000,m². Although the site was occupied continuously from the latter half of the Early Yayoi Period, the nature of the occupation changed from period to period. In the Early Yayoi Period villagers began to build a ditch surrounding an area 270m NS and 160m EW. This ditch was filled in the early part of the Middle Yayoi Period. An outer ditch about 5m wide but only 20cm deep seems to have served as a boundary between the burial area and the

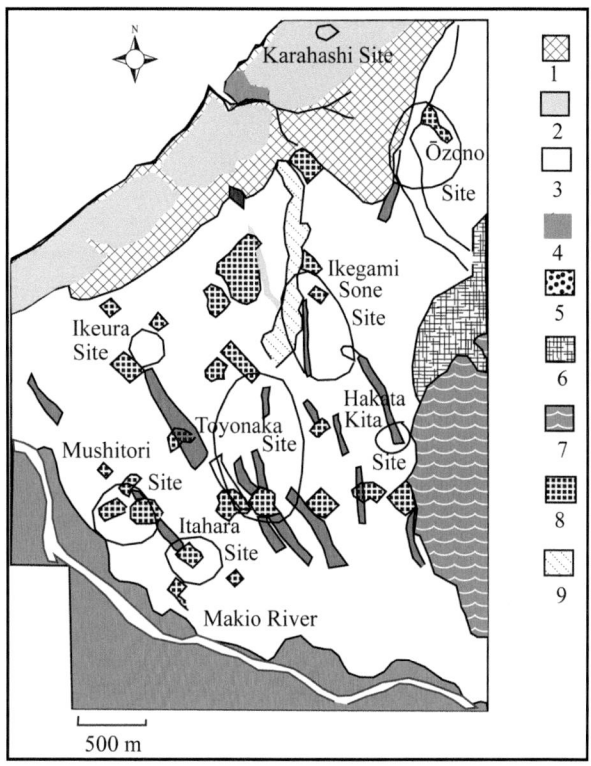

FIGURE A.1. THE IKEGAMI SONE SITE AND SURROUNDING SITES OF THE MIDDLE YAYOI PERIOD. REDRAWN FROM ISHIGAMI 1985, 15. (1) MARSH, SHORELINE. (2) SAND BAR. (3) ALLUVIAL FAN WITH NATURAL TERRACING. (4) FLOOD PLAIN. (5) FAN AREA. (6) SLOPE, NATURAL TERRACE. (7) OLD RIVER COURSE. (8) RECENT RESERVOIR. (9) NATURAL LEVEE. COURTESY OF KUBOSŌ KINEN BIJUTSUKAN.

living area. Outside the ditch, to the SE, were 23 moated burial precincts (*hōkei shūkōbo*), all about the same size, in more than 4 groups, containing a total of 160 burials. About 130m inside the outer ditch there were several ditches of different periods, which were successively filled in. Other parallel ditches have also been recovered but they have not been completely excavated. It appears that boundary ditches were dug as the site expanded and contracted but they were for spatial demarcation rather than defence. The ditches were shallow compared to some defensive ditches excavated in Kyūshū, which were as deep as 5m. In the Late Period, the site appears to have been occupied by several spatially separate groups, but its total size decreased (Akiyama 2006: 28). Only about 15% of the total length of the 1000m of the main ditch has been excavated, leaving many questions (Ishigami 1985: 12).

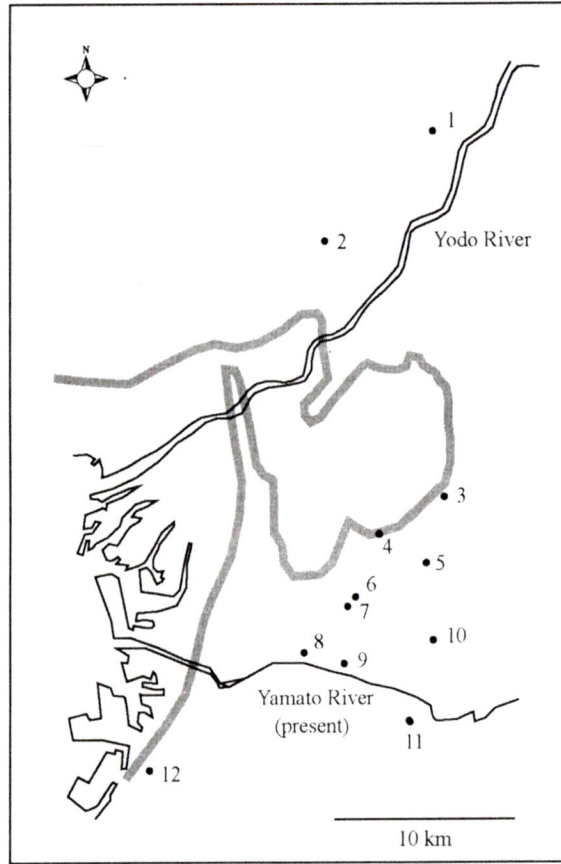

FIGURE A.2. YAYOI PERIOD SITES MENTIONED IN THE TEXT. THE PRESENT SHORELINE OF ŌSAKA BAY, CONSISTING OF HUGE AREAS OF LANDFILL, IS INDICATED, WHILE THE THICK GREY LINE SHOWS THE SHORELINE OF THE EARLY YAYOI PERIOD. (1) AMA. (2) HIGASHI NARA. (3) KITORAGAWA. (4) URIŪDŌ. (5) IKESHIMA FUKUMANJI. (6) KYŪHŌJI. (7) KAMEI. (8) URIWARI. (9) NAGAHARA. (10) ONCHI. (11) HAJINOSATO. (12) YOTSUIKE.

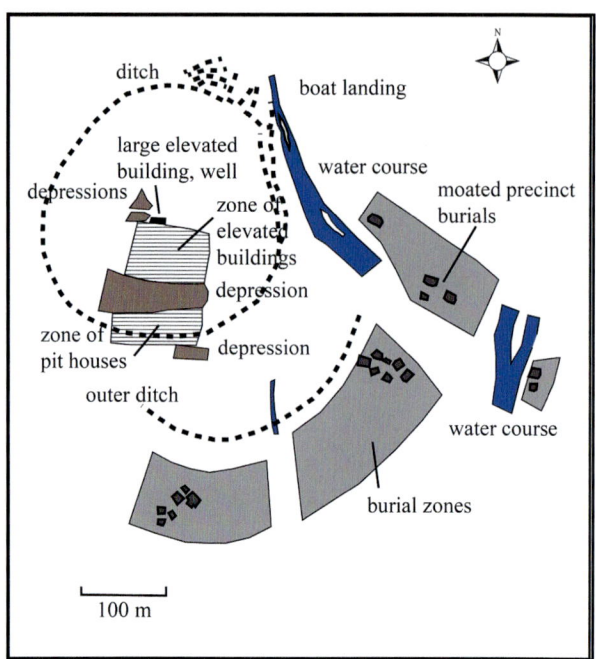

FIGURE A.3. PLAN OF IKEGAMI SONE SITE, SHOWING FEATURES DATING TO THE LATTER HALF OF THE MIDDLE YAYOI. ADAPTED FROM AKIYAMA 2006: 30. COURTESY OF SHINSENSHA PUBLISHERS.

Architectural features in the central area of the site include a large shallow well and a very large central building (Figure A.3). The well is located on the south side of the building in front of the mid point on the building's longitudinal axis. The wall of the well was fashioned from a single trunk of camphor tree (*Cinnamomum camphora*) (Jap. *kusunoki*) with a diameter 1.8 to 1.9m. It appears to have been hollowed with an iron adze judging from the gouge marks on the inner surface (Ikegami Sone Shiseki 1996: 30). At the time of the excavation the water table was about 50-60cm from the surface. The well was filled in, the fill containing what appear to be discarded wooden artifacts, but it is possible that some were religious offerings. Several round post holes were found near the well indicating that it may have been protected by a roof. Pottery sherds from Early to Middle Yayoi were found scattered in the area, and a deliberately buried group of vessels with distinct shape and color were also found. There were also areas of burned soil. Three pits in a line, filled with several hundred sanukite flakes were found;

one of these pits also contained a polished stone adze and red ocher. Another pit contained a polished beveled adze and a cylindrical polished stone object. In addition, a group of five pits containing narrow neck and wide mouth jars were found immediately south of the well, and in a few locations 100m further south. These pits are dated to Yayoi Period IV, the end of the Middle Yayoi Period. The excavators propose that these pits may contain vessels buried after ceremonies connected with the well (Ikegami Sone Shiseki 1996: 30-34). Pits containing whetstones for sharpening reaping knives and jars for trapping octopus (Jap. *takotsubo*), as well as large pottery vessels were also recovered.

Five stages of rebuilding of the large structure were ascertained by stratigraphic analysis of the post holes. These stages have been designated D, A, B, C, and I, with I being the latest. Their estimated floor areas were 55m^2, 87m^2, 109m^2, 52m^2, and 57m^2. Their orientation varied from NW/SE, to E/W. A post hole from Building I has been dated by tree ring dating to 52 BC, and by AMS dating to 60 ± 20 BC (Akiyama 2001, 2007: 553, 567-569). Pottery found in the post hole belongs to Yayoi Period IV, usually dated to the first century AD, but probably earlier by a century (Yoshifusa 2001: 177). The posts were about 60cm in diameter. According to Yoshifusa only about 59 years elapsed from the time of the first building to the final construction. Separate single post holes at each end of the structure are thought to indicate posts that were independent of the structure, running from the ground to the ridge pole. It seems

FIGURE A.4. THE LARGE CENTRAL BUILDING OF THE IKEGAMI SONE SITE, NOVEMBER 2013. R. PEARSON PHOTOGRAPH.

likely that these were symbolic rather than weight bearing (Akiyama 2007: 415-416). A jade curved bead (*magatama*) was recovered in the post hole of the west post. These posts can be seen on the main structures of the Grand Shrine of Ise, said to be exact copies of Late Kofun or Early Kodai Period buildings.

What were the actual appearance and function of this structure? It is often termed *shinden* (temple or shrine). Figure A.4 is a recent photograph of the full size reconstruction of the building on the site.

The actual shape of the building beyond the floor plan is conjectural since only post holes were found. In some reconstructions it is similar to the conjectural reconstruction of the storehouses at Hōenzaka, Ōsaka (see Chapter 5) or the eighth century AD storehouse of the Shosōin, Nara, while in others it is based on representations on Yayoi bronze bells and pottery (Akiyama 2006: 418).

An area some 35 m SSW of the large well and of the same general time period as the large building yielded a few mold fragments for bronze *dōtaku*, areas of burned soil, and what appear to be fragments of the burnt clay walls of furnaces. It is thought to be a bronze casting area. However not all archaeologists have agreed on the extent or time period of the metal working and debate continues about the existence of a separate group of metal casting specialists (Akiyama 2007: 535).

2. Tsudō Shiroyama Kofun

This was the first very large tomb to be built in the Furuichi Group (Ōsaka Furitsu Chikatsu Asuka Hakubutsukan 2006: 41-42). It dates from the late Early Kofun or early Middle Kofun Period (late fourth century AD). It is 208m long and is double moated, the encircling ridge between the two moats being 270m x 190m. In 1912, from the rear round portion, a vertical stone chamber containing a chest-shaped (*nagamochigata*) stone coffin with a special decoration resembling the plates of a tortoise shell, a total of eight (Ichinose et al 2008: 191) or nine (Tanaka 2001: 86) mirrors of several types (deities and beasts, dragons and tigers), bronze whorl decorations (*tomoegata*) and jasper wheel shape bracelets (*sharinseki*) were found. Tsudō Shiroyama is a key site, since it exemplifies the beginning of the Kawachi Dynasty. The Kawachi burials have a particular set of features, derived from Saki and Umami but with new traits. These include the chest-shaped stone coffin, cuirass armor as a grave good, construction of a double moat, and the use of waterbird *haniwa*, and other large *haniwa* forms such as quivers, that must be associated with specific rituals. In general, an enclosure bounded by cylindrical (*entō*) *haniwa* defined the summit of the rear mound in the Early Kofun Period, but later they were placed on additional terraces, in combination with house shaped *haniwa*. In the Middle Kofun Period they were placed on the front rectangular mound and on the various perimeters (Teramura 2004, Fuchinokami 2005).

FIGURE A.5. THE KONDA GOBYŌYAMA KEYHOLE SHAPE TOMB (ZENPOKOENFUN) OF THE FURUICHI TOMB GROUP. FROM ŌSAKA FURITSU CHIKATSU ASUKA HAKUBUTSUKAN 2006: 15. COURTESY OF ŌSAKA FURITSU CHIKATSU ASUKA HAKUBUTSUKAN.

3. Konda Gobyōyama Kofun

This burial mound thought to be Ōjin's tomb is the largest in Japan, not by length but by volume and area. It is thought to belong to Chin, the second Wa king mentioned in the *Song Shu* annals. He was the second king buried in the Furuichi Tomb Group. The only way to date the tomb at present is through the contents of satellite tombs or the *haniwa* chronology (Ōsaka Furitsu Chikatsu Asuka Hakubutsukan 2006: 45-49). Located in the middle of the Furuichi group, the entire mound is stepped in three tiers. The total length of the mound is 415m, width of front portion 300m, height of front square mound 36m, diameter of rear round portion 250m, height of the rear mound portion 35m, and total length including moats and separating ridges 700m (Figure A.5). The two outer ridges between the moats were covered with stone paving and rows of tubular *haniwa*. Objects in the Konda Hachiman Shrine on the north side of the rear mound reputedly found in this tomb include a chest shaped stone coffin and a stone slab from the ceiling of a vertical chamber. However the main portions of the tomb remain unexcavated.

From historical sources, Ōjin should have lived in the latter part of the fourth century, the first year of Ōjin's reign being probably 390 AD. The postulated date of the tomb, based on *sueki* and *haniwa* chronologies, seems to date to the early fifth century (Ōsaka Furitsu Chikatsu 2006: 44). From this tomb there is no report of grey stoneware (*sueki*) from inside the mound, but from the outer ridge between the moats, *sueki* seems to be TK 73 type (Ōsaka Furitsu Chikatsu Asuka Hakubutsukan 2006: 111-112). Absolute dating of TK73 type has been achieved from Heijō Palace where wood from a low layer, in Feature 6030, has been tree ring dated to 412 A.D. Therefore the dating is compatible with the available historical information concerning Ōjin. The nearby Konda Hachiman Shrine, recorded in documents by the eleventh century, was established specifically to honor Ōjin. This old association lends credence to the belief that this tomb is in fact his final resting place (Shiraishi 2011: 14)

A wealth of *haniwa* has been found, including tubular, morning glory, parasol, shield, saddle, house, water bird types, as well as earthenware fish and cuttlefish, Furu type narrow neck jars, *haji* wares, earliest types of *sueki*, wooden hoes, and wooden umbrella like objects about 1 m in diameter. In the 1980's archaeologists found a *haniwa* workshop nearby while working in a nearby river bed (Ichinose et al 2008: 194). The *entō* (tubular) *haniwa* do not have black specks on the outer surface, indicating that they were not fired outside but in an enclosed kiln (Ōsaka Furitsu Chikatsu Asuka Hakubutsukan 2006: 110-111). They must have been made in the early fifth century when

It has been estimated that this tomb took about 15 years to complete, the entire mausoleum probably being completed around the middle of the fifth century AD (Ōsaka Furitsu Chikatsu 2006:110). After the interment the *haniwa* were placed around the tomb.

Excavation in 1983 and ground-penetrating radar survey in 1991 yielded evidence of two rectangular mounds, set like islands in the interior moat, in front of the rectangular portion of the mound, to the left and right of the center longitudinal axis. The east mound was roughly 17m square (Ichinose et al 2008: 191). In addition, aerial laser photography on the Furuichi and Mozu Tomb Groups, undertaken as part of their documentation for their nomination as World Heritage Sites, revealed a rectangular mound on the top of the distal end of the front portion of the mound, while a circular mound was found in a similar location on the Kami Ishitsu Misanzai Tomb of the Mozu Group. The function of these mounds, unknown previously, is not known (Miki 2013). Konda Gobyōyama is surrounded by five satellite mounds. There are two square mounds on both the east and the west sides and a circular mound, Konda Maruyama, to the north (see Figure 5.16).

4. Minegatsuka Kofun

This mound was excavated in the late 1980's in preparation for a historical park (Habikino Shi 1993). It is thought to be of royal class because of its large size and double moat. The total mound length is 96m, while the rear mound portion is 56m in diameter and the width of the front rectangular portion is 74.4m. Ground penetrating radar revealed a vertical stone burial chamber in the center of the rear round mound and the double moat. A second burial was added to the vertical stone chamber by removing the chamber roof. Around the coffin, inside the stone chamber, there were grave offerings in wooden boxes. They included a sword with silver pommel, at least 15 other swords, silver ornaments, 500 glass beads and 560 gilt bronze floral ornaments. There is a possibility that this burial chamber is not the locus of the main burial that could be deeper than this chamber, with a horizontal entrance that has been covered over (Habikino Shi 1993: 83). In this case, the grave offerings for the main personage may be in an undiscovered separate chamber.

The construction of the tomb is estimated to have required 6 years of seasonal labour, with 765 persons working 60 days each year, or 1150 persons working for 3 months each year (Habikino Shi 1993: 80). While Minegatsuka is not very large, it gives a rare glimpse of a burial of a high elite person thought to have royal status. The arrangement of the grave goods shows some similarities to the minor burials of the Daisen Ryō Kofun mentioned below. Although the site has been protected

FIGURE A.6. WATERBIRD HANIWA FROM THE MOAT OF THE KONDA GOBYŌYAMA KOFUN, FURUICHI TOMB GROUP, FIFTH CENTURY AD. TOKYO NATIONAL MUSEUM. COURTESY OF TNM IMAGE ARCHIVES.

new methods of firing *sueki* were in use, using the tunnel kiln which came from the Korean peninsula. Waterbird *haniwa* were found in the surrounding ditches of this tomb (Figure A.6). According to the Imperial Household Agency (Kunaicho), in the Meiji Period, during the dredging of the moat, many examples were found; some are in the Tōkyō National Museum. There are two size groups about 40 cm and 60 cm high. Some specimens in Gakushuin University, donated by the Kunaicho before the Second World War, came from the tomb around 1899. They were also recovered from the Tsudō Shiroyama and Suyama Tombs. From their occurrence they seem to be associated with royal class tombs. In the case of the Suyama Kofun there are other *haniwa* such as house, fence, shield, and parasol (*kinugasa*) types. The diversity of forms suggests that the *haniwa* around this tomb were placed in a complex arrangement. On the ridge between the ditches there were cylindrical, parasol shape, and other kinds of representative *haniwa*. Three fragments of wooden chairs or seats were also recovered (Ōsaka Furitsu Chikatsu Asuka Hakubutsukan 2006: 116).

Figure A.7. The Daisen Ryō Kofun (upper) and Kami Ishitsu Misanzai keyhole shape tombs (zenpokoenfun), of the Mozu Tomb Group. Fifth century AD. The total length of the Daisen Ryō Kofun is 850 m. From Ōsaka Furitsu Chikatsu Asuka Hakubutsukan 2006: 86). Courtesy of Ōsaka Furitsu Chikatsu Asuka Hakubutsukan and Sakai Shi Hakubutsukan.

from commercial development or obliteration since 1974, it is not designated as an imperial tomb.

5. Chino'oka Kofun

This tomb lies on the southwest edge of the Mozu Tomb Group, near the coast. Judging from the *entō haniwa*, it is dated to Period II. This is the earliest dated tomb in the Mozu Tomb group. While it is registered as a National Historic Site, it is not designated as an imperial tomb under the control of the Imperial Household Ministry. It has a *zenpōkōenfun* shape, with three steps and a reconstructed total length of 155m. An excavation in 1972 of the rear portion revealed a clay covered *nagamochi* type coffin of Izumi sandstone. From the top of the clay covering, the following were recovered; three hoe shape bracelets, 18 *sharinseki*, and one bracelet of unknown form. There may have been other artifacts in the clay. In the grave fill. fragments of congealed tuff, different from the stone material of the *nagamochi* type coffin, were recovered, suggesting that there may be more stone coffin burials in the mound (Ichinose et al 2008: 206).

6. Daisen Ryō Kofun

The actual length of the *zenpōkōenfun* is 512 m while the total length, including the triple moat, is 840m (Figures A.7, A.8)

This is Japan's longest tomb, if the triple moat is included. The proportions conform to those of Tsudō Shiroyama. The sides of the tomb were shaped into three steps, and the slopes were faced with stone. The terraces and summit were lined with *haniwa* of clay and wood, and the tomb was surrounded by a triple moat. An enormous amount of co ordinated labor must have been required not only to construct the burial mound, but also to manufacture some 30,000 *haniwa* including human, horse, dog, water bird, and parasol. According to Tsude (2000: 2) the Daisen Ryō Kofun contains 1.400,000 cubic meters of fill. Assuming that in 1 day one person can move about 1 cu m, the hauling of the fill would take 1,400,000 man days. In addition, the tomb was covered with flat paving stones, the installation of which would have required abundant additional labor. If 2,000 people

APPENDIX A

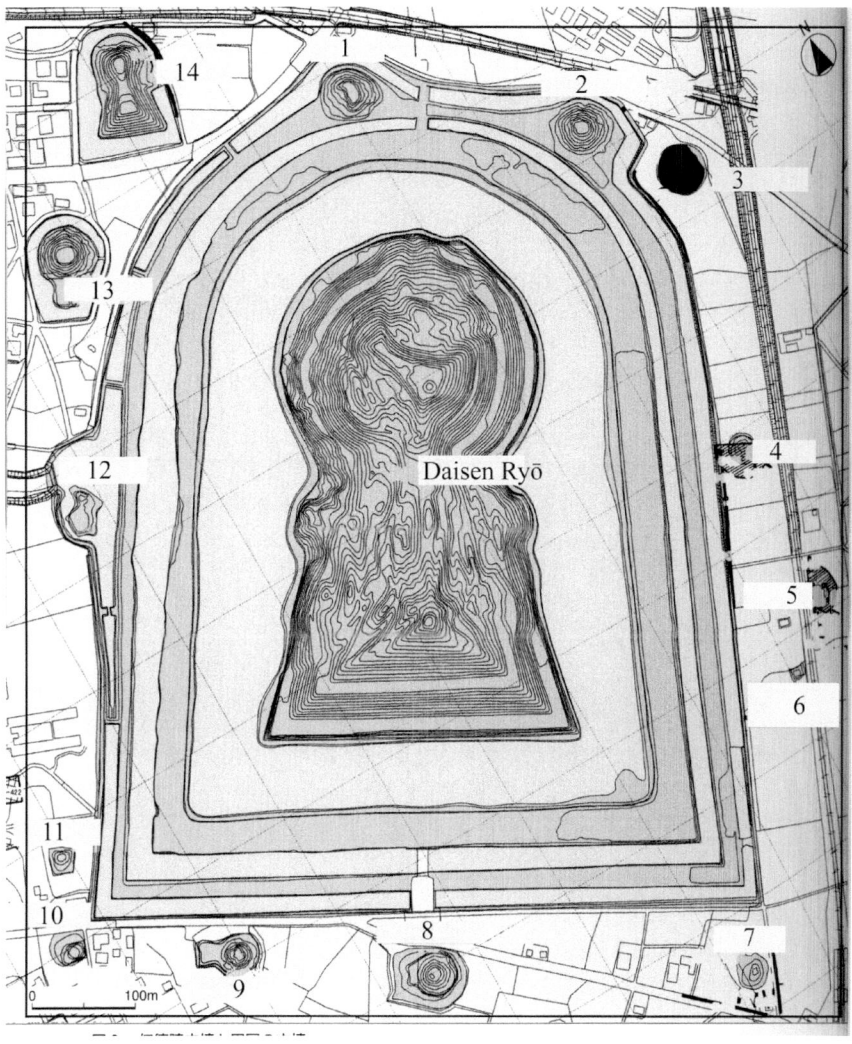

Figure A.8. Daisen Ryō Kofun. Total length of the mound is 512 m, and total length of the site with moats and ridges is 512 m. Surrounding (satellite) tombs. (1) Chayama. (2) Dai'anjiyama. (3) Gen'eimon. (4) Tsukamawari. (5) Kagamiyama. (6) Mozu Yugumo. (7) Shūzuka (8) Magodaiyūyama. (9) Ryūsayama. (10) Kitsuneyama. (11) Dōkameyama. (12) Hinotani. (13) Marukōyama. (14) Nagayama. From Ichinose 2009: 7. Based on data from Hirose and Togawa 2008:165-166. Courtesy of Shinsensha Publishers.

worked daily it would take 16 years to complete the construction of the mound. This estimate is similar to the estimate cited above, for the Konda Gobyōyama Kofun.

There are varying opinions on the date of construction of tomb, as well as the identity of its occupant (Fujii and Kasai 1987: 296-297). One opinion is that the front square part and the objects from the tomb date to the late fifth or early sixth century, and the tomb does not belong to Nintoku. Another opinion is that the front square part of the tomb is substantially earlier, and could belong to the time of Nintoku, thought to be about 430, AD if he is Chin in the *Song Shu*.

Two burials are known. In 1757 AD a stone chamber in the circular rear mound was exposed, probably because of erosion or collapse of the mound fill. There is a description of its discovery in the Edo Period by Arai Hakuseki, an important scholar of Japan's imperial history (Asao et al 1999: 42). In 1872 objects were found when part of the front portion of the mound was eroded. A vertical stone chamber 3.6 to 3.9m long and 2.4m wide, made of river boulders, was roofed with three large stone slabs. Inside the chamber was a *nagamochi* type stone coffin, made of assembled interlocking pieces. The lid was decorated with carved inset rectangles, in turtle shell fashion. The same kind of *nagamochi* type stone coffin was found in the Tsudō Shiroyama Kofun described above. The lid is convex, of the so-called *kamaboko* type. Its material is rhyolitic tuff, from Hyogo Prefecture (Ichinose 2009: 13). Around the coffin were a shield, cup, glass plate, and sword fittings for a broad sword. The shield had copper and iron plates (Asao et al 1999: 42).

Morishita (2009: 25) describes a small collection of artifacts held by the Boston Museum of Fine Arts, consisting of a bronze mirror, a pommel of a sword, two small bronze horse bells and a bronze triple jingle bell. They are said to have come from the Daisen Ryō Kofun but are probably from the smaller associated tombs (Ichinose 2009: 25). The mirror is a Japanese copy of a Chinese Han Dynasty mirror from the mid first century AD, which circulated in Japan from the latter half of the Middle Kofun to the Late Kofun. This type of mirror is numerous, and all examples are identical, being made from a common mold; examples have been found in the Eta Funayama Kofun, Kumamoto Prefecture, Fujinoki Kofun Nara Prefecture, and Inariyama Kofun, Saitama Prefecture. An example was also found in the Tomb of Muryong Wang of Paekche, in Kongju, Korea. These are all tombs of the top level of regional leaders. Morishita (2007) noted that according to Kobayashi Yukio (1961, 1976), they were made in the Southern Dynasty, China, and presented to the Five Kings of Wa. They were used in international relations in East Asia in the fifth and sixth centuries and their distribution within Japan indicates the large area of the islands connected by close political alliances.

A portion of the upper half of the rear mound collapsed in an earthquake in 1399 AD. The section where the collapse occurred was apparently incomplete at the time of construction; therefore it is possible that the *kofun* may have never been completely finished. In a report of the Imperial Household Ministry (Kunaicho) of 2001, it was reported that the west side of the front mound also collapsed, leaving a pile of debris 12m in diameter. It appears that the two front corners were marked with low stone walls, not seen on other *kofun* (Ichinose 2009: 42).

As noted above, many of the Kawachi tombs are copies of each other, at different scales. If the Daisen Ryō Kofun is reduced to 90%, it resembles Konda Gobyōyama Kofun perfectly. If Konda Gobyōyama Kofun is reduced to 93% it is a copy of Kami Ishitzu Misanzai Kofun. The proportions of these tombs are based on the Umami tombs in Nara Prefecture (Ichinose 2009: 48).

In recent research on the Daisen Ryō Kofun, scholars have concluded that the number of *entō* (cylindrical) *haniwa* required was 24,275, with the total estimated to be 30,000, including human, horse, dog, water bird, and parasol forms (Ichinose 2009: 61-81). Undocumented finds presumably from the moats include a human *haniwa* of a shamaness (*mikō*), thought to be the oldest known anthropomorphic *haniwa* in Japan, as well as also fragment of a foot. They may have been part of a *haniwa* arrangement placed at the outer edge of the *kofun*. Remains of *haniwa* have been found in many areas of the outer slopes. All of them lack the black specks in the paste, showing that they were fired in kilns. *Haniwa* were finished by wiping or shaving in regular and sometimes elaborate patterns, using a small slat of regularly grained wood of cypress (*Cryptomeria*) which left striations which match the grain of the individual piece of wood, enabling the detailed matching of patterns on different objects (archaeology.jp. 2014b). There are similarities in the methods of finishing between the *haniwa* in the Daisen Ryō Kofun and those from Konda Gobyōyama, showing that the products from the latter were used as prototypes. The *entō haniwa* from the Daisen Ryō Kofun are smaller than those from the Konda Gobyōyama Kofun, perhaps to accommodate their firing in chamber (*anagama*) kilns. Many of the techniques used in the construction and decoration of the Daisen Ryō Kofun were subsequently followed in other parts of Japan, and seem to have been learned from Kawachi; it served as a center of technical expertise, stimulated by continental migrants. Very large *sueki* jars set on the tomb surface were status symbols. These jars are 62cm high, the mouth is 36cm in diameter, and the body is 62 cm in diameter. The outer surface was beaten and then wiped. An example recovered from the surface of the east side of the mound is dated typologically to the second quarter of the fifth century AD (Ichinose 2009: 74). Surrounding the Daisen Ryō Kofun are 10 satellite mounds, most of which are round or scallop shape, distinctive in form from the satellite mounds of the Konda Gobyōyama Kofun (see Figures A.5, A.9). In the latter case the predominant form is square.

7. Ōtsukayama Kofun

This three-stepped *zenpōkōen* tomb is 168m long; it has a surrounding ditch and on the circular rear portion there is a rectangular area outlined by cylindrical *haniwa* (Fujii and Kasai 1987: 297). It was excavated in 1953. In the round rear portion three burials were recovered, and in the northern part one burial was found in a *nendokaku* wooden coffin set in clay, along with helmets and cuirasses. In the front portion four wooden coffins covered with clay were found, with armour, daggers and swords. The *haniwa* belong to Period II. Beginning in 1949, the mound was gradually demolished for housing construction, the last portion being completely destroyed in 1985 (Ichinose et al 2008: 206).

8. Kurohimeyama Kofun

This *zenpōkōen* tomb is located between the Mozu and Furuichi Tomb Groups. Its present total length is 114m. In addition there were possibly two surrounding moats, now destroyed, that would have added to its length. An excavation was undertaken in 1953; however, the nature of the burial in the summit of the rear mound is not clear. There may have been a vertical chamber with a tuff coffin carved from a single block of congealed tuff, since roof slabs of the same material from a vertical chamber are kept in a nearby shrine along with fragments of iron cuirass, stone spindle whorls, and sherds of *sueki*. They must have come from a chamber in this mound. Judging from the typology of the armor, it must have been part of a votive offering post-dating the chamber (Ichinose et al 2008: 220).

In a position somewhat below the summit of the front mound, a vertical chamber roofed by eight slabs of flat stone was found. The chamber was 4.03m long, 0.83m wide, and 1m high. It contained a huge deposit of armor and weapons including 24 iron cuirasses, 24 helmets, 14 single edge swords 10 double edge swords, 56 iron

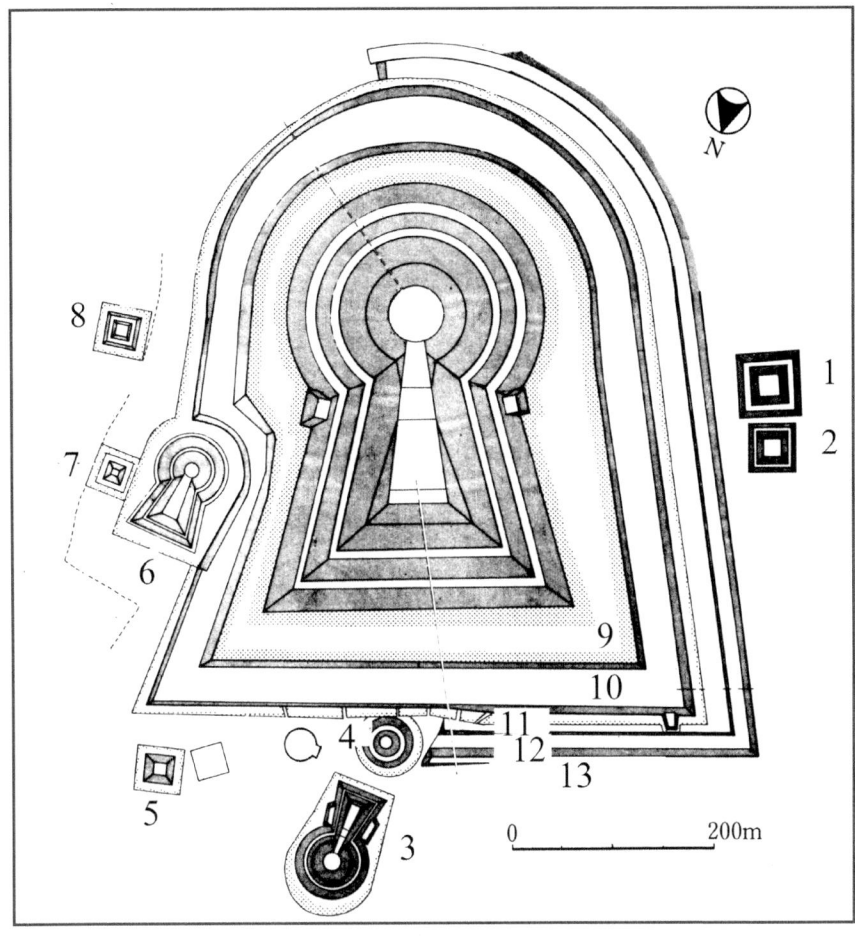

FIGURE A.9. THE KONDA GOBYŌYAMA KOFUN, FURUICHI TOMB GROUP, SHOWING SURROUNDING SATELLITE TOMBS. FROM TANAKA 2001, 149. (1) HIGASHIYAMA. (2) ARIYAMA. (3) ŌTORIZUKA. (4) KONDA MARUYAMA. (5) KYUKINZUKA. (6) NITZUZUKA. (7) BAZUKA. (8) KURIZUKA. (9) INNER MOAT. (10) INNER RIDGE. (11) OUTER MOAT. (12). OUTER RIDGE (13) DITCH FACING OUTER RIDGE. FROM TANAKA 2001: 149. COURTESY OF GAKUSEISHA PUBLISHERS.

arrowheads and 5 iron knives. On the rear mound there was an arrangement of a wide variety of *haniwa*. The *entō haniwa* were of type IV, parallel to the type of those from the Konda Gobyōyama Kofun. Surrounding this mound are six small mounds. Except for one, the Sobayama Kofun, a moated scallop shape mound, 34 m long, with *entō haniwa* of Type V dated to the fifth century AD, their contents are unknown.

9. Konda Maruyama Kofun (Furuichi Group)

The Konda Maruyama Kofun, 50m in diameter, is situated to the north of the front square portion of the Konda Gobyōyama Kofun (Figure A.9), built in the late fifth century AD and is thought to be its satellite mound.

There are many interesting questions concerning Konda Maruyama (Tanaka 2001, 139, Ōsaka Furitsu Chikatsu Asuka Hakubutsukan 2006: 50-53). Tanaka (2001: 138) states that this mound could be an independent burial rather than a satellite. The grave goods indicate that its occupant had power and prestige.

The finds include a clay-surrounded wooden coffin. Artifacts are thought to have been removed from this mound in 1848 AD (Tanaka 2001: 137). They have been retained by the Konda Hachiman Shrine and were registered as National Treasures in 1952. The objects included two gilt bronze saddle bows decorated with dragon motifs (Figure A.10), a gilt bronze bridle piece with mirror shaped plaque, a deer antler sword handle, horse ornaments, and iron arrowheads and cuirass fragments (Tanaka 2001: 139). The gilt bronze horse gear show strong influences from the styles of horse ornaments originating in the three Yan Kingdoms of Northeast China. The saddle bows date to the mid fifth century and probably came from Paekche to Japan, or possibly from Koguryo to Paekche to Japan. They are similar to the saddle bow decorated with dragons found in a tomb in the Hyakutsukabaru Tomb Group of Saitobaru in Miyazaki Prefecture, some 490km to the southwest of the Ōsaka Region (Ōsaka Furitsu Chikatsu Asuka Hakubutsukan 2006: 85). This similarity is thought to indicate a strong relationship between the Kings of Wa and local centers of power.

10. Nonaka Kofun (Furuichi Group)

The Nonaka Kofun was excavated by Ōsaka University in 1964 (Tanaka 1991: 320, Ōsaka Daigaku Kōkogaku

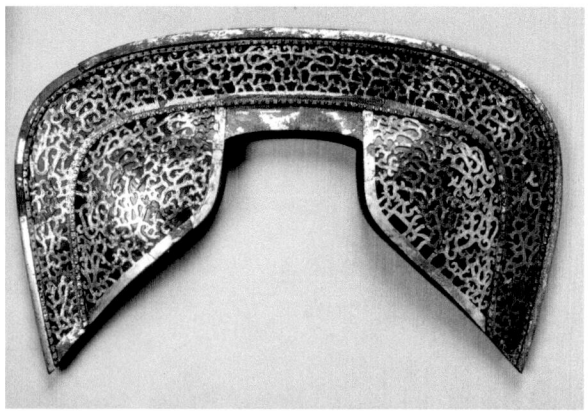

FIGURE A.10. GILT BRONZE SADDLE BOW FROM THE KONDA MARUYAMA KOFUN, FURUICHI TOMB GROUP. FIFTH CENTURY AD. FROM ŌSAKA FURITSU CHIKATSU ASUKA HAKUBUTSUKAN 2006: 50. COURTESY OF KONDA HACHIMAN SHRINE AND ŌSAKA FURITSU CHIKATSU ASUKA HAKUBUTSUKAN.

Kenkyūshitsu 2014, Nakakubo 2014, Takahashi and Nakakubo 2014). It appears to be a satellite tomb of the Hakayama Kofun. The square mound is roughly 37m on each side and 4m in height. At a depth of about 1m from the surface, excavators found what appeared to have been five long wooden boxes thought by some to be coffins and by others to be boxes of offerings. When they were unearthed they consisted of five rows of various kinds of armor, weapons and tools underlain by wooden planks. The sets of armor are shown in Figure A.11. The deposit of Middle Kofun Period weapons and armor is the second richest in Japan.

The first box contained swords and 10 cuirasses and the second, arrowheads, pottery vessels, beads and one cuirass. The third contained a stone mortar and wooden pestle, iron knives and swords; the fourth, iron swords, knives, halberds, adzes and ingots; and the fifth, agricultural tools and ingots. The cuirasses belong to three types (see the discussion of cuirass types in Box 5.7). Two of the types, with riveted triangular plates and riveted horizontal plates, are common in the fifth century AD; a third rare type adds weight to the argument that the undiscovered tomb occupant was of particularly high status similar to that of the occupant of the Kurohimeyama Kofun discussed above. So far only about a dozen examples have been found in Japan, three of which occur in the Nonaka Kofun. This type is made of triangular plates fastened with leather thongs and has a collar that provides protection for the upper back and neck. Two types of helmet were found. The first, the riveted lamellar visored helmet, has been found in other sites, while the second, the leather keeled helmet, has been found only in the Nonaka Kofun. On the top of this helmet there are iron sockets holding feather decoration. It is possible that this is an older type of head gear, used in rituals, but its significance is not clear at present.

From the top of the mound, *haniwa* sherds were recovered, along with small stone replicas (81 knife shaped stone adzes, 2 sickles, and 1spindle whorl.) A concentration of 8800 sherds of earthenware and very early *sueki* were found in an area 0.5m square. The *sueki* sherds include covered dishes of a form rare in Japan and Korea, while many of the vessels bear surface patterns characteristic of various regions of the Korean peninsula. The *haniwa* types included *entō*, morning glory, house, enclosure, saddle, shield, cuirass, and water bird types. Some 41,297 stone beads, sword replicas and *magatama* were discovered as well as a mortar for grinding cinnabar, used in ritual. A total of 36kg of iron ingots in two sizes, 50 to 60g and 120 to 130g, was found, making this the second largest deposit of ingots in Japan, next to the deposit of the Yamato No. 6 Kofun in Nara.

The offerings were deposited into a pit dug into the top of the mound after it was completed (Tanaka 2001: 110) and the mound does not appear to have a central burial. The helmets and cuirasses are in an area about 0.6m below the surface, in the central part of the mound, 6m E/W and 4m N/S. Drawings and photos show a line of cuirasses buried upright. In examples from the Furuichi Group it appears that the mound was built first, then dug into, but the examples from Mozu seem to have offerings that were set in place as the mound was built. The latter three also have offerings set on wooden planks. The three Mozu mounds have different contents: Shichikanyama has weapons, Katonboyama has soapstone objects, and Tsukamawari has beads. There is a different focus in each one. Thus there are many differences in the *baichō* of Furuichi and Mozu.

Tanaka Migaku (1991: 320) concludes that the boxes are coffins originally containing five human burials, particularly since cylindrical beads (*kudatama*) which are personal ornaments, were found in one of them; however this evidence is not very clear. If the mound contains a human burial, it may belong to a powerful individual who owned or controlled many sets of armor or the armor may have been contributed by vassals or confederates. Or the mound may have had a votive function, containing offerings for the individual buried in the Hakayama Kofun (Ōsaka Daigaku Kōkogaku Kenkyūshitsu 2014). The agricultural tools show the attachment of iron blades to wooden tools, increasing their efficiency in heavy soils (Figure 5.12).

11. Tsukamawari Kofun (Mozu Group)

This satellite tomb of the Daisen Ryō Kofun, excavated by Tsuboi Shogoro in the late nineteenth century, is a two stepped circular mound surrounded by a moat. A wooden box, without surrounding clay or human remains, was 3.2m long, 0.5m wide, and only 12cm deep below the surface at the time of excavation. It yielded two bronze mirrors and several iron swords, as well as a variety of

APPENDIX A

FIGURE A.11. IRON CUIRASSES, SHOULDER PROTECTORS AND HELMETS FOUND IN THE NONAKA KOFUN. FROM TAKAHASHI AND NAKAKUBO 2014: 2. COURTESY OF OSAKA DAIGAKU KŌKOGAKU KENKYŪSHITSU.

beads of stone and glass. The finds were a ritual offering rather than a human burial. The *haniwa* belong to Period IV (Ichinose et al 2008: 214-215, Ōtsuka and Kobayashi 1984: 317).

12. Shichikanyama Kofun (Mozu Group)

The Shichikanyama Kofun was excavated in 1913, 1947, and 1952 (Ichinose et al 2008: 214). It seems to be associated with the Kami Ishitzu Nisanzai Tomb (Richu Ryō) since it lies some 120m to the north of it. After excavation, the remaining portions were leveled. It was a round mound, 30m in diameter, built in two steps. On the top was a rectangular area outlined by cylindrical *haniwa*. Inside the tomb there were at least three sets of grave goods. The *haniwa* included tubular *haniwa* with fins, as well as house, shield, armor, and quiver forms. There were four areas each with a wooden coffin set in clay (*nendokaku*), and associated horse gear, armor, swords (150 specimens), iron arrowheads, gilt bronze horse gear, adzes and hand adzes were found in large quantities. In the first one, 1.2m from surface, *haniwa* fragments were found, and there was a clay floor with a wooden box resting on it. The second area was destroyed, so there is not much information. About 0.9m below surface, helmet and cuirass were found, and there was a buried soil layer under them, indicating that they were placed on a former ground surface. The excavators concluded that the compartments were prepared while the tomb was constructed and were of the same age (Tanaka 2001: 110-113).

13. Katonboyama Kofun, Mozu Group

This two-stepped round mound about 50m in diameter is located on the east side the rear mound of the Gobyōyama Kofun (which is different from the Konda Gobyōyama Kofun). Remains of an arrangement of *haniwa*, including house and parasol *haniwa* were found on its summit. At that time a huge quantity of dispersed objects was found. The grave offerings appear to have placed on a large single plank, set on a clay surface. No burial could be located. In addition to two Chinese mirrors dating to the Western Jin Dynasty (Nishikawa 2010: 10-11) there was a huge number of soapstone objects, including four *komochi magatama*, 725 *magatama*, 20,000 *usudama*, a two holed circular object, 20 iron arrowheads, 57 iron adzes, and other iron artifacts. The *haniwa* are not of the usual *entō* type found in other mounds, but seem to match some of the later types found in the moat of the Gobyōyama Kofun. After excavation in 1949 the mound was completely destroyed (Ichinose et al 2008: 214).

14. The Naniwa Palace (Naniwanomiya)

The main buildings were elevated on pillars. Roof tiles and stone platforms, continental attributes, were not present, although there were other buildings with tiled roofs at this time in Naniwa (Miyamoto 2010: 108). However, small post holes around some of the buildings of the Early Naniwa Palace suggest that they may have been surrounded by wooden platforms (Ueki 2009: 94). In the northern portion of the site were the Dairikōden, where the emperor gave audiences, and the Dairizenden, used for state ceremonies. The functions of these two buildings were combined in a single structure from the time of Fujiwara Capital of the Nara Basin (794 to 710 AD). From the time of the Fujiwara Palace, palace buildings were set on Chinese style stone platforms (*kidan*).

In the Early Naniwa Palace, on either side of these two buildings were two large octagonal towers that served to dignify the appearance of the palace, in the manner of palaces of the Korean peninsula and China (Ueki 2009: 52). They are the largest examples of octagonal towers in Japan and reflect Daoist cosmological principles (Naoki and Nakao 2003: 149). To the south side of these two buildings was the administrative area of the capital, the Chōdōin. In a large space approximately 231m x 262m were two rows of buildings lined up on two sides and the southern end. A group of government buildings to the west of the main palace consisted of a separate administrative building and a group of three buildings sharing a common roof (*narabikura*), which must have been some kind of treasury. The only other examples of this building plan occur in the Shosōin and Hōryuji (Ueki 2009: 65). To the south of these buildings was a group of five buildings that also appear to be administrative buildings and related storehouses. On the south and west sides of the palace area, remains of a stockade were found.

To the east of the central buildings of Early Naniwanomiya another group of buildings was found in the 1980s. At first they were thought to be administrative buildings; however excavations in 2005-2006 indicated that they must have had a different purpose. They are set in a walled area about 51m north-south and 31m east-west, and are elevated on posts. They appear to have been used for official banquets, judging from similar examples from later palaces (Ōsaka Shi Bunkazai Kyōkai 2008: 140-142). This distinctive set of buildings commanded a view of Kawachi Lake, which still existed at that time.

A substantial road ran due south from the Naniwa Palace to the bank of the modern course of the Yamato River (Sekiyama 2010b). It must have been built in the fifth century (Chapter 5). On the east side of the road two temples belonging to the Korean royal Paekche clan, a main temple (Kudaradera) and a convent (Kudara Amadera).

The palace was rebuilt some 40 years after its first abandonment and was used as the capital from 726 to 732 and 744 to 745 AD. The later palace, known as the

Figure A.12. Artifacts from metal working workshops associated with Naniwanomiya; clay tuyeres (bellows valves), slag, whetstones, stone bases, and small containers. From Ōsaka 2008: 161. Courtesy of the Ōsaka Shi Hakubutsukan Kyōkai, Ōsaka Shi Bunkazai Kenkyūsho.

Late Period Naniwa Palace, followed roughly the same plan as the Early Period Palace, although unexcavated portions from both periods may show more differences. The Late Period Naniwa Palace had tiled roofs (Yagi 2010: 111-123).

Ravines on the Uemachi Terrace have produced sites protected from the destruction of later building and clearing (Sekiyama 2010c: 85-88). In a buried ravine on the northwest, three hearths and more than six ash concentrations were found, along with bellows valves, bowl shape slag from crucibles, iron scraps, large whetstones, and *sueki* containers for lacquer applied to iron objects. The area was an official iron working site, attached to Naniwanomiya (Figure A.12). In the same ravine was an area where animal hide processing was carried out, judging from the accumulation of animal bones with butchering marks. This deposit is associated with the oldest cultural layer of the Naniwa Palace, suggesting that the animals were originally used as draft animals for palace construction. In another ravine on the northwest, a spring fed pond with a channel constructed of granite blocks was found. The area appears to have been a landscaped garden with a pond, similar to continental examples. The water may have also served an area for raising animals or a hunting preserve. Around Naniwanomiya there would have been facilities for controlling floods from the Ō and Yamato Rivers, as well as engineering works to maintain the Horie Channel and the Naniwa Tsu (Nakao 2010). Finds of Paekche and Silla ceramics at various locations on the Uemachi Terrace attest to substantial interaction with Korea in the Naniwa area (Figure A.13).

16. Sakai Localities

This section contains brief descriptions of some of the major localities within the site of Sakai, organized by the chronological periods mentioned in Chapter 8.

Period I

SKT 21, 61 Small Buildings (Sakai Shi Hakubutsukan 1993: 89)

To the north and west of the central part of Sakai, in an area showing no sign of the burning of AD 1399 and therefore postdating that event, there are the remains of small buildings with stone pillar bases, along with wells and various kinds of pits. (As mentioned above, stone

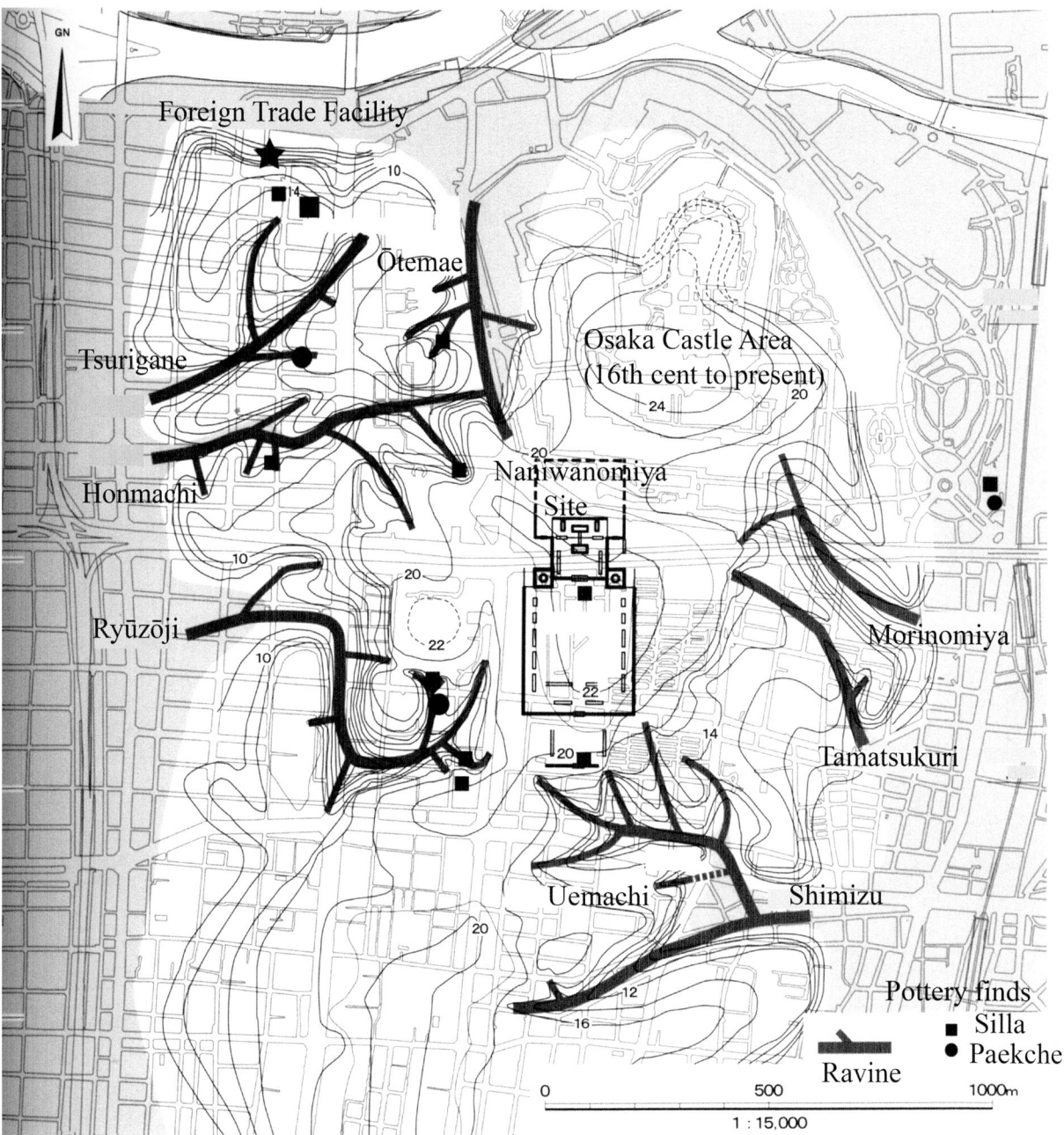

Figure A.13. Map of sites in the area of the Kodai Period Naniwanomiya and Chūsei Period Ōsaka Castle, showing ravines and locations of finds of seventh century AD, Silla and Paekche ceramics. Original prepared by Terai Makoto, Ōsaka Rekishi Hakubutsukan. From Ōsaka Furitsu Yayoi Bunka Hakubutsukan 2008, 78. Courtesy of Terai Makoto and the Ōsaka Furitsu Yayoi Bunka Hakubutsukan.

pillar bases indicate that the original building had a floor raised on pillars, not resting on the ground). The artifacts include earthenware wide mouth storage jars and plates of grey and red earthenware. These were used for storage and serving food. Japanese hard fired ceramics included wide mouth storage jars and shredding and mixing bowls (*suribachi*) (Tsuzuki 2010a) of Bizen ware and bowls, plates, and jars of Tanba and Seto wares. Chinese wares include white ware bowls and plates from Fujian, and celadon bowls, plates, and platters (chargers) from Longquan, Zhejiang Province.

Periods I to V

SKT 39, Residences And Storehouses (Sakai Shi Kyōiku Iinkai 1991a)

This locality is located on a a slightly elevated location, 4.4m above sea level, about 50m from the shore at the time of occupation. The lowest layer is very close to present sea level. The excavation in 1989 of about 50m² in area exposed 15 layers, from the end of the fourteenth century to the eighteenth centuries, with a total depth about 5m. The lowest layer post dates the burning of the city in 1399 AD at the time of the Ōei Rebellion (Ōei no Ran, 1399 AD). The thickest layer is the burned earth layer dating to the year Keicho 20 (1615 AD). From Layer 5, buildings with tile-lined foundations (*senretsu tatemono*) appear (Tsuzuki 2010b). The layout of the streets was set in the latter half of the sixteenth century.

The finding of a long narrow line of grey tile bricks set vertically in the earth indicates a group of storehouses near the shore. This type of storehouse architecture, using vertical grey tiles to line the basement, began at the end of the fifteenth century (Figure 7.6). In Layer 4, dating to the latter half of the sixteenth century, parts of a residential compound (*yashiki*) with a building facing a garden as well as a small entrance garden were recovered. In Layer 3, the thickest layer, dating to the fire of 1615 AD, there are the remains of 7 storehouses and 3 buildings set on pillars, as well as buried large jars used as latrines, and a well. Sherds of tea wares were abundant (Tsuchiyama 1996).

Although Sakai is famous for the rich variety of East Asian trade wares and Japanese glazed ceramics, local earthenware was produced in large quantities and predominated throughout the deposit. In the upper layers, particularly Layer 4, earthenware plates comprised 70% of the entire ceramic assemblage whereas in the lower layers such as Layer 12, they were 90%. The earthenware is primarily reddish low fired earthenware (*haji shitsu doki*). Plates comprised 70% to 90% of all forms. Other vessel forms included flanged cauldrons, lamps, heaters (*hibachi*), jars, very large storage vessels, and vessels for evaporating salt water to make salt. Other clay objects included figurines, weights, and bellows valves. Many vessels of soft grey tile ware, such as plates, flanged cauldrons, ridged bowls for grinding seeds (*suribachi*), heaters and incense burners, were also found.

Chinese wares were the most abundant of the foreign trade wares, comprising half of all the trade wares in Layer 9. Celadon from the first half of the fifteenth century to the first half of sixteenth century comprises 50 to 60% of the glazed ware assemblage. After this period celadon declined and blue and white became popular. In the layer dating to the destruction of 1615 AD, celadon comprises about 10%. Celadon was concentrated in the central area of Sakai, similar to Korean *punchong* wares and other high quality ceramics. Celadon forms were mostly bowls, but there were also plates, jars, and cups (Sakai Shi Hakubutsukan 1993: 91). Within SKT39, storehouse buildings SB301 and SB 302 appear to be storehouses for precious tea utensils. In SB 301 a total of 500 artifacts, primarily ceramics, was recovered (Figure A.14).

SKT 39, SB 302 (Tsuchiyama 1996, Sakai Shi Kyōiku Iinkai 1991a) (Figure A.14).

The top layer contained a relatively small structure SB302, which was burned in 1615. Its dimensions are 3.5 m east to west and 2.2 m north to south. The artifacts were almost completely intact. It appears to have been a storage house for tea utensils, that included large earthenware jars of *haji* and soft paste (*gashitsu doki*), a brazier for heating water, a Bizen ware water jar, a Bizen ware flower vase, a spouted vessel of Karatsu ware, a Mino ware incense burner, a Chinese blue and white jar with lid, a brown glazed jar, a tea mortar, and a bronze incense burner (Sakai Shi Hakubutsukan 1993).

Iron artifacts included plow blades, nails, flanged cauldrons, plates, Nanjing locks (which are secured with a sliding rod), chopsticks, and forceps (*kanshi*). Bronze objects included coins, weights, scales for weighing, Nanjing locks, incense burners, ewers, spoons for measuring tea. The metal objects occur in Layers 2 and 3. In the lower layers, beneath the structure burned in 1615 AD, celadon bowls predominated. Blue and white wares were common from Layer 8 to the surface. The upper layers contained Japanese ceramics such as Tanba, Bizen, Seto, Karatsu, Shigaraki, Imari, Iga, and Tokoname wares. Bizen wares were found in all of the layers, while mortars (*suribachi*) made in Sakai were found in the uppermost two layers. Oribe and Shino tea bowls were found in the top three layers (Tsuzuki 2010c). Some of the major types of ceramics found in Sakai sites are shown in Figures A.16 and A.17.

SKT 39 (SB 301 Tea Master's Tea House, Storehouse (Sakai Shi Hakubutsukan 1993, 63-64).

Architectural remains include a tea house and storage area. This is part of SKT 39. There were about 500 ceramic vessels, all burned, comprising imported ceramics (61%), Japanese ceramics (25%), and local earthenware (14%). Many of the food serving vessels were Fujian blue and white while the storage vessels are Japanese.

SKT 78 Coin Mold Deposit (Sakai Shi Kyōiku Iinkai 1997)

The 1991 excavation contained several living surfaces dating from AD 1615 (Layer 1) to the fire of 1399 AD (Layer 7). In Layers 2 and 3 archaeologists found the merchants' houses and associated features (Sakai Shi Kyōiku Iinkai 1997). Of the total of 3, 841 mold fragments recovered, there were two types, molds for thin plain coins (85 %), and molds for inscribed coins (15%). The inscribed coins comprised 19 types, from Chinese Tang to Northern Song. These types were produced in Sakai in the mid to late sixteenth century (Shimatani 1998).

In the later part of the mediaeval period in every region of Japan there are plain coins of copper, to which was sometimes added tin and/or lead. The plain coins from

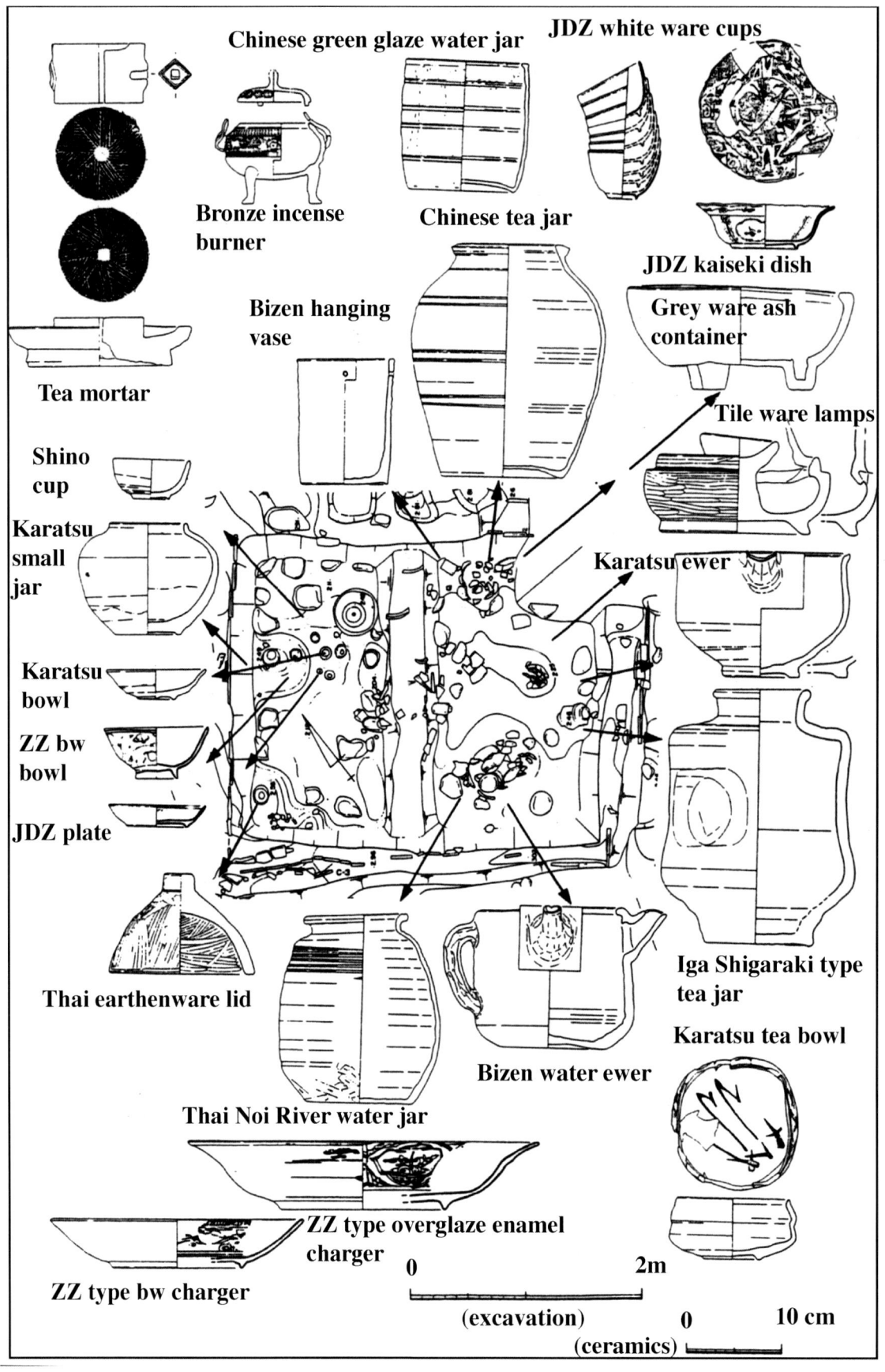

Figure A.14. Ceramics from Layer 3, SB 302, SKT 39, Sakai. From Morimura 2002: 280. Rubbings of the grooved surfaces of the tea mortar (upper right) are shown. The locations of some object are not indicated. The Chinese white, and blue and white, ceramics were produced in Jingdezhen Jiangxi Province (JDZ), and Zhang Zhou (ZZ), Fujian Province, China. Courtesy of Kokuritsu Rekishi Minzoku Hakubutsukan.

APPENDIX A

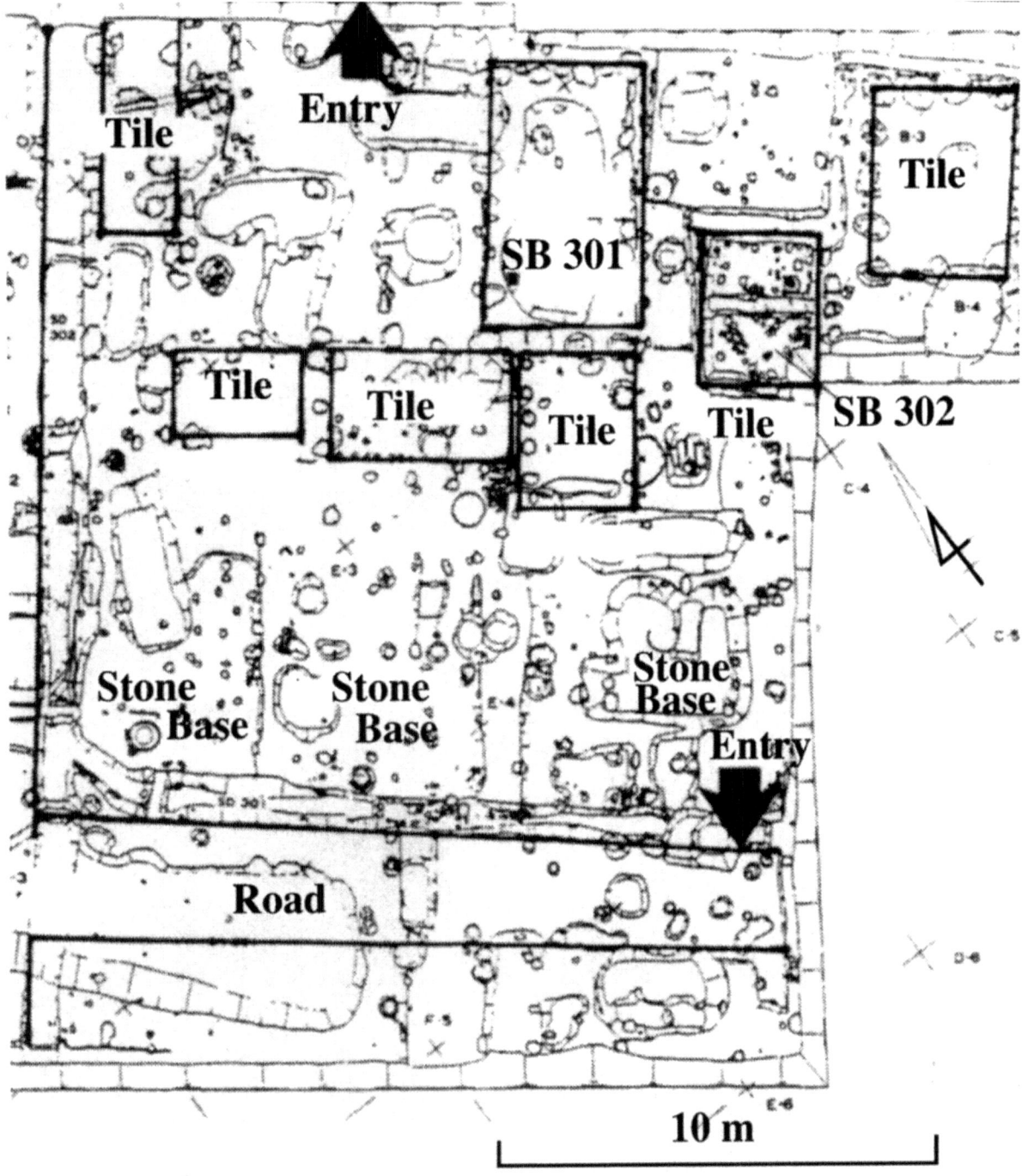

FIGURE A.15. FLOOR PLAN OF LAYER 3 OF SKT 39, SAKAI, SHOWING LOCATION OF BUILDINGS SB 301 AND SB 302. FROM MORIMURA 2002, 279. IN THE FRONT OF THE PROPERTY, NEAR THE ROAD, WERE RESIDENTIAL BUILDINGS WITH RAISED FLOORS SET ON WOODEN PILLARS ON STONE BASES. (INDICATED AS STONE BASE). IN THE REAR WERE MULTI STOREY STOREHOUSES, WITH TILE LINED BASEMENTS (INDICATED AS TILE). FROM MORIMURA 2002: 280. COURTESY OF KOKURITSU REKISHI MINZOKU HAKUBUTSUKAN.

Figure A.16. Tea related ceramics from Sakai sites. From Sakai Shi Hakubutsukan 2006. (1) Chinese Longquan celadon bowl, mid fourteenth century AD (found in Locality SB 3). (2) Black Oribe ware tea bowl, Mino Kilns (SKT 39). (3) Bizen ware water jar (SKT 39). (4) Shigaraki ware water jar (SKT 61). (5) Seto Mino flower vase (SKT 39). (6) Korean grey glazed jar (SB 301). (7) Blue and white box, Zhang Zhou Kilns, Fujian Province, China (SKT 794). (8) Karatsu ware tea bowl (SKT 230). (9) Vietnamese jar (SKT 230). (10) Group of blue and white bowls, Zhang Zhou Kilns, Fujian Province, China (SKT 230). Courtesy of Sakai Shi Kyōiku Iinkai and Sakai Shi Hakubutsukan.

Sakai are of the copper type (based on a comparatively rough compositional analysis) produced in the late sixteenth century (Shimatani 1998).

SKT 200 Residential Area Of Townspeople (Tsuzuki 1994)

There are seven living surfaces, dating from the early to middle fifteenth century to 1615. In the lower layers structures were small raised buildings set on supporting stone bases, along a road, with wells fashioned of soft grey ware circular tiles. Water was stored in large buried Tokoname Ware jars. From Layers 1 to 3, storehouses with tile lined foundations occur (Layer 3 dates to the end of the sixteenth century). Living Surface 5, dating to the first half of sixteenth century, contained the remains of a road built on top of small houses and long narrow *tansaku* lots, indicating a redevelopment of part of the city to smaller holdings.

SKT 361 Metal Casters House (Tsuzuki 1994: 90-95)

In the front portion of the lot there was an open area for working, with a long narrow ditch on one side. Artifacts found on the first living surface dated to the late fifteenth and early sixteenth centuries indicate the presence of metal casting. The structures are linked to the establishment of a Jōdo Shinshū Buddhist Temple and similar casting areas were found in nearby sites, SKT 411, and SKT 39. There was a toilet for each house, on the side of the lot, not at the rear. This indicates that people were engaged in cultivation for which access to night soil is important.

Period V

SKT 19 Commoners' Residential Area (Sakai Shi Kyōiku Iinkai 1984b)

This locality contained deposits from the fire of AD 1615 and yielded a wooden slip (*mokkan*) dating to Tenshō 13 (1588 AD). It appears to be part of a commoners' residential area, containing a stone wall and a stratified deposit. Ceramics were *haji* earthenware, (small plates, shredding bowls (*suribachi*), and braziers (*hibachi*) 47%; Japanese wares (Bizen, Seto, Mino, Karatsu) 17.8%; Chinese and Korean ceramics, 8%; Minato (local) wares 16.5%; local tile wares (*hibachi*) 10.8%.

SKT 47 (Sakai Shi Hakubutsukan 1993)

This area yielded remains of a two storey building (SB04) and many tea ceramics along with the foundations of eight other buildings, all burned in 1615 AD. One of the buildings, 6m x 7m, had a basement lined with grey tiles. On the east side of the building was a two storey building with door and windows. It yielded burned and fallen plaster, a tea grinding mortar, and red earth used in plastering the walls of a tea house as well as the remains of a garden with a built up artificial hill (*chikuyama*). From the stratigraphy, the building was built after 1582 AD. The ceramics are mostly Chinese blue and white, probably reflecting the conservative tastes of the owner since other localities of the same period display a wider variety of wares.

SKT 230, SB01 (Sakai Shi Kyōiku Iinkai1991b)

Several layers were recovered from this warehouse site. The total depth of the excavations was 4m. From Living Surface No. 19, near the bottom, clay weights for fishing nets, flanged earthenware cooking vessels and celadon bowls were found, indicating a relatively simple living pattern in the fifteenth century. In Layer 3, dating to roughly the third quarter of the sixteenth century, a substantial number of Chinese coins were found (Sakai Shi Kyōiku Iinkai 1991b: 34-35). Twenty-three of the 55 illustrated coins come from the Hong Wu (1368 to 1398 AD) and Yong Le (AD 1403 to 1424 AD) eras, reflecting the prosperity of trade, while the others are from the Tang (618 to 906 AD) to Yuan (AD 1260 to 1368 AD) eras, commonly found on Japanese sites. The uppermost living surface was occupied from about 1595 to 1615 AD, the peak period of prosperity. From this layer a total of 410 vessels related to tea consumption were found. Of this assemblage, 71% were blue and white, 12% were Karatsu, and 6% each were Mino and Bizen (Tsuzuki 2010c: 73). Blue and white wares from both Jingdezhen and Zhangzhou were found in large quantities. Non-ceramic artifacts included a deer antler hook for hanging a kettle, and an iron blade for a plough. A special feature is the large number of storage vessels; they include Japanese, Chinese, Thai, Vietnamese, and Korean types. Several different forms of Central Vietnamese tall bottles dating to the sixteenth and seventeenth centuries were found. They are thought to have contained sugar. A group of blue and white helmet shaped bowls (*kabutohachi*) made in Zhangzhou, Fujian, are also notable (Figure A.16 [10]).

SKT 263 (Morimura 2004a, 219)

This site contains the remains of a relatively large building, discovered in 2000. The finds reflect changes in the tea ceremony, in which Sakai merchants began to use Japanese and Southeast Asian wares, but retained their interest in Chinese wares. The finds included Japanese wares such as Karatsu, Bizen, Mino, Shigaraki, Iga, Tanba, and Raku Wares; Chinese wares such as white wares, celadons, blue and white from Zhangzhou and Jingdezhen, overglaze enamelled, South Chinese Three Color (Huanan Sancai) (Figure A.17), and brown wares; and Thai, Vietnamese and Burmese wares (Kanazawa 2004, Morimura 2003a: 2004b). This site exemplifies the trend toward the 'grass hut style" of tea ceremony, a less elaborate form removed from warrior elite control and featuring Japanese and Southeast Asian as well as Chinese ceramics (Slusser 2004). Of particular interest is a group of sherds of blue and white bowls, 10 to 15cm in height and 2 to 3.5cm in diameter. Presumably they were used for tea made from leaves (*sencha*) rather than powder. Two types of stoves for heating water for the tea ceremony were also found.

The main building is a residence, of elevated floor construction. It is flanked by a tea house. In the rear is a three-storey storehouse that, judging from the artifacts recovered, also had a space for tea ritual. It seems that the tea space in the warehouse was for informal use while the separate tea pavilion was for formal use.

FIGURE A.17. STONEWARE PLATE OF SOUTH CHINA THREE COLOR WARE, FOUND IN SS201 FURITSU YAYOI BUNKA HAKUBUTSUKAN AND SAKAI SHI KYŌIKU IINKAI., SAKAI. EARLY SEVENTEENTH CENTURY AD. FROM ŌSAKA FURITSU YAYOI BUNKA HAKUBUTSUKAN 2008: 38. COURTESY OF THE ŌSAKA

Appendix B
Sakai Historical Background

The urban history of Sakai becomes clear from the fourteenth century AD. It was the port of export for large bronze bells and other cast metal artifacts that were a specialty of the Kawachi region, and also a center of learning. In the first 60 years of the fourteenth century, economic growth in Sakai attracted merchants and artisans (Morimura 2006c, Asao 2004). Historical records indicate that in 1368 AD a woodblock edition of the Confucian Analects was published in Sakai (Asao et al 1999: 62-66) confirming that it was a center for the production of high value goods and cultural objects. Wakita (1999: 38) states that in the fourteenth century Sakai served as a collecting point for estate rents paid to aristocrats and temples in Kyōto, and as a port for the Southern Court during the separation of Northern and Southern Courts from 1337 to 1392 AD. At this time the role of manors (*shōen*) as generators of goods and rents remitted directly to owners such as aristocrats and temples declined, as local producers began to sell to urban consumers through distributors and wholesalers (Segal 2011, Wakita 1999: 30).

Many Zen Buddhist temples were built in Sakai in the fourteenth and fifteenth centuries. Some were connected to the large and powerful Shokokuji and Daitokuji temples of Kyōto. When the large temples lost their manors as sources of wealth in the fifteenth and sixteenth centuries and turned to trade to earn revenue (Collcutt 1981: 253-284), it was useful to have representatives in Sakai to participate in trade and to maintain good relations with wealthy patrons.

In the first half of the 150 years of Sakai's greatest prosperity, Sakai was the center for the Ming tributary trade and Ryūkyū trade, while in the second half, trade turned to newly found Japanese silver, guns, weapons and other military goods such as deer skin imported from Taiwan. Despite its relatively small population and area, Sakai exerted disproportionate influence on mediaeval Japan as a center for money lending, intellectual life, and the production of crafts. Tsuzuki (2011a) identifies three different forms of trade which connected Sakai to surrounding areas: (1) relaying trade with Ryūkyū, particularly in the fifteenth century, (2) tributary trade with the Ming Dynasty in the fifteenth to mid sixteenth centuries, and (3) The Red Seal or Tally Trade of the late sixteenth and early seventeenth centuries. The first two types of trade are discussed in Pearson (2013) and the latter type is discussed briefly later in this chapter.

Prominent Buddhist temples in the Kyōto area sponsored trade missions to China in the first half of the fourteenth century to earn revenue for large construction projects. Often the ships left from the port of Hyogo Tsu. The sponsors included not only the Tenryuji Temple of Kyōto and the temple of the Great Daibutsu in Kamakura, but also the Sumiyoshi Shrine (Murai 2005: 113-114). These voyages required certification from the emperor and shōgun that the traders were not pirates, but in fact, they were managed by private traders such as those of Sakai, and were important in the development of burgeoning commerce. There is tantalizing evidence that weapons were a significant aspect of Sakai's trade. Von Verschuer notes that despite official Chinese bans on weapons for most tribute missions, in 1483 AD, the Muromachi government sent 3600 swords as tribute to China, as well as 35,000 swords intended for private trade, and that on another occasion in the fifteenth century Sakai merchants even exported inferior swords in an attempt to increase their profits (causing the Chinese to reduce their price and offer fewer return gifts) (2006: 140-141). A tribute mission of 1539 AD carried 24,862 swords for private sale in Ningbo (2006: 143). Many important aspects concerning the mediaeval shipment of Japanese swords to China are provided in the groundbreaking work of Kobata Atsushi (1941: 388-445).

At the beginning of the fifteenth century AD Sakai became part of the lands controlled by the Hosokawa Clan, powerful administrators in the Shōgun's government in Kyōto (Asao et al 1999: 62). It developed as a trading center for the Inland Sea region (Senboku Kōko Shiryōkan 1996: 2). In the early fifteenth century Ryūkyū ships brought goods from China and Southeast Asia to the port of Hyogo Tsu; from these ships, large black glazed jars from Thailand found their way to nearby Sakai. While the most active period of this trade was from 1429 to 1440, there were a total of 15 voyages from the Ryūkyū Kingdom to the Muromachi Bakufu between 1403 and 1466 AD. In the mid and late fifteenth century, Sakai merchants played a very significant role in the tributary missions sent from Japan to the Ming Court. Generally it is considered that Sakai's Ming-related wealth began in 1467 AD, when Sakai became the home port for the missions (Tsuzuki 1990: 150). The system of sending tribute and receiving goods for trade was complicated and ever-changing, but the profits were enormous. The mid fifteenth century marks the beginning of the period of prosperity for Sakai that lasted about 150 years, until the burning of the city in 1615 AD (Asao et al 1999: 88-92). Goods sent to China from Japan included sulfur, copper, sword blades and screens, while those from China included ceramics, crafts, medicine, books paintings and other Chinese cultural objects (Seki 2002, Tsuzuki 1990: 149).

Under the conditions of the Ming Maritime Prohibition (1368 to 1567 AD), private trade was banned and official trade was limited to tributary trade, at intervals stipulated by Ming officials. Tributary trade involved the submission of tributary gifts to China in exchange for gifts as well as objects to be traded and certain privileges to trade in China (Danjō 2005). The Japanese were restricted to only nineteen trade missions in total from 1410 to 1547 AD (Tanaka 1993: 4-8) while the Kingdom of Ryūkyū sent missions with far greater frequency and relayed the goods it received to Sakai and other Japanese ports. Tribute ships usually carried a Ming envoy, returning to China, as well as a high ranking Buddhist priest or merchant. While the ships usually departed from and returned to the ancient port of Hyogo Tsu, (modern day Kobe) (known as Ōwada no Tomari in the Heian Period (794 to 1185 AD), Sakai merchants were active in provisioning and financing them from at least 1465 AD. Smaller Japanese missions involved one or a few ships and from 50 to 100 persons, but larger missions consisted of as many as nine ships carrying 1200 persons, 350 of whom proceeded to the Ming capital in Peking (Tanaka 1993: 8). The mission of 1467 AD returned on the southern route via Kagoshima and the Pacific coast of Kyūshū and Shikoku, avoiding trouble in the Inland Sea during the Ōnin Wars. The southern route was used extensively by Sakai merchants for travel to the Ryūkyū Kingdom. Their ships often carried Kyōto priests who were engaged in religious and diplomatic activities in ports along the way (Tsunoyama 2000: 60).

During the Ōnin Wars (1467 to 1477 AD) when Kyōto was racked with disturbances and destruction, many aristocrats and townspeople sought refuge in Sakai. In the sixteenth century Sakai continued to be pre-eminent in iron casting, and the production of salt, gunpowder, and fine crafts such as ink stones (Senboku Kōko Shiryōkan 1996: 4). Sakai was the center of a struggle for power in the late 1560's between the Miyōshi Clan, who controlled Sakai, and Oda Nobunaga, who was rising to power. When Oda defeated the Miyōshi, Sakai prepared for retaliation, evacuating women and children and removing treasured tea utensils. The merchant Imai Sōkyū reported that moats were dug and the city was fortified (Watsky 1995: 52, 2004: 22). However Sakai was spared when it paid sufficient "taxes". In 1592 Hideyoshi granted special permission for the Iseya family of Sakai to trade with Southeast Asia (Morimura 2008b: 23). This trade flourished until 1615, and may account in part for the large quantity of Southeast Asian ceramics in sites of this period.

Sakai merchants acted as money lenders for trade and donated substantial sums of money to the large shrines and temples of the Kyōto area. They provided the funds to lease and provision ships from various provincial powers such as the Ōuchi Clan of Kyūshū (Itō 1998), and paid imperial officials and the Ashikaga Shōgunate for the right to participate in the Ming trade which could not be carried out without official sponsorship.

How did this group of merchants come into being? Servants attached to the shrines and temples as handicraft workers became merchants and artisans in the fifteenth century (Morris 1981: 33). Following the devastation of the Ōnin Wars, Sakai merchants donated substantial sums of money for the rebuilding of the Daitokuji Temple in Kyōto (Tsunoyama 2000: 101). Sakai merchants also belonged to the Jishū and Nichiren Buddhist sects. From the middle of the sixteenth century to the beginning of the Tokugawa Period Sakai people were excellent metal casters and produced gunpowder with saltpeter imported from Thailand (Senboku Kōko Shiryōkan 1996: 4). The population of the city was very diverse, including fishermen, farmers, priests, soldiers, merchants, craftsmen, and Chinese and Portugese traders.

The Portugese missionary Luis Frois, who visited the home of the merchant Hibiya Ryōkei in Sakai in 1565 (Morimura 2006c, 5), recounted that his hospitable hosts wore expensive jewelry of pearls, rubies, and diamonds, and also displayed their wealth in valuable tea utensils. He learned that a particular tea container was the most valuable in Japan, valued at the equivalent of 25,000 to 30,000 Portuguese *crusados* (Frois 1966: 97, 102). Sakai merchants were also involved in transporting Chinese coinage to Kyōto, at the time of the Ōnin Wars (AD 1467 to 1477 AD) (Sakai Shi Hakubutsukan 1993: 107). Gun production began shortly after the introduction of guns by the Portuguese in AD 1543, probably travelling on the direct Pacific route from Kagoshima to Sakai. However the scale of production is not well known archaeologically. Japanese silver production rapidly increased in the 1530s, and Sakai became intensively involved in the trade of silver to China (Asao et al 1999: 83). The development of Japan's silver mining industry is claimed by Brown (1951: 96) to be a chief factor in the remarkable economic growth of the latter half of the sixteenth century AD. Sakai merchants were deeply involved in the development of the silver mines.

Suzanne Gay's discussion of mediaeval money lenders in Kyōto is relevant for Sakai (Gay 2001). Social and political upheavals in the later mediaeval period created opportunities for business. In the thirteenth century in Kyōto, *sake* brewers dominated secular money lending while in the later mediaeval period the Five Great Monasteries of Kyōto (Gozan) became prominent lenders. As temples found their estates reduced in the fourteenth century they turned to foreign trade and money lending to create revenue. The money lenders were important members of the community and undertook neighborhood self defense and administration as well as cultural pursuits (Gay 2001: 8). As the demand for credit increased with the expansion of commerce, money lenders met the demand with coinage imported from China, although it was illegal in China to export coinage. They shipped such coinage to Ryūkyū on at least one occasion, in 1471 AD (Uezato 2010). Archaeological discoveries indicate that they were also casting coins. The moneylenders were able to acquire costly tea utensils through defaults on debts (Gay 2001: 196). Morris (1981: 23-36) documents the shift in Sakai from the manor economy to the merchant economy. He states that the leading citizens were the *toimaru*, officials who were posted to supervise rent shipments for estate proprietors. By the fifteenth century they were handling the affairs of more than one patron and were actually independent brokers or businessmen. Some became foreign traders. The local merchant princes (*gosho*) of Sakai were said to show generosity or forbearance (*kanyōsei*) and flexibility (*jūnansei*) through their donations and public involvement (Asao et al 1999: 69). Tsuzuki (1990: 151) mentions that the people of Sakai had a bold and courageous attitude to foreign trade and an independent spirit, and used their commercial power effectively.

These merchants participated in the ruling council (*egōshū*) that managed the internal affairs of Sakai giving it the title of independent city (*jiyū toshi*) (Morimura 2008b), while in fact a similar degree of autonomy occurred among the merchants in many Japanese port cities. The ruling council evolved from shrine guilds (Morris 1981). In the fifteenth century Settsu Sakai (the northern half of Sakai) was under the Sumiyoshi Shrine while Izumi Sakai (the southern half of Sakai) was controlled by the Sekiguchi Shrine, a branch of Sumiyoshi. These organizations had governing councils who organized religious and social activities and managed the collection and payment of taxes, revenues. The *egōshū* was similar to these governing councils in its origin as a shrine guild directing worship of local deities. Despite a degree of financial autonomy, Morris reminds us that ultimate authority still resided with *samurai* overseers of Sakai, who used the services of merchants to provide them with armaments and military supplies for the endless struggles of the period (Morris 1981: 34).

Several generations of Sakai merchants are known from historical records. Kusaba Sainin (1395 to 1486 AD), son of a Southeast Asian immigrant to Sakai, wrote that investors in overseas trade voyages accepted some individual traders as passengers aboard their ships in exchange for one tenth of the value of their imports on return. Sainin advised traders to buy gold or sappanwood in Japan and trade it in China for silk thread that could be sold at a high profit in Japan. In the private trade mission to China in 1453 AD, in which Kusaba was involved, there were nine Japanese ships with a total of 1200 persons on board (Von Verschuer 2006: 124-127). Takeno Jo'ō (1502 to 1555 AD) inherited his father's business dealing in leather goods for warriors (including deer skin from Taiwan). He was an ordained Buddhist priest of the Honganji Sect, and also received training in Zen Buddhism. He became the foremost tea master of Sakai, training followers such as Imai Sōkyū (1520 to 1593 AD), an important civic leader of Sakai, tea master, and trader in fire arms and ammunition.

Imai was known for his close connections with the silver mines of Tajima (Watsky 2004). Throughout the rule of Oda Nobunaga (1534 to 1582 AD), Imai was the leading merchant and tea practitioner in Sakai. His commercial activities were backed by Oda who needed to ship goods from Lake Biwa to the Inland Sea along the Yodo River, where Imai conducted business. Imai organized the production of firearms for the Oda Clan. Imai's business interests included the distribution of goods from his storehouses. In 1554 Imai is known to have made a substantial donation to the Daitokuji Temple in Kyōto. He negotiated the peaceful submission of Sakai to Nobunaga's forces in AD 1569 when the city fortified itself in preparation for battle. Another Sakai merchant, the Christian Konishi Ryūsa, served as Hideyoshi's deputy in Sakai, supplying his campaigns in Kyūshū and Korea. These merchants were involved in manufacturing and trading guns. The most eminent of Sakai's merchant tea masters, Sen no Rikyū, was also an arms merchant who supplied bullets to Oda Nobunaga for his campaign against the Echizen region (Bodart 1977, Watsky 2004: 29). The merchants of Sakai were arms-dealing merchant princes.

Appendix C
Ōsaka's Cultural Heritage and Selected Museums

Urbanization endangers cultural heritage, but without the ravages of urbanization, many remains of the past would remain sleeping in the ground as an unused resource. The surge of urbanization in the Ōsaka region has generated a huge body of information about the past. How does this legacy relate to the life of people living in Ōsaka today? How are sites and artifacts preserved and interpreted?

In the previous chapters I have outlined selected highlights of Ōsaka's archaeological past. I assembled the information from excavation reports and books, visits to sites and museums and the internet. In the dense urban environment of Ōsaka many sites such as Uriūdō and Morinomiya have been destroyed or covered over by urban development. Ōsaka was heavily bombed in World War II, and the post war building of freeways and railway lines has added to the destruction.

Since the 1970s, Ōsaka has under gone rapacious urban development accompanied by enormous archaeological "rescue" operations, many continuing for decades. The extent of urbanization is overwhelming, in comparison to other areas of Japan. There have been thousands of excavations of various sizes, both in preparation for building overpasses, rail lines, and highrise apartments often carried out in narrow spaces in highway road beds or between tall buildings. While the imperial tombs are the largest green areas in the city, entrance to their precincts is restricted to brief visits by archaeologists in the company of officials from the Imperial Household Ministry. It is argued that these are religious sites, not historical or archaeological sites. Okamura (2014a, b) describes *kofun* as symbolic and spiritual assets, linked to mythology, history, and local identity.

Since archaeological research has been undertaken by disparate political jurisdictions and academic specialties, the coherence of the region is difficult to grasp. In addition to the central institutions of Ōsaka Fu, such as the Ōsaka Center for Cultural Heritage (Ōsaka Fu Bunkazai Sentā), there are archaeological branches of departments of education in all of the 40 separate municipal units comprising Ōsaka. The picture of Ōsaka's past is buried in thousands of annual government reports, technical lists, written to conform to the standardized format of Japanese government reports. Difficult to summarize. they are not meant to provide extensive cultural interpretation. Archaeologists supplement these with newspaper articles, site tours during excavations, and various kinds of exhibits and summaries directed to the tax-paying public. Local museums provide a link between archaeologists and the public. Their permanent displays provide easily comprehended narratives of local history while temporary displays introduce the latest finds. In dense urban areas where sites such as Uriūdō and Nagahara have been completely destroyed through excavation and development, small permanent displays in the entrances of public buildings remind citizens of the archaeology of the area (Ichikawa 2007: 39).

In my discussion in this appendix of ten museums in the Ōsaka region, I give a brief description of the physical facility, architectural features, focus, the learning experience it provides, the feeling of its space, and its role in the community. How does archaeological heritage relate to the life of people living in Ōsaka today? How are sites and artifacts preserved and interpreted? Japanese are committed to building *local* museums, which make artifacts and information available in the area in which they were found, in addition to large central museums.

General Historical Museums

Ōsaka Museum Of History

The main historical museum in Ōsaka shares space with NHK Broadcasting in a ten storey building designed by Pelli Clarke Pelli, designers of the International Finance Center in Hong Kong and other international monuments. It is located in the ancient center of the city, between the Naniwa Palace and Ōsaka Castle, the latter reconstructed after World War II. Permanent exhibitions occupy the tenth to seventh floors. From the elevator one enters a multi media orientation center on the tenth floor. Following the presentātion the multi media screen of the center rises to reveal a panoramic view of the palace and castle through huge windows. Then one proceeds into a full scale replica of part of the Dairiden (Audience Hall) of Naniwa Palace (Chapter 7), peopled with life size mannequins in court costumes, lined up by rank.

Western music fills this part of the gallery. Surrounding galleries cover the Yayoi (Chapter 4) to Nara (Chapter 6) Periods. The ninth floor is devoted to the Chūsei and Kinsei periods, with a dynamic mix of scale models, huge pictorials, artifacts, and volunteer guides. The eighth floor is the Archaeological Discovery Center with all kinds of interactive facilities for learning about archaeological methods as well as an extensive open library, including site reports and study area. The space can accommodate large school groups. Pamphlets and signs in the museum are available in Japanese, Chinese,

Appendix C

FIGURE C.1. RECONSTRUCTED STOREHOUSE AT HŌENZAKA, IN FRONT OF THE ŌSAKA MUSEUM OF HISTORY. PHOTO BY R.PEARSON.

Korean, and English. On the day of my last visit, during the week of the Chinese New Years, the galleries were filled with Chinese tourists, who could check all kinds of information in Chinese on their smart phones. In front of the museum is a full scale replica of one of the Hōenzaka Storehouses discussed in Chapter 5 (Figure C.1).

Ōsaka Museum of History

Ōsaka Rekishi Hakubutsukan

1-32 Otemae 4 chome Chuō ku Ōsaka Japan 540-0008

http://www.mus-his.city.Ōsaka.jp/eng/

The Sakai City Museum

Set in a huge park with an attached tea garden, the museum is surrounded by tumuli of the Mozu Group (Chapter 5). In front of the museum park is the Daisen Ryō Kofun, which looks like a forested mountain. The permanent museum exhibitions feature the Mozu Tomb Group, with mural maps and displays of selected artifacts. The second portion of the museum features the mediaeval moated city of Sakai (Chapter 7). The museum also features the innovative modern economy of Sakai. The Sakai Museum functions as a vigorous city museum, curating about five themed exhibits per year, and conducting its own research and publication program. The Mozu Tomb Group that surrounds the Sakai Museum, and the nearby Furuichi Tomb Group, were nominated as World Heritage Sites in 2010.

Sakai City Museum

Sakai Shi Hakubutsukan

www.city.sakai.lg.jp/hakubutu/

Daisen Park, Mozusekiun chō 2 chome, Sakai ku Sakai Shi Ōsaka 590-0802

Ōsaka Furitsu Chikatsu Asuka Museum

Opened in 1994, the museum was designed by Andō Tadao and the building is featured in portfolios of

FIGURE C.2. THE EXTERIOR, STEPPED SURFACE OF THE ŌSAKA FURITSU CHIKATSU ASUKA MUSEUM, DESIGNED BY ANDŌ TADAO. THE MUSEUM IS SET IN A LARGE GARDEN OF FLOWERING PLUMS, DESIGNED BY THE ARCHITECT. PHOTO BY R. PEARSON.

Andō's work. A concrete modernist building, its exterior is formed to represent the sloping, stone paved surface of a keyhole mound (Figure C.2).

The main permanent displays are stunning. Around a massive reconstruction of the Daisen Ryō are examples of every category of artifact of the Kofun Period (Chapter 5). A large reference library of Ōsaka archaeology in the entrance area serves as a research center. The museum supports a vigorous exhibition and publication program. Set in the eastern hills of the edge of the Ōsaka Plain, the museum is somewhat off the beaten path. It sits in a small valley of a forested slope, densely covered with the small Late Kofun burial mounds of the Chikatsu Tomb Group Park. Surrounding it is a garden of flowering plums designed by Andō. The beautiful historical park and outstanding architecture are clearly treasured by local residents. Visiting the museum is a multi-faceted experience.

The display focuses on groups of artifacts and their context in sites and monuments, It shows sequences of construction, burial ritual, and social context. It differs from the Tōkyō National Museum, where archaeological objects are shown as art objects with little information or context, and the National Museum of Japanese History where the emphasis is on historical context provided by models, dioramas, panels, and photos.

Ōsaka Prefectural Chikatsu Asuka Museum

Ōsaka Furitsu Chikatsu Asuka Hakubutsukan

299 Higashiyama, Kanan Chō Minami Kawachi Gun, Ōsaka 585-0001

www.chikatsu-asuka.jp/

Specialized Museums

Senboku Suemura Museum

This museum is devoted to grey fired stoneware, *sueki*, hallmark of the Kofun Period (Chapter 5). Opened in

1970, it features kiln sites of the surrounding Senboku area which were excavated during the construction of suburban residential areas such as Senboku New Town. It is a remarkable museum, devoted to this important ancient ceramic and the discovery of some eight hundred kilns, four hundred of which were excavated. The museum building is a low modern concrete structure, set in an extensive city park surrounding the Ohasu Pond, famous for its lotus flowers, within walking distance of the suburban train station of Midorigaoka and near a huge new children's museum as well as a center for disabled persons.

Sakai City Municipal Senboku Suemura Archaeological Museum

Sakai Shiritsu Senboku Suemura Shiryōkan

http://www.geocities.jp/general_sasaki/sakai-suemura-ni.html

Ōsaka fu Sakai shi Minami ku Wakamatsudai, 2-4 (within the Ōhasu Koen), Ōsaka 590-0116

Ōsaka Prefectural Sayamaike Museum

Designed also by Andō Tadao, this modernist concrete museum celebrates the ancient engineering feat of constructing the Sayama Reservoir (Chapter 7). Its focus is irrigation and water control in the history of the surrounding upland. The mandate of the museum includes the comparative study of water control in eastern Asia. Set in a park at the edge of the ancient reservoir, it features a walled dripping pond feature that must be very attractive to locals during the hot Ōsaka summer. The museum incorporates a huge stratigraphic section of the ancient berm of the reservoir into its display. The priest engineer Chōgen (Chapter 7) is introduced in the museum display. Volunteers work with school groups and the museum supports a vigorous temporary exhibition and publication program.

Ōsaka Prefectural Sayamaike Museum

Ōsaka Furitsu Sayamaike Hakubutsukan

Ōsaka Fu Ōsaka Sayama Shi Ikejiri Naka 2 Chome Ōsaka 589-0007

http://www.sayamaikehaku.Ōsakasayama.Ōsaka.jp/

East Ōsaka Buried Cultural Properties Center (Encountering Excavation)

An archaeological museum attached to the East Ōsaka Buried Cultural Properties Center. Replete with small and low tables for school children, it provides a comprehensive introduction to local archaeology as well as the practice of field archaeology. Countless pull-out drawers contain actual specimens, rather than replicas, which can be handled. They are grouped not only by their chronological and cultural historical attributes but also by their functional and technological features. Abundant text panels and diagrams, as well as work sheets, encourage young visitors to consider the making and uses of artifacts. This museum would thrill any child or adult with an interest in science or history even though its ambience and didactic style might be considered out of date by heritage specialists. Visitors can see field archaeologists working in adjacent rooms in the building. Throughout Japan, municipal archaeologists wear a uniform resembling a construction engineer, identifying them as civil employees. This appearance reinforces the fact that archaeology is a part of the responsibility of the municipal government and is carried out by its employees.

East Ōsaka Buried Cultural Properties Center Encountering Excavation)

(Hakkutsu Fureaikan Higashi Ōsaka Maizō Bunkazai Sentā)

Higashi Ōsaka Shi Minami Shijo Chō, 3-33 Japan 579-8054

http://www.city.higashiŌsaka.lg.jp/0000003611.html

Sakai City Mihara Historical Museum

In an area of highway overpasses and urban arteries clogged with trucks, this local museum includes a little restaurant popular with seniors and families and is adjacent to a large playing field and children's park. Situated in Mihara, the area of ancient metal casters, it features the imposing set of Kofun Period cuirasses from the Kurohimeyama Kofun (Chapter 5) and sites left by the Kawachi metal casters (Chapter 6), including a model of a mold for casting a bell. It offers regular seasonal exhibitions supplemented by informative pamphlets.

The Sakai City Mihara Historical Museum

Sakai Shi Mihara Rekishi Hakubutsukan

Sakai Shi Mihara ku Kuroyama 281 Japan 587-0002

https://www.city.sakai.lg.jp/yoyakuanai/bunrui/bunka/hakubutukan/mcmihara.html

Kashiwara Historical Museum

Set in a park devoted to the Takaida Corridor Tomb Group (Chapter 5) this small local museum has several displays covering the archaeology of the crucial junction of the Yamato and Ishi Rivers. The surrounding empty corridor tombs are easily visible and there are explanatory signs near them. No vandalism is evident. From the surrounding sloping forested park, with a bamboo grove and winter flowering camellias, there are views to the south, of the Furuichi Tomb Group (Chapter 5), oases of green in an endless urban sprawl.

Kashiwara Historical Museum

Kashiwara Shiritsu Rekishi Shiryōkan

Takaida 1598-1, Kashiwara City, Ōsaka Japan 582-1

http://www.city.kashiwara.Ōsaka.jp/bunkazai/shiryōukan/shiryōukan.html

Izumi Sano Historical Museum

Izumi Sano City is a wedge of land that extends from the offshore artificial island of Kansai International Airport to the sparsely populated mountains of Wakayama Prefecture. The main theme of the museum is the mediaeval estate, Hine Shōen (Chapter 7). A huge diorama shows the estate as reconstructed from documentary and archaeological research. The 'traditional' rural landscape, all but lost in the Ōsaka region, is preserved in the Hine area, and the museum sponsors seasonal walking tours that are particularly popular among the many retirees who live in the area. In 2013 a plan was submitted for the landscape preservation of the Ōgi area, the region of the Hine Shōen (Izumi Sano Shi 2013). The cultural heritage of the area, included in the comprehensive plan, includes six localities of shrines and temples, listed as National Historic Sites. The cultural landscape includes vegetation and agricultural land including Kinsei Period reservoirs. Combined with the museum, the cultural heritage preservation area will provide an important respite for local citizens and a vital resource for studying mediaeval estates.

Izumisano Historical Museum

Rekishikan Izumisano

http://www.city.izumisano.lg.jp/shisetsu/rekisi/rekisikan.html

Shijo Higashi 1-295-1, Izumisano Shi, Japan 598-0005

Ōsaka Furitsu Yayoi Hakubutsukan

A museum to celebrate Yayoi Culture and the beginnings of agrarian life in Japan was built near the site of the huge Yayoi village, Ikegami Sone (Chapter 4), saved from destruction with the help of a nationwide group of local citizens and professional archaeologists. On the site, adjacent to the busy Ōsaka-Wakayama Highway, a full scale replica of the huge storehouse found on the site has been erected (Figure A.3). An attached learning center engages the public and school children (Torama 2008). The adjacent museum has several large galleries with definitive interpretive exhibits about Yayoi culture in Ōsaka and other areas, as well as space for temporary exhibitions and a spacious open library. On the ground floor is a fine grand piano, for local concerts in the entrance foyer. The museum sponsors a vigorous program of symposia leading to book-length publications. As in many of the museums mentioned above, video is used to great advantage.

Ōsaka Prefectural Museum of Yayoi Culture

Ōsaka Furitsu Yayoi Bunka Hakubutsukan

http://www.kanku-city.or.jp/yayoi/index.html

4-8-27 Ikegami Chō Izumi City Ōsaka 594-0083 Japan

Archaeological Heritage Management and Public Archaeology

Ōsaka provides a good example of the system of excavation, presentātion, and interpretation, of archaeological resources in Japan, and changes which are occurring through economic, social, and demographic shifts. Based on the principle, "the polluter pays', developers are required by law to pay for the costs of excavation of sites, most of which are completely destroyed in the process. Huge processing and storage facilities were built from the 1970s and 1980s. These house self-governing foundations termed 'centers for buried cultural properties' which shifted the burden of financing and administration away from the boards of education of local governments. The salaries of workers in these centers were incorporated into the budgets of these non-profit foundations (Okamura 2011: 78). In the 1960s and early 1970s amateurs and local community members participated in the excavation process; however as the scale of operations dramatically increased in the late 1970's and 1980's, professional heritage managers were required, producing government reports, media releases, exhibitions, and lectures. Okamura (2011: 81) notes that archaeology became part of Japan's consumer culture. As archaeology became almost completely conducted by government archaeologists in what Matsuda terms archaeological heritage management (AHM), it followed strict bureaucratic requirements, which limited free research and weakened the essential research component of university training (Okamura 2011: 81). Many archaeologists working for government agencies have little time for academic research or the testing of new theories or approaches, or for linking their research to the public in new ways.

The admirable system of heritage preservation and interpretation was built during Japan's prosperity of the 1980s. With economic stagnation, it is difficult to sustain. As in other countries, heritage management must compete with health care and other social services and is being challenged to show that it has some economic value for society. The decline in funding in Japan has been followed by a move to privatize rescue archaeology in order to reduce the size of government. Government agencies are turning to private contractors to carry out excavations required before sites can be developed, rather than retaining large excavation crews. Development companies are expanding into the cultural heritage business by establishing private companies to take on these rescue excavations on contracts from the government, in order to make up for declining revenues brought about by decreasing real estate development. This creates a conflict of interest (Okamura 2014 c,d).

How does the decline in archaeological salvage excavation affect the educational programs and other museum activities in the Ōsaka area and Japan in general (Henshū Iinkai 2008)? From 1997 to 2011, the amount spent on rescue excavations in Japan declined by 40%, as economic development slowed (Sakai 2013). In April, 2008, the government of Ōsaka, faced with rising deficits, proposed the reduction of museum budgets by 50%, along with the closing of the Ōsaka Furitsu Yayoi Bunka Hakubutsukan and the Senboku Shiryōkan, and the transfer of the collections from these museums to the Ōsaka Furitsu Chikatsu Asuka Hakubutsukan. Under public pressure, the governor, Hashimoto Toru, of the neo-conservative Restoration Party, retracted the decision (Hirose 2008). Such an event suggests that support for the Ōsaka museum system was strong, but perhaps not as strong as general as it could be.

Museum admission fees have never paid for more than a fraction of total costs and many Ōsaka museums have no admission fee; however groups who support them have political clout. Two groups provide support for museums in Ōsaka: students, who visited the museums on school visits, and provide some 40% of the visitors, and retirees who are keenly interested in local history and archaeology, often serving as volunteers. However, students only visited the museum on class visits required as part of their school curriculum (Yoshimura 2008). The experience in most cases is passive, rarely leading to an active engagement with archaeology or history. Perhaps the linkages between museums and archaeological facilities and students could be revitalized, to show the relevance of archaeology for teaching science or other fields such as art or digital media.

The bland content of archaeological museums may need revision to engage the public. This can be done by creating novel synergistic exhibits, that link archaeology to new fields of inquiry, and forging interdisciplinary linkages. The latter will take some effort, since university archaeology programs seem to be rooted exclusively in national history with few links to other fields. The Sayamaike Museum has found that its links to ancient engineering, including arch and bridge construction, have public appeal, and are compatible with its broad mandate (Arii 2006).

Is the present system of museums sustainable? Do the museums promote sustainable tourism? What is the impact of nominating sites such as Mozu and Furuichi as World Heritage Sites? Should museums lead as educational innovators instead of being passive repositories with predictable story lines? Who will visit museums when Japan's senior citizens are no longer so numerous? While AHM (Archaeological Heritage Management) practitioners try hard to engage the public, the emerging international field of public archaeology is based on a different structure than the top down pattern followed in Japan. Public archaeology involves the participation of the public in interpretation, and encourages a diversity of interpretations that reflect the diversity of interest groups in the community (Matsuda 2013, Okamura and Matsuda 2008, Matsuda and Okamura 2011). Hodder (2011: 19) states that "archaeological stewardship should be based on dialogue between shareholder groups, and that participation must take place at every level." How will the system of heritage management and public archaeology be reconfigured for the future? The strong points of the museums described here are their immaculate preservation, the creation of high quality spaces, and the interconnectedness of cultural and natural heritage.

Utaka (2013) and Champagain (2013a) noted that Japan's preservation approach could be considered to be 'material based' and monument centric', rather than 'people-oriented' or community-based. The emphasis is on the preservation of the physical site and its authenticity, rather than the living site in its contemporary environment. Sites can become static fossils when neighboring buildings are removed and daily services are restricted, to prevent deterioration or fire. Food stands, bars, restaurants and souvenir stands are regulated and locals are denied access unless they pay admission.

For instance, Utaka (2013) observed that although the Himeji Castle in Himeji City (some distance from Ōsaka), was beautifully preserved and surrounded by attractive green space, and even given World Heritage status, the area around the castle became isolated from daily life and informal activities by locals became restricted. The area lost its neighborly vitality. The castle is important for nostalgia, memory, and emotion, in addition to its history and role in attracting tourists. Its importance for grassroots groups must be acknowledged. Similarly, the vitality of religious sites and regions must be protected; in some cases religious practices are dramatically reduced to save the structure (Champagain 2013b).

I have every confidence that Ōsaka entrepreneurs will create new public spaces and cultural capital that will bring their archaeology into new relationships with the Japanese public. As Japan's reduced population shifts to a more youthful demographic curve, new cultural opportunities for wider and more diversified access will emerge. Perhaps with slower economic development the center of gravity of archaeology will shift toward universities and research institutes which will be linked to international research networks and Ōsaka archaeology will be shared by people around the world in comparative studies.

Glossary

Japanese characters for major site, personal, and place names, and Japanese author's names, and archaeological terms.

Akashi　明石
Akiyama Kōzō　秋山浩三
Akiyama Shingo　秋山進午
Amano Tarō　天野太郎
Amano　天野
Andō Tadao　安藤忠雄
Andoyama　行燈山古墳
Aoyagi Taisuke　青柳泰介
Arii Hiroko　有井宏子
Ariyama　アリ山
Asao Naohiro　朝尾直弘
Asuka Ike　飛鳥池
baichō　倍塚
Ban Yasushi　坂靖
Bingo Sanuki　備後讃岐
Bizen　備前
Bokeyama　ボケ山
bōsei kyō　ぼう制鏡
Bu　武
Chin　珍
Chino'oka　乳の岡
Cho Chul-jae　趙哲済 (Korean)
Chōdōin　朝堂院
Chōgen　重源
Chōshōji　長勝寺
Chūsei　中世
Dai'anji　大安寺
Daidō　大道
Dairikōden　内裏後殿
Dairizenden　内裏前殿
Daisen Ryō　大山陵
Danjō Hiroshi　檀上寛
Doshōmachi　道修町
dōtaku　銅鐸
Dotō　土塔
dozō　土蔵
Echizen　越前
Egōshū　会合衆
Engishiki　延喜式
entō haniwa　円筒埴輪
Eta Funayama　江田船山
Eura Hiroshi　江浦洋
Fuchinokami Ryūsuke　渕ノ上隆介
Fuhonsen　富本銭
Fujii Toshiaki　藤井利章
Fujiidera　藤井寺
Fujinoki　藤の木

Fujio Shin'ichirō　藤尾慎一郎
Fujita Kazutaka　藤田和尊
Fujita Minoru　藤田実
Fujita Saburō　藤田三郎
Fujiwara　藤原
Fujiwara Satoshi　藤原哲
Fukunaga Shin'ya　福永伸哉
Furu　布留
Furuichi　古市
Furuike　古池
gaki　瓦器
gashitsu doki　瓦質土器
Godaigo Tennō　後醍醐王
Gokurakuji Hibiki　極楽寺ヒビキ
Gosashi　五社神
Gose　御所
Habikino　羽曳野
Hagihara Mitsuo　萩原三雄
haji　土師
Haji Minami Ryō　土師南陵
Haji Nisanzai　土師ニサンザイ
haji shitsu doki　土師質土器
Hajidera　土師寺
hajiki　土師器
Hajinosato　土師ノ里
Hakata　博多
Hanada Katsuhiro　花田勝広
haniwa　埴輪
Harunari Hideji　春成秀爾
Hashiguchi Tatsuya　橋口達也
Hashihaka　箸墓
Hashimoto Teruhiko　橋本輝彦
Hayashi Masanori　林正憲
Heijō　平城
Henshū Iinkai　編集委員会
hibachi　火鉢
Hibiya Ryōkei　日比谷了慶
Higashi Ōsaka　東大阪
Higashi Ueno　東上野
Hiki Shōen　日置荘園
Himiko　卑弥呼
Hine Shōen　日根荘園
Hirano　平野
Hirata Yōji　平田洋司
Hirose Kazuo　広瀬和雄
Hishida Tetsuo　菱田哲郎
Hōenzaka　法円坂
hōkei shūkōbo　方形周溝墓
Hokenoyama　ホケノ山
Homutawake　誉田別
Hōraisan　鳳来山

Hōryuji　法隆寺
Hosokawa　細川
Hyakutsukabaru　百塚原
Hyōgo Tsu　兵庫津
Ibaraki　茨城
Ichihara Minoru　市原実
Ichijōdani　一条谷
Ichikawa Hideyuki　市川秀之
Ichikawa Tsukuru　市川創
Ichinose Kazuo　一瀬和夫
Ichinoyama　市の山
iegata sekkan　家形石棺
Iga　伊賀
Iizuka Takeshi　飯塚武司
Ikedadera　池田寺
Ikegami Sone　池上曽根
Ikegami Sone　池上曽根
Ikejiri　池尻
Ikeshima Fukumanji　池島福万寺
Ima Shirotsuka　今城塚
Imai Mayumi　今井真由美
Imai Sōkyū　今井宗久
Imakuma　今熊
Imamura Mineo　今村峰雄
Imari　伊万里
Inariyama　稲荷山
Inoue Tomohiro　井上智博
Inui Tetsuya　乾哲也
Ishi (River)　石
Ishigami Yutaka　石神裕
Ishimura Tomo　石村智
Ishino Hironobu　石野博信
Ishitsu　石津
Ishitsuoka　石津丘
Ishiyama Honganji　石山本願寺
Ishitsuka　石塚
Isogai Fujio　磯貝富士男
Isogawa Shin'ya　五十川伸矢
Itō Koji　伊藤幸司
Iwajuku　岩宿
Izumi　泉
Izumi Sano　泉佐野
Izumiya　和泉屋
Izumori Kō　泉森皎
Jinaimachi　寺内町
Jingū　神功
Jishū　寺宗
Jōdo Shinshū　浄土真宗
jūkan　住館
kabuto　冑
kabutohachi　兜鉢
kachū　甲冑
Kaigawa Katsushi　貝川克士
Kajiyama Hikotarō　梶山彦田郎
Kamei　亀井
Kami Ishitsu Misanzai　上石津ミサンザイ
Kanaseki Hiroshi　金関恕
Kanazawa Yō　金沢陽

kangai shisetsu　館外施設
Karako Kagi　唐古鍵
Karatsu　唐津
Kasai Toshimitsu　笠井敏光
Kashihara　橿原
Kashiwara　柏原
Katonboyama　カトンボ山
Katsuragi　葛城
Kawachi　河内
Kawachi imoji　河内鋳師
Kawachi Kazuhiro　河内一浩
Kawachi nabe　河内鍋
Kawane Yoshiyasu　河音能平
Kaya　伽耶
Ki　紀
Kibi　吉備
Kihara Katsushi　木原克司
Kii　紀伊
Kinsei　近世
Kinugawa Kazunori　絹川一徳
Kishimoto Naofumi　岸本直文
Kita Sadakichi　喜田貞吉
Ko　興
Kō　国府
Kobata Atsushi　小葉田淳
Kobayashi Hiroshi　小林博
Kobayashi Ken'ichi　小林謙一
Kobayashi Saburō　小林三郎
Kobayashi Yukio　小林行雄
Kodai　古代
kofun　古墳
Koganetsuka　黄金塚
Kohama Sei　小浜成
Kojiki　古事記
Kojima Higashi　小島東
Kojita Yasunao　小路泰直
koku　石
komochi magatama　子持勾玉
Konda Gobyōyama　誉田御苗山
Konda Hachiman　誉田八幡
Konda Maruyama　誉田丸山
Konda Shiratori　誉田白鳥
Kondō Yasushi　近藤康司
Kondō Yoshirō　近藤義郎
Kongō　金剛
Konishi Ryūsa　小西隆佐
Kōraibashi　高麗橋
Kōtoku　孝徳
Koyashiroyama　高屋城山
Kudara Amadera　百済尼寺
kudatama　管玉
Kujō　九条
Kumano　熊野
Kumeda Kaibukiyama　久米田貝吹山
Kurosawa Hiroshi　黒沢浩
Kusaba Sainin　草葉西忍
Kusaka Masayoshi　日下雅義
Kuwatsu　桑津

Kyōshima Satoru　京嶋覚
kyoten shūraku　拠点集落
Kyūhōji　久宝寺
Liu Song　劉宋 (Chinese)
magatama　勾玉
Makabe Takahiko　間壁忠彦
Makimuku　纒向
Mametani Hiroyuki　豆谷和之
Mappō　末法
Matsuda Akira　松田陽
Matsuda Jun'ichirō　松田順一郎
Matsugi Takehiko　松木武彦
Matsuo Nobuhiro　松尾信裕
Matsuokayama　松岡山
Mesuriyama　メスリ山
Miki Hiroshi　三木弘
Minami Hideo　南秀雄
Minami Kawachi　南河内
Minato　湊
Minegatsuka　峰ケ塚
Mino　美濃
Miyake Yonekichi　三宅米吉
Miyamoto Kōji　宮本康治
Miyamoto Sachiko　宮本佐知子
Miyaoka Masanobu　宮岡昌宣
Miyoshi　三好
Mizoguchi Kōji　溝口孝司
Mizuno Masayoshi　水野正好
Mononobe　物部
Mori Tsuyoshi　森毅
Morii Sadao　森井貞雄
Morimoto Susumu　森本晋
Morimura Ken'ichi　森村健一
Morinomiwa　森の宮
Morioka Hideto　盛岡秀人
Morishita Shōji　森下章司
Mozu　百舌鳥
Murai Shōsuke　村井章介
Murakami Takashi　村上陸
Murakawa Yukihiro　村川行弘
Nagahara Takamane　長原高回
Nagahara　長原
nagamochigata sekkan　長持形石棺
Nagaō　長大
Nagaoka　長岡
Nagasone　長曽根
Nagayoshi Kawanabe　永吉川辺
Nagazumi Yōko　永積洋子
Nakakubo Tatsuo　中久保辰夫
Nakamura Hiroshi　中村博司
Nakao Yoshiharu　中尾芳治
Nakaoka Masaru　中岡勝
Nakatsuyama　中津山
Nakayamatsuka　中山塚
Nanban Fuki　南蛮吹
Nangō　南郷
Naniwa Horie　難波堀江
Naniwa Tsu　難波津

Naniwanomiya　難波宮
Nankai　南海
Naoki Kōjirō　直木孝次郎
narabikura　並び倉
Narutaki　鳴滝
nendokaku　粘土郭
Nichiren　日蓮
Nihon Shoki　日本書紀
Niiro Izumi　新納泉
Niki Hiroshi　仁木宏
nimōsaku　二毛作
Nintoku　仁徳
Nishikawa Toshikatsu　西川寿勝
Nishimoto Toyohiro　西本豊弘
Nishitonozuka　西殿塚
Nishiurahashi　西浦橋
Niwatori　鶏
Nojima Hisashi　野島永
Nonaka　野中
Ōbadera　大庭寺
Oda Nobunaga　織田信長
Odagi Fujimi　小田木富慈実
Ogasawara Shigeru　小笠原茂
Ōgata　大県
Ogura Tetsuya　小倉徹也
Ōjin　応神
Oka Misanzai　岡ミサンザイ
ōkabe tatemono　大壁建物
okabe yoroi　頸甲
Okamura Katsuyuki　岡村勝行
Ōkawa　大川
Okinaga　息長
Onchi　恩智
Oribe　織部
Osawa Ken'ichi　小沢健一
Ōtsu　大津
Ōtsudō　大津道
Ōtsuka Hatsushige,　大塚初重
Ōuchi　大内
Ōwada no Tomari　大和田泊
Ōyamato　大大和
Ozaki Hiromasa　尾嵜大真
Rennyo　蓮如
Ryōnan Kita　陵南北
Sahara Makoto　佐原真
Sai　濟
Saikudani　細工谷
Saitobaru　西都原
Sakaehara Towao　栄原永遠
Sakai Hideya　坂井秀弥
Sakai Ryūichi　坂井龍一
Sakamoto Minoru　坂本稔
Saki Ishitsuyama　佐紀石津山
Saki Misasagiyama　佐紀陵山
Saki　佐紀
Sakurai Chausuyama　桜井茶臼山
sankakuen shinjūkyō　三角縁神獣鏡
Sano　佐野

San　讃
Sayama　狭山
Sefukuji　施福寺
Seike Akira　清家章
Seki Shūichi　関周一
Sekiguchi　関口
Sekimoto Yumiko　関本優美子
Sekiyama Hiroshi　積山洋
Senboku　泉北
senretsu tatemono　專列建物
Seto　瀬戸
Settsu　摂津
Settsu　摂津
sharinseki　車輪石
Shibuya Mukōyama　渋谷向山
Shichikanyama　七観山
Shigaraki　信楽
Shikinzan　紫金山
Shimada Akira　嶋田章
Shimatani Kazuhiro　嶋谷和彦
Shimogaki Hitoshi　下垣仁志
Shin Yakushiji　新薬師寺
Shin'ike　新池
Shinjō　新城
Shino　志野
Shinpukuji　真福寺
Shinshū Honkyō　真宗本教
Shiragayama　白髪山
Shiraishi Kōji　白石耕治
Shiraishi Ta'ichirō　白石太一郎
Shiroyama　城山
Shitara Hiromi　設楽博己
Shitennōji　四天王寺
shōen　荘園
shōgun　将軍
Shokokuji　諸国寺
Shōtoku　聖徳
Sobayama　側山古墳
Soga Riuemon　蘇我理右衛門
Sumitomo Tomomichi　住友友以
Soga　曽我
Song Shi　宋史 (Chinese)
Song Shu　宋書 (Chinese)
sueki　須恵器
Suemura　陶村
Sugahara Yūichi　菅原雄一
Sukigara Toshio　鋤柄俊夫
Sumitomo Masatomo　住友政友
Sumitomo　住友
Sumiyoshi　住吉
Sumiyoshi Sairei Zu Byōbu　住吉祭礼図屏風
Sumiyoshinotsu　住吉津
suribachi　摺鉢
Suyama　巣山
Suzuki Yasutami　鈴木靖民
Tadeiyama　田出井山
Taira no Kiyomori　平清盛
Tajihidō　丹比道

Tajima　田島
Takahashi Teruhiko　高橋照彦
Takatsuki　高槻
Takeno Jō'ō　武野 紹鴎
Takesue Jun'ichi　武末純一
Takeuchi　竹内
Tamateyama　玉手山
Tanabe　田辺
Tanaka Migaku　田中箕学
Tanaka Shinsaku　田中晋作
Tanaka Takeo　田中健夫
Tanba　丹波
Tanioka Takashi　谷岡能史
tankō　短甲
Tenmu　天武
Tennōji　天王寺
Tenri Gareri　天理ガレリ
Tenryūji　天竜寺
Terai Makoto　寺井誠
Teramura, Hirofumi　寺村裕史
Terasawa Kaoru　寺澤薫
Tobi Chausuyama　外山茶臼山
Tōdaiji　東大寺
Togawa Yoshikazu　十川良和
Tokoname　常滑
Tokugawa Ieyasu　徳川家康
Tokushima　徳島
tomoegata　巴型
toraijin　渡来人
Torama Asami　虎間麻美
tottaimon　突帯文
Toyoshima Naohiro　豊島直博
Toyotomi Hideyori　豊臣秀頼
Toyotomi Hideyoshi　豊臣秀吉
Toyo　臺與
Tsubai Ōtsukayama　椿井大塚山
Tsuchiyama Takeshi　土山健史
Tsude Hiroshi　都出比呂志
Tsudō Shiroyama　津堂城山古墳
Tsugiyama Jun　次山惇
Tsujimoto Yūya　辻本裕也
Tsujio Ei'ichi　辻尾榮市
Tsukamawari　塚回
Tsukuriyama　造山
Tsunoyama, Sakae　角山榮
Tsuzuki Shin'ichirō　續伸一郎
Uchida Kusuo　内田九州男
Uchida Toshihide　内田俊秀
Ueda Masa'aki　上田正昭
Ueda Takashi　上田陸司
Ueki Hisashi　植木久
Uemachi　上町
Uezato Takashi　上里陸
Umami　馬見
Ume　梅
Urabe Yukihiro　卜部行弘
Uriūdō　瓜生堂
Uriwari　瓜破

Uwanabe　ウワアナベ
Wada　和田
Wada Seigo　和田晴吾
Wadō Kaichin　和同開珎
Wakabayashi Kunihiko　若林邦彦
Wakasa Tōru　若狭徹
Wani　王仁
Watanabe Tsu　渡辺津
Wei Zhi　魏志
Yagi Hisae　八木久栄
Yamakawa Hitoshi　山川均
Yamato　大和
Yamato Yanagimoto　大和柳本

Yamauchi Noritsugu　山内紀嗣
yashiki　屋敷
Yashimatsuka　八島塚
Yasuda Yoshinori　安田喜憲
Yasumura Toshifumi　安村俊史
Yayoi　弥生
Yoko (River)　除
Yoneda Fumitaka　米田文孝
Yoshimura Ken　吉村健
Yoshinogawa　吉野川
Yotsuike　四つ池
Zenmyōji　善明寺
zenpōkōenfun　前方後円墳

References Cited

academics3 . 2014. *Kō iseki (Kō site)* website accessed Sept 22 2014 http://academic3.plala.or.jp/fujinan/fujisi/bunkazai/koiseki.htm

Akiyama, Kōzō. 2001. "B.C. 52 nen to Yayoi doki" sono ato --Ikegami Sone Iseki no nenrin nendai (After the "Yayoi pottery dated to 52 BC " -- tree ring dating of the Ikegami Sone Site) *Kōkogaku Janaru* 472: 6-10.

Akiyama, Kōzō. 2006. *Yayoi Jitsu Nendai to Toshi Ron no Yukue: Ikegami Sone Iseki (True Dating of Yayoi and Present State of the Urban Center Theory: the Ikegami Sone Site).* Tōkyō, Shinsensha.

Akiyama, Kōzō. 2007. *Yayoi Ōgata Nōkō Shūraku no Kenkyū (Study of Large Yayoi Farming Settlements).* Tōkyō, Aoki Shoten.

Akiyama, Shingo. 1985. Makioyama Sefukuji Kyozuka Gun no chōsa. In Izumi Shi Kubosō Kinen Bijutsukan (ed.), *Tokubetsu Ten Shisei 30 Shūnen Kinen, Koganetsuka Kofun, Sefukuji Kyozuka no Ihō (Special Exhibition on the 30th Anniversary of the Municipal System. Treasures from the Koganetsuka Kofun and the Sutra Mound of the Sefukuji*: 55-76. Izumi Shi, Izumi Shi Kubosō Kinen Bijutsukan.

Amano, Tarō. 1996. Ōsaka Ishiyama Honganji Jinaichō puranu no fukugen ni kansuru kenkyū (Study relating to the reconstruction of the plan on the Jinaimachi (Temple town complex) of the Ishiyama Honganji, Ōsaka. *Jinbun Chiri* 48 (2): 22-41.

Amino, Yoshihiko. 2012. *Rethinking Japanese History.* Ann Arbor, Center for Japanese Studies, University of Michigan.

Amstutz, G. 1991. *The Honganji Institution 1500 to 1570. The Politics of Pure Land Buddhism in Late Mediaeval Japan.* PhD Dissertation, Princeton University. Ann Arbor, University Microfilms International.

archaeology.jp. 2014a. *Makimuku iseki (Makimuku site)* website accessed Sept 2014 http://archaeology.jp/sites/2010/makimuku.htm

archaeology.jp. 2014b. *Kofun period research trends 2009.* website accessed Sept. 14 2014. http://archaeology.jp/publication/trends/Kofun-2009.pdf

Arii, Hiroko. 2006. Tasha no monozashi (Another viewpoint). *Kōkogaku Kenkyū* 53(1): 11-14.

Asao, Naohiro. 2004. Kokusai minato ichi: Sakai (International commercial port: Sakai). *Asahi Hyakka Nihon no Rekishi (Special Volume, Chūsei Kara Kinsei e: Dejima to Tōjin Machi (From Mediaeval to Pre Modern: Dejima and Chinese communities)* 31: 260-265.

Asao, Naohiro, Sakaehara Towao, Niki Hiroshi, and Kojita Yasunao. 1999. *Sakai no Rekishi (History of Sakai).* Tōkyō, Kadokawa Shoten.

Ban,Yasushi. 2009. *Kofun Jidai no Isekigaku: Yamato Ōken no Shihai Kōzō to Haniwa Bunka (Study of Sites of the Kofun Period; the Structure of Power of the Yamato Polity and Haniwa Culture).* Tōkyō: Yūzankaku.

Ban Yasushi and Aoyagi Taisuke. 2011. *Katsuragi no Ōto Nangō Iseki Gun (The capital of the Katsuragi, Nangō Site Group).* Tōkyō, Shinsensha.

Barnes, G. L. 1987. The role of the *be* in state formation. In E. Brumfiel and T. Earle (eds.), *Production, Exchange, and Complex Societies*: 86-101. Cambridge, Cambridge University Press.

Barnes, G.L. 1988. *Protohistoric Yamato.* Ann Arbor, Center for Japanese Studies, University of Michigan.

Barnes, G.L. 1993. *China, Korea, and Japan: The Rise of Civilization in East Asia.* London, Thames and Hudson.

Barnes, G.L. 2000. Archaeological armor in Korea and Japan; styles, technology, and social setting. *Journal of East Asian Archaeology* 2:3/4: 61-95.

Barnes, G.L. 2007. *State Formation in Japan: Emergence of a 4th Century Ruling Elite.* London, Routledge.

Barnes, G.L. 2014. A hypothesis for Early Kofun Rulership. *Japan Review* 27: 3-29.

Barnes, G.L. 2015. *The Archaeology of East Asia. The Rise of Civilization in China, Korea, and Japan.* Oxford, Oxbow Books.

bell.jp 2014. *Mozu Kofungun (Mozu Tomb Group)* website accessed Sept. 22 2014 http://bell.jp/pancho/travel/furuiti-mozu%20kofungun/mozu-kofungun.htm

Bodart, B. 1977. Tea and counsel: the political role of Sen Rikyū. *Monumenta Nipponica* 32(1): 49-74.

Braudel, F. 1982. *Civilization and Capitalism, 15th to 18th Centuries. The Wheels of Commerce, Volume II* London, Collins.

Brown, D. M. 1951. *Money Economy in Mediaeval Japan: A Study in the Use of Coins.* Far Eastern Association, Monograph 1. New Haven, Far Eastern Association.

bunarinn.fc2web.com.2014. *Nara Ken Gose Shi (Nara Prefecture Gose City;* web site accessed Sept. 14 2014 http://bunarinn.fc2web.com/kodaitatemono/hibiki/katuragihibiki.htm

Campbell, R.B. 2009. Toward a network and boundaries approach to early complex polities: the Late Shang Case. *Current Anthropology* 50: 6: 821-848.

Champagain, N. K. 2013a. Introduction: contexts and concerns in Asian heritage management. In K. D. Silva and N.K. Champagain (eds.), *Asian Heritage Management: Contexts, Concerns, and Prospects*: 1-30. London, Routledge.

Champagain, N., K. 2013b. Heritage management in the Buddhist context. In K. D. Silva and N.K. Champagain (eds.), *Asian Heritage Management: Contexts, Concerns, and Prospects*: 49-64. London, Routledge.

Chō, Chorje. 2008. Zō ga ita Uemachi no umi (Uemachi sea and fossil elephants). In Ōsaka Shi Bunkazai Kyōkai (eds.), Ōsaka *no Iseki*: 18-19. Ōsaka, Ōsaka Shi Bunkazai Kyōkai.

Collcutt, M. 1981. *Five Mountains: The Rinzai Zen Monastic Instuitution in Mediaeval Japan*. Cambridge, Cambridge University Press.

Collcutt, M. 1990. Mediaeval Shōen. In K. Yamamura, J. Hall, M. Jansen, D. Twitchett and H. Kanai (eds.), *The Cambridge History of Japan Volume 3 Mediaeval Japan*: 89-127. Cambridge, Cambridge University Press.

Como, M. 2009. *Weaving and Binding: Immigrant Gods and Female Immortals in Ancient Japan*. Honolulu, University of Hawaii Press.

Danjō, Hiroshi. 2005. Mindai kaikin no jitsuzō (A true image of the Ming Prohibition). In Murai Shōsuke and Rekishigaku Kenkyūkai (eds.), *Minato Machi to Kaiiki Sekai*: 145-177. Tōkyō, Aoki Shoten.

Earle, T. 1997. *How Chiefs Come to Power*. Stanford, Stanford University Press.

Edwards, W. 2000. Contested access: the Imperial Tombs in the Postwar Period. *Journal of Japanese Studies* 26 (2): 371-392.

Edwards, W. 2006. Introduction, Tsude Hiroshi, Early state formation in Japan. In J. Piggott (ed.), *Capital and Countryside in Japan 300 – 1180*: 13-15. Ithaca, Cornell University East Asia Program.

Edwards, W. 2013. Kofun Period research trends 2009 Japan Arch Assoc (Walter Edwards 2013 Translator's Note) website accessed July 11 2015. http://archaeology.jp/publication/trends/Kofun-2009.pdf

Eura, Hiroshi. 1996. Kawachi Heiya no suiden kaihatsu (Development of rice paddies on the Kawachi Plain). *Gekkan Bunkazai* 398: 40-43.

Eura, Hiroshi. 2007. Naniwa tsu to Shiragi doki (Naniwa Port and Silla pottery). In Ōsaka Furitsu Yayoi Bunka Hakubutsukan (ed.), *Hakkutsu Sareta Ōsaka 2007; Suito Ōsaka no Kokusai Kōryūshi (Ōsaka Excavations 2007; History of International Trade of Ōsaka, Water City)*: 72-79. Izumi Shi, Ōsaka Furitsu Yayoi Bunka Hakubutsukan.

Eura, Hiroshi. 2012. *Himiko no Jidai no Nōkō Gijutsu (Agricultural Technology at the Time of Himiko)* Powerpoint for lecture at the Ōsaka Furitsu Yayoi Hakubutsukan Jan 15 2012. http/inoues.net/study/aguliculture.html. web site accessed Sept. 25 2014.

Frois, L. 1966. *Nihon Shi (History of Japan)*. translated by Yanagiya Takeo. Tōkyō, Heibonsha.

Fuchinokami, Ryūsuke. 2005. Kofun ni okeru tsukuridashi shūhen ibustugun no yōso (The nature of artifact groups in the area of the front rectangular portion of *kofun*). *Kōkogaku Kenkyū* 52(3): 54-73.

Fujii Toshiaki and Kasai Toshimitsu. 1987. Tennō Ryō Jiten (Dictionary of Imperial Mausolea). In *Rekishi Dokuhon Tokushu, Tennō Ryō to kyūto (Dictionary of Imperial Mausolea, Special Issue, Imperial Tombs and Capitals)* pp. 286-339. Tōkyō, Shin Jinbutsu Oraisha.

Fujiidera Shi. 2015. Ketsujō mimikazari no nazō No. 62. website accessed Sept. 14 2014. www.fujiidera.Ōsaka.jp/rekishi kanko/kodai kara nomes

Fujio, Shin'ichirō. 2000 Appendix 1: The relationship between Kaya and Silla and western Japan in terms of iron production from the first century BC to the sixth century AD. *Journal of East Asian Archaeology* 2: 96-121.

Fujio, Shin'ichirō. 2009. Kosho nendai o mochi ita Yayoi shūrakuron (Yayoi settlement theory using calibrated dates). *Kokuritsu Rekishi Minzoku Hakubutsukan Kenkyū Hōkoku* 149:135-161.

Fujio, Shin'ichirō. 2011. *(Shin) Yayoi Jidai 500 Nen Hayakatta Inasaku (New) Yayoi Period Paddy Rice Cultivation 500 Years Earlier)*. Tōkyō, Yoshikawa Kōbunkan.

Fujita, Saburō. 2012. *Karako Kagi Iseki (The Karako Kagi Site)*. Tōkyō, Dōseisha.

Fujita, Kazutaka. 2006. *Kofun Jidai no Ōken to Gunji (Royal Power and Warfare in the Kofun Period)*. Tōkyō, Gakuseisha.

Fujita, Minoru. 2000. Jinaimachi Ōsaka (Ishiyama) to sono chiriteki kankyō (The geographical environment of Ishiyama, Jinaimachi, Ōsaka. In Watanabe Takeshi Kanchō Taishoku Kinen Ronshū Kankōkai (Committee for the retirement publication for Director Watanabe Takeshi) (ed.), Ōsakajō to Jōkamachi (Ōsaka Castle and Castle Town): 369-393. Kyōto, Shibunkaku Shuppan.

Fujiwara, Satoshi. 2002. Yayoi shūraku no nōgyō keizairyoku (Agricultural economic power of Yayoi villages). *Kōkogaku Kenkyū* 49(3): 106-118.

Fukunaga, Shin'ya. 1999. Kofun no shutsugen to chuō seiken no girei kanri (Appearance of kofun and management of ritual by the central authority). *Kōkogaku Kenkyū* 46(2): 53-72.

Fukunaga, Shin'ya. 2004. Social changes from the Yayoi to the Kofun Periods. In Society for Archaeological Studies (ed.), *Cultural Diversity and the Archaeology of the Twenty First Century*: 141-149. Okayama, Society for Archaeological Studies.

Fukunaga, Shin'ya. 2005. *Sankakuen Shinjūkyo no Kenkyū (Study of Triangular Rim Mirror with Animals and Deities)*. Ōsaka, Ōsaka Daigaku Shuppankai.

Fukunaga, Shin'ya. 2008. Kofun shutsugenki no Yamatogawa to Yodogawa (The Yamato and Yodo Rivers in the period of the emergence of the Kofun Tombs). In Shiraishi Ta'ichirō (ed.), *Kinki Chihō ni okeru Ōgata Kofungun no Kisoteki Kenkyū (Fundamental Study of the Large Tombs of the Kinki Region)*: 439-450. Nara, Nara Daigaku Bunkakubu Bunkazai Gakka.

Fukunaga, Shin'ya. 2014. Kofun jidai no seiritsu to Hashihaka Kofun (The formation of the Kofun Period and the Hashihaka Kofun). In Sakurai Shi Bunka Isan Katsuyō Jikkō Iinkai (ed.), *Shinpojiumu [Hashihaka Saikō] Happyō Yōshi (Summary of Lectures of the Symposium, [Re examination of Hashihaka]*: 37-43. Sakurai, Sakurai Shiritsu Maizō Bunkazai Sentā.

Gay, S. 2001. *The Money Lenders of Mediaeval Kyōto*. Honolulu, University of Hawaii Press.

geocities.jp. 2014. *Hineshō Iriyamada Mura (Hineshō Iriyamada Village)* Web site accessed Sept. 14 2014. http://book.geocities.jp/eiji71ura/hinesou.html

Grossberg, K. A. 1981. *Japan's Rennaissance: The Politics of the Muromachi Bakufu.* Cambridge, Council on East Asian Studies.

Habikino Shi Kyōiku Iinkai. 1993. *Kawachi Furuichi Kofungun Minegatsuka Kofun Gaihō (Summary Report of the Minegatsuka Burial Mound, Furuichi Burial Mound Group, Kawachi)*. Tōkyō, Yoshikawa Kōbunkan.

Hall, J. 1966. *Government and Local Power in Japan, 500 to 1700: A Study based on Bizen Province.* Princeton, Princeton University Press.

Hall, J. 1991. Introduction. In J. Hall (ed.), *The Cambridge History of Japan*, Volume 4, :1-39. Cambridge, Cambridge University Press.

Hanada, Katsuhiro. 2002. *Kodai no Tetsu Seisan to Toraijin (Ancient Iron Production and Continental Immigrants)*. Tōkyō, Yūzankaku.

Harunari, Hideji. 1975. Jimmu Ryō wa itsu tskurareta no ka (When was the Jimmu Tennō Mausoleum built?). *Kōkogaku Kenkyū* 84: 59-82.

Harunari, Hideji, Kobayashi Ken'ichi, Sakamoto Minoru, Imamura Mineo, Ozaki Hiromasa, Fujio Shin'ichirō, and Nishimoto Toyohiro. 2011. Kofun jidai shutsugenki no tanso 14 nendai sokutei (Radiocarbon dating the beginning of the Kofun Period) *Kokuritsu Rekishi Minzoku Hakubutsukan Kenkyū Hōkoku* 163:176-xx.

Hashiguchi, Tatsuya. 1995. Yayoi Jidai no tatakai (Yayoi Period warfare). *Kōkogaku Kenkyū* 42(1): 54-77.

Hashimoto, Teruhiko. 2010. Makimuku iseki (Makimuku site). In Bunka Chō, (ed.), *Hakkutsu Sareta Nihon 2010 (Japanese Islands Excavated 2010)*: 31-34. Tōkyō, Asahi Shinbun Shuppan.

hct.zaq.ne.jp. 2014. Ōsaka *heiya no hensen (Changes in the* Ōsaka *Plain)* website accessed Sept. 22 2014. http://www.hct.zaq.ne.jp/agua/preyamato-river/anime.html

Henshū Iinkai. 2008. Kongō no maizō bunkazai hogo taisei no arikata ni tsuite, hōkoku (Concerning the future state of the cultural properties protection system, report) *Kōkogaku Kenkyū* 55(1): 101-116.

Higashi Ōsaka Shi Kyōiku Iinkai. 2009. *Higashi* Ōsaka *no Rekishi to Bunkazai (History and Cultural Pr*operties *of East* Ōsaka*)*. Higashi Ōsaka, Higashi Ōsaka Shi Kyōiku Iinkai.

hineno.org. 2014. *Hine shōen (Hine manor)* website accessed Sept 22 2014. http://www.hineno.org/REKISIKN.HTM

Hirai, Kiyoshi. 1998. *Hoian no kōkogaku chōsa; Betonamu no Nihonmachi.* Tōkyō. Shōwa Joshi Daigaku Kokusai Bunka Kenkyūjo.

Hirose, Kazuo. 1983. Kawachi Furuichi Daikō no nendai to sono igi (The date of the Furuichi Great Ditch and its significance). *Kōkogaku Kenkyū* 29(4): 53-68.

Hirose, Kazuo. 1984. Kodai no kaihatsu (Development in the Kofun Period*). Kōkogaku Kenkyū* 30: 340-72.

Hirose, Kazuo. 1998. Yayoi toshi no seiritsu (The development of Yayoi urban centers). *Kōkogaku Kenkyū* 45(3): 34-56.

Hirose, Kazuo. 2004a Jōron (Introduction). In Bunka Chō (ed.), Kinai no Kyōdai Kofun to Sono Jidai (The Gigantic Tombs of the Kinai and Their Period). *Kikan Kōkogaku* Spec Pub 14: 10-15.

Hirose, Kazuo 2004b. Kinai itsutsu dai kofungun no Shosō (Several aspects of the five great Kofun groups of the Kinai region). In Hirose Kazuo (ed.), Kinai no Kyōdai Kofun to Sono Jidai (The Gigantic Tombs of the Kinai and Their Period). *Kikan Kōkogaku* Spec Pub 14: 16-26.

Hirose, Kazuo. 2004c. Zenpōkōenfun kokka ron josetsu (Introduction to the theory of the keyhole tomb state). In Kōkogaku Kenkyūkai (ed.), *Bunka no Tayosei to Hikaku Kōkogaku (Cultural Diversity and Comparative Archaeology)*, ed., pp. 251-260. Okayama, Kōkogaku Kenkyūkai.

Hirose, Kazuo. 2008. Ōsaka Fu no hakubutsukan no jōken to kadai (Present situation and problems regarding Ōsaka museums). *Kōkogaku Kenkyū* 55(1): 1-7.

Hirose, Kazuo 2013. Kofun jidai no shūchō (Chiefs in the Kofun Period). *Kokuritsu Rekishi Minzoku Hakubutsukan Kenkyū Hōkoku* 175:162.

Hirose Kazuo, Isao Iba (eds). 2006. *Yayoi Jidai no Ōgata Tatemono to sono Tenkai (Large Buildings of the Yayoi Period and their Development)*. Shiga, Sanraisu Shuppan.

Hishida, Tetsuo. 2007. *Kodai Nihon Kokka Keisei no Kōkogaku. (Archaeology of the Formation of the Ancient Japanese State).* Kyōto, Kyōto Daigaku Gakujutsu Shuppankai.

Hishida, Tetsuo. 2010a. Kofun jidai no te kōgyō seisan (Craft production in the Kofun Period). In Kishimoto Naofumi (ed.), *Shiseki de Yomu Nihon no Rekishi 2 (Reading Japanese Archaeology at Historic Sites) 2 Kofun Jidai (Kofun Period)*: 212-238. Tōkyō, Yoshikawa Kōbunkan.

Hishida, Tetsuo. 2010b. Kofun Jidai Kinai no toraikei bunbutsu (Cultural objects of foreign immigrant type found in the Kinai Region in the Kofun Period). *Kobunka Dansō* 66: 43-54.

Hodder, I. 2011. Is a shared past possible? The ethics and practice of archaeology in the twenty-first century. In A. Matsuda and K. Okamura, (eds.), *New*

Perspectives in Global Public Archaeology: 19-28. New York, Springer Science and Business Media.

Hosoya, L. A. 2009. Sacred commonness: an archaeological approach to Yayoi social stratification: the 'central building model' and the Ikegami Sone Site. *Senri Ethnological Studies* 73: 99-178.

Hurst, C. 2009. The Heian Period. In W. Tsutsui, (ed.), *A Companion to Japanese History*: 30-46. Oxford, Blackwell Publishing e book.

Ichihara, Minoru. 1975 Ōsaka Sōgun to Ōsaka Heiya (Ōsaka Layer Group and Ōsaka Plain). *Urban Kubota* 11:26-29.

Ichikawa Tsukuru, Matsuda Jun'ichiro, Ōgura Tsutsuya, Chō Chul-jae, Tsujimoto Yūya and Hirata Yōji. 2011. Ko kankyō to ningen katsudō no kankei ha'aku ni mukete: Ōsaka shi Uemachi Daichi hokubu o daizai toshite (For the comprehension of the correlation of palaeoenvironment and human activities in the northern part of the Ōsaka Uemachi upland). *Bunkazai Kenkyūsho Kenkyū Kiyō* 13 (2001): 11-38.

Ichikawa, Hideyuki. 2009. *Rekishi no Naka no Sayamaike (Sayama Pond in History)*. Ōsaka, Seibundō.

Ichikawa, Tsukuru. 2007. Uriūdō shūhen o aruku (Walking around the vicinity of the Uriūdō site). In Ōsaka Shi Bunkazai Kyōkai (ed.), *Naniwa Kōkogaku Sanpo (A Walk Through Naniwa Archaeology)*: 39-47. Ōsaka, Gakuseisha.

Ichimoto, Yōshimi. 2014. Ichisuka Kofungun to Chikatsu Asuka Hakubutsukan (The Ichisuka Kofun group and the Chikatsu Asuka Museum). In Ichinose Kazuo, Fukunaga Shin'ya, and Hōjō Yōshitaka (eds.), *Kofun Jidai no Kōkogaku (10). Kofun Jidai to Gendai Shakai (Archaeology of the Kofun Period, Kofun and Contemporary Society)*: 185-193. Tōkyō, Dōseisha.

Ichinose, Kazuo. 2005. *Daiōbo to Zenpōkōenfun (Tombs of the Great Kings and Keyhole Shape Mounds)*. Tōkyō, Yoshikawa Kōbunkan.

Ichinose, Kazuo. 2009. *Kofun Jidai no Shinboru: Nintoku Ryō Kofun (Symbol of the Kofun Period: Nintoku Mausoleum Tumulus)*. Tōkyō, Shinsensha.

Ichinose, Kazuo, Togawa Yoshikazu, and Kawachi Kazuhiro. 2008. Furuichi, Mozu Kofun Gun no jūyō kofun no gaiyō (Summary of important tombs in the Furuichi and Mozu tomb groups). In Shiraishi, Ta'ichirō (ed.), *Kinki Chihō ni okeru Ōgata Kofungun no Kisoteki Kenkyū (Fundamental Study of the Large Tombs of the Kinki Region)*: 188-221. Nara, Nara Daigaku Bungakubu Bunkazai Gakka.

Ichinose, Kazuo and Togawa Yoshikazu. 2008. Osaka Fu oyobi Kaku Shichōson ni yoru Chōsa (Investigations in each City, Township, and Village in Ōsaka Fu). In Shiraishi, Ta'ichirō (ed.), *Kinki Chihō ni okeru Ōgata Kofungun no Kisoteki Kenkyū (Fundamental Study of the Large Tombs of the Kinki Region)*: 121-172. Nara, Nara Daigaku Bungakubu Bunkazai Gakka.

Iizuka, Takeshi. 2004. Yayoi Jidai no mokkisei o meguru shomondai (Some problems concerning the production of wooden implements in the Yayoi Period). *Kōkogaku Kenkyū* 51(1): 34-54.

Ikegami Sone Shiseki Shitei 20 Shūnen Kinen Jigyō Jikkōinkai. 1996. *Yayoi no Kangō Toshi to Kyōdai Shinden (Yayoi Moated Villages and Shrines)*. Izumi Shi, Ikegami Sone Shiseki Shitei 20 Shūnen Kinen Jigyō Jikkōinkai.

Imai Mayumi, Morioka Hideto. 2012. Yayoi shūraku ni shimeru tekki kōba no tokushitsu (Special features of iron workshops found in Yayoi settlements). *Kōkogaku Janaru* (631): 26-29.

Inoue, Tomohiro. 2007. Suiden inasaku juyōki no Kawachi Heya (The Kawachi Plain in the period of acceptance rice paddy cultivation). *Gekkan Bunkazai* 527: 22-27.

Inui, Tetsuya. 2006. Shiseki: Ikegami Sone Iseki (Historic site: the Ikegami Sone Site). *Kōkogaku Janaru* 541: 32-35.

Ishigami, Yutaka. 1985. Kangō shūraku toshite Ikegami Sone. In Izumi Shi Kubosō Kinen Bijutsukan (ed.), *Tokubetsu Ten Shisei 30 Shūnen Kinen, Koganezuka Kofun, Sefukuji Ino chō (Special exhibition on the 30th anniversary of the Municipal System, Treasures from the Koganetsuka Kofun and the Sutra Mound of the Sefukuji (Temple)*: 11-28. Izumi Shi, Kubosō Kinen Bijutsukan.

Ishimura, Tomo. 2010. Seizoku nishū ōken no kōzō (Structure of dual paramountship. *Kōkogaku Kenkyū* 57(3): 37-49.

Ishino, Hironobu. 2005a. San seiki no [toshi] Makimuku (The third century [urban center] Makimuku). In Ishino Hironobu (ed.), *Yamato Makimuku Iseki (The Makimuku Site, Yamato)*: 63-84. Tōkyō, Gakuseisha.

Ishino, Hironobu. 2005b. Henkaku ki no Makimuku to sōki kofun (The period of change of Makimuku and incipient *kofun*). In Ishino Hironobu (ed.), *Yamato Makimuku Iseki (The Makimuku Site, Yamato)*: 29-62. Tōkyō, Gakuseisha.

Ishino, Hironobu. 2006. Sankakuen shinjūkyō no fukuso ichi to nendai (The position in grave goods and date of the triangular rim beast and deity mirror). In Nara Rekishi Chiri no Kai (ed.), *Sankakuen Shinjūkyō; Yamataikoku, Wakoku (The Triangular Rim Beast and Deity Mirror: Yamataikoku and Wakoku)*: 10-33. Tōkyō, Shinsensha.

Isogai, Fujio. 2001. *Chūsei Nōgyō to Kikō: Suiden no Nimosaku (Mediaeval Agriculture and Climate; the Development of Paddy Multicropping)*. Tōkyō, Yoshikawa Kōbunkan.

Isogawa, Shin'ya. 1992. Kodai, Chūsei no itetsu imono (Cast iron objects from the Kodai and Chūsei Periods). *Kokuritsu Rekishi Minzoku Hakubutsukan Kenkyū Hōkoku* 46: 1-80.

Isogawa, Shin'ya. 2004. Chūsei no kinzoku seisan to ryūtsū (The production and distribution of metals in

the mediaeval period). *Rekishi Dokuhon* 49 (6): 222-224.
Itō, Koji. 1998. Ōuchi shi no Nichi Min bōeki to Sakai (The Japan Ming trade of the Ōuchi Clan and Sakai). *Isutoria* 16: 47-69.
Itō, Koji. 2008 . Sumitomo Dōfusho de no seiren sagyo (Smelting at the Sumitomo Copper Refinery) In Ōsaka Shi Bunkazai Kyōkai (ed.), *Ōsaka no Iseki*: 262-263. Ōsaka, Ōsaka Shi Bunkazai Kyōkai.
Izumi Sano Shi. 2013. *Izumi Sano Shi Hineshō no Sato Ōgi Chiiki Keikan Kaikaku (Plan for Preservation of Landscape of the Ōgi Valley Region*. Izumi Sano: Izumi Sano Shi. *www.city.izumisano.lg.jp/.../ keikankeikaku-all.pdf*
Izumori, Kō. 2006. *Kawachi no Kodō to Kofun o Manabu Hito no Tame ni (For Those Who Would Learn about Kawachi Roads and Tombs)*. Kyōto, Sekai Shisōsha.
Kaigawa, Katsushi. 2013. Minato Iseki (Minato Site). In Ōsaka Shi Bunkazai Kyōkai (ed.), *Rekishi hakkutsu Ōsaka 2012 (Historical excavations Ōsaka 2012)*: 44. Ōsaka, Ōsaka Furitsu Chikatsu Asuka Hakubutsukan.
Kajiyama Hikotarō, Ichihara Minoru. 1986. *Ōsaka Heiya no Oitachi (Life History of the Ōsaka Plain)*. Tōkyō, Aoki Shobō.
Kanazawa, Yō. 2004. Porutugaru tsuji no mita keisei ki no cha kaiseki (Kaiseki cuisine in the tea ceremony in its formative period as observed by a Portugese translator). *Idemitsu Bijutsukan Kanpō* 126: 54-63.
Kashihara Kōkogaku Kenkyūsho. 1977. *Niizawa Sentsuka 126 go fun (The Niizawa Senzuka Tomb No. 126*. Nara, Nara Ken Kyōiku Iinkai.
Kashihara Kōkogaku Kenkyūsho 2013. Ōgata seitetsu no iseki (Ōgata iron working site)
Pdf file accessed Sept. 22 2014 http://www.infokkkna.com/ironroad/dock/iron/4iron12.pdf
Kashiwara Shi Kyōiku Iinkai. 1997. *Ōgata no Tetsu (Iron of Ōgata)*. Kashiwara, Kashiwara Shi Kyōiku Iinkai.
Kashiwara Shiritsu Rekishi Shiryōkan. 1994. *Jōmon Jidai no Hajime Koro (Around the Beginning of the Jōmon Period)*. Kashiwara, Kashiwara Shiritsu Rekishi Shiryōkan.
Kashiwara Shiritsu Rekishi Shiryōkan. 2012. *Takaida Yokoanangun (The Takaida Corridor Tomb group)*. Kashiwara, Kashiwara Shiritsu Rekishi Shiryōkan.
Kashiwara Shiritsu Rekishi Shiryōkan. 2013. *Kawachi Ōhashi (The Great Kawachi Bridge)*. Kashiwara, Kashiwara Shi Rekishi Hakbutsukan.
Kawane, Yoshiyasu. 2002. *Ōsaka no Chūsei Zenki (The Early Chūsei Period of Ōsaka)*. Ōsaka, Seibundō Shuppan.
Kidder, J. E. 2007. *Himiko and Japan's Elusive Chiefdom of Yamatai; Archaeology, History, and Mythology*. Honolulu, University of Hawaii Press.
Kihara, Katsushi. 2000. Naniwa Kyō: Setouchi to kyō no hajimari (The Naniwa Capital; beginning of Setouchi and Kyō). In Watanabe Takeshi Kanchō Taishoku Kinen Ronshū Kankōkai (Committee for the retirement publication for Director Watanabe Takeshi) (ed.), *Ōsakajō to Jōkamachi (Ōsaka Castle and Castle Town)*: 341-367. Kyōto, Shibunkaku Shuppan.
Kihara, Katsushi. 2007. Kodai miya toshi to shūhen kankyō no hōzen; Naniwa Kyō to kodai Ōsaka heiya o jirei toshite (Ancient capital cities and preservation of surrounding environments; case study of the Naniwa Capital and the Ōsaka Plain). *Rekishi Chirigaku* 49:5-18.
Kikuchi, Sei'ichi. 2003. *Betonamu Nihonmachi no Kōkogaku*. Tōkyō. Koshi Shoin.
Kinugawa, Kazunori. 2008a. Ōsaka saikō no kyūsekki (The oldest Palaeolithic tools in Ōsaka). In Ōsaka Shi Bunkazai Kyōkai (ed.), *Ōsaka no Iseki (Ōsaka Sites)*: 22-23. Ōsaka, Ōsaka Shi Bunkazai Kyōkai.
Kinugawa, Kazunori 2008b. Setouchi gihō to Kō kei naifugata sekki (The Setouchi technique and the Kō Type stone knife) In Ōsaka Shi Bunkazai Kyōkai (ed.), *Ōsaka no Iseki (Ōsaka Sites)*: 24-25. Ōsaka, Ōsaka Shi Bunkazai Kyōkai.
Kishimoto, Naofumi. 1989. Sankakuen shinjūkyō no seisaku kōjingun (Craft groups that produced triangular rim beast and deity mirrors). *Shirin* 72:5: 1-42
Kishimoto, Naofumi. 2008. Zenpōkōenfun no futatsu keibetsu to ōken kōzō (Two lines of keyhole shaped tombs and the structure of royal authority). In Shiraishi, Ta'ichirō (ed.), *Kinki Chihō ni okeru Ōgata Kofungun no Kisoteki Kenkyū (Fundamental Study of the Large Tombs of the Kinki Region)*: 459-464. Nara, Nara Daigaku Bungakubu Bunkazai Gakka.
Kishimoto, Naofumi. 2010a. Wakoku no keisei to zenpōkōenfun no kōyū (The formation of Wakoku and the federations of the keyhole shape tombs). In Kishimoto Naofumi (ed.), *Shiseki de Yomu Nihon no Rekishi 2 (Reading Japanese Archaeology at historic sites) 2 Kofun Jidai (Kofun Period)*: 14-46. Tōkyō, Yoshikawa Kōbunkan.
Kishimoto, Naofumi. 2010b. Kawachi seiken no jidai (The period of Kawachi power). In Kishimoto Naofumi (ed.), *Shiseki de Yomu Nihon no Rekishi 2 (Reading Japanese Archaeology at Historic Sites) 2 Kofun Jidai (Kofun Period)*, ed., pp. 47-75. Tōkyō, Yoshikawa Kōbunkan.
Kishimoto, Naofumi. 2013. Dual kingship in the Kofun Period as seen from the keyhole tombs. (translated by Joseph Ryan) *UrbanScope* 4 (2013): 1-21.
Kobata, Atsushi. 1939. *Chūsei Nantō Tsūkō Bōeki Shi no Kenkyū (Study of Mediaeval Diplomatic Exchange in the Southern Islands)*. Tōkyō, Nihon Hyōronsha.
Kobata, Atsushi. 1941, *Chūsei Ni Shi Tsūkō Bōeki no Kenkyū (Study of mediaeval Japan-China Diplomatic Exchange)*. Tōkyō, Nihon Hyōronsha.
Kobayashi, Ken'ichi. 1990. Hohei to kihei (Infantry and cavalry). In Shiraishi Ta'ichirō (ed.), *Kofun Jidai no Kōgei (Industrial Arts of the Kofun Period)*: 141-153. Tōkyō, Kōdansha.

Kobayashi, Yukio. 1961. *Kofun Jidai no Kenkyū (Study of the Kofun Period)*. Tōkyō, Aoki Shoten.

Kobayashi, Yukio. 1976. *Kofun Bunka Ronkō (Study of the Kofun culture)*. Tōkyō, Heibonsha.

Kobayashi, Yukio. 2006. Thesis on duplicate mirrors introduced and interpreted by Walter Edwards, In J. Piggott (ed.), *Capital and Countryside in Japan 300 – 1180*: 58-73. Ithaca, Cornell University East Asia Program.

Kōeki Zaidan Hōjin Ōsaka Fu Bunkazai Sentā. 2012. *Kitoragawa Iseki (The Kitoragawa Site)*. Ōsaka, Ōsaka Fu Bunkazai Sentā.

Kohama, Sei. 2006. Tenji kaisetsu (Explanation of the exhibition). In Ōsaka Furitsu Chikatsu Asuka Hakubutsukan (ed.), *Ōjin Dai Ō no Jidai (The Period of the Great King Ōjin)*: 15-87. Ōsaka, Ōsaka Furitsu Chikatsu Asuka Hakubutsukan.

Kondō, Yasushi. 2011. Shiseki Dotō (Historic Site, Earth Pagoda). In Ōsaka Furitsu Chikatsu Asuka Hakubutsukan (ed.), *Rekishi Hakkutsu Ōsaka (Historical Excavations Ōsaka)*: 49. Ōsaka, Ōsaka Furitsu Chikatsu Asuka Hakubutsukan

Kondō, Yoshirō. 1983. *Zenpōkōenfun no Jidai (The Age of Keyhole Shape Tumulus)*. Tōkyō, Iwanami Shoten.

Kurosawa, Hiroshi. 2012. Yayoi shūraku kara mita seidōki seisaku no dōkō (Movements in bronze implement making in Yayoi settlements. *Kōkogaku Janaru* (631): 21-25.

Kusaka, Masayōshi. 1980. *Rekishi Jidai no Chikei Kankyō (Topography and Environment of the Historical Period)*. Tōkyō, Kokon Shoin.

Kusaka, Masayōshi. 2012. *Chikei kara Mita Rekishi (History Seen from Geomorphology)*. Tōkyō, Kōdansha.

Kyōshima, Satoru. 2007a. Dai fukugo iseki Nagahara Iseki ni tsuite (Concerning the large complex Nahgahara Site). In Ōsaka Shi Bunkazai Kyōkai (ed.), *Naniwa Kōkogaku Sanpo (A Walk Through Naniwa Archaeology)*: 24-39. Ōsaka, Ōsaka Shi Bunkazai Kyōkai.

Kyōshima, Satoru. 2007b. Edazeni to Kudara Amadera no Saikudani Iseki to Okachiyama Kofun (The branch coin mold and the Saikudani Site of the Kudara Convent and the Okachiyama Kofun). In Ōsaka Shi Bunkazai Kyōkai (ed.), *Naniwa Kōkogaku Sanpo (A Walk through Naniwa archaeology)*: 126-133. Tōkyō, Gakuseisha.

Lee, D. 2014. Keyhole shaped tombs in the Yongsan River Valley; representations of frontier politics. *Kankoku Joshi Gakkotsu* 83: 69-90.

Makabe, Tadahiko. 1994. *Sekkan kara Kofun Jidai o Kangaeru (Considering the Kofun Period from Stone Coffins)*. Tōkyō, Dohōsha.

Mametani, Kazuyuki. 2012. Ōgata tatemono no seikaku ni tsuite no kyōjitsu (The truth about the nature of large buildings). *Kōkogaku Janaru* (631): 12-15.

Matsuda, Akira. 2013. Paburiku akeoloji no kanten kara mita kōkogaku, bunkazai, bunkazai isan (Archaeology, cultural properties, and cultural heritage management seen from the point of view of public archaeology). *Kōkogaku Kenkyū* 60(2): 19-33.

Matsuda A. and K. Okamura. 2011. Introduction: New Perspectives in Global Public Archaeology. In K. Okamura and M. Matsuda (eds.), *New Perspectives in Global Public Archaeology*: 1-18. New York, Springer Science and Business Media.

Matsugi, Takehiko. 1995. Yayoi Jidai no sensō to Nihon Rettō shakai no hatten katei (Yayoi Period warfare and the process of social evolution in the Japanese Islands). *Kōkogaku Kenkyū* 41(4): 25-26.

Matsuo, Nobuhiro. 2000. Ōsakajōnai no daikō (Large moats inside Ōsaka Castle). In Watanabe Takeshi Kanchō Taishoku Kinen Ronshū Kankōkai (Committee for the Retirement Publication for Director Watanabe Takeshi (ed.), *Ōsakajō to Jōkamachi (Ōsaka Castle and Castle Town)*: 61-90. Kyōto, Shibunkaku Shuppan.

Matsuo, Nobuhiro. 2003. Sengoku jidai no Ōsaka: Jinaimachi kara jōkamachi (Ōsaka in the Sengoku Period; from temple town to castle town). In Ono Masatoshi and Haghihara Mitsuo (ed.), *Sengoku Jidai no Kōkogaku (Archaeology of the Sengoku Period)*: 83-92. Tōkyō, Koshi Shoin.

Matsuo, Nobuhiro. 2006. Uemachi Daichi shūhen no chūsei shūraku (Mediaeval villages in the vicinity of the Uemachi Terrace). In Sakaehara Towao and Hiroshi Niki (eds.), *Naniwanomiya kara Ōsaka e (From Naniwanomiya to Ōsaka Castle)*: 141-166. Ōsaka, Koshi Shoin.

Matsuo, Nobuyuki. 2008a. Kawachi Wan no kishibe no shūraku (Villages on the shore of Kawachi Bay). In Ōsaka Shi Bunkazai Kyōkai (ed.), *Ōsaka no Iseki (Ōsaka Sites)*: 38,39. Ōsaka, Ōsaka Shi Bunkazai Kyōkai.

Matsuo, Nobuyuki. 2008b. Sumitomo Dōfusho no kōzō (The structure of the Sumitomo copper refinery). In Ōsaka Shi Bunkazai Kyōkai (ed.), *Ōsaka no Iseki (Ōsaka Sites)*, ed. pp. 260-261. Ōsaka, Ōsaka Shi Bunkazai Kyōkai.

Matsuo, Nobuyuki. 2010. Sumitomo Dōfushoato no hakkutsu chōsa to Kinsei kōkogaku (The Sumitomo copper refinery site excavation and Kinsei archaeology). *Sumitomo shiryō sosho geppō* (http://www.shiryōkan.jp/geppou/pages/25th_1. html) 25:xx.

Miki, Hiroshi. 2013. Mozu, Furuichi Kofungun kōkū rēza sokuryozū (Aerial laser map of the Mozu and Furuichi Tomb Groups. In Ōsaka Furitsu Chikatsu Asuka Hakbutsukan (ed.), *Rekishi Hakkkutsu Ōsaka 2012. (Historical Excavations Ōsaka 2012)*: 30-40. Ōsaka, Ōsaka Furitsu Chikatsu Asuka Hakubutsukan.

Minami, Hideo. 2008. Hakkutsu de wakaru machiya no hattatsu (The development of townspersons' houses as seen from archaeology). In Ōsaka Shi Bunkazai Kyōkai (ed.), *Ōsaka no Iseki (Ōsaka Sites)*: 264-265. Ōsaka, Ōsaka Shi Bunkazai Kyōkai.

Miyamoto, Kōji. 2008. Sumiyoshi Tsū to Sumiyoshi no seisui (The rise and fall of Sumiyoshi and Sumiyoshi Port). In Ōsaka Shi Bunkazai Kyōkai (ed.), *Ōsaka no Iseki (Ōsaka Sites)*: 186-187. Ōsaka, Ōsaka Shi Bunkazai Kyōkai.

Miyamoto, Sachiko. 2010. Zenki Naniwanomiya izen no kawara (Roof tiles predating the Early Period Naniwanomiya). In Sekiyama Hiroshi (ed.), *Higashi Ajia ni okeru Naniwanomiya to Kodai Naniwa no Kokusaiteki Seikaku ni kansuru Sōgō Kenkyū (Team Study of the Ancient Naniwa Palace and its International Relations) Kaken Project No. 18320131, 2006-2009, Final Report)*: 97-109. Ōsaka, Ōsaka Shi Bunkazai Kyōkai.

Miyaoka, Masanobu. 2012. Tōkan kara miru Kinai to Kibi (Kinai and Kibi areas as seen from ceramic coffins). *Kōkogaku Kenkyū* 59(1): 60-80.

Mizoguchi, K. 2009. Nodes and edges: a network approach to hierarchisation and state formation in Japan. *Journal of Anthropological Archaeology* 28: 14-26.

Mizoguchi, Kōji. 2012. Shutsuji to kyōjū o meguru Yayoi shūrakuron (Yayoi settlements as seen from descent and residence). *Kōkogaku Janaru* 631: 7-11.

Mizoguchi, K. 2013. *The Archaeology of Japan; from the Earliest Rice Farming Villages to the Rise of the State*. Cambridge: Cambridge University Press.

Mizuno, Masayoshi. 2006. Wakoku Jo Ō Himiko oyobi ōto to Yamato (Himiko Queen of Wa, the Royal Capital and Yamato). In Nara Rekishi Chiri no Kai (ed.), *Sankakuen Shinjūkyō; Yamataikoku, Wakoku (The Triangular Rim Beast and Deity Mirror: Yamataikoku and Wakoku)*: 34-89. Tōkyō, Shinsensha.

Mizuno Masayoshi and Ishino Hironobu. 2006a. Wakoku Jo Ō Himiko jidai kara zenpōkōenfun no jidai e. In Nara Rekishi Chiri no Kai (ed.), *Sankakuen Shinjūkyō; Yamataikoku, Wakoku (The Triangular Rim Beast and Deity Mirror: Yamataikoku and Wakoku)*: 97-112. Tōkyō, Shinsensha.

Mizuno, Masayoshi, Ishino Hironobu. 2006b. Korumu: sankakuen shinjūkyō no shurui to keitō (Varieties and geneaology of the triangular rim beast and deity mirror). In Nara Rekishi Chiri no Kai (ed.), *Sankakuen Shinjūkyō; Yamataikoku, Wakoku (The Triangular Rim Beast and Deity Mirror: Yamataikoku and Wakoku)*, ed., pp. 90-97. Tōkyo: Shinsensha.

Mori Tsuyoshi and Mametani Kazuyuki. 2000. Kōkogaku kara mita senba no seiritsu to tenkai (The birth and development of the field of battle, seen from archaeology). In Watanabe Takeshi Kanchō Taishoku Kinen Ronshū Kankōkai (Committee for the Retirement Publication for Director Watanabe Takeshi) (ed.), *Ōsakajō to Jōkamachi (Ōsaka Castle and Castle Town)*: 91-116. Kyōto, Shibunkaku Shuppan.

Morii, Sadao. 2001. Kinki chihō no kangō shūraku (Moated villages in the Kinki area). In Ōsaka Furitsu Yayoi Bunka Hakubutsukan (ed.), *Yayoi Jidai no Shūraku (Yayoi Period Villages)*: 135-155. Tōkyō, Gakuseisha.

Morimoto, Susumu. 2012. Yayoi Jidai no fundō (Weights of the Yayoi Period). *Kōkogaku Kenkyū* 59 (3): 67-75.

Morimoto, Tetsu. 2011. Ryōbo kofun no maisō shisetsu no girei (Burial facilities and rituals in the imperial tombs). In Ōsaka Furitsu Chikatsu Asuka Hakubutsukan (ed.), *Mozu Furuichi no Ryōbo Kofun (The Imperial Tombs of Mozu and Furuichi)*: 132-137. Ōsaka, Ōsaka Furitsu Chikatsu Asuka Hakubutsukan.

Morimura, Ken'ichi. 1989. Sakai Kangō toshi ni okeru chūkinsei tōjiki yoroku (A consideration of mediaeval and premodern ceramics from the moated city of site of Sakai). *Tōyō Tōji* 19: 4: 47-63.

Morimura, Ken'ichi. 1998. Sakai ni okeru bōeki tōji (Trade ceramics from Sakai). In Nihon Kōkogaku Kyōkai (ed.), *Nihon Kōkogaku Kyōkai 1998 Nendo Taikai Kenkyū Happyō Shiryō (Research Paper Materials, Japan Archaeological Association 1998 Meetings)*: 123-135. Okinawa, Nihon Kōkogaku Kyōkai 1998 Nendo Okinawa Taikai Jikkōinkai.

Morimura, Ken'ichi. 2000. Kōkogaku kara mita Azuchi-Momoyama Jidai: Sakai shutsudo no nanshitsu shiyū tōki (The Azuchi Momoyama Period as seen from archaeology; low fired glazed pottery from Sakai) *Hagoromo Kokubun* 13 (3): 1-22.

Morimura, Ken'ichi. 2002. Jūgō – jūnana seiki ni okeru Tōnan Ajia tōjiki kara mita tōji no Nihon bunka shi (The ceramic culture history of Japan seen from fifteenth to seventeenth century Southeast Asian ceramics). *Kokuritsu Rekishi Minzoku Hakubutsukan Kenkyū Hōkoku* 94: 251-296.

Morimura, Ken'ichi. 2003a. Sakai shutsudo Betunamu jiki ni yoru Kinsei chanoyu sutairu no kakuritsu -- 16 seiki matsuba-- 1615 nen ni oite (Vietnamese ceramics found in Sakai and the establishment of the premodern style of tea ceremony from the late sixteenth century to AD 1615). *Showa Joshi Daigaku Kokusai Bunka Kenkyūsho Kiyō* 9: 139-146.

Morimura, Ken'ichi. 2003b. Kōkogaku kara mita Kōrai chawan (Chōsen Ōcho tōji chawan) (Korean tea bowls seen from archaeology (Tea bowls of the Choson Dynasty). In Kōrai Chawan Kenkyūkai (ed.), *Kōrai Chawan; Ronkō to Shiryō (Koryo Tea Bowls; Study and Debate)*: 147-157. Kyōto, Kawara Shoten.

Morimura, Ken'ichi. 2004a. Kokusai bōeki toshi Sakai no kinsei toshi kenchiku to yashiki no kōsei (The Kinsei (premodern period) architecture and composition of residences in the international trading city of Sakai. *Kansai Kinsei Kōkogaku Kenkyū* XII: 186-225.

Morimura, Ken'ichi. 2004b. *Sakai kara shutsudo shita Tai, Betunamu tōji. (Thai and Vietnamese ceramics found in Sakai)* Paper presented at the Symposium, Tōjiki ga hanaseru kōryū; Kyūshu, Okinawa kara shutsudo shita Tōnan Ajia san tōjiki (Symposium on Southeast Asian archaeology 2004. Interrelations between Kyūshu and Southeast Asia through Southeast Asian ceramics found in Kyūshu and Okinawa. Kagoshima, Kagoshima Daigaku Maizō Bunkazai Chōsashitsu.

Morimura, Ken'ichi. 2004c. Chajin no toshi: Sakai shutsudo no Ao Oribe (City of tea masters; green Oribe ware found in Sakai). In Mino Tōki Rekishikan (ed.), *Oribe no Ryūtsūen o Horu; Nishi Nihon (Excavating the Area of Circulation of Oribe Ware, Western Japan)*: 46-105. Tōki Shi, Mino Tōki Rekishikan.

Morimura, Ken'ichi. 2005a. Izumi Kuni ("Kuni" of Izumi). In Kodai Tsūrō Kenkyūkai (ed.), *Nihon Kodai Tsūrō Jiten (Dictionary of Ancient Roads of Japan)*: 34-40 Tōkyō, Yagi Shoten.

Morimura, Ken'ichi. 2005b. Jūyon - jūgō seiki no Ryūsenyō kei seiji; hennen to Sakai bōeki shisutemu (Celadons from Longquan type kilns of the fourteenth and fifteenth centuries; dating and the Sakai trading system. *Sangyō, Shakai, Ningen* 6:43-51.

Morimura, Ken'ichi. 2005c. Bizenyaki wa, itsu sakai ni kita ka? soshite chanoyu no taisei e -- rekishi ga Bizenyaki no dokusosei o umidashita (When did Bizen ceramics come to Sakai? and toward the success of the tea ceremony--history created by the originality of Bizen ceramics). In Bizen Shi Rekishi Minzoku Shiryōkan (ed.), *Bizenyaki Kenkyū Saizensen (Most Recent Advances in Bizenware Studies) II*: 61-81. Bizen, Bizen Shi Rekishi Minzoku Shiryōkan.

Morimura, Ken'ichi. 2006a. Sakai: kodai dōro ami no midokoro (Sakai: highlights of the ancient road network in the Kodai Period). In Kodai (ed.), *Takenouchi Kaidō o Arukō (Let's Walk Along the Takenouchi Highway)*: 1-2. Ōsaka, Kodai.

Morimura, Ken'ichi. 2006b. Ajia no kaito; Sakai no shin rekishi zō (Maritime city of Asia: A new historical image of Sakai). *Ōsaka Shunyu* 122:22-28.

Morimura, Ken'ichi. 2006c. Sakai Kangō Toshi Iseki no rekishi zō (The historical image of the Sakai moated city site). *Ōsaka Fu Maizō Bunkazai Kenkyūkai Shiryō* 53:1-14.

Morimura, Ken'ichi. 2006d. Bizenyaki no kako, genzai, mirai Bizenyaki: Momoyama Bunka no katachi ni ikiru (The past, present, and future of Bizen Ware: living in the style of Momoyama Culture. In Bizen Shi Rekishi Minzoku Shiryōkan (ed.), *Bizen Forum: Bizen Yaki Umi no Michi, Yume Fuorumu 2006 (Bizen Forum, Bizen Ware: Sea Routes, Vision Forum)*: 61-81. Bizen, Bizen Shi Kyōiku Iinkai.

Morimura, Ken'ichi. 2006e. Bizenyaki no susa; genzai, yūrai Bizenyaki. Momoyama Bunka no katachi ni ikiru (The past, present, and future of Bizenyaki living in the form of Momoyama Culture). *Bizen Shi Rekishi Shiryōkan Kiyō* 8:109-124.

Morimura, Ken'ichi. 2006f. Jūroku seiki no matsuyo kara jūnana seiki shoto no Sakai ni okeru sencha no shutsugen (The appearance of the custom of drinking tea prepared from leaves (*sencha*) in Sakai from the latter half of the sixteenth century to the seventeenth century) In Kitani Yoshinobu Sensei Kinen Ronshū Kankōkai (ed.), *Kitani Yoshinobu Sensei Koki Kinen Ronshū (Essays in Commemoration of the Retirement of Professor Kitani Yoshinobu*: 451-458. Ōsaka, Kitani Yoshinobu Sensei Kinen Ronshū Kankōkai.

Morimura, Ken'ichi. 2008a. Kawachi Ōchō ryōenron (The debate about the Kawachi royal mausolea) In Tsuzuya Fuminori (ed.), *Ōken to Buki to Shinkō (Royal Authority, Weapons, and Religion)*: 120-130. Tōkyō, Dōseisha.

Morimura, Ken'ichi. 2008b. Jiyū toshi Sakai (The free city, Sakai). *Taiyō* 155: 23-29.

Morimura, Ken'ichi. 2009a. Chūkinsei toshi Sakai ni okeru toshi saigai (Urban disasters in mediaeval and premodern Sakai). In Edo Iseki Kenkyūkai (ed.), *Saigai to Edo Jidai (Disasters and the Edo Period)*: 40-72. Tōkyō, Yoshikawa Kōbunkan.

Morimura, Ken'ichi. 2009b. Shōshū Yō (Zhangzhou Kilns). In Itō Ikutarō (ed.), *Chūgoku Yakimono Nyūmon (Introduction to Chinese Ceramics) Taiyō, Special Edition*: 187-190. Tōkyō, Heibonsha.

Morimura, Ken'ichi. 2009c. Jūgō, jūroku seiki no Nichū cha bunka to sappo taisei (Japan China tea culture of the 15th and 16th centuries and the tributary system. In Ningbo Dongya Cha Wenhua Yanjiu Zhongxin (ed.), *Di er tze haishang cha lu juhui wenshu (Papers of the second conference on the maritime route of tea)*: 79-88. Ningbo, Ningbo Dongya Cha Wenhua Yanjiu Zhongxin.

Morimura, Ken'ichi. 2009d. Chūsei no Sakai to bōeki tōji (Mediaeval Sakai and trade ceramics). In Bukkyō Daigaku Shukyō Bunka Mujiumu: (ed.), *Umi o Koeta Tōjiki to Cha Bunka Shinpojiumu Happyō Yōshi (Materials from the Symposium, Ceramics and Tea Culture Which Crossed the Sea)*: 9-12. Kyōto, Bukkyō Daigaku Shukyō Bunka Mujiumu.

Morimura, Ken'ichi. 2011. Sakai ni okeru chaji to Bizen mono (Bizen objects and tea ceremony activities in Sakai). *Bizen Rekishi Fuorumu 2011 Shiryōshu (Materials from the Bizen History Forum 2011)*: 41-58.

Morimura, Ken'ichi. 2014. Suemura to *sueki* no seiritsu nendai ni tsuite (Concerning Suemura and the date of the beginning of *sueki* production). *Kanshikikei Doki Kenkyū* XIII: 153-184.

Morishita, Shōji. 2007. Dō kagami seisan no henyo to kōryū (Interaction and transformation of bronze mirror production). *Kōkogaku Kenkyū* 54(2): 34-49.

Morishita, Shōji. 2009. Korumu (Column). In Ichinose Kazuo (ed.), *Kofun Jidai no Shinboru: Nintoku Ryō Kofun (Symbol of the Kofun Period: Nintoku Mausoleum Tumulus)*: 25. Tōkyō, Shinseisha.

Morris, D. 1981.The city of Sakai and urban autonomy In Bardwell Smith and George Elison (ed.), *Warlords,*

Artists and Commoners: Japan in the Sixteenth Century: 7-22. Honolulu, University of Hawaii Press.

Murai, Shōsuke. 2005. Jisha zōei ryō tosen o minaosu: bōeki, bunka, kōryū, chinsen (A review of voyages to Tang to raise money for building temples and shrines: trade, culture, exchange, and sunken ships), In Rekishigaku Kenkyūkai and Murai Shōsuke (eds.), *Minato Machi to Kaiiki Sekai (Port Towns and the Maritime World)*: 113-143. Tōkyō, Rekishigaku Kenkyūkai.

Murakami, Takashi. 2008. Hakkutsu chōsa de yomigaetta [kodōzuroku] no sekai (Reconstructing the world of the Kodōzuroku. *Sumitomo Shiryō Sosho Geppō* 23 ((http://www.shiryōkan.jp/geppou/pages/23th_1.html). Web site accessed October 10 2014.

Murakawa, Yukihiro. 1991.Wa ōken to Kawachi chiiki (The royal power of Wa and the Kawachi area). In Murakawa Yukihiro and Kobayashi Hiroshi (eds.), *Kawachi Chiiki Shi: Sōron Hen (Kawachi Regional History: General Discussion)*: 59-79. Ōsaka, Ōsaka Keizai Hōka Daigaku Shuppanbu.

Murakawa Yukihiro and Kobayashi Hiroshi. 1995. *Yayoi Jidai no Ōsaka Wan Engan: Kawachi Chiiki Shi Yayoi Hen (The Shore of Ōsaka Bay in the Yayoi Period: Kawachi Regional History, Yayoi Section)* Ōsaka, Ōsaka Keizai Hōka Daigaku Shuppanbu.

Nagai, Masahiro. 2010. Sakai Kangō Toshi Iseki ni okeru Bizen jiki no shutsugen to tenkai (The appearance and development of Bizen Ware in the Sakai Moated City Site). *Kansai Kinsei Kōkogaku Kenkyū* 18: 131-146.

Nagazumi, Yōko 2001 *Shūinsen (Red Tally Trade)*. Tōkyō, Yoshikawa Kōbunkan.

Nakakubo, Tatsuo. 2014. Ōsaka Fu Fujiidera Shi Nonaka Kofun (The Nonaka Kofun, Fujiidera City, Ōsaka). *Kōkogaku Kenkyū* 61(1): 96-98.

Nakamura, Hiroshi. 2000. Hideyoshi no Ōsakajō kakuchō koji ni tsuite – Bunroku sannen no sōko fushin (The expansion of Ōsaka castle under Hideyoshi; the construction of features in Bunroku 3). In Watanabe Takeshi Kanchō Taishoku Kinen Ronshū Kankōkai (Committee for the Retirement Publication for Director Watanabe Takeshi) (ed.), *Ōsakajō to Jōkamachi (Ōsaka Castle and Castle Town)*: 23-42. Kyōto, Shibunkaku Shuppan.

Nakamura, Hiroshi. 2001. *Izumi Suemura Kama no Rekishiteki Kenkyū (Historical Study of the Izumi Suemura Kilns)*. Tōkyō, Fuyō Shobō Shuppan.

Nakamura, Hiroshi. 2006. *Senboku Kyūryō ni Hirogaru Sueki Yo: Suemura Iseki Gun (Sueki Kilns Along the Senboku Slope—the Suemura Site Group)*. Tōkyō, Shinsensha.

Nakao, Yoshiharu. 2010. Kodai Naniwa to Naniwa Tsu ni tsuite (Ancient Naniwa and the Ancient Port). In Sekiyama Hiroshi (ed.), *Higashi Ajia ni okeru Naniwanomiya to Kodai Naniwa no Kokusaiteki Seikaku ni kansuru Sōgō Kenkyū (Team Study of the Ancient Naniwa Palace and its International Relations) Kaken Project No. 18320131, 2006-2009, Final Report*: 7-28. Ōsaka, Ōsaka Shi Bunkazai Kyōkai.

Nakao, Yoshiharu. 2007. Kodai no Naniwa to Naniwa Tsu ni Tsuite. In Ōsaka Furitsu Yayoi Bunka Hakubutsukan (ed.), *Hakkutsu Sareta Ōsaka 2007; Suito Ōsaka no Kokusai Kōryūshi (Ōsaka Excavations 2007; History of International Trade of Ōsaka, Water City)*: 84-91. Izumi Shi, Ōsaka Furitsu Yayoi Bunka Hakubutsukan.

Nakaoka, Masaru. 2006. Hine Shō iseki no chōsa kekka (Results of excavations at Hine Shō). Ōsaka *Fu Maizō Bunkazai Kenkyūkai Dai 53 Kai Shiryō*: 15-26.

Nakaoka, Masaru. 2013. Tsuchimaru Ameyama jōato (Tsuchimaru Ameyama fortification site). In Ōsaka Furitsu Chikatsu Asuka Hakubutsukan (ed.), *Rekishi Hakkutsu Ōsaka 2012 (Historical Excavations Ōsaka 2012)*: 64. Ōsaka, Ōsaka Furitsu Chikatsu Asuka Hakubutsukan.

Naoki Kojirō, Nakao Yōshiharu. 2003. *Kodai Naniwa to Naniwanomiya (Ancient Period Naniwa and the Naniwa Palace)*. Tōkyō, Gakuseisha.

Nature. 2014. Nature jobs, spotlight on Ōsaka. website accessed October 10 2014. www.nature.com/naturejobs/science/articles/10.1038/nj 0433

Niiro, Izumi. 2011. Zenpōkōenfun no sekkei genri shiron (Essay on the principles of design of zenpōkōenfun). *Kōkogaku Kenkyū* 58(1): 16-36.

Nishikawa, Toshikatsu. 2006. Koko made susunda sankakuen shinjūkyō kenkyū (Studies of triangular rim beasts and deities mirrors to the present). In Nara Rekishi Chiri no Kai (ed.), *Sankakuen Shinjūkyō; Yamataikoku, Wakoku (The Triangular Rim Beast and Deity Mirror: Yamataikoku and Wakoku)*: 113-142. Tōkyō, Shinsensha.

Nishikawa, Toshikatsu. 2010. Hantō no shinshutsu shita Wa ō no gundan (The Wa Kings' army that advanced to the Korean Peninsula) In Nishikawa Toshikatsu, Tanaka Shinsaku (eds.), *Wa Ō no Gundan (The Military Corps of the Wa Kings)*: 9-80. Tōkyō, NHK Books.

North, D. C. 1981. *Structure and Change in Economic History*. New York, W.W. Norton.

Odagi, Fujimi. 2007a. Komagawa, Imagawa no nagare ni sotte (Sites along the Koma and Ima Rivers). In Ōsaka Shi Bunkazai Kyōkai (ed.), *Naniwa Kōkogaku Sanpo (A Walk Through Naniwa Archaeology)*: 66-76. Tōkyō, Gakuseisha.

Odagi, Fujimi. 2007b. Kinsei Hirano kangō toshi no han'ei (The prosperity of the Hirano Moated City in the Kinsei Period). In Ōsaka Shi Bunkazai Kyōkai (ed.), *Naniwa Kōkogaku Sanpo (A Walk Through Naniwa Archaeology)*: 56-65. Tōkyō, Gakuseisha.

Odagi, Fujimi 2008a. Yūkei sentōki ishiwari no tekuniku (Technique for flaking stone points). In Ōsaka Shi Bunkazai Kyōkai (ed.), *Ōsaka no Iseki (Ōsaka Sites)*: 26-27. Ōsaka, Ōsaka Shi Bunkazai Kyōkai.

Odagi, Fujimi 2008b. Morinomiya Iseki, Kawachi Wan kara Kawachi Kata e (The Morinomiya Site, from Kawachi Bay to Kawachi Lagoon). In Ōsaka Shi Bunkazai Kyōkai (ed.), *Ōsaka no Iseki (Ōsaka Sites)*: 36-37. Ōsaka, Ōsaka Shi Bunkazai Kyōkai.

Odagi, Fujimi. 2008c. Hirano Gō: Kinsei no machinami o ima ni tsutaeru Hirano Gō (The Hirano area: telling about house rows of the Kinsei Period) In Ōsaka Shi Bunkazai Kyōkai (ed.), *Ōsaka no Iseki (Ōsaka Sites)*: 268-269. Ōsaka, Ōsaka Shi Bunkazai Kyōkai.

Ogasawara, Shigeru. 1995. Ten o aite ni shita rekishi gakusha Miyazaki Ichisada no koseki (The historian who became a partner of heaven, the interest of Miyazaki Ichisada in world history) *Asteion* 35: 180-197.

Okamura, K. 2011. From object centered to people focused: exploring the gap between archaeologists and the public in contemporary Japan. In K. Okamura and A. Matsuda (ed.) *New Perspectives in Global Public Archaeology*: 77-86. New York, Springer Science and Business Media.

Okamura, Katsuyuki. 2014a. Kofun jidai no shimin shakai (Kofun period and popular society) In *Kofun to gendai shakai (Kofun and contemporary society)*, ed. Ichinose Kazuo, Fukunaga Shin'ya and Hōjō Yoshitaka, pp. 43-56. Tōkyō. Dōseisha.

Okamura, Katsuyuki. 2014b. Gendai kōkogaku to komunikēshion (Contemporary archaeology and communication). *LINK* 6: 10-19.

Okamura, K. 2014c. Ethics of commercial archaeology. In C. Smith (ed.), *Encyclopedia of Archaeology*: 2482-2485. New York, Springer.

Okamura K. 2014d. Japan: Cultural Heritage Management Education. In C. Smith (ed.), *Encyclopedia of Archaeology*: 4156-4160. New York, Springer.

Okamura Katsuyuki and Matsuda Akira. 2008. Henkaku ki no kōkogakusha (Archaeologists at the time of change). *Kōkogaku Kenkyū* 55(1): 81-84.

Okauchi, Mitsuzane. 1986. Mounded tombs in East Asia from the 3rd to 7th centuries AD. In Pearson, R., G. Barnes, and K. Hutterer (eds.), *Windows on the Japanese Past*: 127-148. Ann Arbor, Center for Japanese Studies, University of Michigan.

Ōsaka Daigaku Kōkogaku Kenkyūshitsu 2014. *Nonaka iseki (Nonaka site)* web site accessed Sept. 14 2014. www.let.osaka-u.ac.jp/kouKou/nonaka/about/about 02.01.html

Ōsaka Fu Bunkazai Kenkyūsho. 2014a. *Saikudani iseki (Saikudani site)* website accessed Sept. 22 2014. http://www.occpa.or.jp/iKō/naniwa_info/naniwa_gaiyōu/iKō_03_01_01.html

Ōsaka Fu Bunkazai Kenkyūsho. 2014b. *Nakanoshima Kurayashiki Ato Chōsa NX13-Ichiji Genchi Setsumeikai Shiryō (Materials for the Site Exhibition at Excavation NX13-1 of the Nakanoshima Warehouses)* (2 pp). Ōsaka, Ōsaka Fu Bunkazai Kenkyūsho.

Ōsaka Fu Bunkazai Sentā. 2007. *Sakai Kangō Toshi Iseki (SKT 959) no chōsa (The Investigation of Site SKT 959 of the Moated City Sakai) (Handout for site excavation visitors)*. Ōsaka, Ōsaka Fu Bunkazai Sentā.

Ōsaka Fu Bunkazai Sentā. 2013a. Kokunai saikō ishi no fundō, Kamei Iseki (The oldest stone weights found in Japan, Kamei Site). Web site accessed Sept. 25 2014. www.youtube.com/watch?v=o7jcPozVNO1.

Ōsaka Fu Bunkazai Sentā. 2013b. *Ōsaka Joato no Hakkutsu Chōsa, Heisei 25 Nen 11 Gatsu 23 Nichi Genchi Setsumeikai (Excavations of Ōsaka Castle, On Site Public Explanation, November 23 2014 Handout)*. Ōsaka, Ōsaka Fu Bunkazai Sentā.

Ōsaka Fu Bunkazai Sentā. 2014. *Ōsaka Furitsu Seijin Byō Sentā Seibi Jigyō ni Tomonau Ōsaka Jōato Genchi Kōkai Shiryō* (Materials for the *Site Exhibition at the Excavation of* Ōsaka *Castle in Conjunction with Facilities at the Ōsaka Municipal Adult Disease Center*) (2 pp). Ōsaka, Ōsaka Fu Bunkazai Sentā.

Ōsaka Furitsu Chikatsu Asuka Hakubutsukan. 1994. *Ōsaka Furitsu Chikatsu Asuka Hakubutsukan Josetsu Tenji Zuroku (Catalogue of Permanent Display of the Ōsaka Prefectural Chikatsu Asuka Museum)*. Ōsaka: Ōsaka Furitsu Chikatsu Asuka Hakubutsukan.

Ōsaka Furitsu Chikatsu Asuka Hakubutsukan. 2006. *Ōjin Dai Ō no Jidai (The Period of the Great King Ōjin)*. Ōsaka, Ōsaka Furitsu Chikatsu Asuka Hakubutsukan.

Ōsaka Furitsu Chikatsu Asuka Hakubutsukan. 2013a. *Kōkogaku kara Mita Nihon no Kokka to Kodai Bunka (The Japanese Ancient State and Culture as Seen from Archaeology)*. Ōsaka, Ōsaka Furitsu Chikatsu Asuka Hakubutsukan.

Ōsaka Furitsu Chikatsu Asuka Hakubutsukan. 2013b. *Kōkogaku kara Mita Suikō Chō (The Suikō Dynasty seen from Archaeology)*. Ōsaka, Ōsaka Furitsu Chikatsu Asuka Hakubutsukan.

Ōsaka Furitsu Sayamaike Hakubutsukan. 2007. *Kokudo o Hiraita Kanamonotachi (Tools for Opening the Land)*. Ōsaka, Ōsaka Furitsu Sayamaike Hakubutsukan.

Ōsaka Furitsu Yayoi Bunka Hakubutsukan. 2008. *Hakkutsu Sareta Ōsaka 2007: Suito no Kokusai Koryū Shi (Ōsaka Excavations 2007: History of International Trade of Ōsaka Water City)*. Izumi, Ōsaka Furitsu Yayoi Bunka Hakubutsukan.

Ōsaka Shi Bunkazai Kyōkai. 2008. *Ōsaka Iseki: Shutsudohin wa Kataru Naniwa Hakkutsu Monogatari (Ōsaka Sites: from Objects and Sites, the Excavation Account of Naniwa*. Ōsaka, Kuramoto Sha.

Osawa, Ken'ichi. 2006. Chūsei Uemachi Daichi no shūkyōteki yōsō (Religious aspects of the Uemachi Daichi in the Chūsei Period) In Sakaehara Towao and Hiroshi Niki (eds.), *Naniwanomiya kara Ōsakajō e (From Naniwanomiya to Ōsaka Castle)*:167-189. Ōsaka, Koshi Shoin.

Ōtsuka Hatsushige and Kobayashi Saburō (ed). 1984. *Kofun Jiten (Kofun Dictionary)*. Tōkyō, Tōkyōdō Shuppan.

Pai, H. 2013. *Heritage Management in Japan and Korea*. Seattle, University of Washington Press.

Paine, R. T. and. A. Soper. 1981. *The Art and Architecture of Japan*. Baltimore, Penguin Books.

Pearson, R. 1981. Social Complexity in Chinese Coastal Neolithic Sites. *Science* 213: 1078-1086.

Pearson, R. 1992. *Ancient Japan*. New York, Braziller.

Pearson, R. 2013. *Ancient Ryūkyū: An Archaeological Study of Island Communities*. Honolulu, University of Hawaii Press.

Piggott, J. 1997. *The Emergence of Japanese Kingship*. Stanford, Stanford University Press.

Piggott, J. 2009. Review of State Formation in Japan: Emergence of a Fourth Century Ruling Elite, by G.L. Barnes. *Journal of Japanese Studies* 35:2: 413-419. Quickcal ver.1.5. 2015. Website accessed July 6 2015. www.calpal-online.de.

Rekishikan Izumi Sano. n.d. *Rekishikan Izumi Sano Josetsu Tenji Annai (Izumi Sano Historical Museum Guide to Permanent Exhibitions)*. Izumi Sano, Rekishikan Izumi Sano.

Robb, J. 2010. Beyond Agency. *World Archaeology*. 42(4): 493-520.

Rosenfield, J. M. 2010. *Portraits of Chōgen*. Leiden, Brill.

Ryavec, C. 1978. *Political Jurisdiction in the Sengoku Daimyo Domain, Japan, 1477 to 1573*. Phd Dissertation, Columbia University. Ann Arbor, UMI.

Ryan, J. 2011 Makimuku Site. www/http/japanesearchaeology.com.2011/05/ makimuku iseki. Website accessed September 25 2014.

Sahara Makoto and Kanaseki Hiroshi. 1975. *Inasaku no Hajimari (The Beginning of Rice Cultivation)*. Tōkyō, Kōdansha.

Sakai, Hideya. 2013. Iseki chōsa to hogo no 60 nen (60 years of site investigation and preservation). *Kōkogaku Kenkyū* 60(2): 5-18.

Sakai, Ryūichi. 2001. Yayoi shakai to jōhō netsuwāku (Yayoi society and communication network). In Sakaehara Towao and Hiroshi Niki (eds.), *Yayoi jidai no shūraku (Yayoi Period villages)*: 18-25. Tōkyō, Gakuseisha.

Sakai Shi Hakubutsukan. 1993. *Hakata to Sakai (Hakata and Sakai)*. Sakai, Sakai Shi Hakubutsukan.

Sakai Shi Hakubutsukan. 2006. *Chadogu Haiken (Looking at Tea Ceremony Utensils)*. Sakai, Sakai Shi Hakubutsukan.

Sakai Shi Hakubutsukan. 2010. *Yomigaeru Chūsei Toshi Sakai: Hakkutsu Kekka to Shutsudohin (Bringing to Life the Mediaeval City of Sakai; Results of Excavations and Excavated Objects)*. Sakai, Sakai Shi Hakubutsukan.

Sakai Shi Kyōiku Iinkai. 1984a. *Tōki Senzuka 29 go fun Hakkutsu Chōsa Gaiyō Hōkokusho (Summary Report of Excavations of the Tōki Senzuka Mound No. 29)*. Sakai, Sakai Shi Kyōiku Iinkai.

Sakai Shi Kyōiku Iinkai. 1984b. *Sakai Kangō Toshi Iseki Hakkutsu Chōsa Hōkoku; Ichi no Machi Higashi 4 chome SKT 19 Chiten (Report of the Excavation of Sakai Moated City, Locality SKT 19, Ichi no Machi Higashi 4 chome, SKT 19)*. Sakai, Sakai Shi Kyōiku Iinkai.

Sakai Shi Kyōiku Iinkai. 1991a. *Sakai Kangō Toshi Iseki Chōsa Gaiyō Hōkoku: SKT 39 Jiten: Sakai Shi Kumano Chō Nishi 2 Chō (Summary Report of Excavations of the Sakai Moated City: Locality 39, Sakai City, Kumano Chō, Ward 2)*. Sakai, Sakai Shi Kyōiku Iinkai.

Sakai Shi Kyōiku Iinkai. 1991b. *Sakai Shi Kangō Toshi Iseki Chōsa Gaiyō Hōkoku: SKT 230, 289, 292 Chiten (Summary Report of Excavations of the Sakai Moated City City. Localities 230, 289, 292)*. Sakai, Sakai Shi Kyōiku Iinkai.

Sakai Shi Kyōiku Iinkai. 1997. *Sakai Shi Bunkazai Chōsa Gaiyō Hōkoku Dai 61 Satsu (Outline Report of the Investigations of Cultural Properties of Sakai City No. 61)*. Sakai, Sakai Shi Kyōiku Iinkai.

Sakai Shi Kyōiku Iinkai. 1999. *Nagasone Iseki (Nagasone Site)*. Sakai Shi, Sakai Shi Kyōiku Iinkai.

Sakai Shi Kyōiku Iinkai. 2008. *Mozu Kofungun no Chōsa 1 (Investigation of the Mozu Tombs 1)*. Sakai, Sakai Shi Kyōiku Inkai.

Sakai Shi Kyōiku Iinkai. 2009. *Mozu Kofungun no Chōsa 2 (Investigation of the Mozu Tombs 2)*. Sakai, Sakai Shi Kyōiku Iinkai.

Sakai Shi Mihara Chō Rekishi Hakubutsukan. 2012. *Kawachi Imoji (Kawachi Metal Casters)*. Museum pamphlet (2 pp). Sakai Shi, Sakai Shi Mihara Chō Rekishi Hakubutsukan.

Samurai Archives 2015. website accessed May 19 2015. http://wiki.samurai-archives.com/ index.php ? title = Ōsaka_castle

Schortman, E.M. 2014. Networks of power in archaeology. *Annual Review of Anthropology* 2014. 43: 167-182

Schramm, C. J. 2010. Foreword. In D. S. Landes, J. Mokyr, and W. Baumol (eds.), *The Invention of Enterprise: Entrepreneurship from Ancient Mesopotamia to Modern Times*, ed. pp. vii-viii. Princeton, Princeton University Press.

Segal, E. 2011. *Coins, Trade, and the State: Economic Growth in Early Mediaeval Japan*. Cambridge, Harvard University Asia Center, Harvard University Press.

Seike, Akira. 1999. Kofun jidai shūhen maisōbo kō; Kinai no haniwa kan o chūshin ni (Consideration of peripheral burials of the Kofun Period In Tsude Hiroshi (ed.), *Kokka Keisei Ki no Kōkogaku (Archaeology of the Period of State Development)*: 231-260. Ōsaka, Ōsaka Daigaku Kōkogaku Kenkyūshitsu.

Seki, Shūichi. 2002. Karamono no ryūtsū to shohi (Distribution and consumption of Chinese goods).

Kokuritsu Rekishi Minzoku Hakubutsukan Kenkyū Hōkoku 92:87-111.

Sekimoto, Yumiko. 2011. Mozu, Furuichi kofun gun to entō haniwa kenkyū (Mozu and Furuichi tomb groups and the study of cylindrical *haniwa*). In Ōsaka Furitsu Chikatsu Asuka Hakubutsukan (ed.), *Mozu Furuichi no Ryōbo Kofun (The Imperial Tombs of Mozu and Furuichi)*: 138-143. Ōsaka, Ōsaka Furitsu Chikatsu Asuka Hakubutsukan.

Sekiyama, Hiroshi. 2004. Ōsaka wan engan no Kofun jidai doki seien (Kofun period salt production (using ceramic evaporating vessels) in the Ōsaka Bay region). In Hirose Kazuo (ed.), *Kinai no Kyōdai Kofun to sono Jidai (The Gigantic Tombs of the Kinai and their Period) Kikan Kōkogaku Special Publication 14:* 109-120.

Sekiyama, Hiroshi. 2010a. *Naniwa Kyō to Kudara Ō shi (History of Naniwa Kyō and the Paekche royal clan)* In Sekiyama Hiroshi (ed.) *Higashi Ajia ni okeru Naniwanomiya to Kodai Naniwa no Kokusaiteki Seikaku ni kansuru Sōgō Kenkyū (Team Study of the Ancient Naniwa Palace and its International Relations) Kaken Project No. 18320131, 2006-2009, Final Report*: 125-143. Ōsaka, Ōsaka Shi Bunkazai Kyōkai.

Sekiyama, Hiroshi. 2010b. Naniwa Daidō to Naniwa Kyō (The Naniwa Great Road and the Naniwa Capital). In Sekiyama Hiroshi (ed.), *Higashi Ajia ni okeru Naniwanomiya to Kodai Naniwa no Kokusaiteki Seikaku ni Kansuru Sōgō Kenkyū (Team Study of the Ancient Naniwa Palace and its International Relations) Kaken Project No. 18320131, 2006-2009, Final Report,* ed. pp. 69-78. Ōsaka, Ōsaka Shi Bunkazai Kyōkai.

Sekiyama, Hiroshi. 2010c. Fukutosei shita no Naniwa Kyō (Naniwa Capital under the system of multiple capitals). In Sekiyama Hiroshi (ed.), *Higashi Ajia ni okeru Naniwanomiya to Kodai Naniwa no Kokusaiteki Seikaku ni kansuru Sōgō Kenkyū (Team study of the Ancient Naniwa Palace and its International Relations) Kaken Project No. 18320131, 2006-2009, Final Report:* 79-96. Ōsaka, Ōsaka Shi Bunkazai Kyōkai.

Sen, Rikyū. 1998. *The Japanese Way of Tea, from its Origins to Sen Rikyū.* Translated by Dixon Morris. Honolulu, University of Hawaii Press.

Senboku Kōko Shiryōkan. 1996. *Jiyū toshi; Sakai (Free City; Sakai).* Sakai, Senboku Kōko Shiryōkan.

Shibata, Kazuya. 2011. Yamatogawa Imaike Iseki (Yamatogawa Imaike Site) In *Osaka Furitsu Chikatsu Asuka Hakubutsukan (ed.), Rekishi Hakkutsu Osaka (Historical Excavations Osaka)*, 42-43. Osaka, Osaka Furitsu Chikatsu Asuka Hakubutsukan.

Shimada, Akira. 1985. Izumi Koganetsuka Kofun. In Kubosō Kinen Bijutsukan (ed.), *Tokubetsu Ten shisei 30 Shūnen Kinen, Koganetsuka Kofun, Sefukuji Kyozuka no Chō (Special Exhibition on the 30th Anniversary of the Municipal System (Treasures from the Koganetsuka Kofun and the Sutra Mound of the Sefukuji (Temple)*: 29-54. Izumi Shi, Kubosō Kinen Bijutsukan.

Shimatani, Kazuhiko. 1998. Chūsei no *mumonsen* to sono seibun sosei (Coins without inscriptions (plain coins) and their composition). *Kikan Kōkogaku* 62:71-74.

Shimatani, Kazuhiko. 1999. Sakai shi zeni no nazo (The puzzle of Sakai coins.) In Asao Naohiro, Sakehara Towao, Niki Hiroshi, and Kojita Yasunari (eds.) *Sakai no Rekishi (History of Sakai)*: 122-124. Tōkyō, Kadokawa Shoten.

Shimatani, Kazuhiko. 2003. *Mochusen* no seisan to fukyū (The production and diffusion of counterfeit coins), In Ono Masatoshi and Hagihara Mitsuo (eds.), *Sengoku Jidai no Kōkogaku (Archaeology of the Sengoku Period)*: 529-540. Tōkyō, Koshi Shoin.

Shimatani, Kazuhiko. 2010. Chūsei Sakai no kangō o meguru shomondai (Some problems concerning the moat of Sakai). *Chūsei Toshi Kenkyū* 15:103-120.

Shimogaki, Hitoshi. 2010. *Sankukuen Shinjūkuyō Kenkyū Jiten (Dictionary for the Study of the Triangular Rim Mirrors Decorated with Deities and Beasts).* Tōkyō, Yoshikawa Kōbunkan.

Shimogaki, Susumu. 2012. Kofun jidai shūchōbo keitōron no keitō (The geneaology of the reconstruction of genealogies of chiefly tombs of the Kofun Period). *Kōkogaku Kenkyū* 59(2): 56-70.

Shiraishi, Kōji. 2004. Suemura to sueki seisan (Suemura and sueki production). In Hirose Kazuo (ed.), *Kinai no Kyōdai Kofun to sono Jidai (The Gigantic Tombs of the Kinai and their Period). Kikan Kōkogaku Special Publication 14:* 96-108.

Shiraishi, Ta'ichirō. 1989. Kyōdai kofun no zōei (Construction of the very large tombs). In Shiraishi Ta'ichirō (ed.), *Kofun: Kodai o Kangaeru (Mounded tombs: Thinking About the Past)*: 73-106. Tōkyō, Yoshikawa Kōbunkan.

Shiraishi, Ta'ichirō. 2006. Furuichi kofun gun no seiritsu to Yamato Ōken (The development of the Furuichi Kofun Group and Yamato royal power). In Ōsaka Furitsu Chikatsu Asuka Hakubutsukan (ed.), *Ōjin Dai Ō no Jidai (The Period of the Great King Ōjin)*: 6-14. Ōsaka, Ōsaka Furitsu Chikatsu Asuka Hakubutsukan.

Shiraishi, Ta'ichirō. 2008. Wakoku Ōbo zōeichi ido no imi suru mono (Making sense of the shift of the burial place of the Wa kings). In Shiraishi Ta'ichirō (ed.), *Kinki Chihō ni Okeru Ōgata Kofungun no Kisoteki Kenkyū (Fundamental Study of the Large Tombs of the Kinki Region)*: 451-457. Nara, Nara Daigaku Bungakubu Bunkazai Gakka.

Shiraishi, Ta'ichirō. 2009. *Kōkogaku Kara Mita Wakoku (The Country of Wa Seen from Archaeology).* Tōkyō, Dai'ichi Shobō.

Shiraishi, Ta'ichirō. 2011. Mozu, Furuichi no ryōbo kofun ni tsuite (Concerning the imperial tombs of Mozu and Furuichi) In Ōsaka Furitsu Chikatsu Asuka

Hakubutsukan (ed.), *Mozu, Furuichi no Ryōbo Kofun (The Imperial Tombs of Mozu and Furuichi)*: 8-17. Ōsaka, Ōsaka Furitsu Chikatsu Asuka Hakubutsukan.

Shitara, Hiromi. 2009. Hottate munamochibashira to sorei saishi (Buildings with free standing *munamochibashira* ridge pole support posts and ancestor ritual). *Kokuritsu Rekishi Minzoku Hakubutsukan Kenkyū Hōkoku* 149: 55-90.

Slusser, D. 2004. The transformation of tea practice in sixteenth century Japan. In M. Pitelka (ed.), *Japanese Tea Culture: Art, History, and Practice*: 39-59. London, Routledge Curzon.

Sugahara, Yūichi. 2006. Sue no chiiki sa to gijutsu kakusan (Regional differences in kiln groups producing *sue* ware and the diffusion of technology). *Kōkogaku Kenkyū* 53(1): 47-61.

Sugimoto, Atsunori. 2007. Yayoi no ōgata funkyūbo to kokusai kōryū no mura, Kami Iseki shūhen (A Yayoi Period large burial mound and village of international exchange, the Kami Site vicinity). In Ōsaka Shi Bunkazai Kyōkai (ed.), *Naniwa Kōkogaku Sanpo (A Walk Through Naniwa Archaeology)*: 47-55. Tōkyō, Gakuseisha.

Sukigara, Toshio. 1999. *Chūsei Sonraku no Chiiki Sei no Kōkogakuteki Kenkyū (Archaeological Study of the Regional Nature of Mediaeval Villages)*. Tōkyō, Daikōsha.

Sugiyama, Jun. 2010. Ōken to kōeki no kyōten. In Kishimoto Naofumi (ed.) *Shiseki de Yomu Nihon no Rekishi (2) Kofun no Jidai (Reading Japanese Archaeology at Historic Sites (2) Kofun Period)*: 160-181. Tōkyō, Yoshikawa Kōbunkan.

Sumitomo Corporation News. 1979. *From the History of Sumitomo*. Ōsaka, Sumitomo Corporation.

Sumitomo Group. 2014. *Sumitomo history* http://www.sumitomo.gr.jp/english/history/index07html. Web site accessed June 24 2014.

Suzuki, Yasutami. 2002. Wakoku to Higashi Ajia (The country of Wa and East Asia). In Suzuki Yasutami (ed.), *Wakoku to Higashi Ajia. Nihon no Jidai Shi (The Country of Wa and East Asia: Historical Periods of Japan) Vol. 2:* 7-88. Tōkyō, Yoshikawa Kōbunkan.

Takahashi Teruhiko and Nakakubo Tatsuo, eds. 2014. *Nonaka Kofun to 'Wa no Go Ō' no Jidai (The Nonaka Kofun and the Period of the 'Five Kings of Wa'*. Ōsaka, Ōsaka Daigaku Shuppan Kai.

Takesue Jun'ichi, Morioka Hideto and Shitara Hitomi. 2011. *Yayoi Jidai; Rettō no Kōkogaku (Yayoi Period: Archaeology of the Archipelago)*. Tōkyō, Kawade Shobō Shinsha.

Tanaka, Manabu. 2011. Tsuka Ana Kofun (Tsuka Ana Kofun). In Ōsaka Furitsu Chikatsu Asuka Hakubutsukan (ed.), *Rekishi Hakkutsu Ōsaka (Historical Excavations Ōsaka)*: 28-29. Ōsaka, Ōsaka Furitsu Chikatsu Asuka Hakubutsukan.

Tanaka, Migaku. 1991. *Wajin Sōran (Disturbances of the Wa People)*. Tōkyō, Shūeisha.

Tanaka, Shinsaku. 2001 *Mozu, Furuichi Kofungun no Kenkyū (Study of the Mozu and Furuichi Burial Mound Groups)*. Tōkyō, Gakuseisha.

Tanaka, Shinsaku. 2009. *Tsutsugata Dōki no Seiken Kōtai (Change in Power and Tubular Bronze Artifacts)*. Tōkyō, Gakuseisha.

Tanaka, Shinsaku. 2010. Buki, bugu kara fukugen suru Kofun Jidai no jōbigun (Reconstructing the standing army of the Kofun Period from weapons and armor). In Tanaka Shinsaku and Nishikawa Toshikatsu (eds.), *Wa Ō no Gundan (The Military Corps of the Wa Kings)*: 81-172. Tōkyō, NHK Books.

Tanaka, Shinsaku. 2012. Nokogugata sekisei mokeihin no shutsugen to sono tenkai (Appearance and development of stone replicas of agricultural tools). *Kōkogaku Janaru* 624: 19-23.

Tanaka Shinsaku and Nishikawa Toshikatsu. 2010. Mozu, Furuichi Kofungun no seiroku o hikiita jinbutsu (The people who commanded the power of the Mozu and Furuichi Tomb Groups). In Tanaka Shinsaku and Nishikawa Toshikatsu (eds.), *Wa Ō no Gundan (The Military Corps of the Wa Kings)*: 189-222. Tōkyō, NHK Books.

Tanaka, Takeo. 1993. Ken Min sen to Sakai (The ships dispatched to Ming, and Sakai). In *Hakata to Sakai (Hakata and Sakai)*: 4-8. Sakai, Sakai Shi Hakubutsukan.

Tanioka, Takashi. 2008. Kokikō deita kara mita koko iseki ni okeru kyōsui konseki (Palaeoclimatological approach to archaeological flood evidence). *Kōkogaku Kenkyū* 55(2): 82-93.

Tenri Gareri. 2013. *Furu Iseki Ten (The Furu Site Exhibition)*. Tōkyō: Tenri Gareri.

Teramura, Hirofumi. 2004. *Entō haniwa* retsu no hensen to sono igi (Alignments of *entō haniwa* cylinders and their significance). *Kōkogaku Kenkyū* 51(2): 76-96.

Terasawa, Kaoru. 2005. Makimuku iseki to shoki Yamato seiken (The Makimuku site and the early period of Yamato political authority). In Ishino Hironobu (ed.), *Yamato Makimuku Iseki (The Yamato Makimuku Site)*: 86-122. Tōkyō, Gakuseisha.

Torama, Asami. 2008. Ikegami Sone Yayoi gakushukan no raishi man nana nen (Full seven years since the opening of the Ikegami Sone Learning Center). *Kōkogaku Kenkyū* 55(1): 12-16.

Totman, C. 1989. *The Green Archipelago: Forestry in Pre-Industrial Japan*. Berkeley, University of California Press.

Totman, C. 1993. *Early Modern Japan*. Berkeley, University of California Press.

Totman, C. 2000. *A History of Japan*. Oxford, Blackwell Publishers.

Toyoshima, Naohiro. 2000. Tekki sono shisetsu no seikaku (The nature of buried offerings of iron artifacts). *Kōkogaku Kenkyū* 46 (4): 76-92.

Troost, C. K. 1997. Peasants, elites, and villages in the fourteenth century. In J. Mass (ed.), *The Origins of*

Japan's Mediaeval World: 91-112. Stanford, Stanford University Press.

trussell.com 2015. Fuhonsen coin. website accessed September 20 2015. www. trussel.com/prehist/news 102 htm

Tsuchiyama, Takeshi. 1996. Sakai shutsudo tōjiki sosei ni tsuite – SKT 39 chiten no chōsa o chūshin ni (The ceramic assemblage from Sakai, with particular reference to those coming from SKT 39). In Tōki Shi Mino Tōjiki Rekishi Kan (ed.), *Tokubetsu Ten: Sakai Shū no Yakimono (The Ceramics of the Populace of Sakai)*: 40-43. Tōki, Mino Tōjiki Rekishi Kan.

Tsude, Hiroshi. 1989a. *Nihon Nōkō Shakai no Seiritsu Katei: (The Process of Development of Agricultural Society in Japan)*. Tōkyō, Iwanami Shoten.

Tsude, Hiroshi. 1989b. Kofun no tanjō to shūen (Birth and death of kofun). In Tsude, Hiroshi (ed.), *Kofun Jidai no Ō to Minshū (King and People of the Kofun Period)*: 27-34. Tōkyō, Kōdansha.

Tsude, Hiroshi. 2000. *Ōryō no Kōkogaku (The Archaeology of Royal Tombs)*. Tōkyō, Iwanami Shinsho.

Tsude, Hiroshi. 2006. Early state formation in Japan (introduced and interpreted by Walter Edwards). In J. Piggott (ed.), *Capital and Countryside in Japan 300 – 1180*: 15-53. Ithaca, Cornell University East Asia Program.

Tsujio, Ei'ichi. 2000. Kosugi Tsugimura ga kaita Naniwa Itachigawa shutsudo no kuribune ezu (The drawing by Kosugi Tsugimura of the dugout canoe found in the Itachi River, Naniwa) In Watanabe Takeshi Kanchō Taishoku Kinen Ronshū Kankōkai (Committee for the Retirement Publication for Director Watanabe Takeshi) (Ed.), *Ōsakajō to Jōkamachi (Ōsaka Castle and Castle Town)*: 319-339. Kyōto, Shibunkaku Shuppan.

Tsujita, Jun'ichirō. 2007. *Kagami to Shoki Yamato Seiken (Mirrors and the Initial Yamato Political Power)*. Tōkyō, Suirensha.

Tsujita, Jun'ichirō. 2014. Sekai no naka no Kofun Jidai kenkyū (Kofun Period Studies in global perspective). *Kōkogaku Kenkyū* 61:3: 15-28.

Tsunoda, Ryusaku and L.C. Goodrich (ed). 1951. *Japan in the Chinese Dynastic Histories: Later Han Through Ming Dynasties*. South Pasadena, D. and Ione Perkins.

Tsunoyama, Sakae. 2000. *Sakai: Umi no Toshi Bunmei (Sakai: Civilization of a Maritime City)*. Sakai, PHP Kenkyūsho.

Tsuzuki, Shin'ichiro. 1990. Sakai no han'ei to bunka. In Tsuda Hideo (ed.), *Zusetsu: Ōsaka Fu no Rekishi (Illustrated History of Ōsaka)*: 149-158. Tōkyō, Kawade Shobō Shinsha.

Tsuzuki, Shin'ichiro. 1993. 'Chūsei toshi Sakai' no kūkan kōsei - sono kōkogakuteki fukugen (Archaeological reconstruction of the spatial structure of the 'Mediaeval City of Sakai'. *Hakata* 2: 67-76.

Tsuzuki, Shin'ichirō. 1994. Chūsei toshi Sakai: toshi kūkan to kōzō (The mediaeval city Sakai; urban space and structure. *Chūsei Toshi Kenkyū* 1:79-118.

Tsuzuki, Shin'ichirō. 2007. Minami no kuni yori Sakai e hakobareshi [yakimono] kō (Consideration of ceramics brought to Sakai from southern countries). In Ōsaka Furitsu Yayoi Bunka Hakubutsukan (ed.), *Hakkutsu Sareta Ōsaka 2007; Suito Ōsaka no Kokusai Kōryūshi (Ōsaka Excavations 2007; History of International Trade of Ōsaka, Water City)*: 92-97 Izumi, Ōsaka Furitsu Yayoi Bunka Hakubutsukan.

Tsuzuki, Shin'ichirō. 2010a. Sakai Kangō Toshi iseki kara shutsudo shita "koneru, orosu" yakimono (Ceramics for mixing and grating found in the Sakai Moated City Site) *Bizen Shi Rekishi Minzoku Shiryōkan Kiyō* 12: 47-60.

Tsuzuki, Shin'ichirō. 2010b. Kōwan toshi Sakai ni okeru zō ikō; senretsu tatemono no kentō (Storage pits of the port city of Sakai; an examination of tile based buildings with tile lined basements). In Senda Yōshihiro and Yata Toshifumi (eds.), *Toshi to Jōkan no Chūsei (The Chūsei Period of Cities and Castles)*:. 229-254. Tōkyō, Koshi Shoin.

Tsuzuki, Shin'ichirō. 2010c. Sakai shutsudo no cha tō (Tea ceramics excavated from Sakai). *Kikan Kōkogaku* 110: 75-78.

Tsuzuki, Shin'ichirō. 2010d. Sakai Kangō Toshi Iseki kara shutsudo shita Betunamu tōjiki (Vietnamese ceramics found in the Sakai Moated City Site). In Kikuchi Sei'ichi and Abe Yurikō (eds.), *Umi no Michi to Kōkogaku; Indoshina Hantō kara Nihon e (Maritime Routes and Archaeology; from the Indochina Peninsula to Japan*: 232-247. Tōkyō, Koshi Shoin.

Tsuzuki, Shin'ichirō. 2010e. Bōeki toshi Sakai shutsudo no tōjiki (Trade ceramics excavated from the trading city of Sakai). *Kikan Kōkogaku* 110:79-83.

Tsuzuki, Shin'ichirō. 2011a. Sakai Kangō Toshi iseki ni okeru ryūtsū no yōsō (The nature of circulation in the Sakai Moated City Site). In Nihon Chūsei Doki Kenkyūkai (ed.), *Kōkogaku to Muromachi Sengoku Ki no Ryūtsū (Circulation in the Muromachi and Sengoku Periods)*: 93-117. Tōkyō, Koshi Shoin.

Tsuzuki, Shin'ichirō. 2011b. Sakai Kangō Toshi Iseki kara shutsudo shita Chūgoku sei tōjiki no yōsō ni tsuite (soan) (Aspects of Chinese ceramics excavated from the Sakai Moated City Site (basic introduction). *Hakata Kenkyūkai Ki 20 Shūnen Tokubetsu Go*: 3-12.

Tsuzuki, Shin'ichirō. 2012a. Sakai Kangō Toshi Iseki ni okeru "Nanban Bōeki Ki" no bōeki tōji (Trade Ceramics from the "Period of Nanban Trade" in the Sakai Moated City Site). *Bōeki Tōji Kenkyū* 32: 66-75.

Tsuzuki, Shin'ichirō. 2012b. Sakai Kangō Toshi Iseki kara shutsudo shita cha tō -- Bizenyaki ni tsuite (Concerning tea ceramics --Bizen Ware-- from the Sakai Moated City Site). In Sakai Shi Hakubutsukan (ed.), *Sakai Shutsudo no Chatō -- Bizenyaki (Tea ceramics from Sakai, Bizen Ware)*: 3-7. Sakai, Sakai Shi Hakubutsukan.

Uchida, Kusuo. 2000. Ōsakajō kenkyū no ayumi (A walk through Ōsaka Castle studies). In Watanabe Takeshi Kanchō Taishoku Kinen Ronshū Kankōkai (Committee for the Retirement Publication for Director Watanabe Takeshi) (ed.), *Ōsakajō to Jōkamachi (Ōsaka Castle and Castle Town)*: 23-42. Kyōto, Shibunkaku Shuppan.

Uchida, Toshihide. 2004. Chūsei no dō o megutte (Concerning mediaeval copper) *Rekishi Dokuhon* 49 (6): 226-227.

Ueda, Masa'aki. 2007. Kawachi Ōchō to Mozu Kofun Gun. *Higashi Ajia no Kodai Bunka* 131: 2-21.

Ueda, Takashi. 2011. "Kawachi Imoji" no katsudo to Chōgen (Activities of the "Kawachi Imoji" and Chōgen) *Ōsaka Furitsu Sayamaike Hakubutsukan Kenkyū Hōkoku* 7: 69-76.

Ueki, Hisashi. 2009. *Naniwanomiya Ato (The Site of the Naniwa Palace)*. Tōkyō, Dōseisha.

Uezato, Takashi. 2010. Ko Ryūkyū no kinkōhin seisan no ryūtsū (The production and exchange of metal work of Ko Ryūkyū). *Nihon no Bijutsu* 533: 84-94.

Urabe, Yukihiro. 2006. Kinai no zenpōkōhōfun o kangaeru (Considering the front and rear square mound burials of the Kinai). *Kōkogaku Janaru* 551: 31-35.

Utaka, Y. 2013. The Himeji Castle World Heritage Site; challenges of sustaining memories of a revered heritage in Japan. In K. D. Silva and N.K. Champagain (eds.), *Asian Heritage Management: Contexts, Concerns, and Prospects*: 143-156. London, Routledge.

Van Goethem, E. 2008. *Nagaoka: Japan's Forgotten Capital*. Leiden, Brill.

Von Verschuer, C. 2006. *Across the Perilous Seas: Japanese Trade with China and Korea from the Seventh to Seventeenth Centuries* (translated by Kirsten Lee Hunter). Ithaca, Cornell University.

Wada, S. 1986. Political interpretation of stone coffin production in protohistoric Japan. In R. Pearson, G. Barnes, K. Hutterer (eds.), *Windows on the Japanese Past: Studies in Archaeology and Prehistory*: 349-374. Ann Arbor, University of Michigan Center for Japanese Studies.

Wada, Seigo. 2003. Kofun jidai no seigyō to shakai (Kofun Period subsistence and society). *Kōkogaku Kenkyū* 50(3): 43-56.

Wada, Seigo. 2014. *Kofun Jidai no Sōsei to Takaikan (Kofun Period Burial Assemblage and View of the Other World)*. Tōkyō, Yoshikawa Kōbunkan.

Wakabayashi, Kunihiko. 2001. Yayoi Jidai daikibo shūraku no hyōka; Ōsaka heiya no Yayoi jidai chiiki iseki gun a chūshin ni (An appraisal of large scale settlements of the Yayoi Period; an analysis based on Middle Yayoi sites of the Ōsaka Plain. *Nihon Kōkogaku* 12: 35-54.

Wakabayashi, Kunihiko. 2005. Hōkei shūkōbo gun to shūraku (Groups of moated precinct burials and villages). *Kōkogaku Janaru* 534: 9-13.

Wakabayashi, Kunihiko. 2006. Kyūryō ue Yayoi shūraku to fukugo shakai no kakudai (Yayoi hilltop villages slopes and the expansion of Yayoi plural society). *Kodai Bunka* 58(2): 96-105.

Wakabayashi, Kunihikō. 2008. Shūraku to shūdan (2) Kinki (Village and social group (2) Kinki). In Shitara Hitomi, Fujio Shin'ichirō and Matsumoto Takehiko (eds.), *Yayoi jidai no kōkogaku (8) shūraku kara yomu Yayoi shakai (Archaeology of the Yayoi Period (Volume 8) Reading Yayoi Society from Village Sites)*: 36-37. Tōkyō, Dōseisha.

Wakabayashi, Kunihiko. 2009. Shūraku bunritsu pataan o hensen kara mita Yayoi shakai (Yayoi society seen from changes in the pattern of village distribution). *Kokuritsu Rekishi Minzoku Hakubutsukan Kenkyū Hōkoku* 149: 33-53.

Wakasa, Toru. 2007. *Kofun Jidai no Suiri Shakai no Kenkyū (Kofun Period Irrigation Society)*. Tōkyō, Gakuseisha.

Wakita, H. 1999. Ports, markets, and mediaeval urbanism in the Ōsaka region. In J.L. McClain, and Wakita Osamu (eds.), *Ōsaka, the Merchant's Capital of Early Modern Japan*: 22-43. Ithaca, Cornell University Press.

Wang, Z. (Zhenping) 2005. *Ambassadors from the Island of the Immortals*. Honolulu, University of Hawaii Press.

Wang, Zhongshu. 1992. *Sankakuen Shinjūkyō (Mirror with Triangular Rim and Beasts and Deities)*. Tōkyō, Gakuseisha.

Watsky, A. 1995. Commerce, politics, and tea; the career of Imai Sōkyū. *Monumenta Nipponica* 50(1): 47-65.

Watsky, A. 2004. Commerce, politics, and tea: the career of Imai Sōkyū (1520-1593). In M. Pitelka (ed.), *Japanese Tea Culture: Art, History, and Practice*: 18-38. London, Routledge Curzon.

weblio.jp. 2014. *Hine Shō iseki (Hine Shō site)* website accessed Sept. 22 2014. http://www.weblio.jp/content/%E6%97%A5%E6%A0 %B9 %E8%8D%98% E9%81%BA%E8%B7%A1

Willey, G., P. Phillips. 1958. *Method and Theory in American Archaeology*. Chicago, University of Chicago Press.

Wilson, R. 2003. Plastic, graphic, and plain: Mino ceramics from the Momoyama Period. *Orientations* 34 (10): 14-19.

Yagi, Hisae. 2010. Kōki Naniwanomiya no yanegawara o megutte (Concerning the roof tiles of the Late Period Naniwanoiya). In Sekiyama Hiroshi (ed.), *Higashi Ajia ni okeru Naniwanomiya to Kodai Naniwa no Kokusaiteki Seikaku ni Kansuru Sōgō Kenkyū (Team Study of the Ancient Naniwa Palace and its International Relations) Kaken Project No. 18320131, 2006-2009, Final Report*: 111-123. Ōsaka, Ōsaka Shi Bunkazai Kyōkai.

Yamakawa, Hitoshi. 1998. Chūsei shūraku no ronri (The Logic of mediaeval village sites). *Kōkogaku Kenkyū* 45(2): 104-123.

Yamamura, K. 1990. The Growth of Commerce. In K. Yamamura, J. Hall, M. Jansen, D. Twitchett, and H. Kanai (eds.), *The Cambridge History of Japan Volume 3 Mediaeval Japan*: 344-395. Cambridge, Cambridge University Press.

Yamauchi, Noritsugu. 2008. *Kofun jidai no Furu Iseki (The Furu Site in the Kofun Period)*. Nara Joshi Daigaku 21seiki COE puroguramu hōkokushu note URL 19:39-60. Website http://nwudir.lib.nara-wu.ac.jp/dspace/handle/10935/2512. Accessed October 21 2014.

Yasuda, Yoshinori. 1977. Wakoku ran ki no shizen kankyō (The natural environment at the time of the Wa Disturbance. *Kōkogaku Kenkyū* 23:83-99.

Yasuda, Yoshinori. 1978a. Ōsaka Fu Kawachi Heiya ni okeru kako ichiman sanzen nenkan no shokusei hensen to kochiri (Vegetational history and palaeogeography of the Kawachi Plain for the last 13,000 years). *Daiyonki Kenkyū (The Quaternary Research)* 16(4): 211-229.

Yasuda, Yoshinori. 1978b. *Prehistoric Environment of Japan; Palynological Approach*. Sendai, Institute of Geography, Tohoku University.

Yasuda, Yōshinori. 1980a. Uriūdō iseki no deido no kafun bunseki II (Pollen analysis of mud samples from the Uriūdō site II). In Ōsaka Fu Bunkazai Sentā (ed.), *Uriūdō: Kinki Jidōsha Tenri-Suita Sen Kensetsu ni Tomanau Maizō Bunkazai Hakkutsu Gaiyō Hōkokusho (Summary Report of Excavations of Buried Cultural Properties in Association with the Construction of the Kinki Tenri-Suita Highway)*: 427-436. Ōsaka, Ōsaka Fu Bunkazai Sentā.

Yasuda, Yoshinori. 1980b. Onchi Iseki shūhen no kokankyō no fukugen (Reconstruction of the ancient environment in the vicinity of the Onchi Site I). In Ōsaka Fu Bunkazai Sentā (ed.), *Uriūdō: Kinki Jidosha Tenri-Suita Sen Kensetsu ni Tomanau Maizō Bunkazai Hakkutsu Gaiyō Hōkokusho (Summary Report of Excavations of Buried Cultural Properties in Association with the Construction of the Kinki Tenri-Suita Highway)*: 227-252. Ōsaka, Ōsaka Fu Bunkazai Sentā.

Yasumura, Toshifumi. 2008a. Tamateyama Kofungun (Tamateyama Kofun Group). In Shiraishi Ta'ichirō (ed.) *Kinki Chihō ni okeru Ōgata Kofungun no Kisoteki Kenkyū (Fundamental Study of the Large Tombs of the Kinki Region)*: 20-22. Nara, Nara Daigaku Bungakubu Bunkazai Gakka.

Yasumura, Toshifumi. 2008b. Furuichi Kofungun no seiritsu to Tamateyama Kofungun (The formation of the Furuichi Tomb Group and the Tamateyama Kofun Group) In Shiraishi Ta'ichirō (ed.), *Kinki Chihō ni okeru Ōgata Kofungun no Kisoteki Kenkyū (Fundamental Study of the Large Tombs of the Kinki Region)*: 465-472. Nara, Nara Daigaku Bungakubu Bunkazai Gakka.

Yoneda, Fumitaka. 2006. Kawachi Kō iseki no igi to ibutsu (The significance and artifacts of the Kō Site. *Occasional Paper No. 2, Chiiki Renkei Kikaku dai'ichi Kan, Kawachi Kō Iseki Satogaeri Ten.* Ōsaka, Kansai Daigaku Naniwa Ōsaka Bunka Yusan Kenkyū Sentā.

Yoshifusa, Yasuyuki. 2001. Ima yomigaeru Yayoi no kunimura (Reconstructing Yayoi country and villages). In Ōsaka Furitsu Yayoi Bunka Hakubutsukan (ed.) *Yayoi Jidai no Shūraku (Yayoi Period Villages)*: 176-196. Tōkyō, Gakuseisha.

Yoshimura, Ken. 2008. Hakugaku no renkei no jōken to kadai (Collaboration between museum and school; present condition and problems). *Kōkogaku Kenkyū* 55(1): 7-12.

Zaidan Hojin Ōsaka Shi Bunka Kyōkai. 1996. *Shitennōji Kyūkedai Iseki Hakkutsu Chōsa Hōkokusho (Report of Excavations of the Kyūkedai Site, Shitennōji)*. Ōsaka, Zaidan Hojin Ōsaka Shi Bunka Kyōkai.

Index

A

abrader 14
aerial laser photography 85
Ama Site 20
Amano River 58
Andō Tadao 105, 106, 107
Andoyama Kofun 24, 30
Arai Hakuseki 87
Archaeological Discovery Center 104
armor iii, 5-6, 23, 26, 30, 32, 46-47, 51, 70, 83, 88, 88, 90, 91, 92, 116, 128
Asuka Ike Site 46
Asuka Period 26, 39, 46, 53, 58
Awatsu SZ Type ii, 13-14
Azuchi Momoyama Period 61, 122

B

baichō (satellite mound) 23, 37, 43, 51, 90, 111
base camp 14
bead production 6, 18, 44
bellows valves iv, 18, 43, 46, 64, 93, 95
bird *haniwa* 25, 36, 83-86, 88, 90
Bizen Ware v, 94-95, 98, 123-124, 129-130
blue and white ware 71, 73, 76, 95, 96, 98, 99
Boston Museum of Fine Arts 87
bronze arrowhead 18, 32, 43
bronze casting 18, 20, 83
bronze earrings 38, 39
bronze sockets 26, 90
Bu 33, 111
Buddha Hall 54
Buddhism 3-4, 27, 38, 53, 59, 62, 103, 116
buke yashiki 73
burial mounds 5, 25-26, 30-32, 37, 43, 51, 78, 106
Burmese Wares 99

C

camphor tree 82
canals 5-6, 23, 49-51, 58-59, 78
carracks 72
central buildings (Yayoi) 15, 18, 19, 82, 83, 92
chamber *(anagama)* kiln 88
chert 13
chest shaped stone coffin 84
chiefs' residence 18-20, 44, 48
Chikatsu Asuka region 50
Chin 33, 84, 87, 111
Chinese mirrors 21, 28, 92
Chino'oka Kofun 31, 36-37, 86
Chōgen iii, 3, 58-59, 64, 107, 111, 126, 130

Chōshōji Temple 64
Chūsei Period 1, 111-iv, 5, 39, 55-56, 59-62, 70, 72-73, 77, 79, 94, 120, 125, 129
clay mold 28, 64
clay net weight 54
coffin ii, 25-26, 30-32, 38, 43, 83-89, 92, 130
coin mold 95, 121
coins 53, 55, 65, 70-71, 95, 97, 99, 103, 116, 126-127
coins, thin plain 53, 55, 65, 70-71, 95, 97, 99, 103, 116, 126-127
communal well being 51, 79
confederacy 25, 27, 33
counterfeit coins 70-71, 127
craft production 6, 18, 23, 26, 39, 48-49, 61-62, 118
crucible 64, 90
cuirass vi, 32, 43, 46, 83, 88-90, 92
cuirass, horizontal plate vi, 32, 43, 46, 83, 88-90, 92
cuirass, triangular plate vi, 32, 43, 46, 83, 88-90, 92
cypress wood striations 88

D

dai ō 26, 121, 125, 127
Dairikoden 92
Dairizenden 92
Daisen Ryō Kofun 33, 36, 37, 39, 44, 85-88, 90, 105-106
Daitokuji 101, 103
Daoism 27, 28, 78, 92
deer skin 101, 103
diatoms 11-12
disasters iv, 65, 68, 123
Doshōmachi 75, 80
dōtaku 18, 20, 27, 83, 111
Dotō Site 3, 53, 59
double cropping 4, 61
dozō 75, 111
dry field 15
dual authority 30, 75

E

early state 6, 15, 25, 28, 78, 117, 129
Early Yayoi iv, 3, 9, 16, 20-21, 81-82
Earthquake 11, 22, 65, 78, 88
East Osaka Buried Cultural Properties Center (Encountering Excavation) (Hakkutsu Fureaikan Higashi Osaka Maizo Bunkazai Senta) 107
eboshi 64
egōshū 103
elite residential compounds 6, 51
Engishiki 3, 25, 33, 111
entō haniwa 32, 39, 40, 83-84, 86, 88, 89, 90. 92

entrepreneurs 5-7, 23, 59, 61, 77, 80, 110
entrepreneurship, productive 5, 77, 79-80, 126
entrepreneurship, unproductive 5, 77, 79-80, 126
environmental data 1, 22

F

Final Jōmon Period 3, 9, 14, 16, 17
finger nail impression 13
Five Kings of Wa ii, vi, 3, 25, 33-34, 88, 128
footed stand 41
Fuhonsen 55, 111, 129
Furu Site 44, 128, 131
Furu Type 26, 84
Furuichi Canal 58
Furuichi Tomb Group ii-iv, 13, 35, 39, 44, 50, 84-85, 89-90, 105, 108, 131
Furuike Site 9

G

galactic polity 4, 78
galleons 72
gashitsu doki 63, 95, 111
Goboyama Kofun 43
Godaigo Tennō 66, 111
Gokurakuji Hibiki Site 47
Goshaji Kofun 31
gosho 103
Goshu coin 32
gozoku 39
granite 68, 93
grey tile ware 95
guns 70, 101-103
Gyoki 59

H

Haji Minami Ryō Site 44
Haji Nisanzai Kofun 36
Haji no Sato Site 39, 44
hajiki 54, 62, 111
Hakayama Kofun 90
hakusai kyō 27, 28
Han Dynasty 29, 87
haniwa iii-iv, vi, 5, 25-26, 29-30, 32, 36, 38-41, 43-44, 51, 78-79, 83-86, 88-90, 92, 111, 116, 126-128
haniwa coffin 43
haniwa surface specks 40, 84
haniwa types 40, 84
Hashihaka Kofun iii, 27, 29, 37-38, 78, 118
Hashinaka 31
hearth 13, 43, 62, 93
Heian Period 4, 11, 59, 62, 64, 102, 119
helmet iii, 46-47, 90, 92, 99
Hibiya Ryōkei 102
Higashi Nara Site 18
Higashi Ueno Site 44

Hiki Shōen 3, 39, 62-63, 111
Himeji Castle 109, 130
Himiko 3, 25, 27, 29-30, 33, 35, 78, 111, 117, 120, 122
Hine Shōen 3, 62, 64, 108, 111, 118
Hirano Site 72
hitogata 51
hoe shape bracelet 32, 86
Hōenzaka Site 49
Hoi An 80
hōkei shūkōbo 21, 81, 111, 130
Homutawake 32, 111
Honganji Buddhist Sect 61
Horie iii, 50, 55=56, 59, 93, 113
horizontal burial chamber 26, 37, 85
horizontal ridge (*tottaimon*) 16
horse raising 39
horticulture 2, 15
Hōryuji 54-56, 92, 112
Hosokawa Clan 101
house shape stone coffin 31, 38
Huzhou Type mirror 59
Hyōgo Tsu 112

I

Ichijodani 73
ideology 23, 27-28, 31, 51, 78
iegata sekkan 31, 112
Ikedadera 58, 112
Ikegami Sone Site iv, 19-20, 81-83, 116, 119
Ikejiri 58, 107, 112
Ikeshima Fukumanji Site 17, 78
Ikoma Mountain Range 8, 55
Imai Sōkyū 102
Imakuma River 58
immigrants iii, 2, 5, 23, 38-39, 41, 44, 46, 48-49, 51, 53, 55, 58-59, 77, 118
Imperial Tombs vi, 1, 25, 35-38, 104, 117, 122, 127-128
Initial Jōmon Period 13, 14
iron casting 3, 61, 64
iron cauldron 64
iron ingot 23, 32, 43, 46, 76, 90
iron sand 43-44
irrigation 5, 6, 16, 18, 23, 51, 53, 58, 59, 61, 78, 107
Ishi River iii, 32, 50, 58
Ishiyama Honganji 3, 6-7, 49, 61-62, 70, 72-73, 77, 80, 112, 116
Ishisuka Tomb Group 38
Iwajuku Site 13
Izumi sandstone iii, 58-59, 68, 86
Izumisano Historical Museum (Rekishikan Izumisano) 108

J

Jiangsu Province 14
Jinaimachi 72-73, 112, 116-117, 121
Jingdezhen v, 59, 71, 96, 99

133

Jingū 54
Jimmu Tennō 25
Jishū Sect 102
jitō 62
jiyū toshi 103, 123, 127
jōbigun 26, 128
Jōmon figurines 16
Jōmon Period 1, 9-10, 13-17, 39, 120
jōri field iii, 50, 63
jūkan 44, 112
jūnansei 103

K

kabuto 46, 112
kabutohachi 99, 112
kachū 46, 112
kaiseki ryōri 72, 96
Kaiyuan Tongbao 70
Kamakura Period 4
Kamei Site 21, 125
Kami Ishitsu Misanzai Kofun 36-37, 85-86
kangai shisetsu 54, 112
Kansai Innovative Comprehensive Global Strategic Special Zone 80
kanshi 95
kanyōsei 103
Kanzaki River 56
Karako Kagi Site 117
Kashiwara Historical Museum (Kashiwara Shiritsu Rekishi Shiryokan) 107, 108
Katonboyama Kofun 92
Katsuragi Clan 44, 47
Kawachi Bay ii, 9-10, 13-14, 17, 121, 125
Kawachi Dynasty 33, 83
Kawachi imoji 64, 112, 126, 130
Kawachi Lagoon 9-11, 50, 77, 125
Kawachi Lake 9-11, 50, 53, 55, 92
Kawachi nabe 64, 112
Kawachi Plain 8-11, 17, 20, 31, 37, 44, 70, 117, 119, 131
Kaya 28, 41, 43, 46, 112, 117
Kentōshi 55, 79
kesshōhengan 20
Ki River 48, 61
kidan 92
Kijima Type 13
Kinsei Period I, 5, 43, 61, 70, 70-75, 108, 124-125
kinugasa haniwa 85
Kitoragawa Site 20, 21
Ko 33, 112, 119, 130
kō ii, 3, 6, 13-14, 112, 116, 120, 126, 129, 131
Kō Site ii, 13-14, 116, 131
kobyakusho 63
Kodai Period iii-iv, 4-5, 7, 50, 53, 56, 61-62, 64, 79, 83, 94, 123
kofun i-iv, 1-13, 19-21, 23, 25-33, 35-41, 43-54, 58-59, 70, 76, 78-79, 83-92, 104-107, 112, 116-131
kofun construction 5, 23, 33, 36, 37, 39

kofun moats 36, 39, 83-84, 87-88
Kofun Period i, iii, 4-5, 7-8, 10-13, 19-21, 23, 25-28 30-33, 37-41, 43-53, 58-59, 70, 78-79, 83, 90, 106-107, 116-121 124-131
Kofun Period army 26, 51, 78
Kofun Period chronology 24, 26-32, 34
Kofun Period tomb groups 24-38
kofun roof slabs 87-88
Koganetsuka Kofun 28, 32, 50, 116, 119, 127
Koguryo 33, 89
Kojiki 3, 25, 33, 112
Kojima Higashi Site 43
Konda Gobyōyama Kofun 35, 37, 39, 41, 46, 50, 54, 84-85, 87-89
Konda Hachiman Shrine iv, 84, 89-90
Konda Maruyama Kofun iv, 89-90
Konda Shiratori Site 44
Konishi Ryūsa 103
Kōraibashi 55
Korean ceramics 49, 53, 55, 99
Korean style house 44
Kosaka Site 41
Koseto 62
Kōtoku Emperor 55
Kōya 50, 58-59, 65
Kudara Amadera iii, 55-56, 92, 112, 121
kudatama 90, 112
Kumano 58-59, 62, 64-66, 79, 112, 126
Kunaicho (Imperial Household Ministry) 85, 88
Kumeda Kifukuyama Kofun 24, 32
Kurohimeyama Kofun 24, 36, 88, 90, 107
Kurokawa Type 15
Kusaba Sainin 103, 112
Kuwazu Site ii, 15
kyōten shūraku 18, 20

L

lake deposits 9, 11, 12
large central building iv, 18, 82-83
large wall building 44
Late Paleolithic Period ii, 12
level kiln iii, 42
Little Ice Age 61
Liu Song Dynasty 33
Longquan Kilns 71
Luis Frois 102

M

magatama 18, 32, 44, 83, 90, 92, 112-113
Makimuku Site 19-20, 27, 116, 118-119, 126, 128
Manila 80
Mappō 59, 113
Markets 4, 6, 65, 73, 79-80, 130
Menam Noi Kilns 71
Mesuriyama Kofun 29
metal casting iii, 3, 55, 61-64, 68, 70, 73, 834, 99

Mi-Son wares 71
Middle Jōmon Period 9
Middle Yayoi ii, iv, 10-11, 15, 18-22, 43, 51, 77-78, 81-82, 130
migrants 39, 51, 55, 88
Mihara Chō 55, 62, 64, 70, 126
mikō (shamaness), 88
military rulers 4, 31, 51, 61, 78
Minato Site 43, 120
Minato Wares 99
Minegatsuka Kofun 85, 118
Ming tributary trade 101
mirror ii, 27-29, 32, 59, 89, 117, 119, 122-124, 130
mirror, triangular rim ii, 27-29, 32, 59, 87, 89, 117, 119, 124-124, 130
miyake 25-26, 113
Miyake Yonekichi 25, 113
Miyazaki Ichisada 77, 125
moat 111-iv, 18-19, 29, 39-40, 66, 68-70, 72-73, 83, 85-86, 89-90, 92, 127
moated burial precinct 6, 19, 20, 81
moated village 19, 81
mochihakobu kan 26
mokkan 55, 99
mold fragments 70, 83, 95
money lending 101-102
Mononobe Clan 44
Morinomiwa Site 4, 9
Mount Ikoma 8, 13
Mozu Tomb Group iii-iv, 36, 39, 44, 47, 50, 54, 86, 105, 116
Muromachi Period 4

N

Nagahara Site ii, 12, 16, 44, 78
Nagahara Tomb Group 38
Nagahara Type ii, 16
nagamochigata sekkan ii, 25, 30-31, 113
Nagaoka 55, 79, 113, 130
Nagasone Ditch iii, 50
Nagayoshi Kawanabe Site 9, 16, 50
Nanban Fuki Technique 75
Nangō Site iii, 44, 47-48, 116
Naniwa i, iii, 3, 6-7, 33, 39, 46, 49-56, 58-59, 61-62, 72-73, 79, 92-93, 104, 113, 117, 119-122, 124-125, 127-131
Naniwa Daidō 58, 127
Naniwa Horie iii, 50, 55-56, 113
Naniwa Palace, Early iii, 3, 7, 50, 53-55, 59, 61, 72-73, 79, 92-93, 104, 122, 124, 127, 130
Naniwa Palace, Late iii, 3, 7,50, 53-55, 59, 61, 72-73, 79, 92-93, 104, 122, 124, 127, 130
Naniwanomiya iii-iv, 49, 53, 55, 57, 59, 77, 79, 92-94, 113, 121-122, 124-127, 130
Nanjing lock 95
Nankai Road 50
nanushi 63

Nara Basin 8, 15, 19-20, 22-23, 25-27, 31, 33, 35-36, 38, 44, 47-48, 50-51, 53, 55, 65-66, 77-78, 92
Nara Period 1, 4, 44
narabikura 92, 113
Narutaki Site 48, 49
Nauman elephant 13
nenbangan 20
nendokaku 26, 31-32, 88, 92, 113
network 1,4, 6, 21, 63, 66, 116, 122-123, 126
Nichiren Sect 102
Nihon Shoki ii, 3, 25, 33-34, 113
Nimōsaku 61, 113
Ningbo 101, 123
Nishitonozuka 29-31, 113
Nonaka Kofun iv, 44, 89-91, 124, 128

O

Ō River 53, 62,
Ōbadera Site 41
ōbo 26, 127
obsidian 13, 32, 82
ocher
octagonal towers 92
Oda Nobunaga 3, 66, 70, 73, 77, 102-103, 113
Ōgata Site 44
Oi Site 55
Ōjin 32-33, 54, 84, 113, 121, 125, 127
Onchi Site 11, 131
Ongagawa Type 16
Onin Wars 3
Onodera 59
Oribe Ware v, 98, 123
Ōsaka Castle 72
Ōsaka Castle building stages 72, 74
Ōsaka Museum of History (Osaka Rekishi Hakubutsukan) 105
Ōsaka Plain ii, 1, 6, 11-12, 15, 17, 19-20, 25, 28, 32, 37, 51, 58, 78, 106, 118-120, 130
Ōsaka Prefectural Chikatsu Asuka Museum (Osaka Furitsu Chikatsu Asuka Hakubutsukan) 105-106
Ōsaka Prefectural Museum of Yayoi Culture (Osaka Furitsu Yayoi Bunka Hakubutsukan) 108
Ōsaka Prefectural Sayamaike Museum (Osaka Furitsu Sayama Ike Hakubutsukan) 107
oshighata mon 13
Ōtsu Road 50
Ōtsukayama Kofun 36, 43, 50, 88
Ōuchi Clan 102, 120
Ōwada no Tomari 102, 113
Ōyamato Kofun Group 30, 24, 31

P

Paekche iv, 28, 33, 44, 52-55, 59, 88-89, 92-94, 127
Paekche Clan 55, 92
paramount chief iii, 48
paving stones 46, 86

pillar base 68, 73, 93, 94, 97
pit house 47, 54
pollen analysis iii, 10-11, 131
ports 1, 7, 23, 49-51, 53-55, 59, 61-62, 70, 80, 102, 130
post holes 62, 82-83, 92
pottery types 14, 44, 31
prestige goods 6, 14, 23, 25, 27, 46, 79
Prince Shōtoku 62
project vii, 6, 58, 122, 124, 127, 130
punchong ware 71
Pure Land Buddhism 62, 116

Q

Qing wares 76
Queen Mother of the West ii, 27, 29

R

radar, ground penetrating 85
reaping knife 16, 19, 20, 45, 82
Rennyo 62, 72, 113
rice paddies ii, 16-17, 61, 77, 117
rice weevil (*Sitophilus linearis*) 15
ritsuryō 26
roads iii, 5-6, 23, 33, 49-51, 53, 58, 66, 69, 79, 120, 123
roof tiles 54-55, 58, 79, 92, 122, 130
Ryōnan Kita Site 44
Ryūkyū Kingdom 71, 101-102

S

saddle bow iv, 89-90
Sai 33, 113
Saikudani iii, 55-56, 113, 121, 125
Saishoyama Site 56
Saitobaru 89, 113
Sakai I, iii-v, vii, 1, 3, 6-8, 18, 20, 31, 33, 36, 39, 41, 43, 50, 53, 55, 58-59, 61-73, 75, 77, 79-80, 86, 93-103, 105, 107, 109, 113, 116, 120, 122-130
Sakai City Mihara Historical Museum (Sakai Shi Mihara Rekishi Hakubutsukan) 107
Sakai City Municipal Senboku Suemura Archaeological Museum (Sakai Shiritsu Senboku Suemura Shiryokan) 107
Sakai City Museum (Sakai Shi Hakubutsukan) 105
Sakai Locality SKT 19 99
Sakai Locality SKT 21 93
Sakai Locality SKT 39 94, 95-97
Sakai Locality SKT 78 45
Sakai Locality SKT 200 97
Sakai Locality SKT 263 99-100
Sakai Locality SB 301 95
Sakai Locality SB 302 95-96
Sakai Locality SKT 361 99
Sakai Moated City 3, 123-124, 126, 129-130
Sakai periods 93-100
sake 102

Saki Tateretsu Tomb Group 24
Saki Tomb Group 31, 38
salt production 39, 43, 127
samurai 4, 64, 71, 73, 75, 103, 126
San 33, 114, 119, 123
sandstone mold 18, 20, 58
sanukite 13, 82
Sayama Reservoir iii, 3, 50, 53, 58-59, 64, 107
scepter 32
sea level change 8
secondary burials 47
sediments 8, 11, 55
Sefukuji Sutra Mound 53, 59
Sekiguchi Shrine 66, 103
Sen no Rikyū 103
Senboku upland 2, 8, 41, 106
senretsu tatemono 95, 114, 129
Senri Terrace 8
set of armor 46, 47, 88, 90
Seto Ware 71, 94, 95, 98, 99
Setouchi Technique 6, 120
sharinseki 32, 83, 86, 114
Shichikanyama Kofun 92
Shin'ike kilns 39
shinden 18, 83, 119
shinmei 19
Shino Ware 71-73, 95-96
Shinpukuji Casting Site 64
Shitennōji iii, 50, 53-54, 58, 62, 73, 77, 114, 131
shōen iii, 3-4, 39, 56, 61-65, 69, 101, 108, 111, 114, 117-118
Shoki Imari Ware 73
Shokokuji 101, 114
Shōmu Emperor 55
Shosōin 83, 92
side blow technique ii, 13
Silla iv, 43, 55, 93-94, 117
silver 38, 72, 75-76, 85, 101-103
size rank 19
slag iv, 43-44, 46, 55, 64, 93
slit ring jade earrlng 14
social stratification 18, 119
sodality 19, 77
Soga Clan 55,
Soga Riuemon 75, 114
Song Shu 3, 33, 84, 87, 114
South China Three Color Ware v, 100
steatite bead 38
stemmed point 13, 14
stone rod 16
stoneware ceramics 23
storage facilities 6, 23, 108
storehouse iv-v, 19, 48-49, 63, 83, 95, 100, 105, 108
sueki iii, vi, 26-27, 38-44, 46, 49-50, 58, 63, 84-85, 88, 90, 93, 106, 114, 123-124, 127
Suemura Kiln Group 3
suetsukeru kan 26
Suita upland 8

Sumitomo Copper Refinery 75, 120-121
Sumiyoshi Sairei Zu Byobu 68
Sumiyoshi Shrine iii, 49-50, 53-54, 66, 69, 77, 101, 103
suribachi 94-95, 99, 114
sutra mound 58, 116, 119, 127
sword 32, 44, 46, 59, 85, 87, 89-90. 101

T

Takaida Corridor Tomb Group 38, 107, 120
takara no ichi 66
Takeno Jō'ō 114
Takenouchi Road 50
takotsubo 82
Tamateyama Tomb Group 3, 24, 32
tameike 61
Tanabe Clan 44, 55
Tanabe Site 44
Tanba Ware 71, 94, 95, 99
tansaku 70, 90
tatara 44
Tea Ceremony 71-73, 77, 80, 99, 120, 122-123, 126
tea mortar v, 95-96
tea pavilion 100
tea utensils 71, 95, 103-103
tenmoku 71
Tenmu Emperor 55
Thai wares 71, 99
Tile iv-v, 68-69, 95, 97, 99, 129
TK 73 Type grey stoneware 27, 41, 84
Tobi Chausuyama Kofun 29
Todaiji 3, 55-56, 58, 64
toimaru 103
Tokoname 62, 69, 95, 99, 114
Tokugawa Clan 5
Tokugawa Period 1, 7, 72, 80, 102
tomoegata 26, 32, 83, 114
topological theory 78
toshi-teki 62
Toyotomi Hideyori 114
Toyotomi Hideyoshi 3, 70, 72-73, 114
tree ring dating 33, 58, 82, 116
triangular concave based point 14
tribute missions to China 61, 71, 101
Tsubai Ōtsukayama Kofun 43
tsubo 63
Tsukamawari Kofun 90
Tsukuriyama Kofun 36
tubular *haniwa* iii, 29, 40, 84, 92
tunnel kiln 41, 85
tuyeres (bellows valves) 18, 43, 46, 64, 93, 95

U

Uemachi Terrace iii, 7-8, 11, 49-50, 53, 55-56, 62, 73, 93, 121
Umami Tomb Group 47
umbrella pine 9-10, 20
Uriūdō Site ii, 10-11, 21, 131

Uriwari Site 56, 81, 82

V

vegetation changes 9,
vertical burial chamber 30-32, 36, 38
Vietnamese wares 71
villages ii, 1, 4, 6, 9-11, 13, 15-16, 18-22, 41, 4853, 61, 63-64, 77-78, 81, 117, 119, 121-122, 126, 128-131
volcanic tuff 31, 38

W

Wadō Kaichin 55
warehouse sites 39, 49, 61, 66, 68, 70
waruizeni 70
Watanabe Tsu 58, 62, 115
water bird *haniwa* 83-85, 86, 88, 90
weapons 5-6, 21, 23, 26-28, 30, 32, 38, 43-44, 46, 48, 51, 70, 79, 88, 90, 101, 123, 128
Wei Dynasty 27, 33
Wei Zhi 3, 27, 33, 115
well iii-iv, 8, 13-15, 18-19, 23, 26, 30-32, 37-39, 43-44, 46, 48, 51-53, 55, 58-59, 62-63, 65-66, 69-71, 73, 75-80, 82-84, 87-88, 90, 92-93, 95, 99, 101-102, 104, 107-108
wet rice cultivation 6. 17, 78
wooden box burial offering 43, 90, 92
wooden chair 85
wooden coffin 26, 31-32, 88-89, 92
wooden spade 21
wooden umbrella 84
World Heritage Site 85, 105, 109

Y

Yagai Site 41
Yamataikoku 27, 119, 122, 124
Yamato River iii, 8-9, 17, 20, 35, 39, 44, 50, 53, 58, 62, 92
Yamato Seiken 27, 128-129
Yamato Yanagimoto Tomb Group 38
Yayoi chronology vi, 16
Yayoi Period i-ii, iv, 1, 10-11, 15-23, 26, 28-29, 39, 43, 48, 51, 61, 77-78, 81-82, 117-119, 121-122, 124, 126, 128, 130-131
Yayoi urban center 18
Yodo River iii, 7-8, 11, 14, 50, 53, 62, 73, 77, 103
yōkai 63
Yoke River 58
Yongsan River Valley 25, 121
Yotsuike Site 19, 81
Yūryaku 33

Z

zenpōkōenfun 23, 31, 35-36, 38, 86, 115, 118-122, 124
Zhangzhou blue and white 71
zōkei 63